THE
AUTHORITY

EARTH INFERNO
and other stories

Earth Inferno:

Writer: Mark Millar Pencils (issues #17-18): Chris Weston
Pencils (issues #19-20): Frank Quitely Inks (issues #17-18): Garry Leach
Inks (issues #19-20): Trevor Scott Colors: David Baron
Letters: Bill O'Neil Editor: John Layman

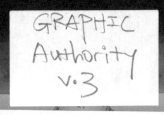

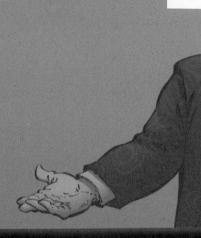

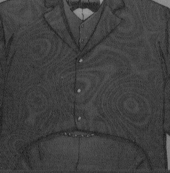

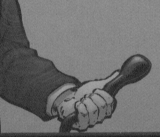

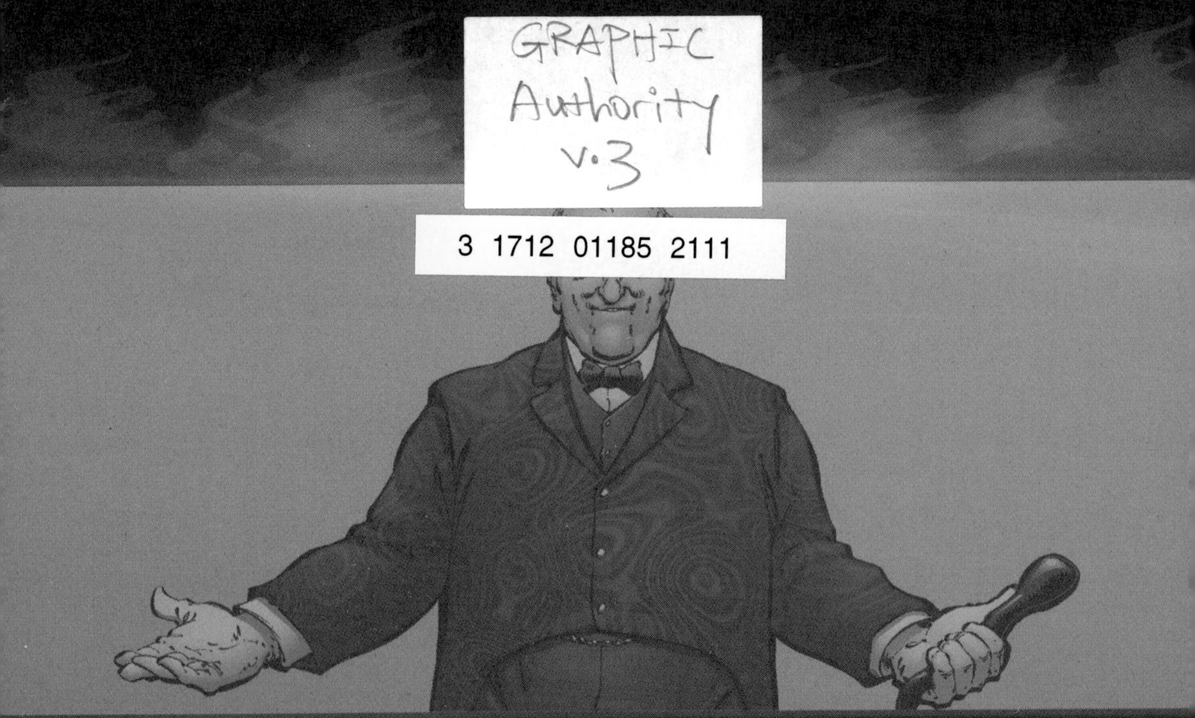

Devil's Night Annual 2000:

Writer: Joe Casey Pencils: Cully Hamner
Inks: Ray Snyder with
Cully Hamner and Mark Irwin
Colors: David Baron Letters: Naghmeh Zand
Editor: John Layman

Isolation:

Writer: Paul Jenkins Pencils: Georges Jeanty
Inks: Karl Story Colors: Brian Stelfreeze
Letters: Kathleen @ Fishbrain
Editor: John Layman

Orbital:

Writer: Warren Ellis Pencils: Cully Hamner
Inks: Karl Story Colors: Brian Stelfreeze
Letters: John Costanza Editor: John Layman

Cover by: Frank Quitely, Trevor Scott and David Baron

Original series editor:
John Layman

Collected Edition editors:
John Layman and Jeff Mariotte

Collected Edition Design:
Larry Berry

The Authority created by: Warren Ellis and Bryan Hitch

THE AUTHORITY: EARTH INFERNO & OTHER STORIES Published by WildStorm Productions. ISBN# 1-56389-854-3.

THE AUTHORITY

EARTH INFERNO

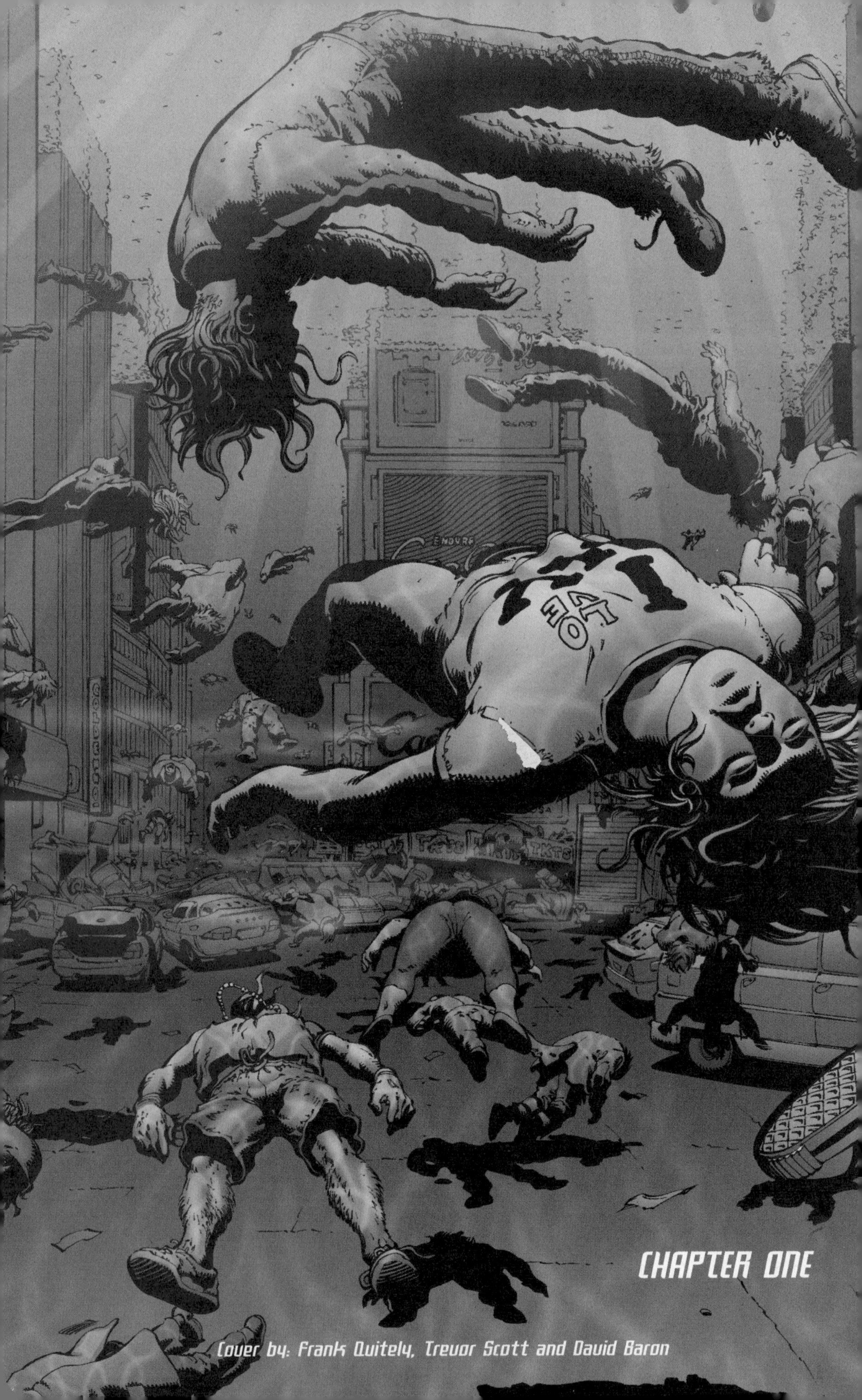

CHAPTER ONE

Cover by: Frank Quitely, Trevor Scott and David Baron

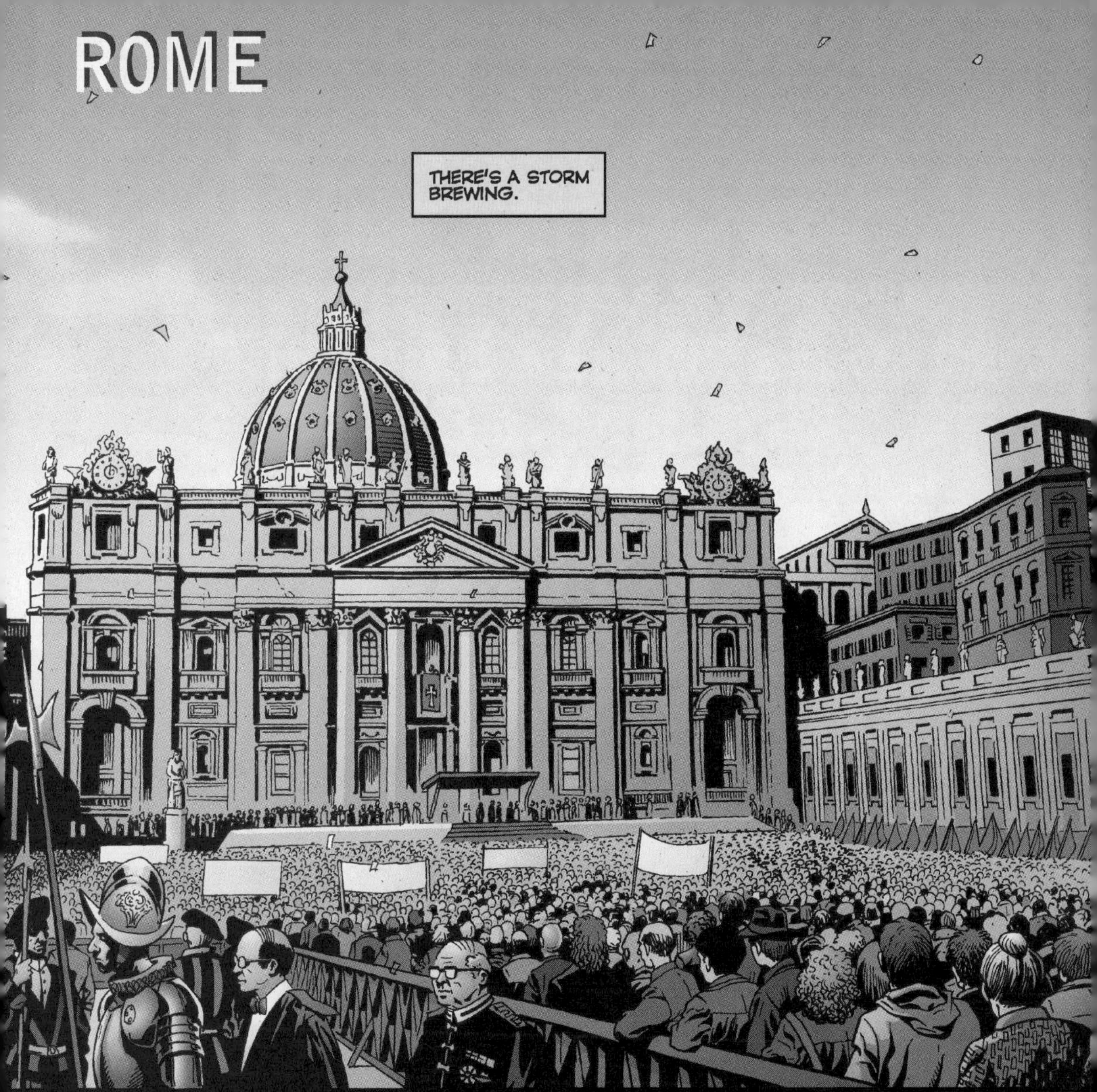
ROME
THERE'S A STORM BREWING.

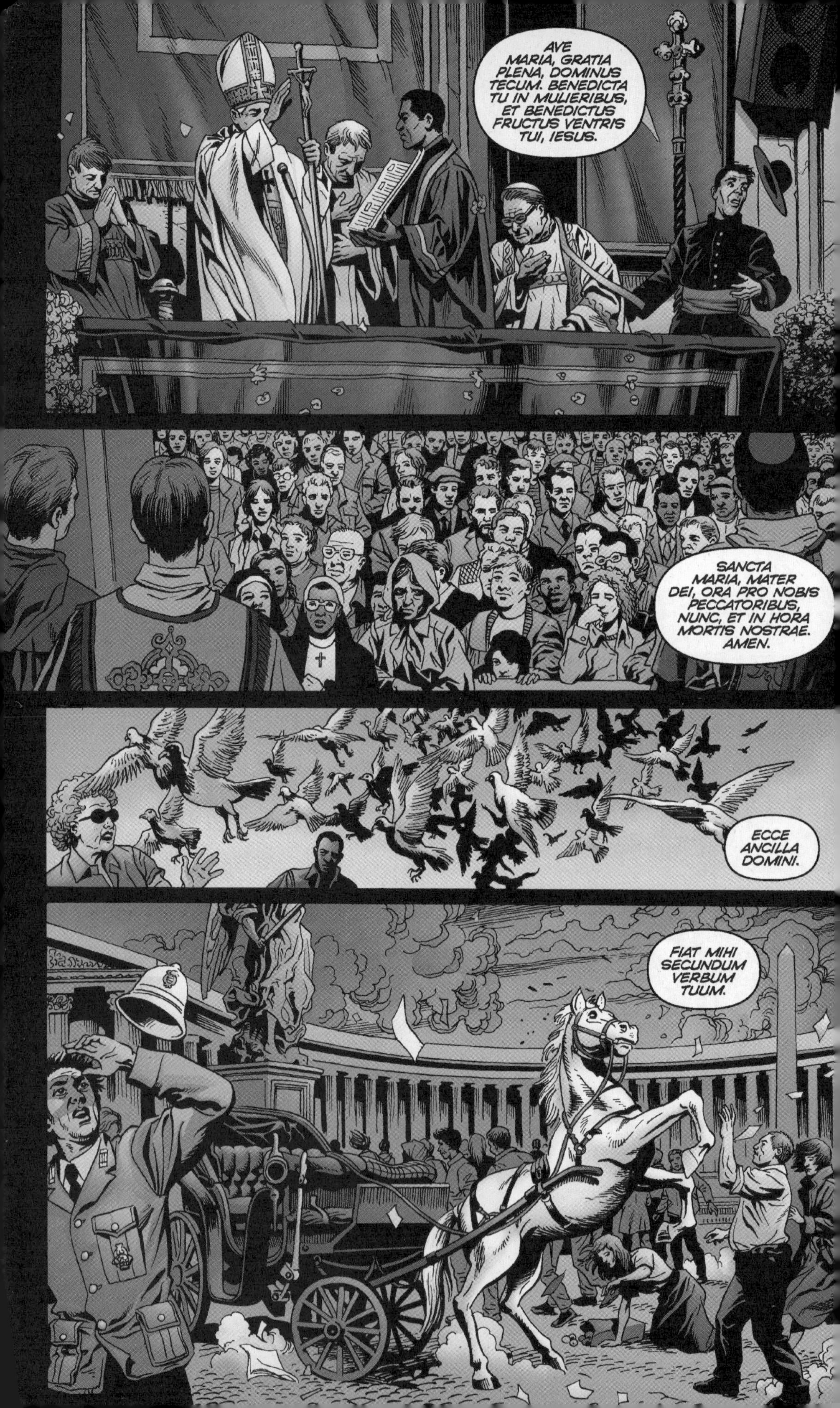
AVE MARIA, GRATIA PLENA, DOMINUS TECUM. BENEDICTA TU IN MULIERIBUS, ET BENEDICTUS FRUCTUS VENTRIS TUI, IESUS.
SANCTA MARIA, MATER DEI, ORA PRO NOBIS PECCATORIBUS, NUNC, ET IN HORA MORTIS NOSTRAE. AMEN.
ECCE ANCILLA DOMINI.
FIAT MIHI SECUNDUM VERBUM TUUM.

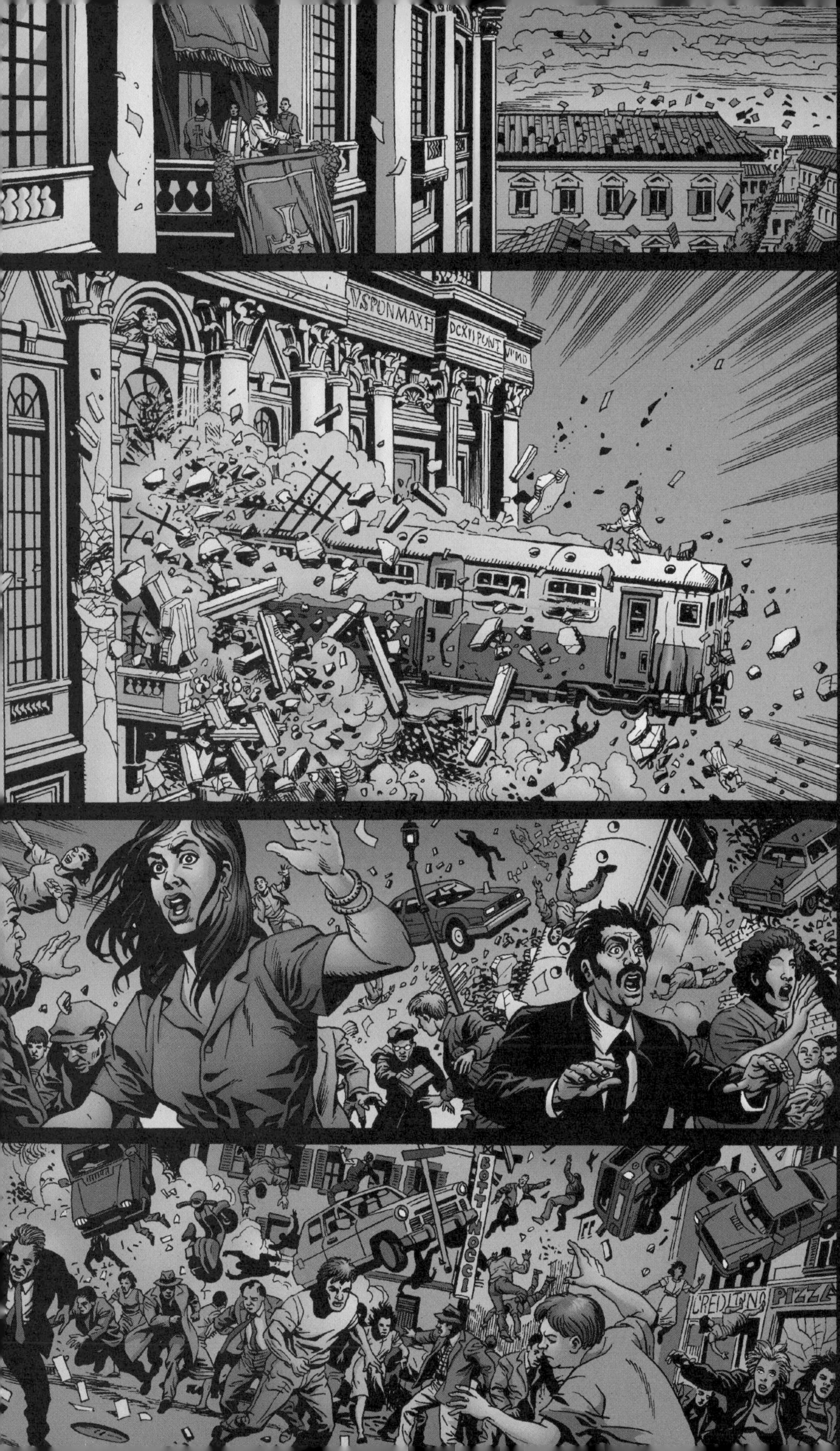

V.S.PON MAX H
DCXVI PONT
VI MD
BOTT NOCCI
PIZZA

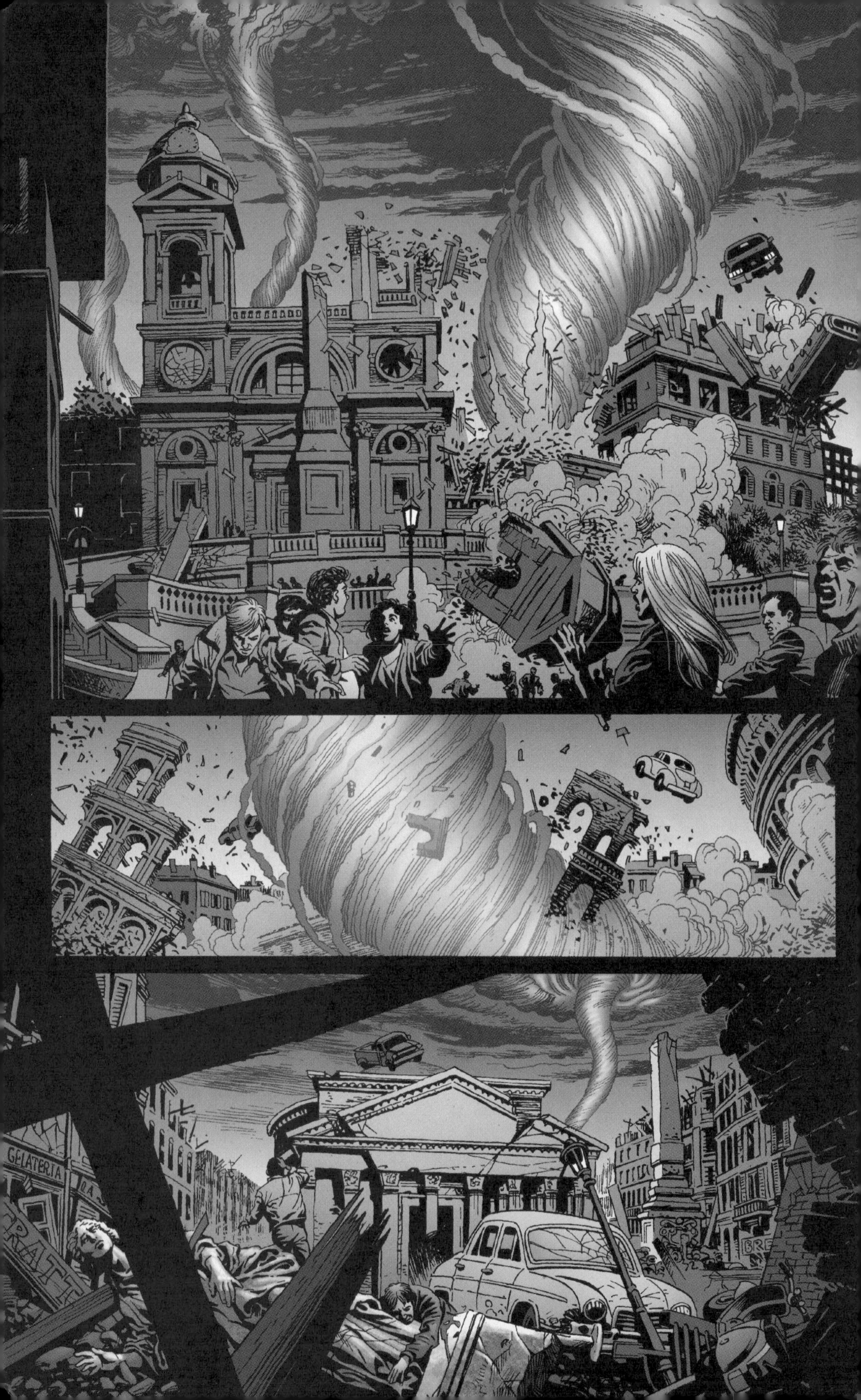
GELATERIA

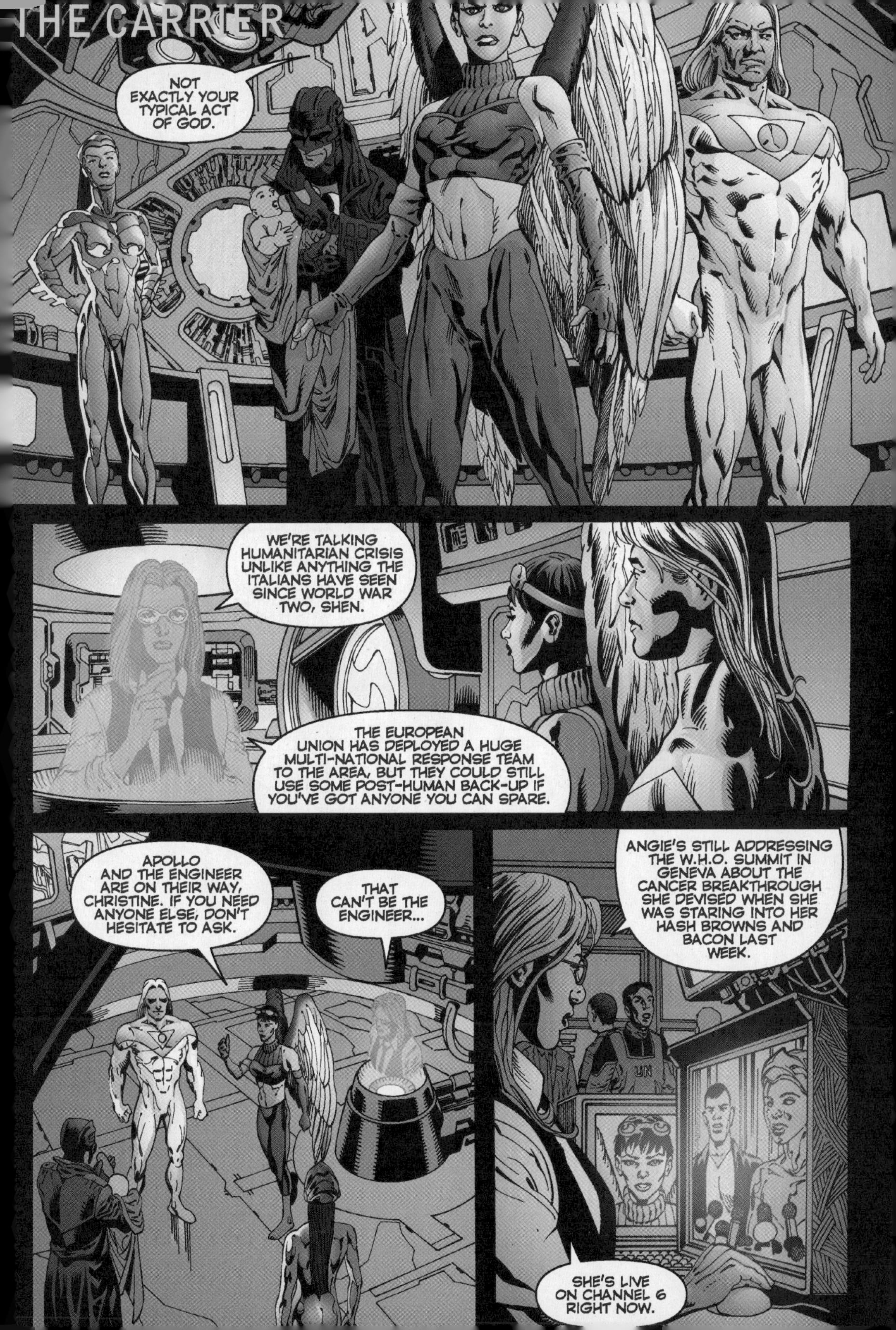

THE CARRIER
NOT EXACTLY YOUR TYPICAL ACT OF GOD.
WE'RE TALKING HUMANITARIAN CRISIS UNLIKE ANYTHING THE ITALIANS HAVE SEEN SINCE WORLD WAR TWO, SHEN.
THE EUROPEAN UNION HAS DEPLOYED A HUGE MULTI-NATIONAL RESPONSE TEAM TO THE AREA, BUT THEY COULD STILL USE SOME POST-HUMAN BACK-UP IF YOU'VE GOT ANYONE YOU CAN SPARE.
APOLLO AND THE ENGINEER ARE ON THEIR WAY, CHRISTINE. IF YOU NEED ANYONE ELSE, DON'T HESITATE TO ASK.
THAT CAN'T BE THE ENGINEER...
ANGIE'S STILL ADDRESSING THE W.H.O. SUMMIT IN GENEVA ABOUT THE CANCER BREAKTHROUGH SHE DEVISED WHEN SHE WAS STARING INTO HER HASH BROWNS AND BACON LAST WEEK.
SHE'S LIVE ON CHANNEL 6 RIGHT NOW.

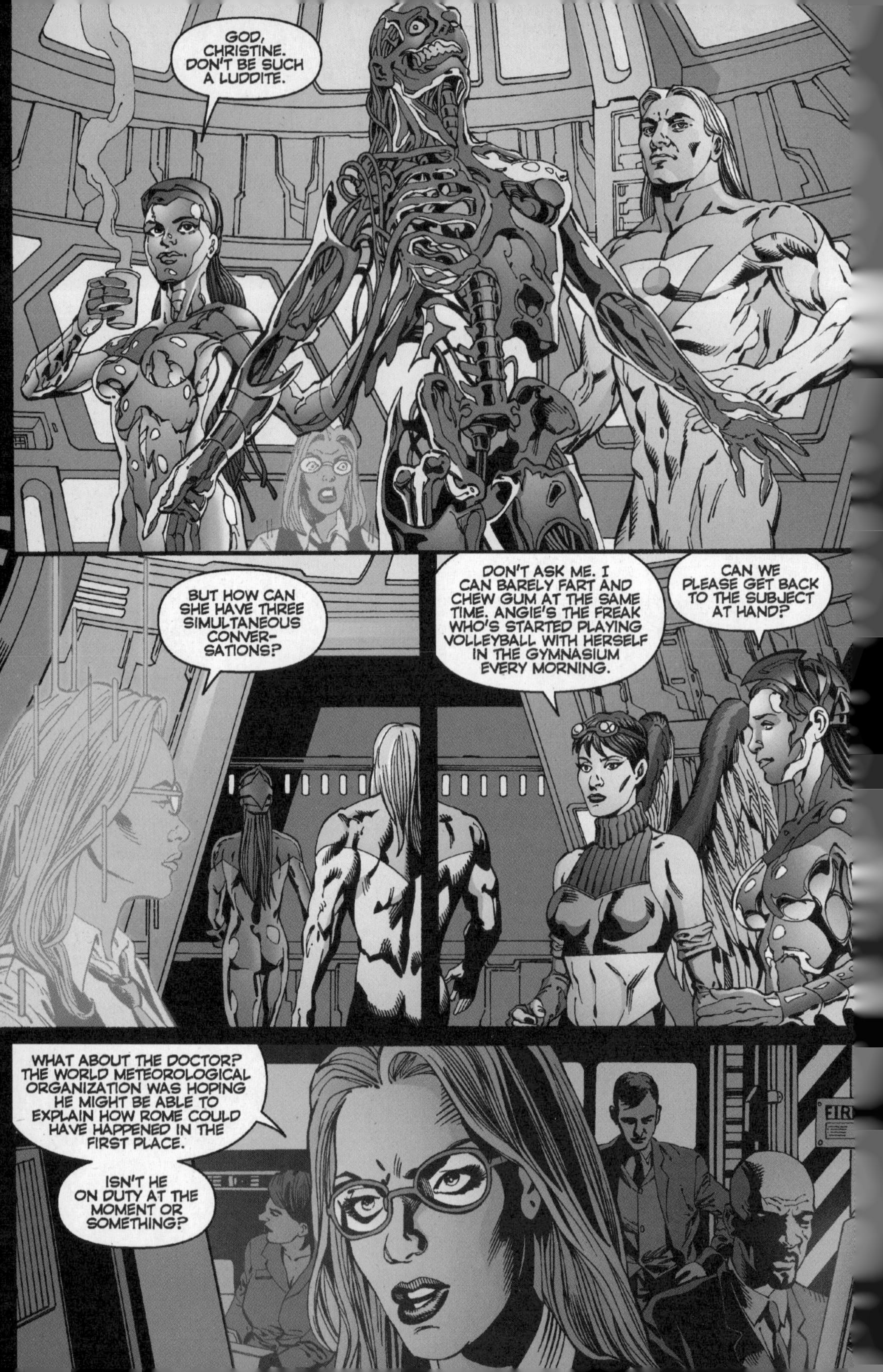

GOD, CHRISTINE. DON'T BE SUCH A LUDDITE.
BUT HOW CAN SHE HAVE THREE SIMULTANEOUS CONVER-SATIONS?
DON'T ASK ME. I CAN BARELY FART AND CHEW GUM AT THE SAME TIME. ANGIE'S THE FREAK WHO'S STARTED PLAYING VOLLEYBALL WITH HERSELF IN THE GYMNASIUM EVERY MORNING.
CAN WE PLEASE GET BACK TO THE SUBJECT AT HAND?
WHAT ABOUT THE DOCTOR? THE WORLD METEOROLOGICAL ORGANIZATION WAS HOPING HE MIGHT BE ABLE TO EXPLAIN HOW ROME COULD HAVE HAPPENED IN THE FIRST PLACE.
ISN'T HE ON DUTY AT THE MOMENT OR SOMETHING?

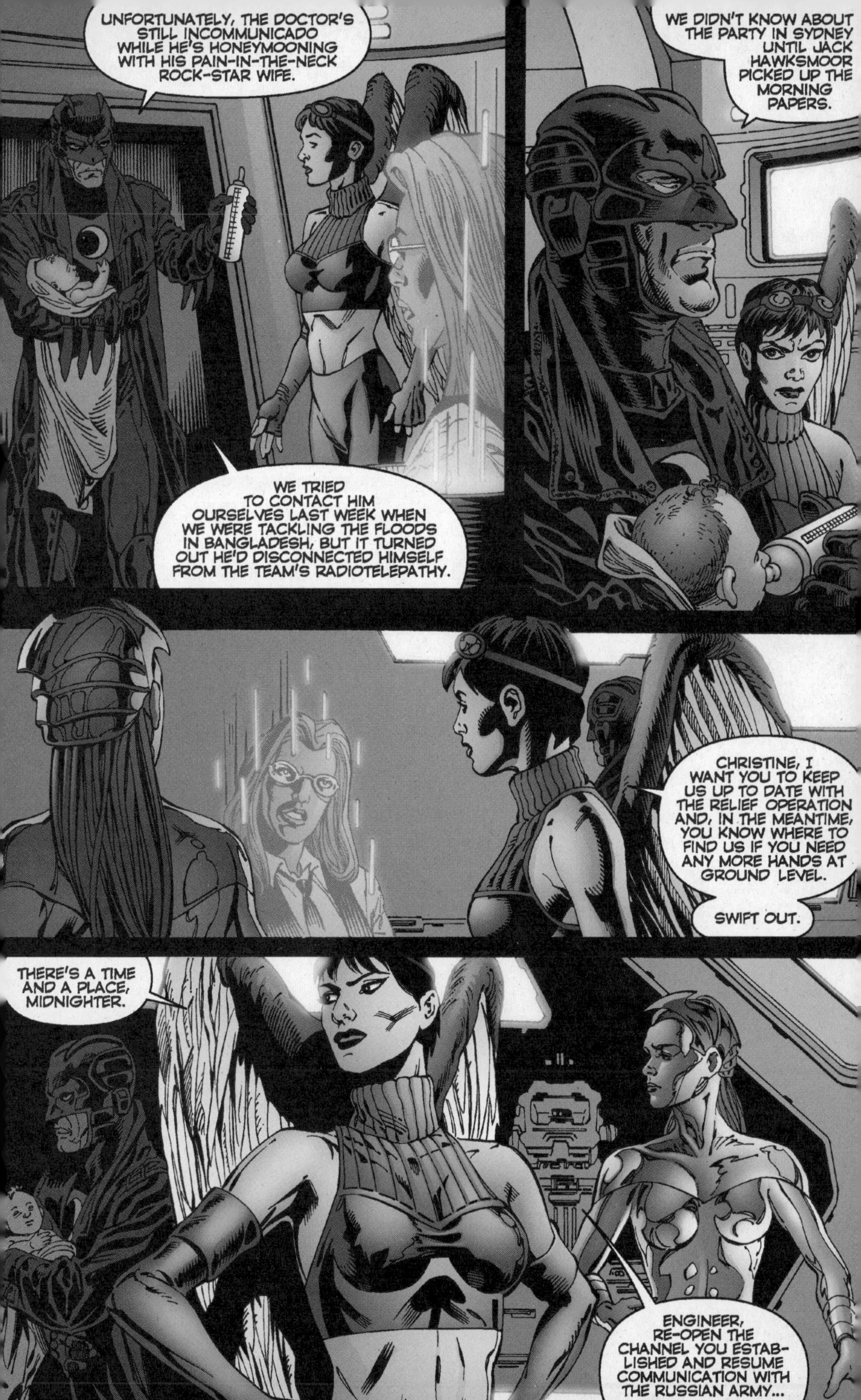
UNFORTUNATELY, THE DOCTOR'S STILL INCOMMUNICADO WHILE HE'S HONEYMOONING WITH HIS PAIN-IN-THE-NECK ROCK-STAR WIFE.
WE TRIED TO CONTACT HIM OURSELVES LAST WEEK WHEN WE WERE TACKLING THE FLOODS IN BANGLADESH, BUT IT TURNED OUT HE'D DISCONNECTED HIMSELF FROM THE TEAM'S RADIOTELEPATHY.
WE DIDN'T KNOW ABOUT THE PARTY IN SYDNEY UNTIL JACK HAWKSMOOR PICKED UP THE MORNING PAPERS.
CHRISTINE, I WANT YOU TO KEEP US UP TO DATE WITH THE RELIEF OPERATION AND, IN THE MEANTIME, YOU KNOW WHERE TO FIND US IF YOU NEED ANY MORE HANDS AT GROUND LEVEL.
SWIFT OUT.
THERE'S A TIME AND A PLACE, MIDNIGHTER.
ENGINEER, RE-OPEN THE CHANNEL YOU ESTAB-LISHED AND RESUME COMMUNICATION WITH THE RUSSIAN ARMY...

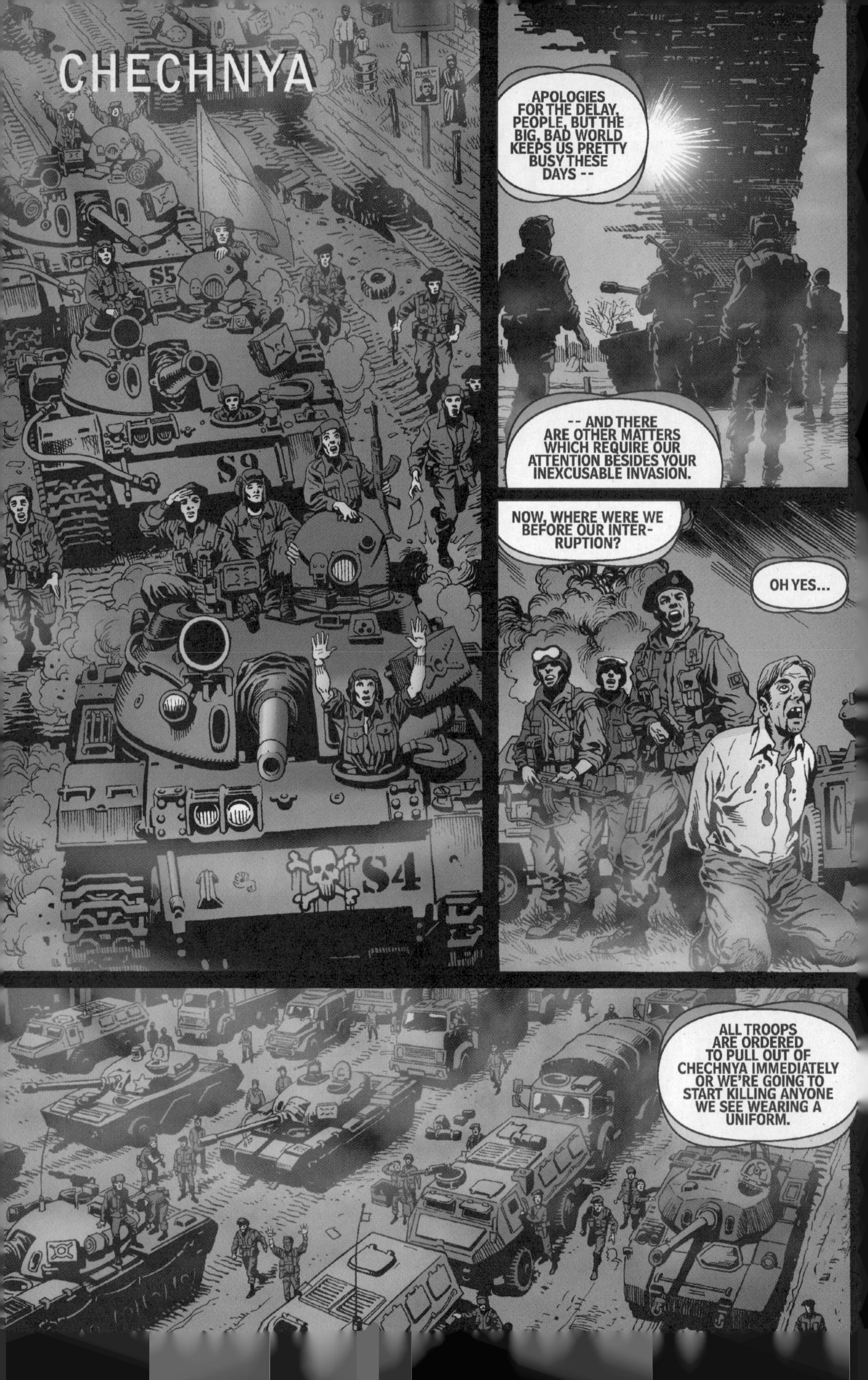
CHECHNYA
APOLOGIES FOR THE DELAY, PEOPLE, BUT THE BIG, BAD WORLD KEEPS US PRETTY BUSY THESE DAYS --
-- AND THERE ARE OTHER MATTERS WHICH REQUIRE OUR ATTENTION BESIDES YOUR INEXCUSABLE INVASION.
NOW, WHERE WERE WE BEFORE OUR INTER-RUPTION?
OH YES...
ALL TROOPS ARE ORDERED TO PULL OUT OF CHECHNYA IMMEDIATELY OR WE'RE GOING TO START KILLING ANYONE WE SEE WEARING A UNIFORM.

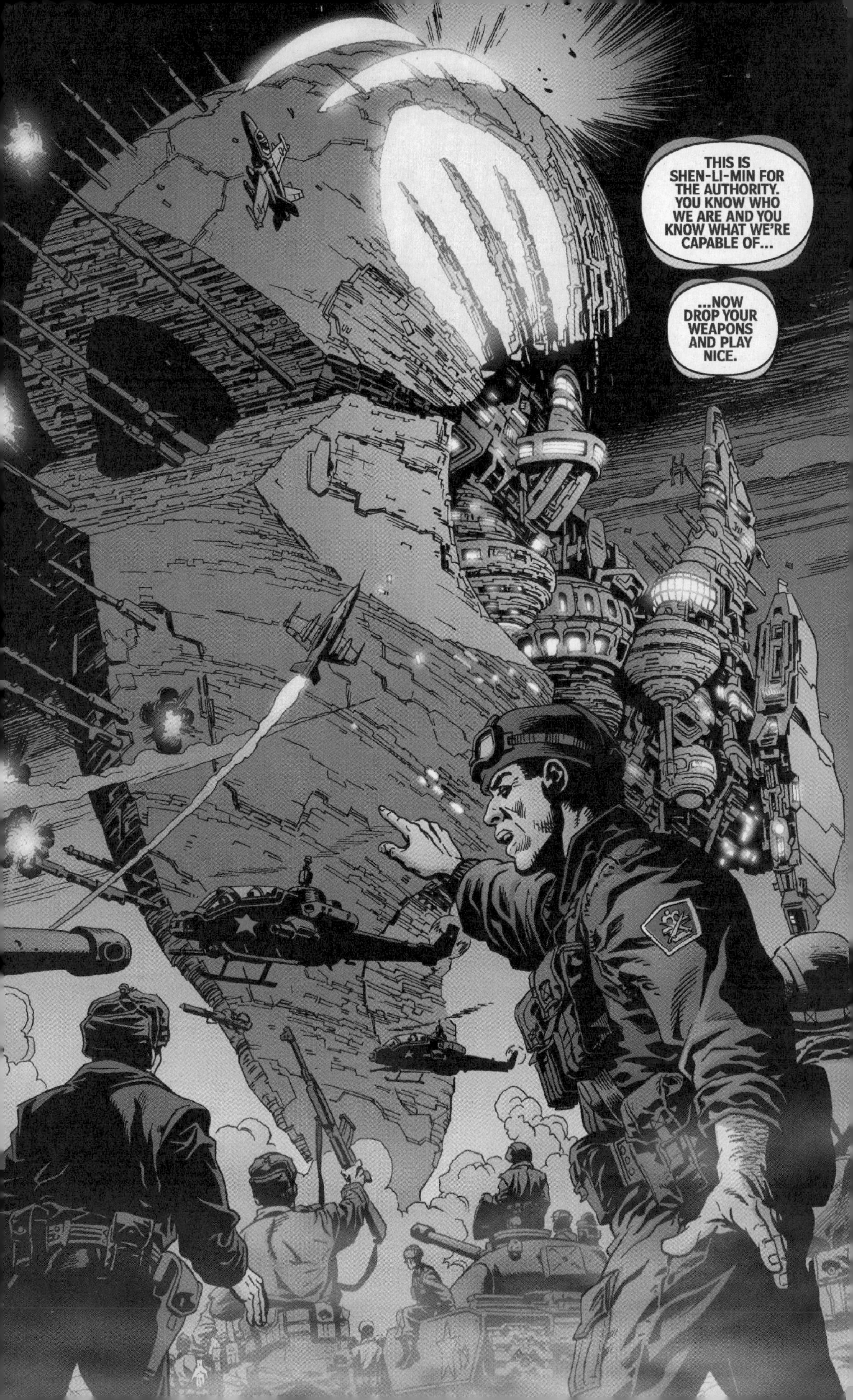
THIS IS SHEN-LI-MIN FOR THE AUTHORITY. YOU KNOW WHO WE ARE AND YOU KNOW WHAT WE'RE CAPABLE OF...
...NOW DROP YOUR WEAPONS AND PLAY NICE.

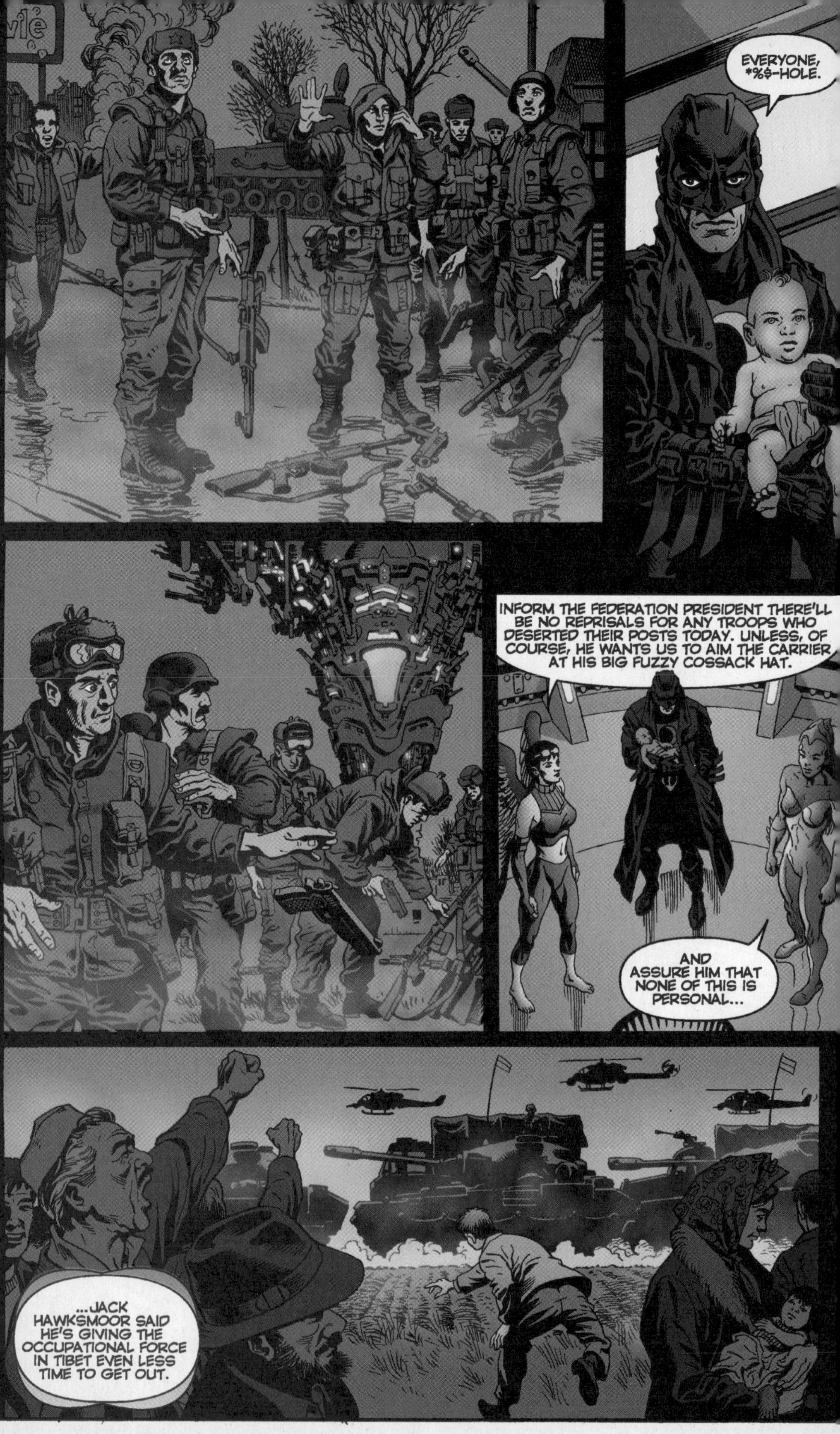
EVERYONE, *%$-HOLE.
INFORM THE FEDERATION PRESIDENT THERE'LL BE NO REPRISALS FOR ANY TROOPS WHO DESERTED THEIR POSTS TODAY. UNLESS, OF COURSE, HE WANTS US TO AIM THE CARRIER AT HIS BIG FUZZY COSSACK HAT.
AND ASSURE HIM THAT NONE OF THIS IS PERSONAL...
...JACK HAWKSMOOR SAID HE'S GIVING THE OCCUPATIONAL FORCE IN TIBET EVEN LESS TIME TO GET OUT.

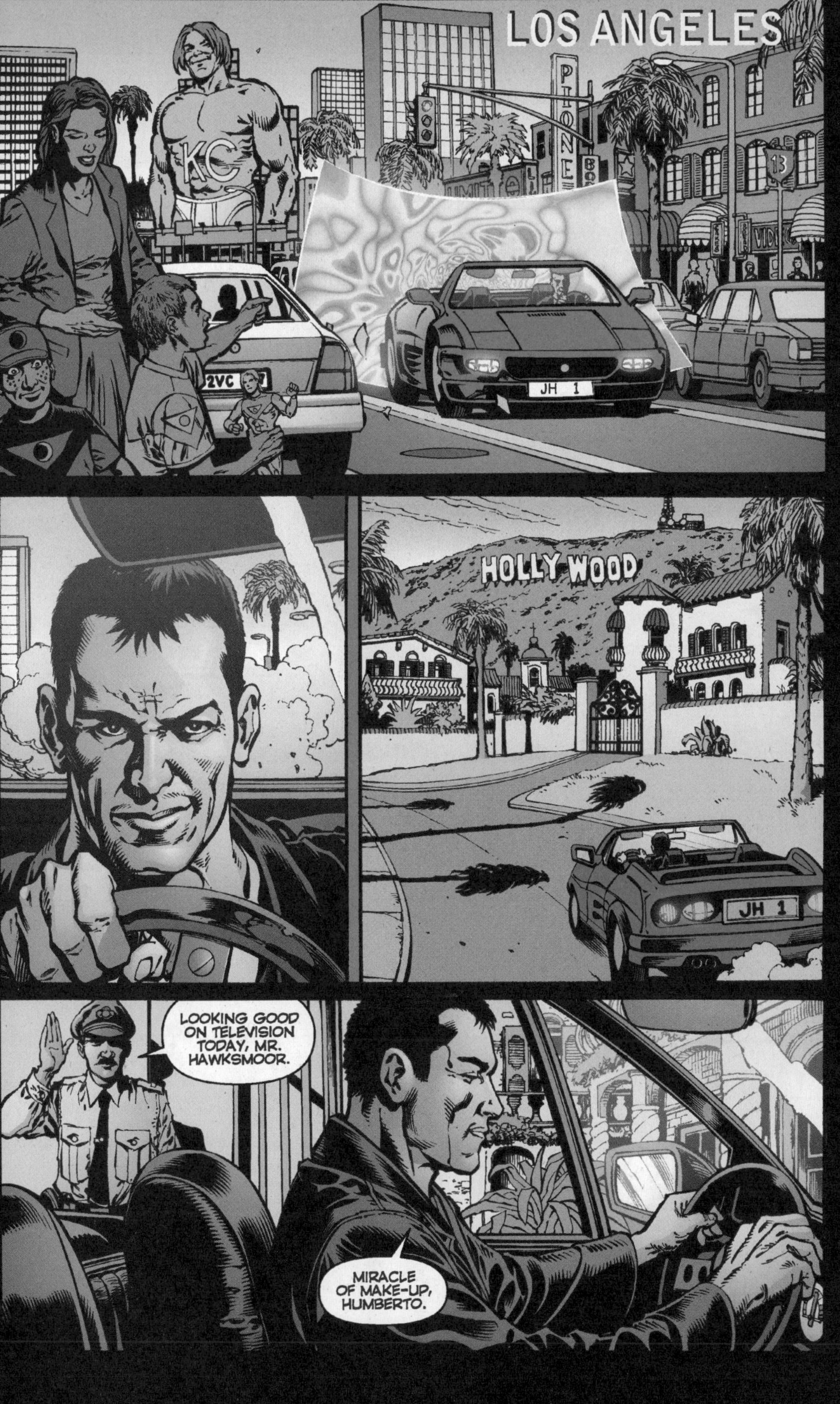
LOS ANGELES
KC
JH 1
HOLLYWOOD
JH 1
LOOKING GOOD ON TELEVISION TODAY, MR. HAWKSMOOR.
MIRACLE OF MAKE-UP, HUMBERTO.

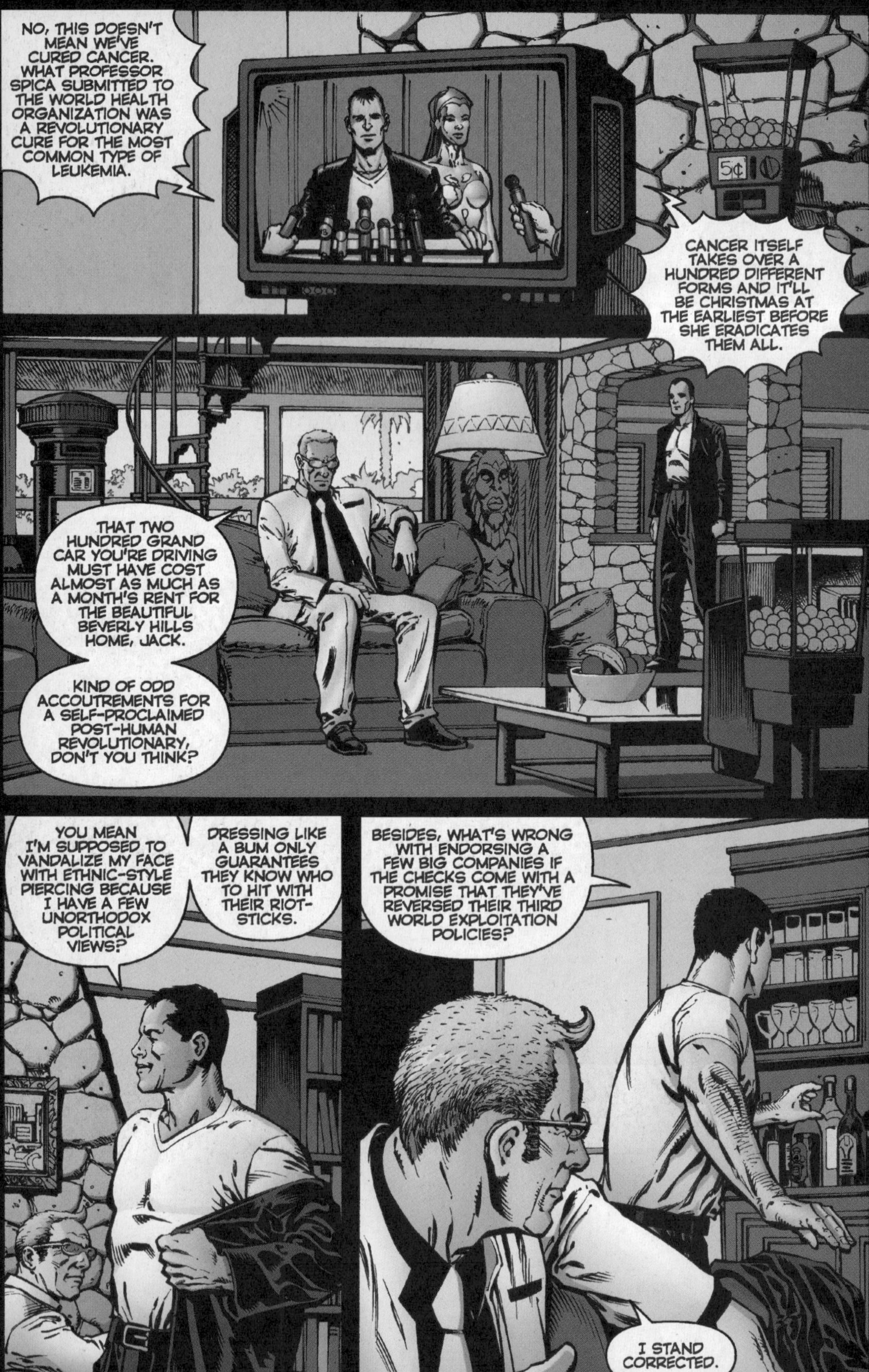
NO, THIS DOESN'T MEAN WE'VE CURED CANCER. WHAT PROFESSOR SPICA SUBMITTED TO THE WORLD HEALTH ORGANIZATION WAS A REVOLUTIONARY CURE FOR THE MOST COMMON TYPE OF LEUKEMIA.
5¢
CANCER ITSELF TAKES OVER A HUNDRED DIFFERENT FORMS AND IT'LL BE CHRISTMAS AT THE EARLIEST BEFORE SHE ERADICATES THEM ALL.
THAT TWO HUNDRED GRAND CAR YOU'RE DRIVING MUST HAVE COST ALMOST AS MUCH AS A MONTH'S RENT FOR THE BEAUTIFUL BEVERLY HILLS HOME, JACK.
KIND OF ODD ACCOUTREMENTS FOR A SELF-PROCLAIMED POST-HUMAN REVOLUTIONARY, DON'T YOU THINK?
YOU MEAN I'M SUPPOSED TO VANDALIZE MY FACE WITH ETHNIC-STYLE PIERCING BECAUSE I HAVE A FEW UNORTHODOX POLITICAL VIEWS?
DRESSING LIKE A BUM ONLY GUARANTEES THEY KNOW WHO TO HIT WITH THEIR RIOT-STICKS.
BESIDES, WHAT'S WRONG WITH ENDORSING A FEW BIG COMPANIES IF THE CHECKS COME WITH A PROMISE THAT THEY'VE REVERSED THEIR THIRD WORLD EXPLOITATION POLICIES?
I STAND CORRECTED.

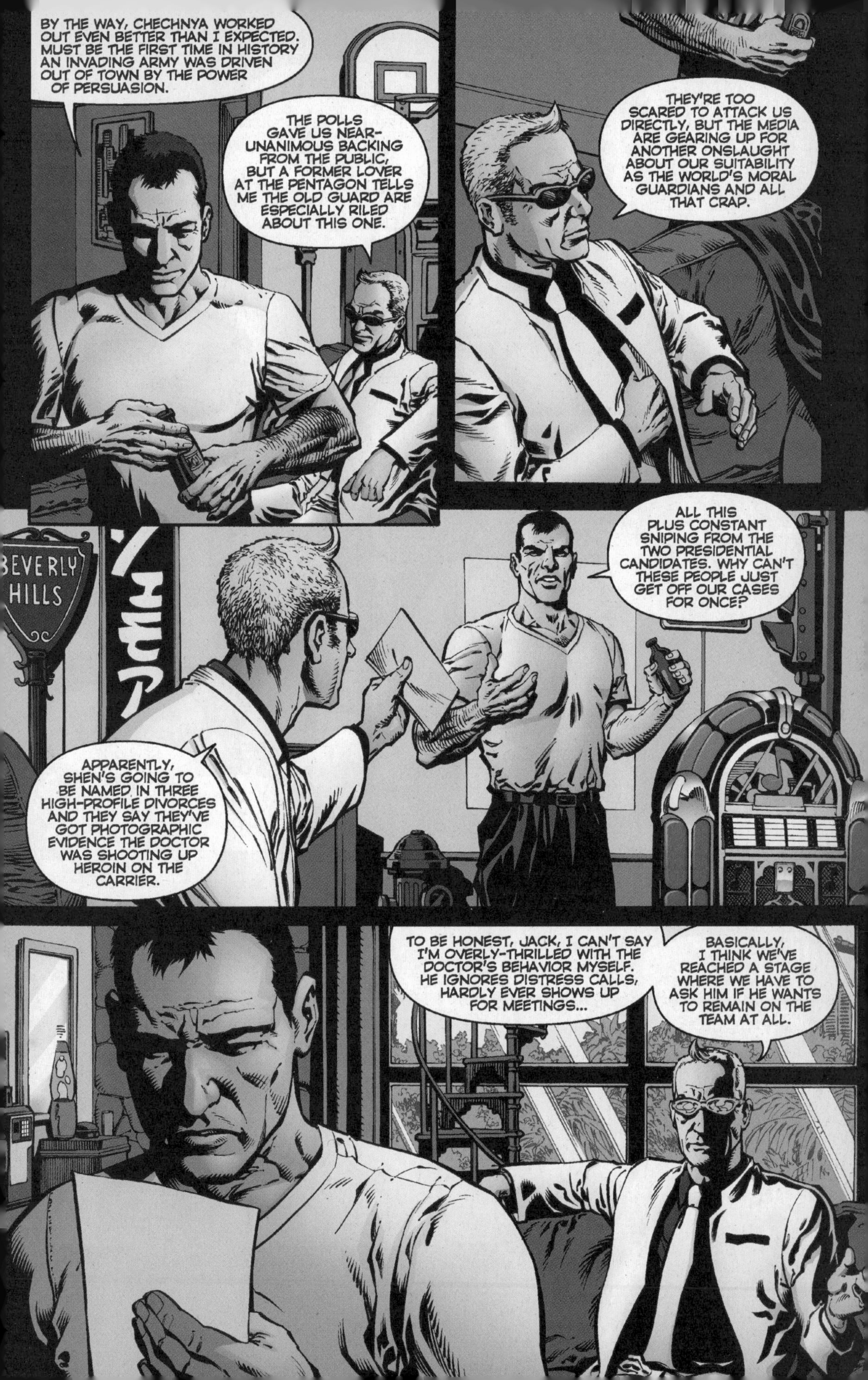
BY THE WAY, CHECHNYA WORKED OUT EVEN BETTER THAN I EXPECTED. MUST BE THE FIRST TIME IN HISTORY AN INVADING ARMY WAS DRIVEN OUT OF TOWN BY THE POWER OF PERSUASION.
THE POLLS GAVE US NEAR-UNANIMOUS BACKING FROM THE PUBLIC, BUT A FORMER LOVER AT THE PENTAGON TELLS ME THE OLD GUARD ARE ESPECIALLY RILED ABOUT THIS ONE.
THEY'RE TOO SCARED TO ATTACK US DIRECTLY, BUT THE MEDIA ARE GEARING UP FOR ANOTHER ONSLAUGHT ABOUT OUR SUITABILITY AS THE WORLD'S MORAL GUARDIANS AND ALL THAT CRAP.
BEVERLY HILLS
ALL THIS PLUS CONSTANT SNIPING FROM THE TWO PRESIDENTIAL CANDIDATES. WHY CAN'T THESE PEOPLE JUST GET OFF OUR CASES FOR ONCE?
APPARENTLY, SHEN'S GOING TO BE NAMED IN THREE HIGH-PROFILE DIVORCES AND THEY SAY THEY'VE GOT PHOTOGRAPHIC EVIDENCE THE DOCTOR WAS SHOOTING UP HEROIN ON THE CARRIER.
TO BE HONEST, JACK, I CAN'T SAY I'M OVERLY-THRILLED WITH THE DOCTOR'S BEHAVIOR MYSELF. HE IGNORES DISTRESS CALLS, HARDLY EVER SHOWS UP FOR MEETINGS...
BASICALLY, I THINK WE'VE REACHED A STAGE WHERE WE HAVE TO ASK HIM IF HE WANTS TO REMAIN ON THE TEAM AT ALL.

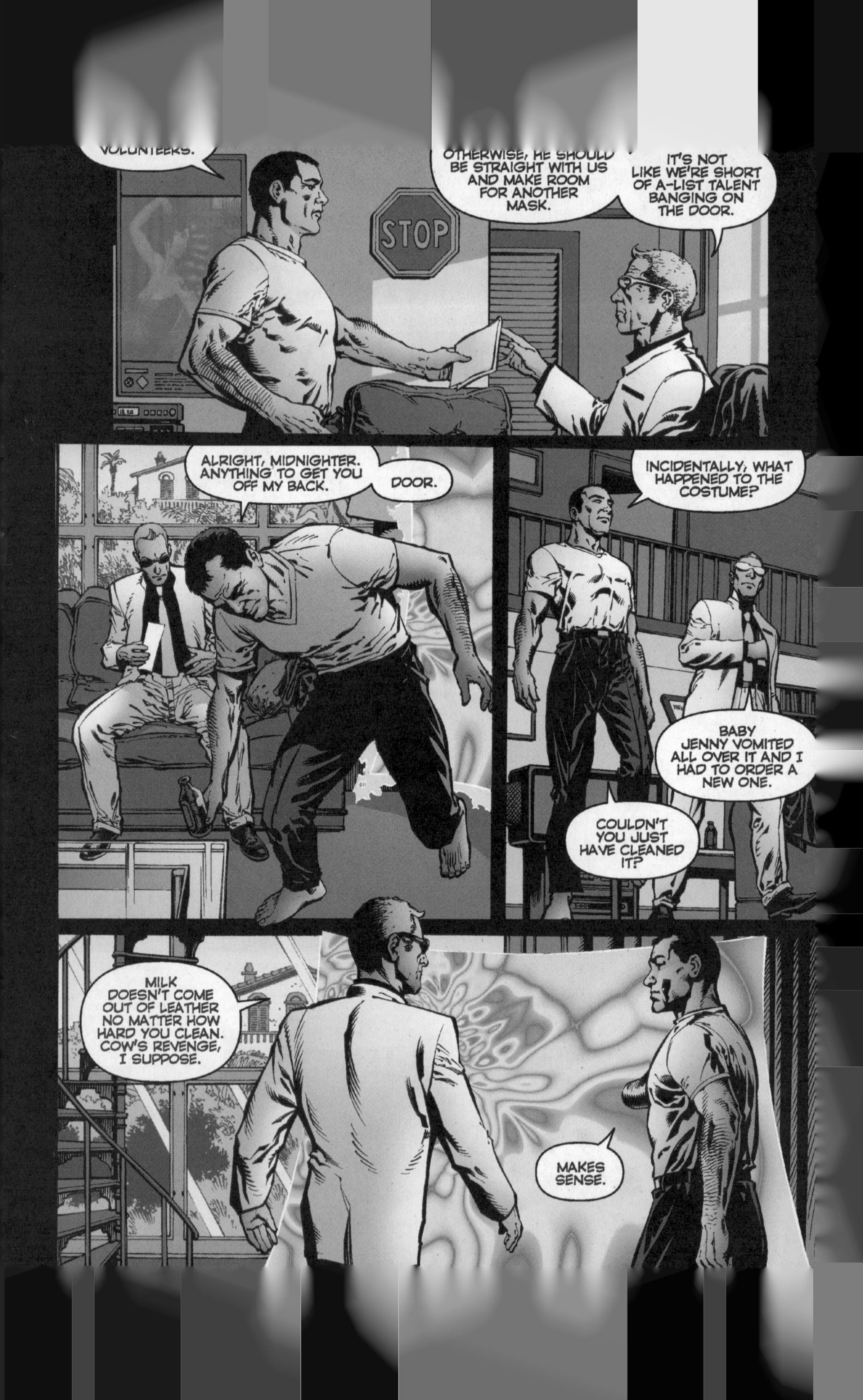
VOLUNTEERS.
OTHERWISE, HE SHOULD BE STRAIGHT WITH US AND MAKE ROOM FOR ANOTHER MASK.
IT'S NOT LIKE WE'RE SHORT OF A-LIST TALENT BANGING ON THE DOOR.
STOP
ALRIGHT, MIDNIGHTER. ANYTHING TO GET YOU OFF MY BACK.
DOOR.
INCIDENTALLY, WHAT HAPPENED TO THE COSTUME?
BABY JENNY VOMITED ALL OVER IT AND I HAD TO ORDER A NEW ONE.
COULDN'T YOU JUST HAVE CLEANED IT?
MILK DOESN'T COME OUT OF LEATHER NO MATTER HOW HARD YOU CLEAN. COW'S REVENGE, I SUPPOSE.
MAKES SENSE.

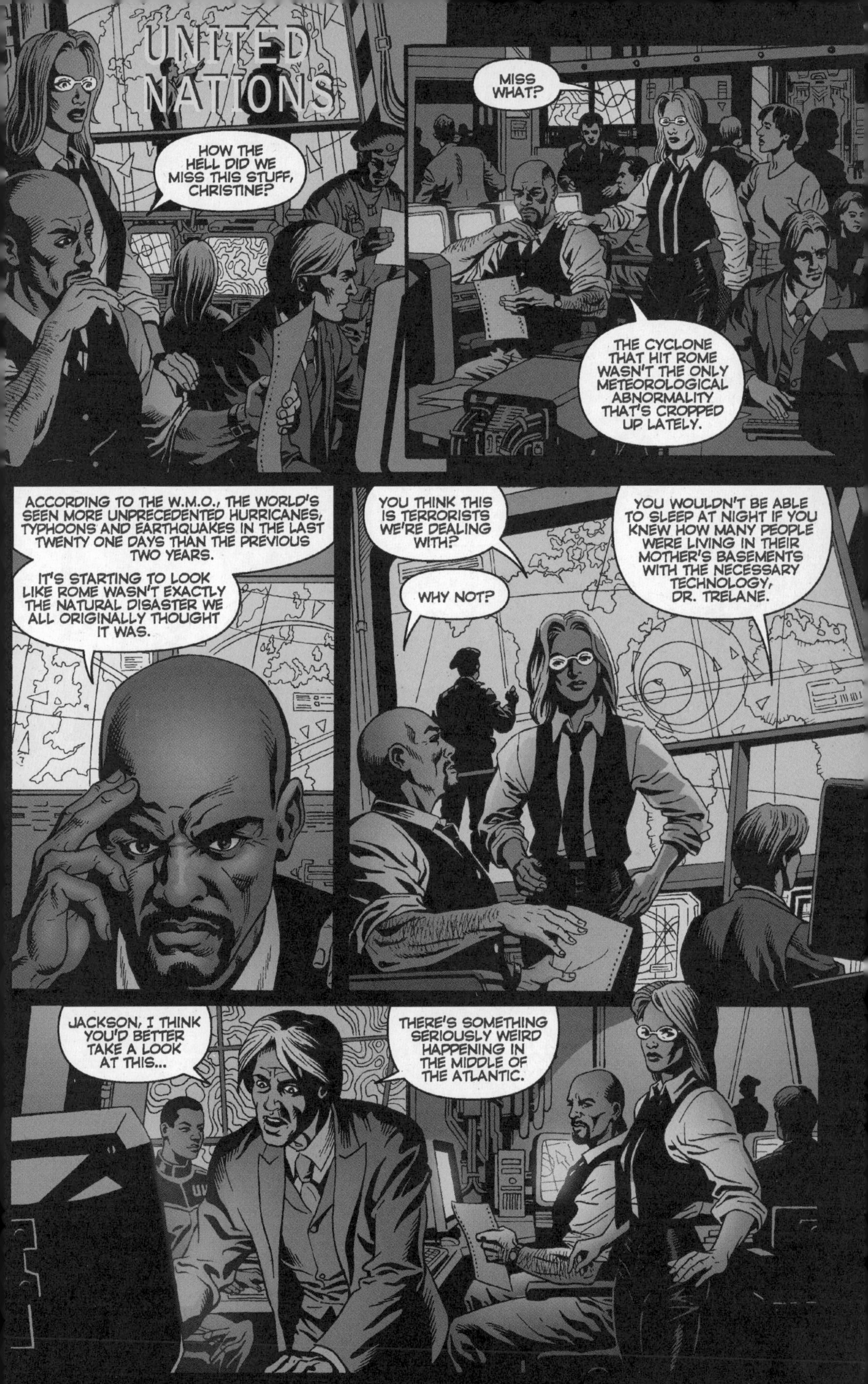
UNITED NATIONS
HOW THE HELL DID WE MISS THIS STUFF, CHRISTINE?
MISS WHAT?
THE CYCLONE THAT HIT ROME WASN'T THE ONLY METEOROLOGICAL ABNORMALITY THAT'S CROPPED UP LATELY.
ACCORDING TO THE W.M.O., THE WORLD'S SEEN MORE UNPRECEDENTED HURRICANES, TYPHOONS AND EARTHQUAKES IN THE LAST TWENTY ONE DAYS THAN THE PREVIOUS TWO YEARS.
IT'S STARTING TO LOOK LIKE ROME WASN'T EXACTLY THE NATURAL DISASTER WE ALL ORIGINALLY THOUGHT IT WAS.
YOU THINK THIS IS TERRORISTS WE'RE DEALING WITH?
WHY NOT?
YOU WOULDN'T BE ABLE TO SLEEP AT NIGHT IF YOU KNEW HOW MANY PEOPLE WERE LIVING IN THEIR MOTHER'S BASEMENTS WITH THE NECESSARY TECHNOLOGY, DR. TRELANE.
JACKSON, I THINK YOU'D BETTER TAKE A LOOK AT THIS...
THERE'S SOMETHING SERIOUSLY WEIRD HAPPENING IN THE MIDDLE OF THE ATLANTIC.

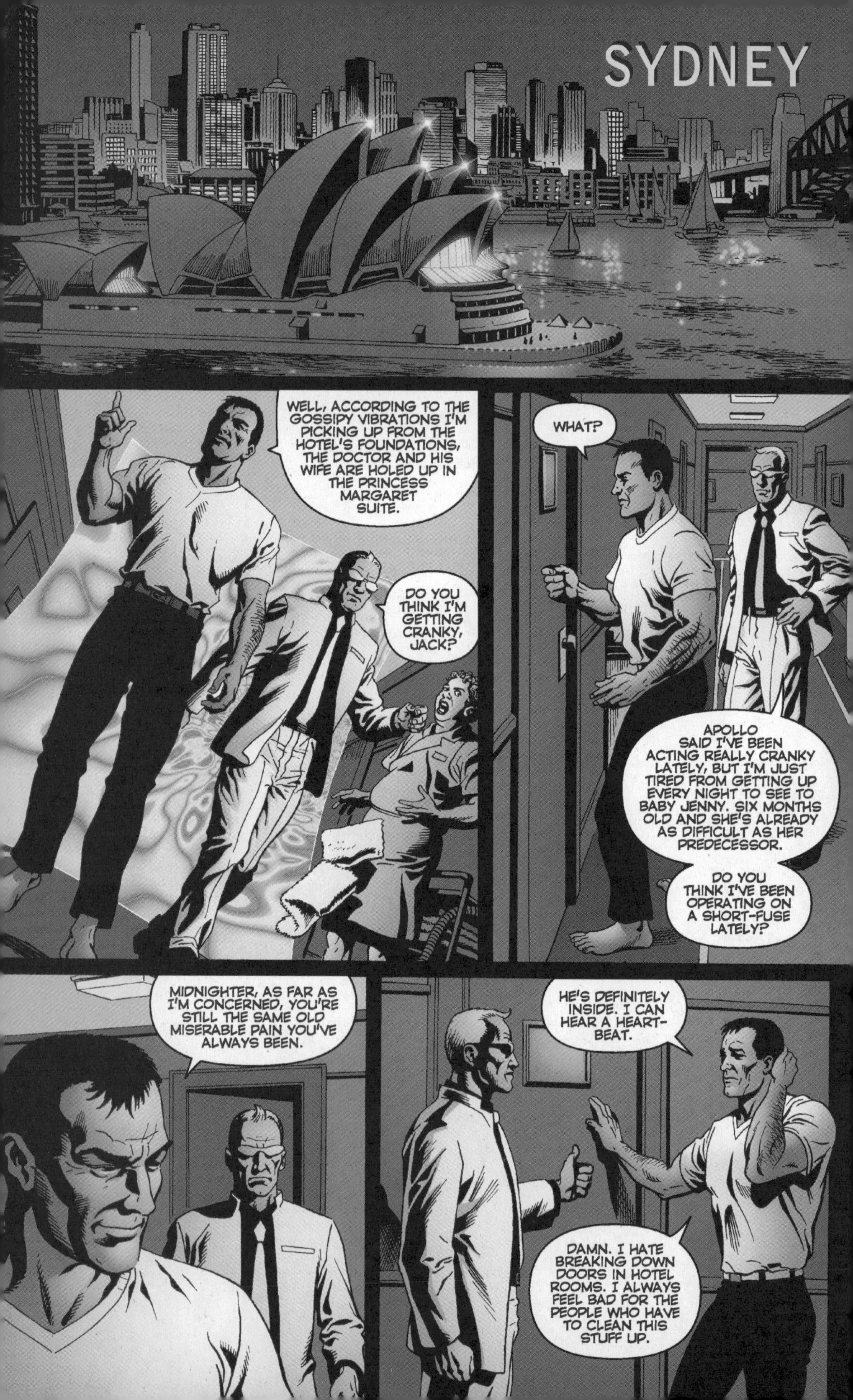
SYDNEY
WELL, ACCORDING TO THE GOSSIPY VIBRATIONS I'M PICKING UP FROM THE HOTEL'S FOUNDATIONS, THE DOCTOR AND HIS WIFE ARE HOLED UP IN THE PRINCESS MARGARET SUITE.
DO YOU THINK I'M GETTING CRANKY, JACK?
WHAT?
APOLLO SAID I'VE BEEN ACTING REALLY CRANKY LATELY, BUT I'M JUST TIRED FROM GETTING UP EVERY NIGHT TO SEE TO BABY JENNY. SIX MONTHS OLD AND SHE'S ALREADY AS DIFFICULT AS HER PREDECESSOR.
DO YOU THINK I'VE BEEN OPERATING ON A SHORT-FUSE LATELY?
MIDNIGHTER, AS FAR AS I'M CONCERNED, YOU'RE STILL THE SAME OLD MISERABLE PAIN YOU'VE ALWAYS BEEN.
HE'S DEFINITELY INSIDE. I CAN HEAR A HEART-BEAT.
DAMN. I HATE BREAKING DOWN DOORS IN HOTEL ROOMS. I ALWAYS FEEL BAD FOR THE PEOPLE WHO HAVE TO CLEAN THIS STUFF UP.

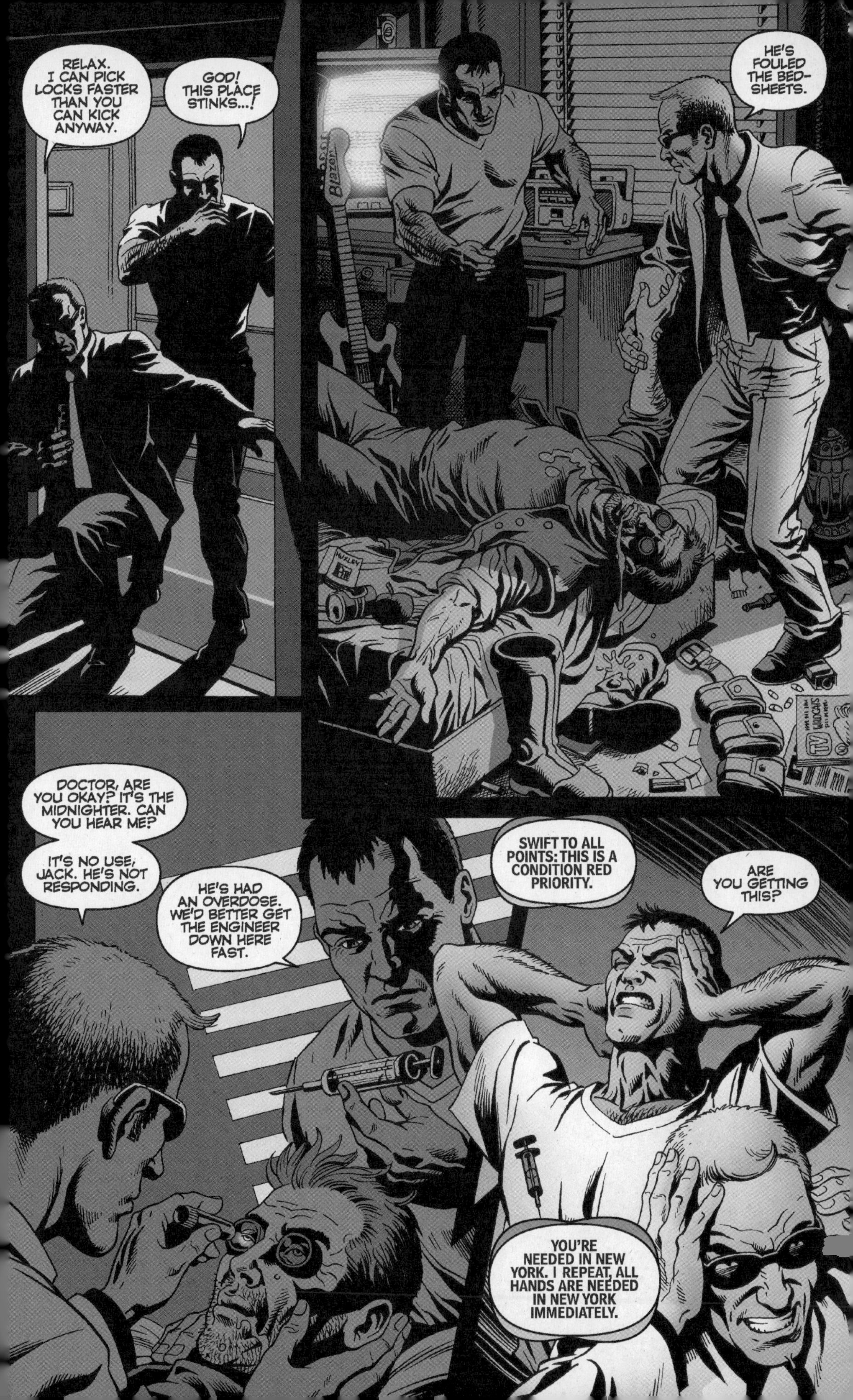

RELAX. I CAN PICK LOCKS FASTER THAN YOU CAN KICK ANYWAY.
GOD! THIS PLACE STINKS...!
HE'S FOULED THE BED-SHEETS.
DOCTOR, ARE YOU OKAY? IT'S THE MIDNIGHTER. CAN YOU HEAR ME?
IT'S NO USE, JACK. HE'S NOT RESPONDING.
HE'S HAD AN OVERDOSE. WE'D BETTER GET THE ENGINEER DOWN HERE FAST.
SWIFT TO ALL POINTS: THIS IS A CONDITION RED PRIORITY.
ARE YOU GETTING THIS?
YOU'RE NEEDED IN NEW YORK. I REPEAT, ALL HANDS ARE NEEDED IN NEW YORK IMMEDIATELY.

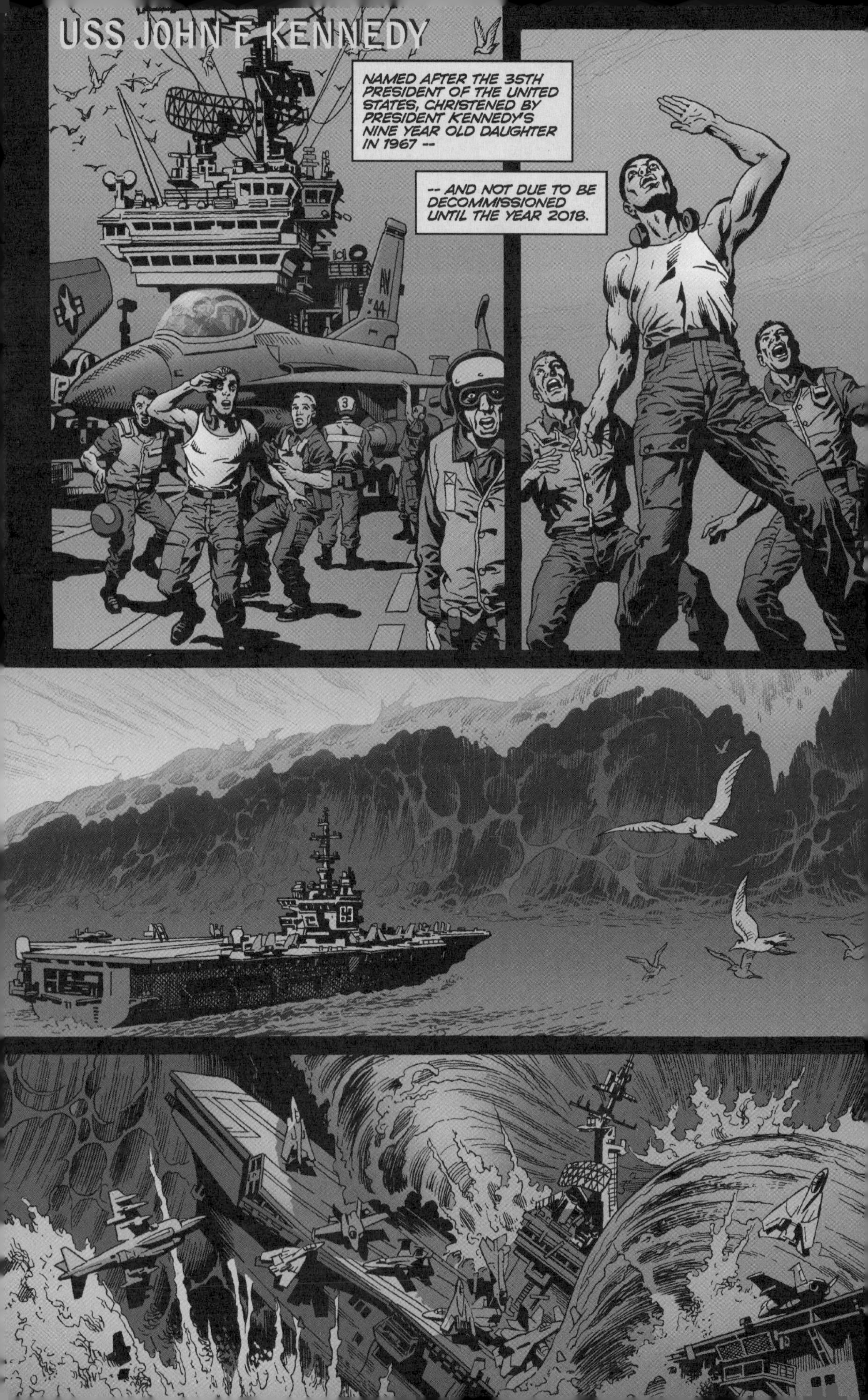
USS JOHN F. KENNEDY
NAMED AFTER THE 35TH PRESIDENT OF THE UNITED STATES, CHRISTENED BY PRESIDENT KENNEDY'S NINE YEAR OLD DAUGHTER IN 1967 --
-- AND NOT DUE TO BE DECOMMISSIONED UNTIL THE YEAR 2018.

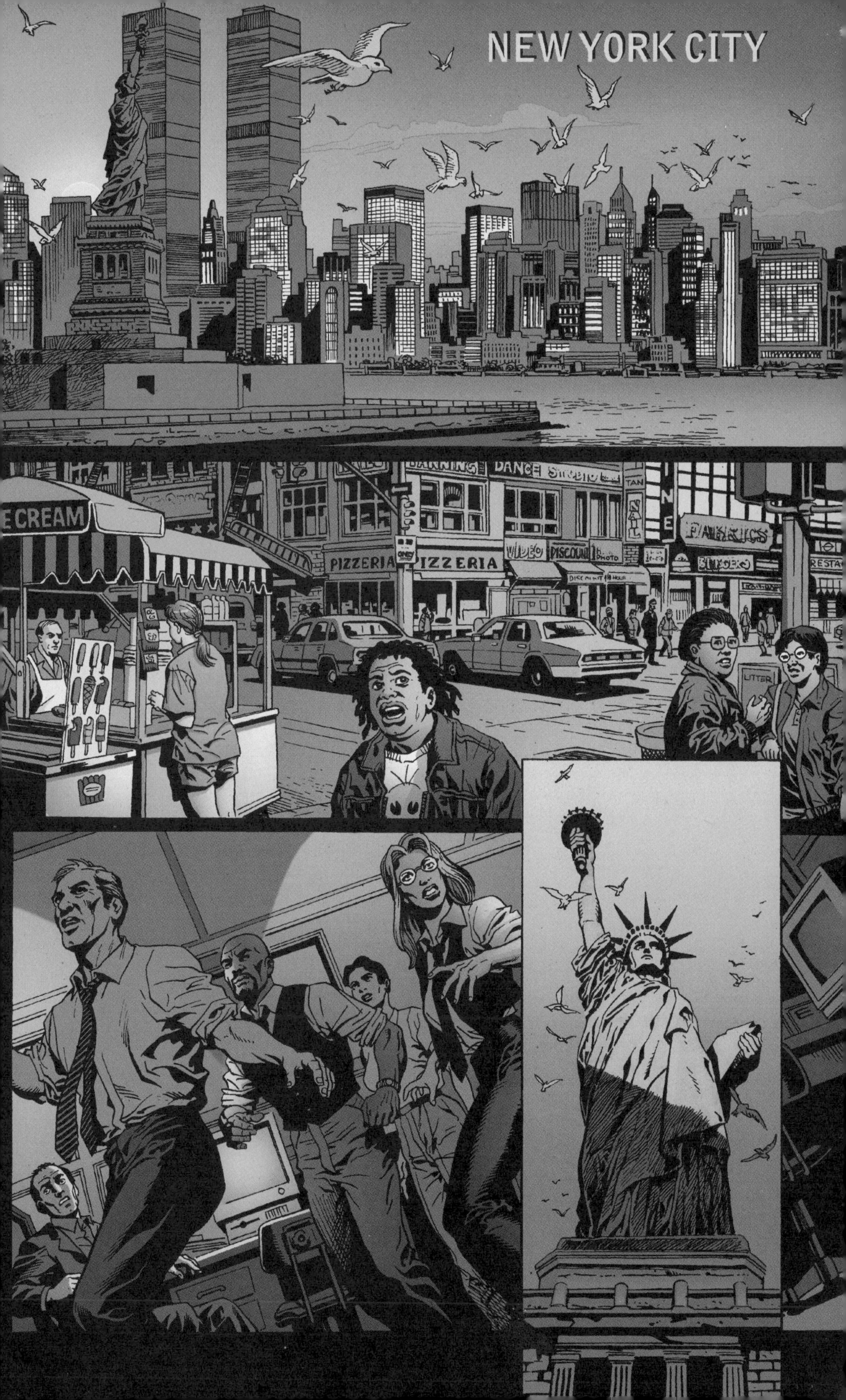
NEW YORK CITY
E CREAM
PIZZERIA
PIZZERIA
VIDEO
LITTER

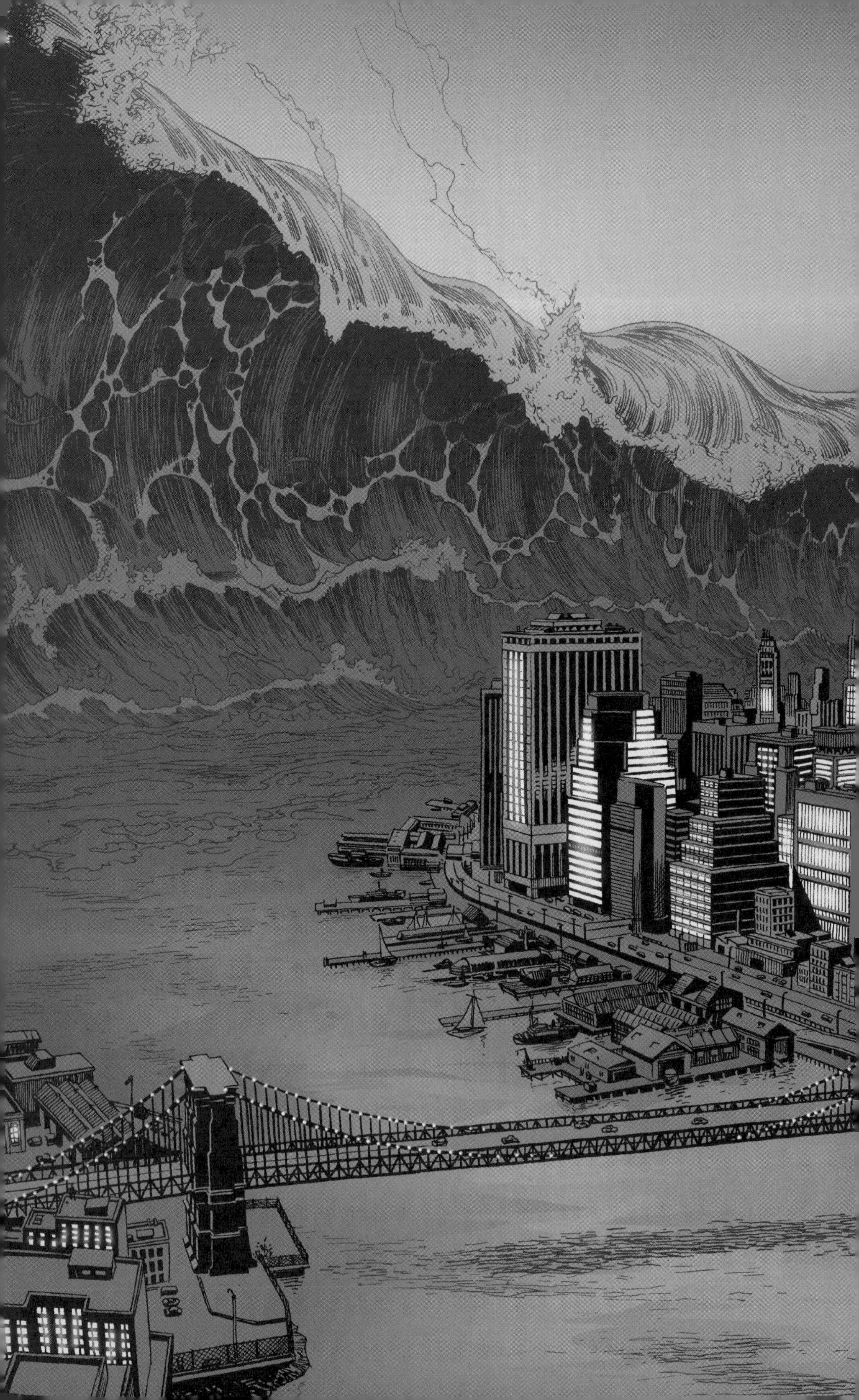

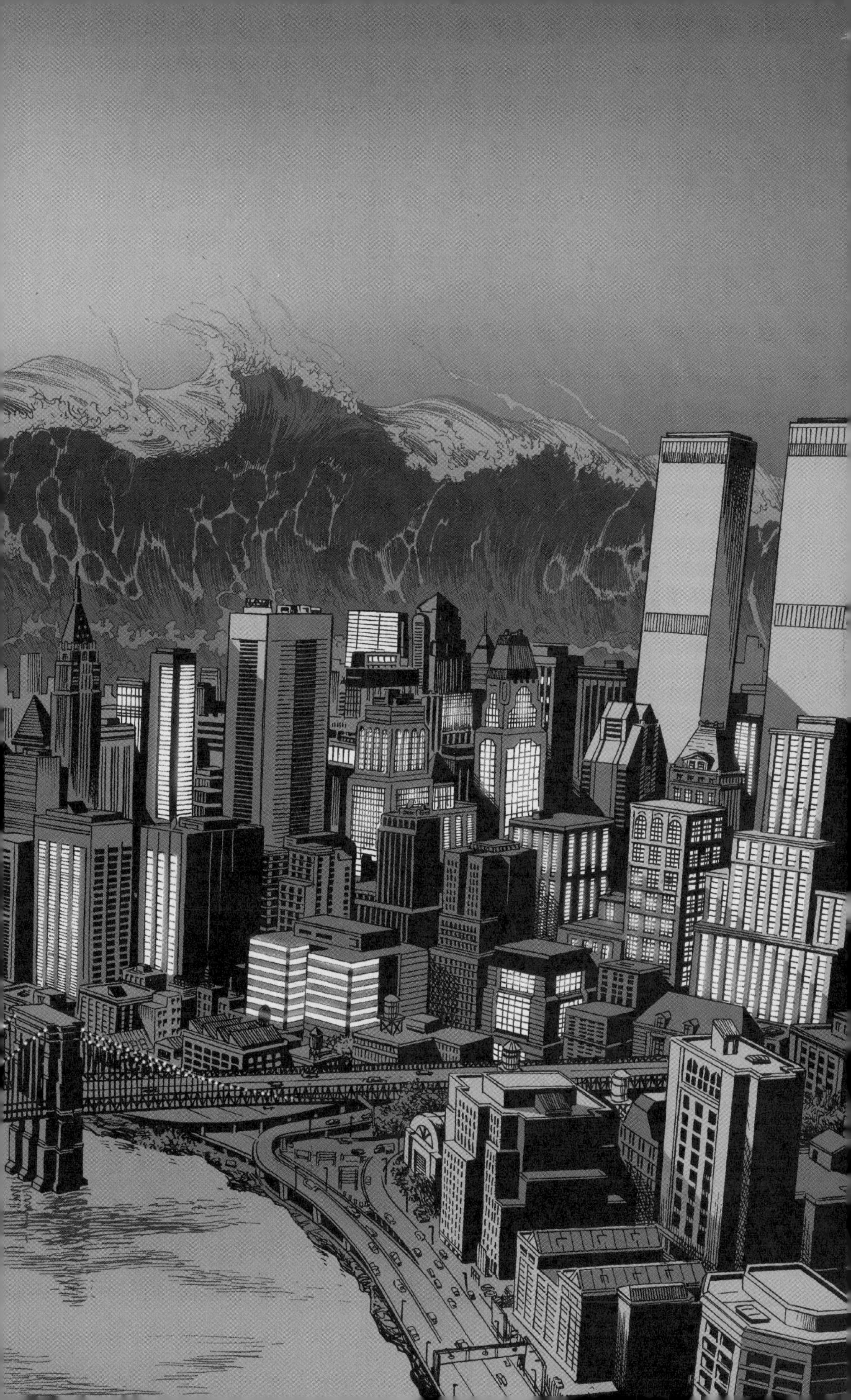

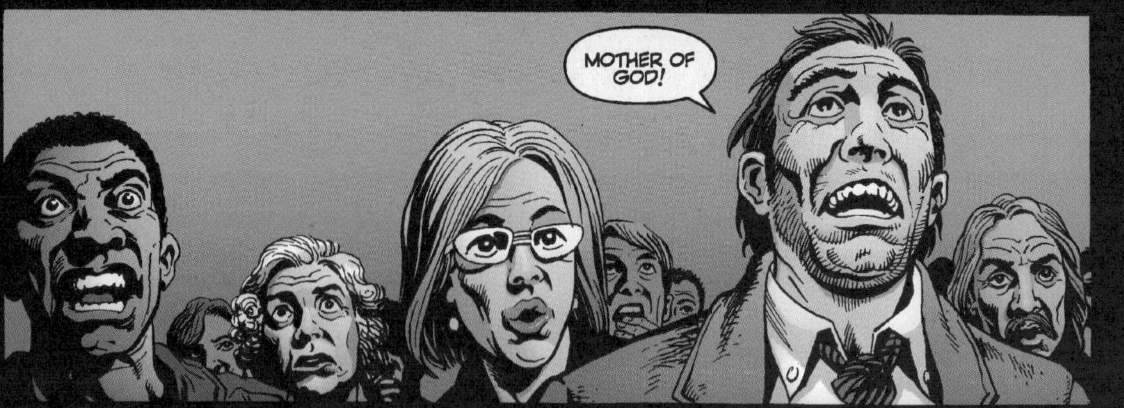
MOTHER OF GOD!

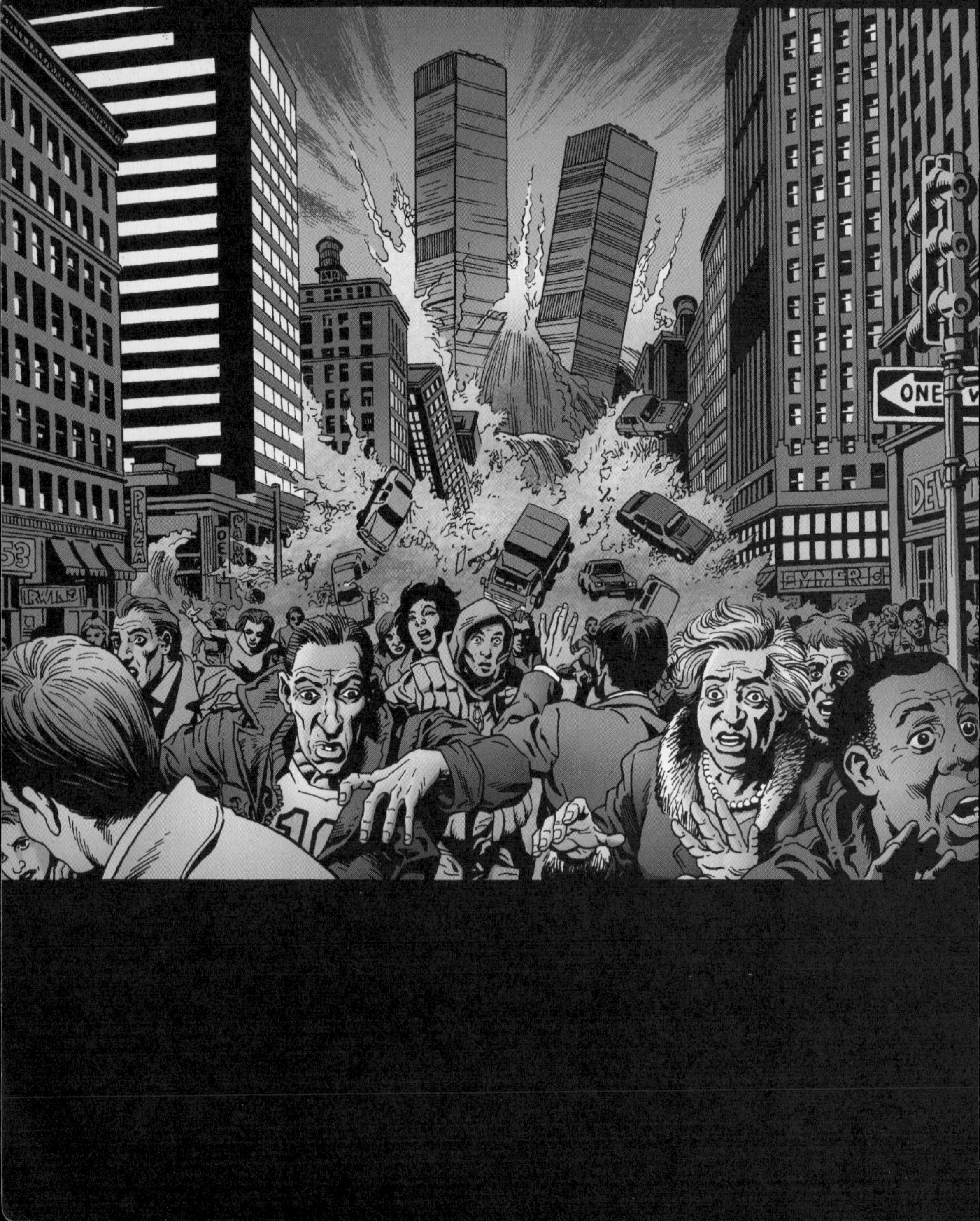
PLAZA
ONE

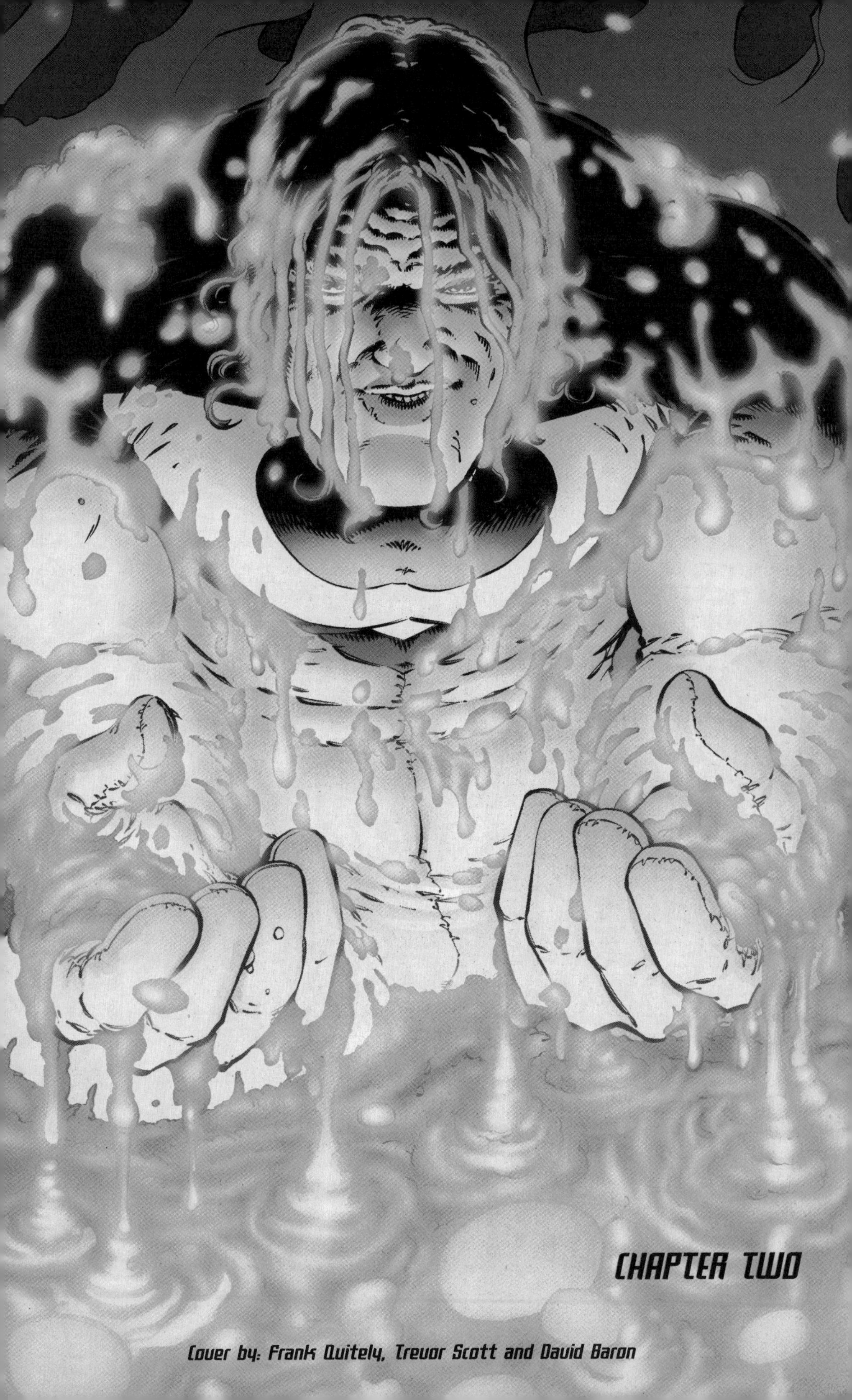

CHAPTER TWO

Cover by: Frank Quitely, Trevor Scott and David Baron

NEW YORK CITY

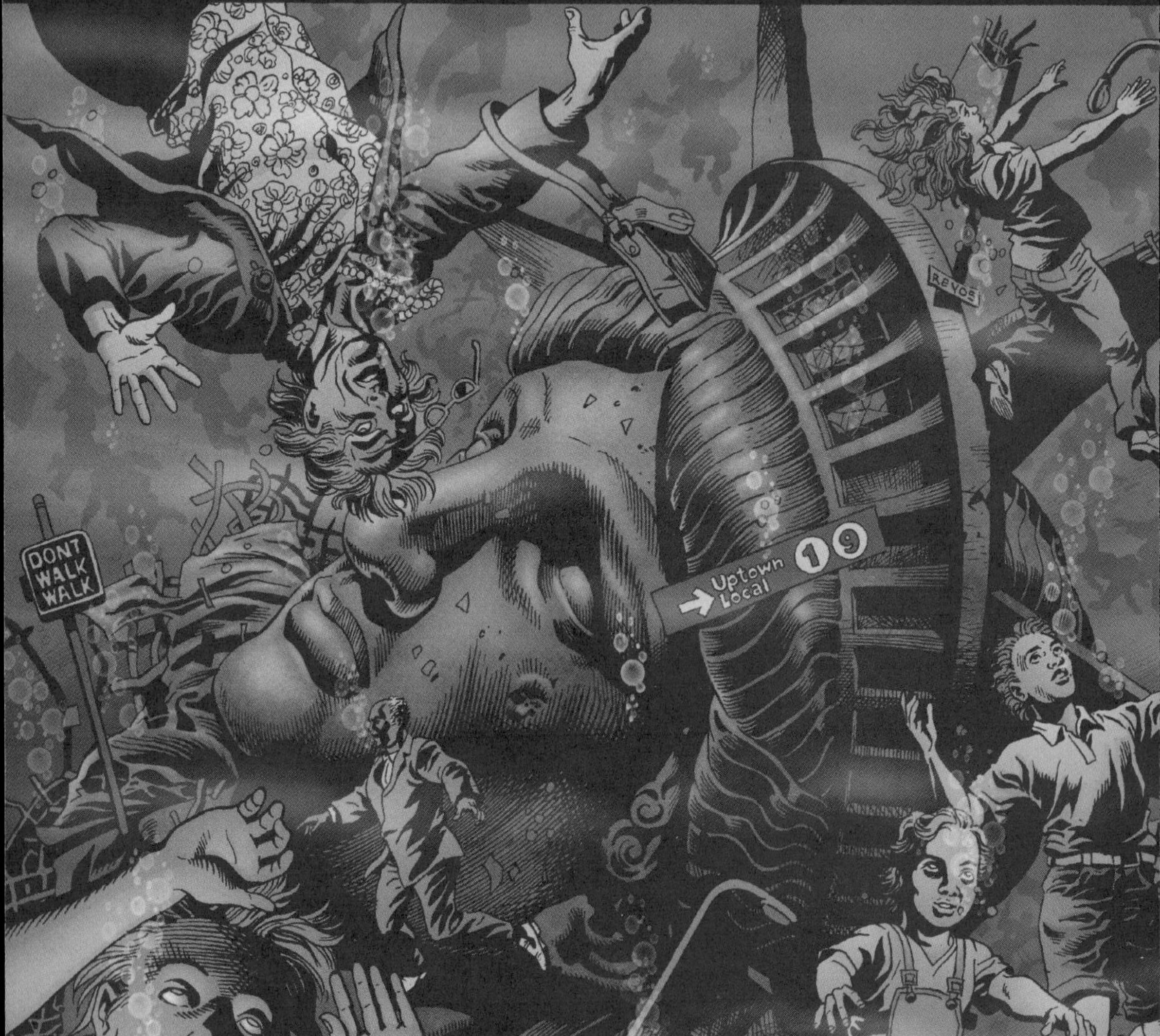
DON'T
WALK
WALK
Uptown
Local
1
9

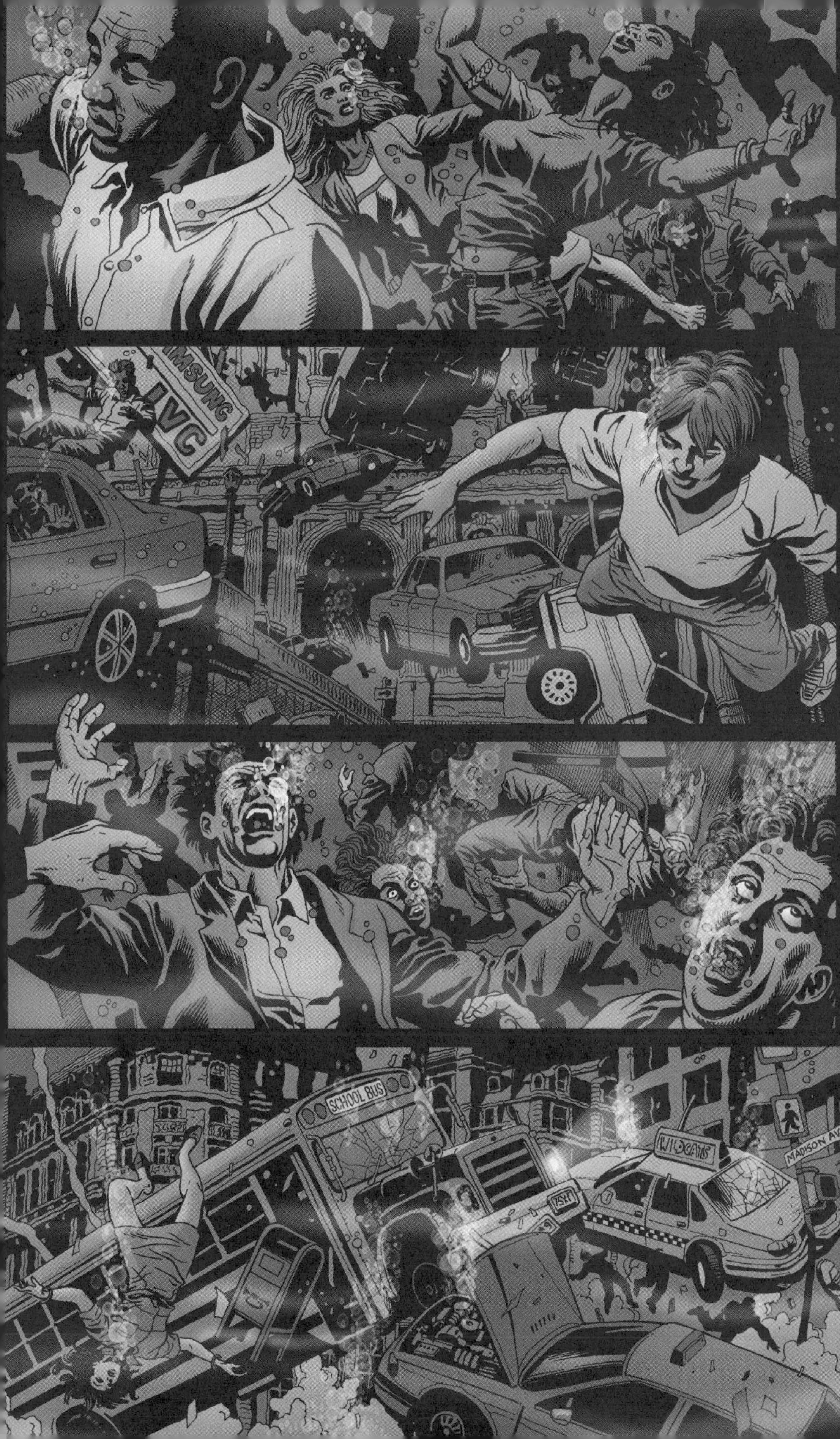
SCHOOL BUS
WILDCATS
MADISON AVE

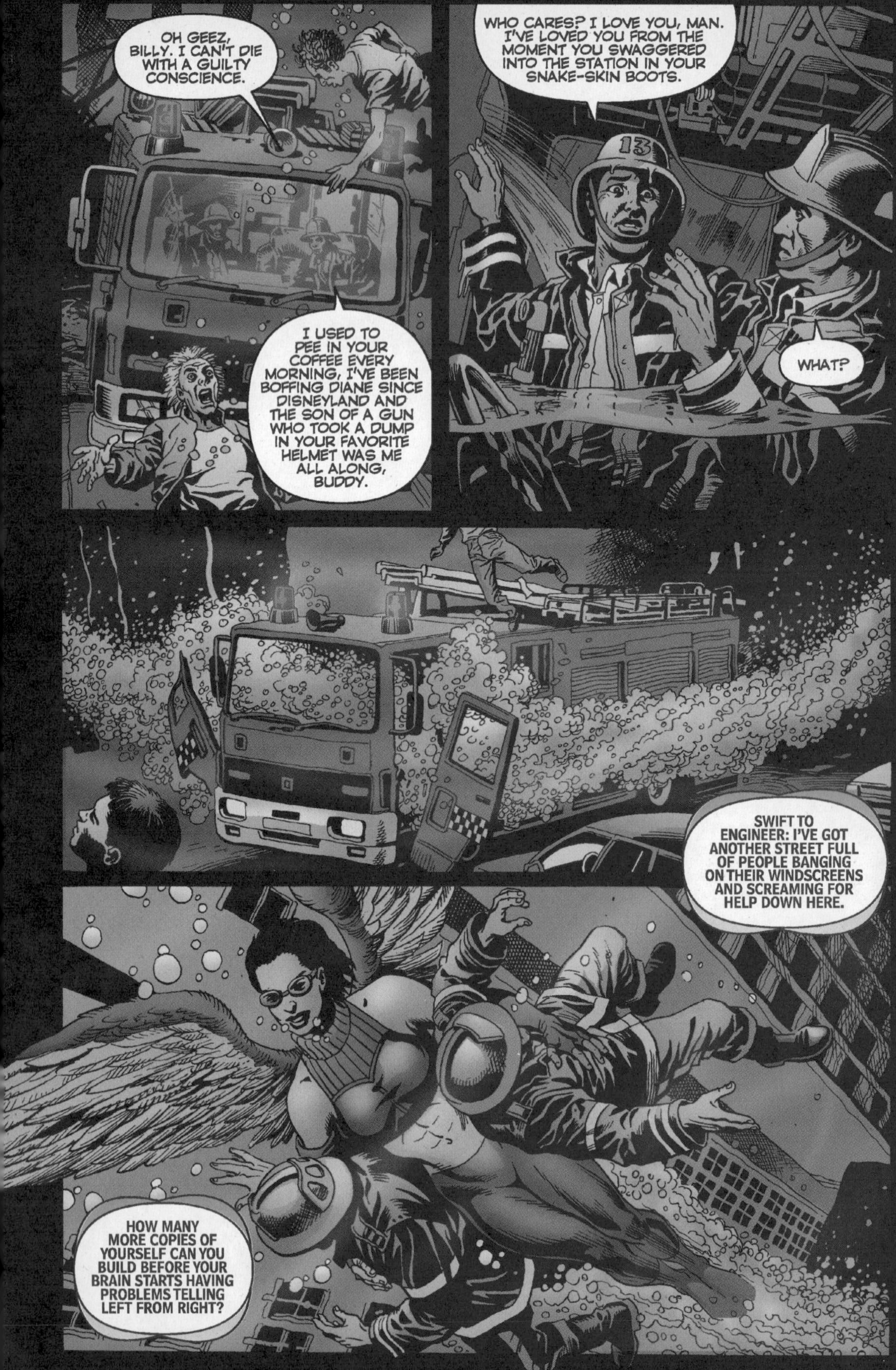
OH GEEZ, BILLY. I CAN'T DIE WITH A GUILTY CONSCIENCE.
I USED TO PEE IN YOUR COFFEE EVERY MORNING, I'VE BEEN BOFFING DIANE SINCE DISNEYLAND AND THE SON OF A GUN WHO TOOK A DUMP IN YOUR FAVORITE HELMET WAS ME ALL ALONG, BUDDY.
WHO CARES? I LOVE YOU, MAN. I'VE LOVED YOU FROM THE MOMENT YOU SWAGGERED INTO THE STATION IN YOUR SNAKE-SKIN BOOTS.
13
WHAT?
SWIFT TO ENGINEER: I'VE GOT ANOTHER STREET FULL OF PEOPLE BANGING ON THEIR WINDSCREENS AND SCREAMING FOR HELP DOWN HERE.
HOW MANY MORE COPIES OF YOURSELF CAN YOU BUILD BEFORE YOUR BRAIN STARTS HAVING PROBLEMS TELLING LEFT FROM RIGHT?

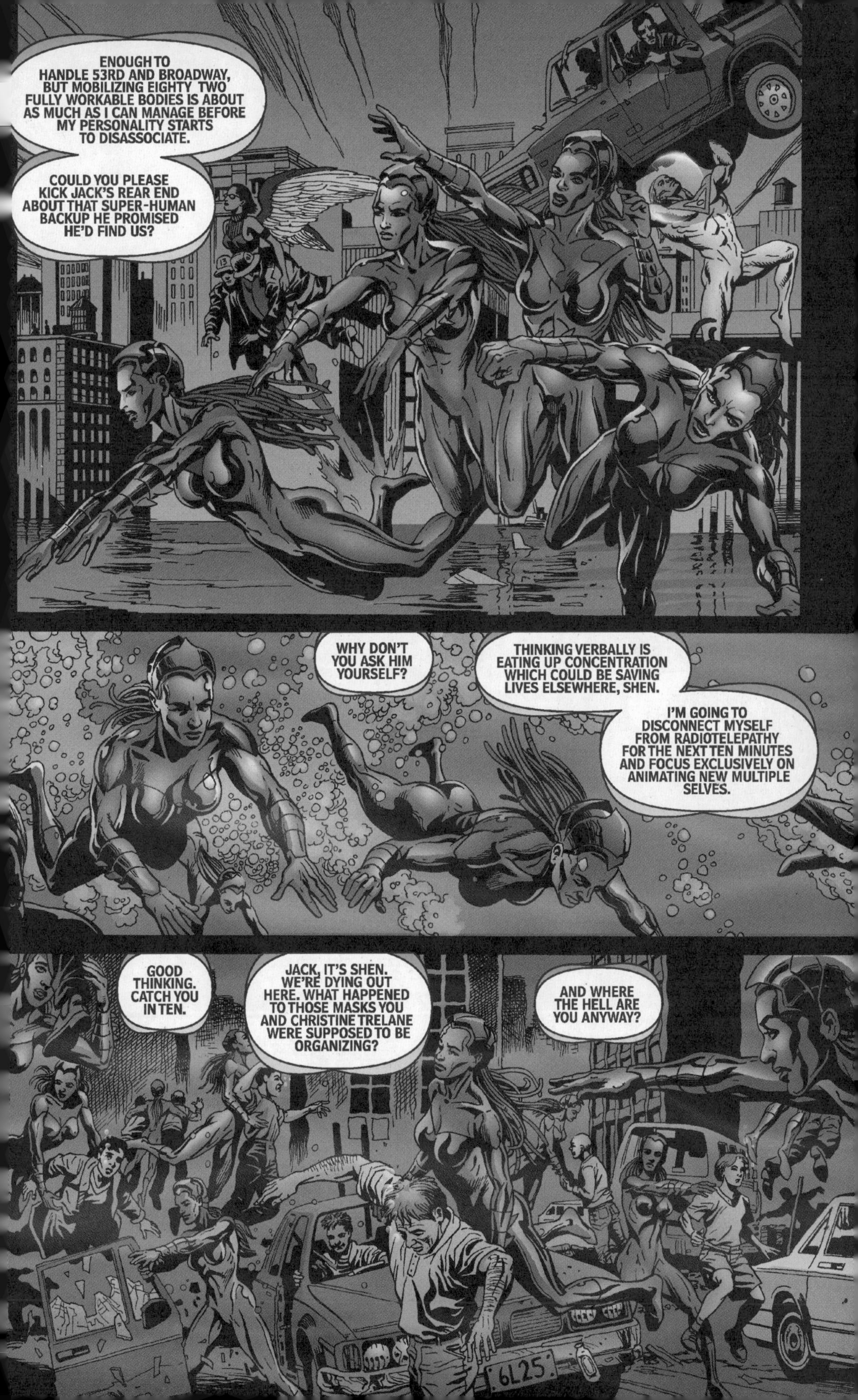
ENOUGH TO HANDLE 53RD AND BROADWAY, BUT MOBILIZING EIGHTY TWO FULLY WORKABLE BODIES IS ABOUT AS MUCH AS I CAN MANAGE BEFORE MY PERSONALITY STARTS TO DISASSOCIATE.
COULD YOU PLEASE KICK JACK'S REAR END ABOUT THAT SUPER-HUMAN BACKUP HE PROMISED HE'D FIND US?
WHY DON'T YOU ASK HIM YOURSELF?
THINKING VERBALLY IS EATING UP CONCENTRATION WHICH COULD BE SAVING LIVES ELSEWHERE, SHEN.
I'M GOING TO DISCONNECT MYSELF FROM RADIOTELEPATHY FOR THE NEXT TEN MINUTES AND FOCUS EXCLUSIVELY ON ANIMATING NEW MULTIPLE SELVES.
GOOD THINKING. CATCH YOU IN TEN.
JACK, IT'S SHEN. WE'RE DYING OUT HERE. WHAT HAPPENED TO THOSE MASKS YOU AND CHRISTINE TRELANE WERE SUPPOSED TO BE ORGANIZING?
AND WHERE THE HELL ARE YOU ANYWAY?
6L25

THE CARRIER

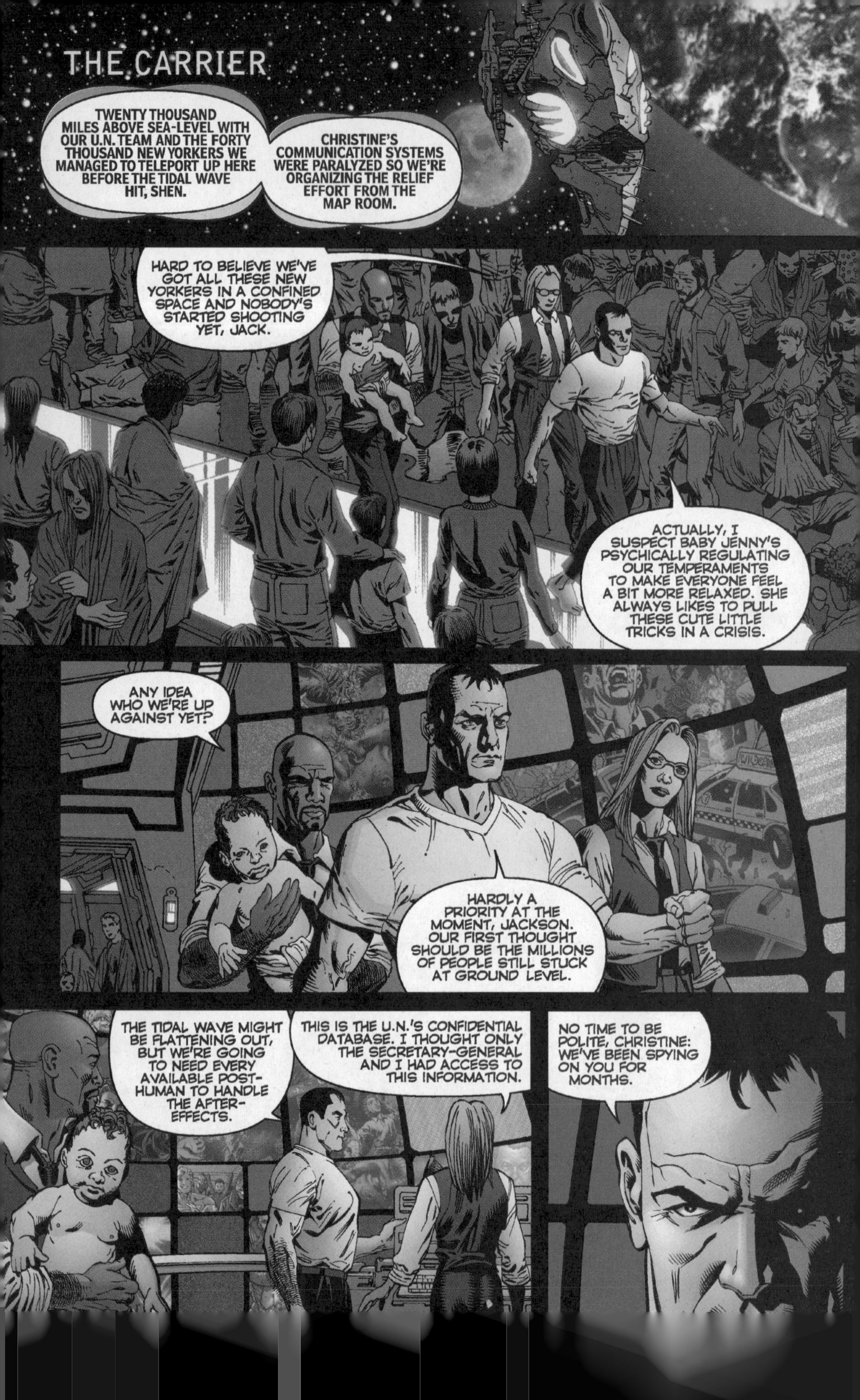
TWENTY THOUSAND MILES ABOVE SEA-LEVEL WITH OUR U.N. TEAM AND THE FORTY THOUSAND NEW YORKERS WE MANAGED TO TELEPORT UP HERE BEFORE THE TIDAL WAVE HIT, SHEN.
CHRISTINE'S COMMUNICATION SYSTEMS WERE PARALYZED SO WE'RE ORGANIZING THE RELIEF EFFORT FROM THE MAP ROOM.
HARD TO BELIEVE WE'VE GOT ALL THESE NEW YORKERS IN A CONFINED SPACE AND NOBODY'S STARTED SHOOTING YET, JACK.
ACTUALLY, I SUSPECT BABY JENNY'S PSYCHICALLY REGULATING OUR TEMPERAMENTS TO MAKE EVERYONE FEEL A BIT MORE RELAXED. SHE ALWAYS LIKES TO PULL THESE CUTE LITTLE TRICKS IN A CRISIS.
ANY IDEA WHO WE'RE UP AGAINST YET?
HARDLY A PRIORITY AT THE MOMENT, JACKSON. OUR FIRST THOUGHT SHOULD BE THE MILLIONS OF PEOPLE STILL STUCK AT GROUND LEVEL.
THE TIDAL WAVE MIGHT BE FLATTENING OUT, BUT WE'RE GOING TO NEED EVERY AVAILABLE POST-HUMAN TO HANDLE THE AFTER-EFFECTS.
THIS IS THE U.N.'S CONFIDENTIAL DATABASE. I THOUGHT ONLY THE SECRETARY-GENERAL AND I HAD ACCESS TO THIS INFORMATION.
NO TIME TO BE POLITE, CHRISTINE: WE'VE BEEN SPYING ON YOU FOR MONTHS.

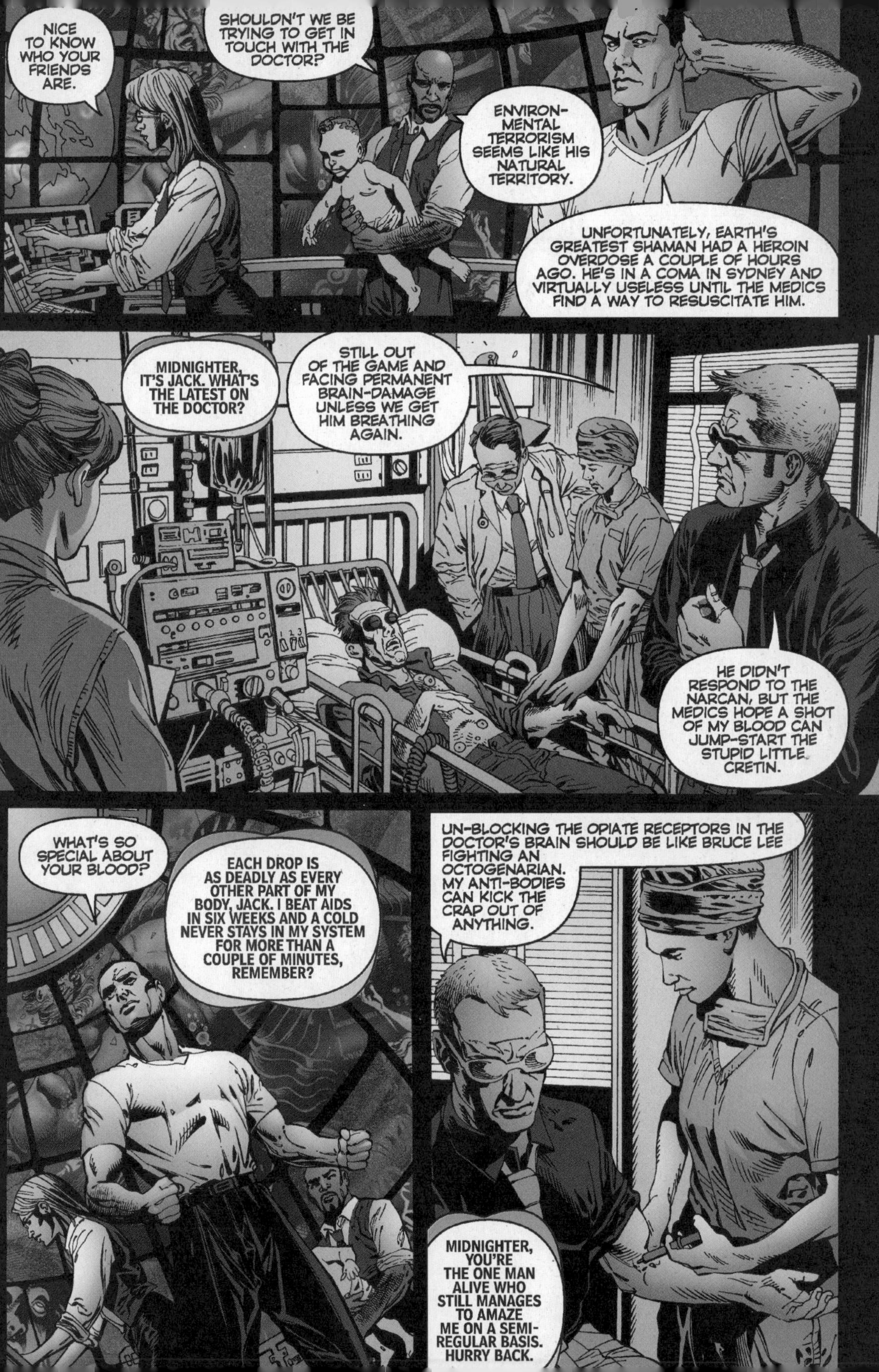
NICE TO KNOW WHO YOUR FRIENDS ARE.
SHOULDN'T WE BE TRYING TO GET IN TOUCH WITH THE DOCTOR?
ENVIRON-MENTAL TERRORISM SEEMS LIKE HIS NATURAL TERRITORY.
UNFORTUNATELY, EARTH'S GREATEST SHAMAN HAD A HEROIN OVERDOSE A COUPLE OF HOURS AGO. HE'S IN A COMA IN SYDNEY AND VIRTUALLY USELESS UNTIL THE MEDICS FIND A WAY TO RESUSCITATE HIM.
MIDNIGHTER, IT'S JACK. WHAT'S THE LATEST ON THE DOCTOR?
STILL OUT OF THE GAME AND FACING PERMANENT BRAIN-DAMAGE UNLESS WE GET HIM BREATHING AGAIN.
HE DIDN'T RESPOND TO THE NARCAN, BUT THE MEDICS HOPE A SHOT OF MY BLOOD CAN JUMP-START THE STUPID LITTLE CRETIN.
WHAT'S SO SPECIAL ABOUT YOUR BLOOD?
EACH DROP IS AS DEADLY AS EVERY OTHER PART OF MY BODY, JACK. I BEAT AIDS IN SIX WEEKS AND A COLD NEVER STAYS IN MY SYSTEM FOR MORE THAN A COUPLE OF MINUTES, REMEMBER?
UN-BLOCKING THE OPIATE RECEPTORS IN THE DOCTOR'S BRAIN SHOULD BE LIKE BRUCE LEE FIGHTING AN OCTOGENARIAN. MY ANTI-BODIES CAN KICK THE CRAP OUT OF ANYTHING.
MIDNIGHTER, YOU'RE THE ONE MAN ALIVE WHO STILL MANAGES TO AMAZE ME ON A SEMI-REGULAR BASIS. HURRY BACK.

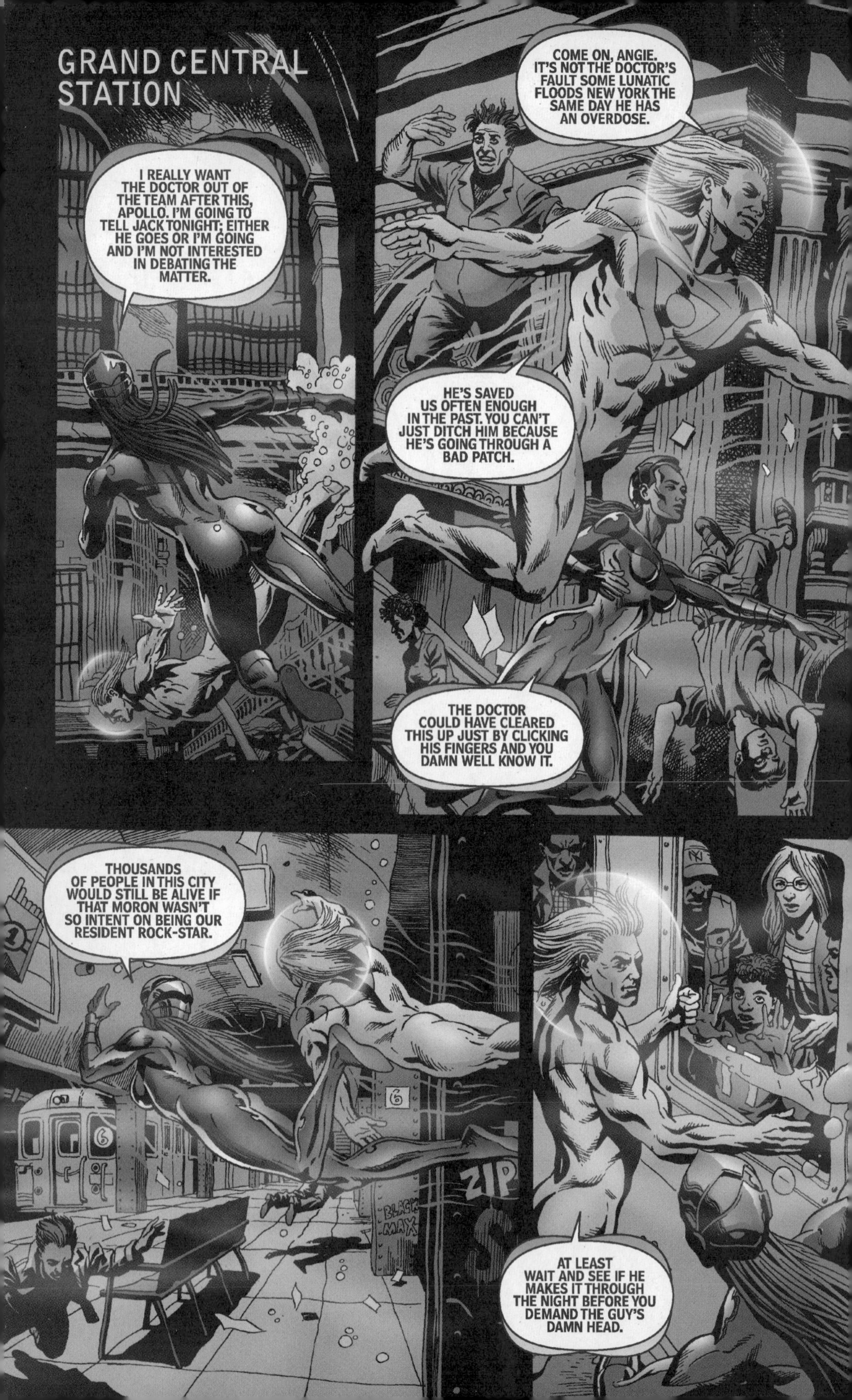
GRAND CENTRAL STATION
I REALLY WANT THE DOCTOR OUT OF THE TEAM AFTER THIS, APOLLO. I'M GOING TO TELL JACK TONIGHT; EITHER HE GOES OR I'M GOING AND I'M NOT INTERESTED IN DEBATING THE MATTER.
COME ON, ANGIE. IT'S NOT THE DOCTOR'S FAULT SOME LUNATIC FLOODS NEW YORK THE SAME DAY HE HAS AN OVERDOSE.
HE'S SAVED US OFTEN ENOUGH IN THE PAST. YOU CAN'T JUST DITCH HIM BECAUSE HE'S GOING THROUGH A BAD PATCH.
THE DOCTOR COULD HAVE CLEARED THIS UP JUST BY CLICKING HIS FINGERS AND YOU DAMN WELL KNOW IT.
THOUSANDS OF PEOPLE IN THIS CITY WOULD STILL BE ALIVE IF THAT MORON WASN'T SO INTENT ON BEING OUR RESIDENT ROCK-STAR.
AT LEAST WAIT AND SEE IF HE MAKES IT THROUGH THE NIGHT BEFORE YOU DEMAND THE GUY'S DAMN HEAD.

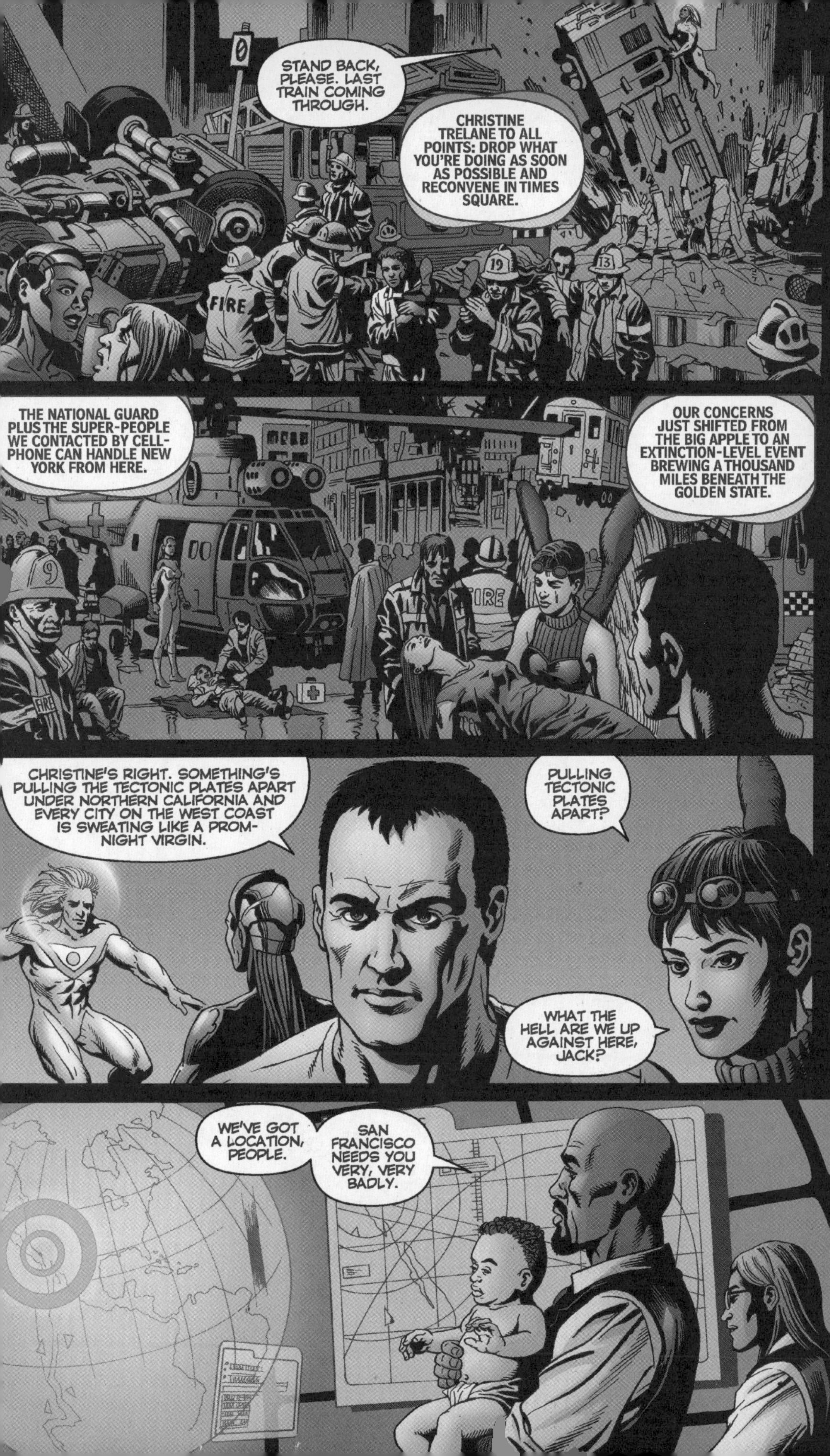
STAND BACK, PLEASE. LAST TRAIN COMING THROUGH.
CHRISTINE TRELANE TO ALL POINTS: DROP WHAT YOU'RE DOING AS SOON AS POSSIBLE AND RECONVENE IN TIMES SQUARE.
FIRE
THE NATIONAL GUARD PLUS THE SUPER-PEOPLE WE CONTACTED BY CELL-PHONE CAN HANDLE NEW YORK FROM HERE.
OUR CONCERNS JUST SHIFTED FROM THE BIG APPLE TO AN EXTINCTION-LEVEL EVENT BREWING A THOUSAND MILES BENEATH THE GOLDEN STATE.
CHRISTINE'S RIGHT. SOMETHING'S PULLING THE TECTONIC PLATES APART UNDER NORTHERN CALIFORNIA AND EVERY CITY ON THE WEST COAST IS SWEATING LIKE A PROM-NIGHT VIRGIN.
PULLING TECTONIC PLATES APART?
WHAT THE HELL ARE WE UP AGAINST HERE, JACK?
WE'VE GOT A LOCATION, PEOPLE.
SAN FRANCISCO NEEDS YOU VERY, VERY BADLY.

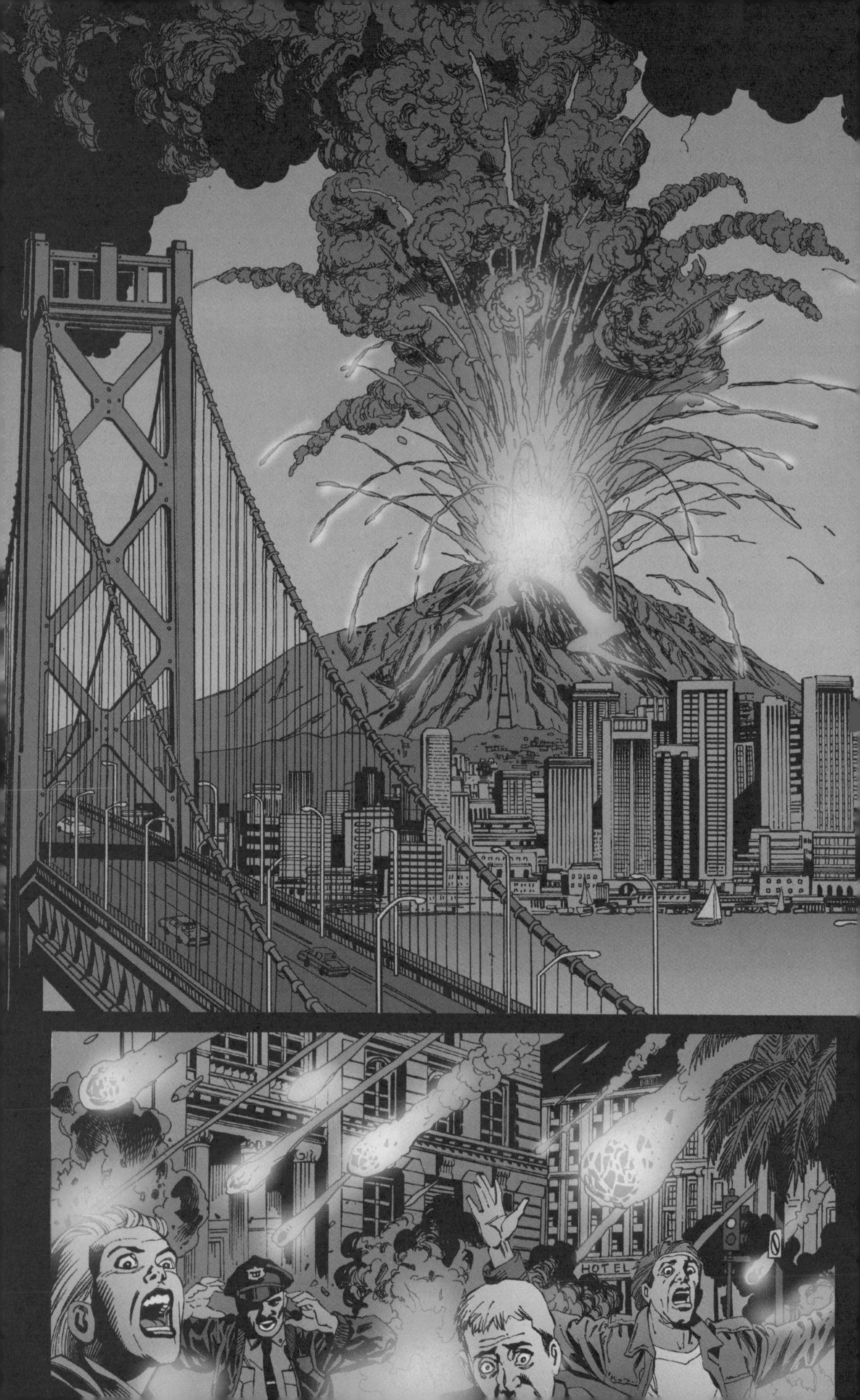
HOTEL

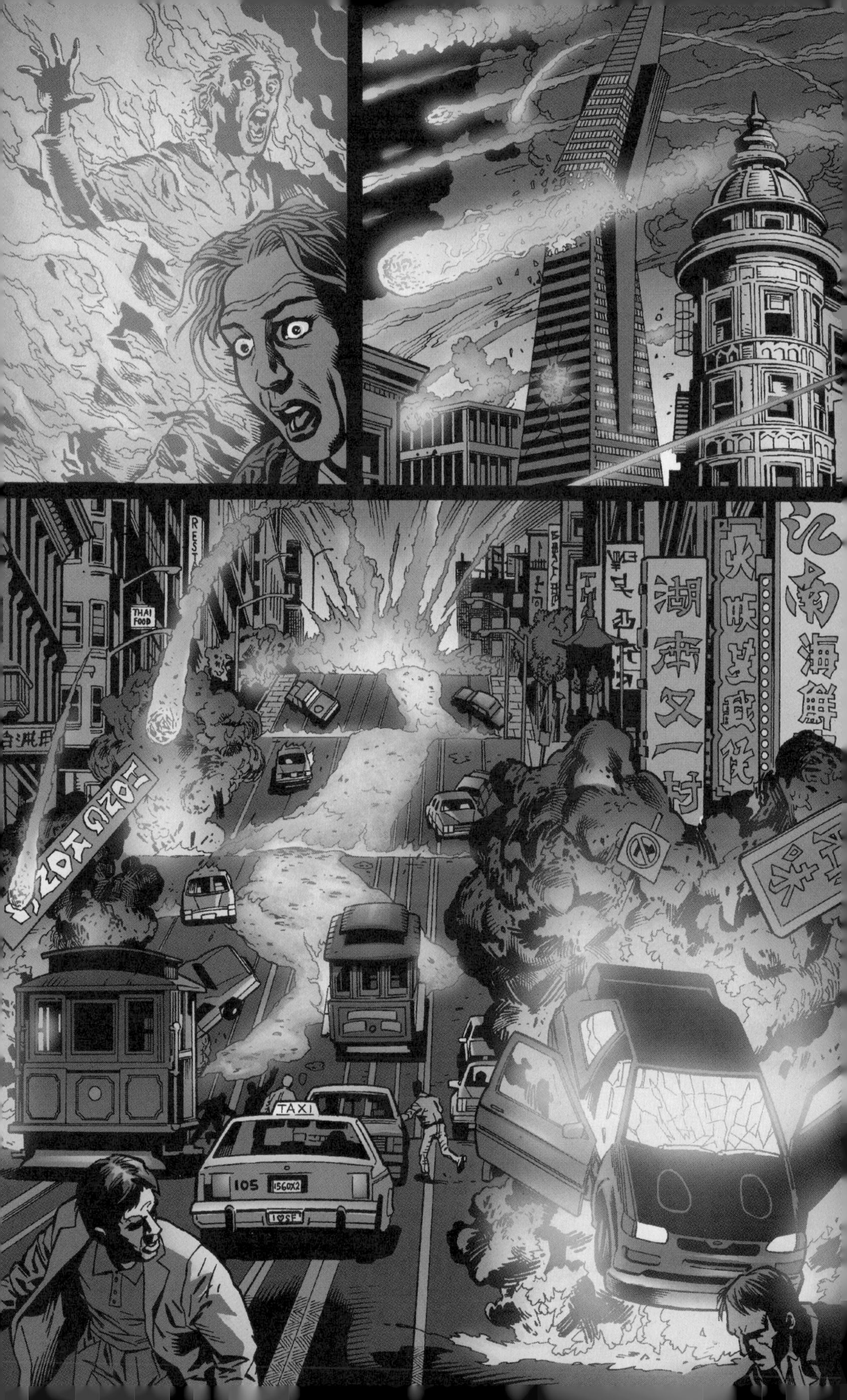
THAI FOOD
TAXI
105
1560X2

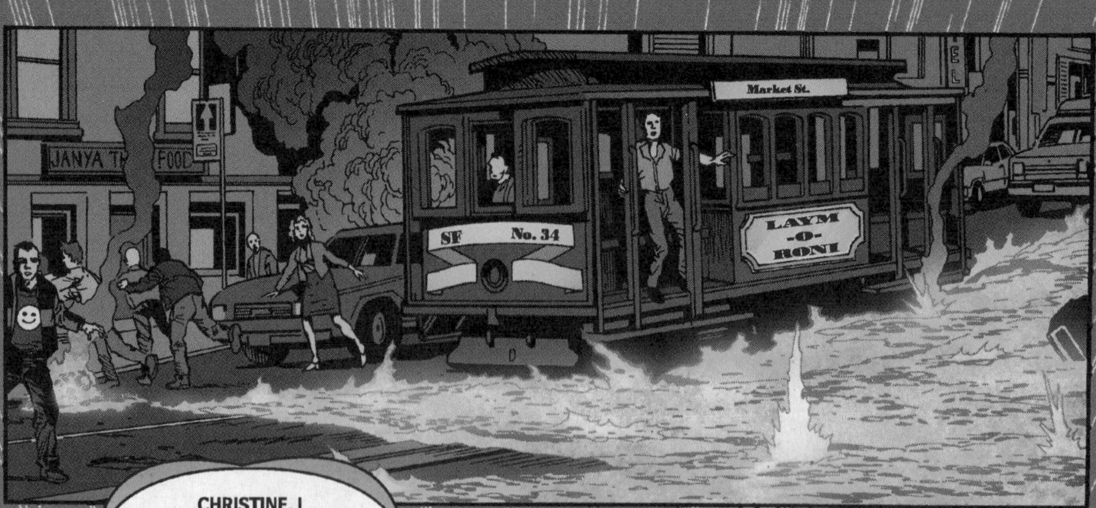
JANYA TH
FOOD
Market St.
SF No. 34
LAYM -O- RONI

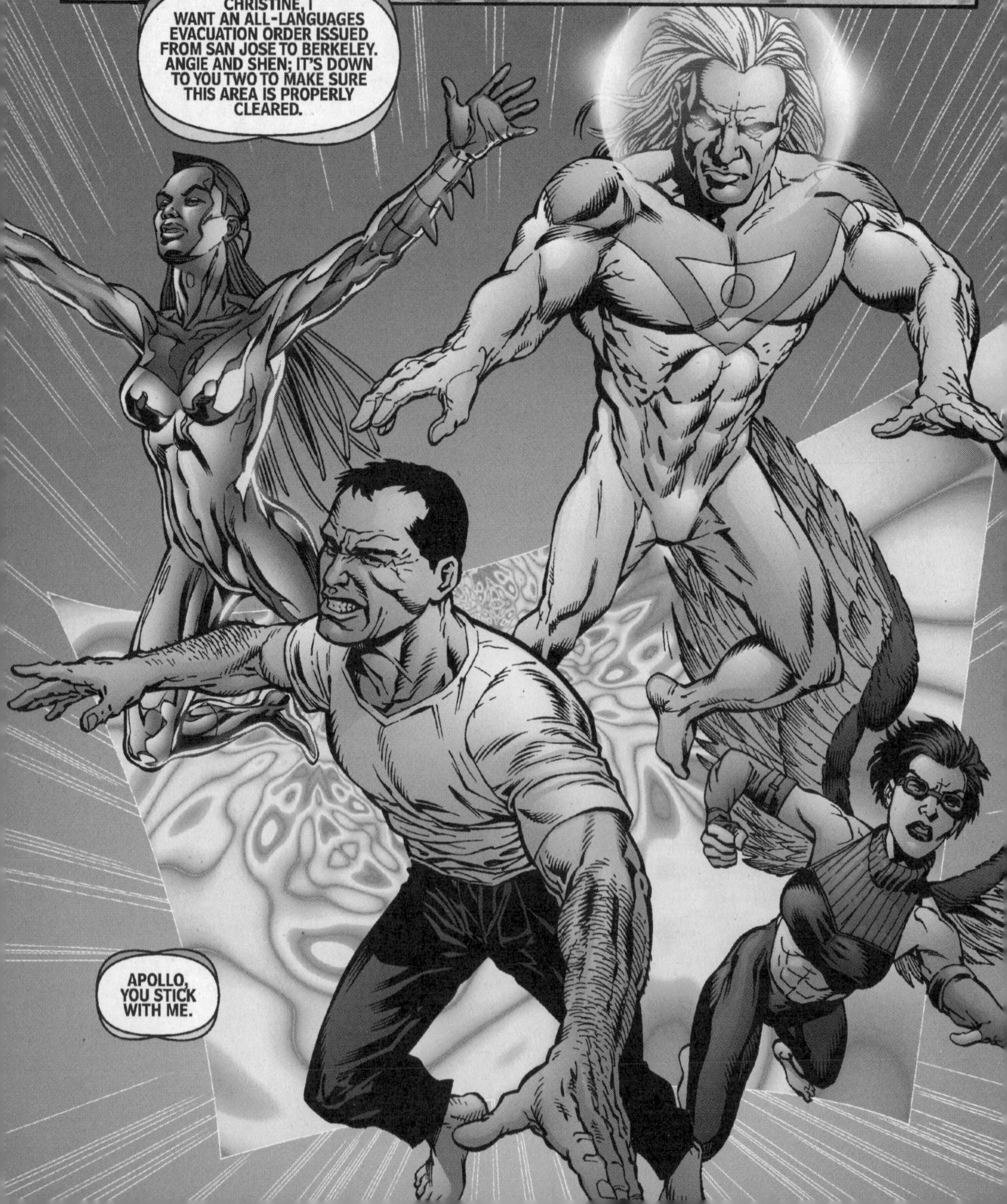
CHRISTINE, I WANT AN ALL-LANGUAGES EVACUATION ORDER ISSUED FROM SAN JOSE TO BERKELEY. ANGIE AND SHEN; IT'S DOWN TO YOU TWO TO MAKE SURE THIS AREA IS PROPERLY CLEARED.
APOLLO, YOU STICK WITH ME.

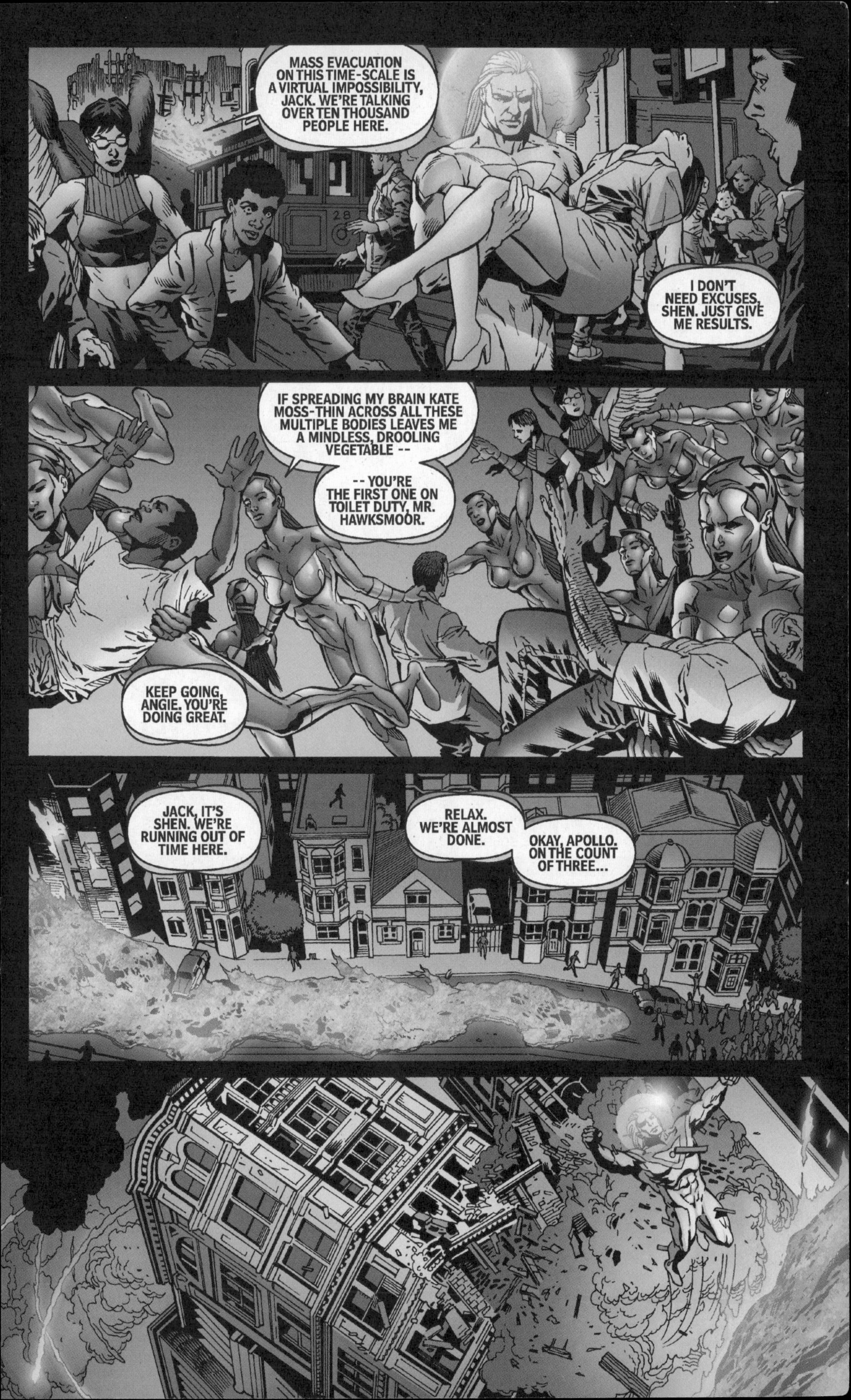
MASS EVACUATION ON THIS TIME-SCALE IS A VIRTUAL IMPOSSIBILITY, JACK. WE'RE TALKING OVER TEN THOUSAND PEOPLE HERE.
I DON'T NEED EXCUSES, SHEN. JUST GIVE ME RESULTS.
IF SPREADING MY BRAIN KATE MOSS-THIN ACROSS ALL THESE MULTIPLE BODIES LEAVES ME A MINDLESS, DROOLING VEGETABLE --
-- YOU'RE THE FIRST ONE ON TOILET DUTY, MR. HAWKSMOOR.
KEEP GOING, ANGIE. YOU'RE DOING GREAT.
JACK, IT'S SHEN. WE'RE RUNNING OUT OF TIME HERE.
RELAX. WE'RE ALMOST DONE.
OKAY, APOLLO. ON THE COUNT OF THREE...

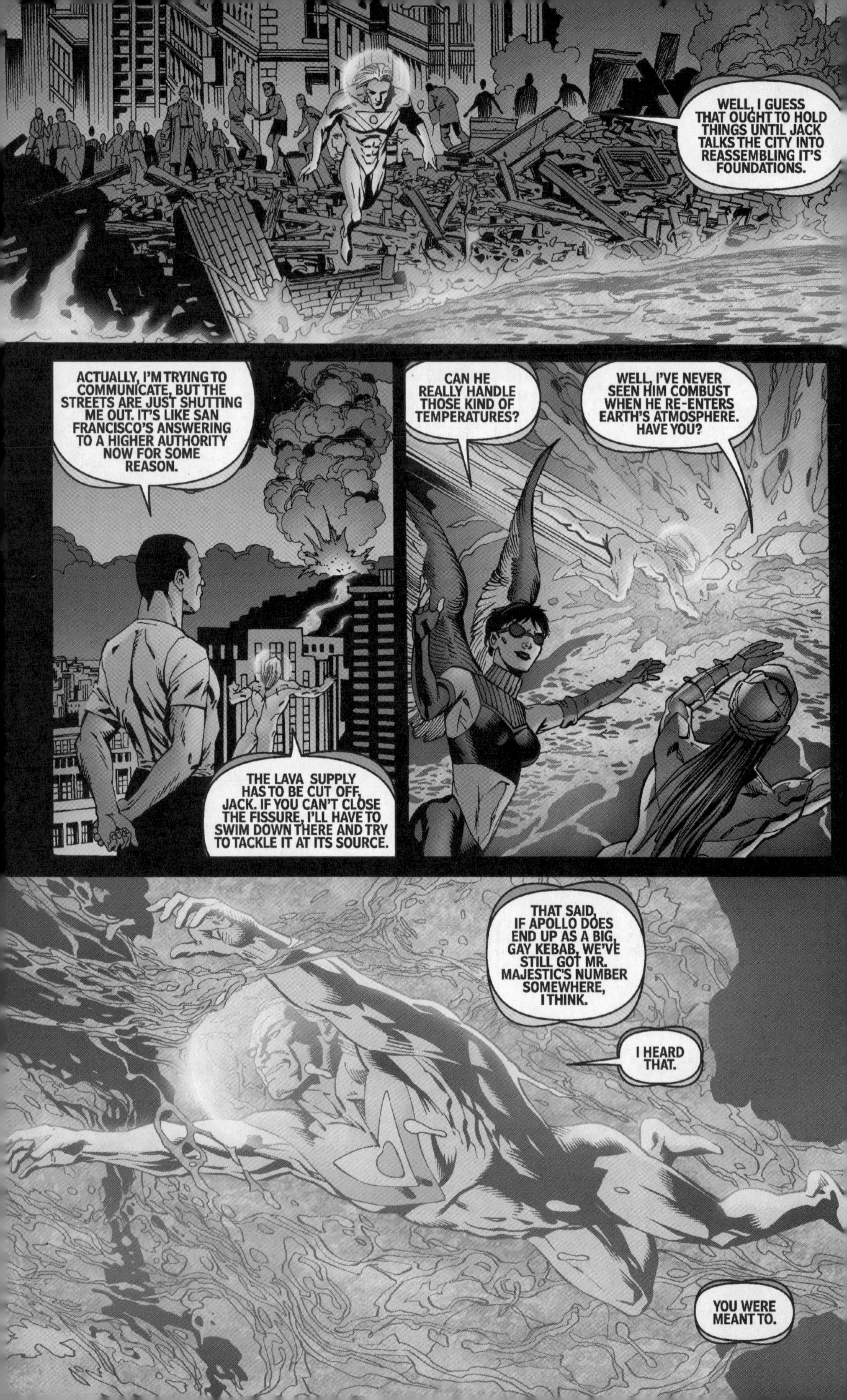
WELL, I GUESS THAT OUGHT TO HOLD THINGS UNTIL JACK TALKS THE CITY INTO REASSEMBLING IT'S FOUNDATIONS.
ACTUALLY, I'M TRYING TO COMMUNICATE, BUT THE STREETS ARE JUST SHUTTING ME OUT. IT'S LIKE SAN FRANCISCO'S ANSWERING TO A HIGHER AUTHORITY NOW FOR SOME REASON.
THE LAVA SUPPLY HAS TO BE CUT OFF, JACK. IF YOU CAN'T CLOSE THE FISSURE, I'LL HAVE TO SWIM DOWN THERE AND TRY TO TACKLE IT AT ITS SOURCE.
CAN HE REALLY HANDLE THOSE KIND OF TEMPERATURES?
WELL, I'VE NEVER SEEN HIM COMBUST WHEN HE RE-ENTERS EARTH'S ATMOSPHERE. HAVE YOU?
THAT SAID, IF APOLLO DOES END UP AS A BIG, GAY KEBAB, WE'VE STILL GOT MR. MAJESTIC'S NUMBER SOMEWHERE, I THINK.
I HEARD THAT.
YOU WERE MEANT TO.

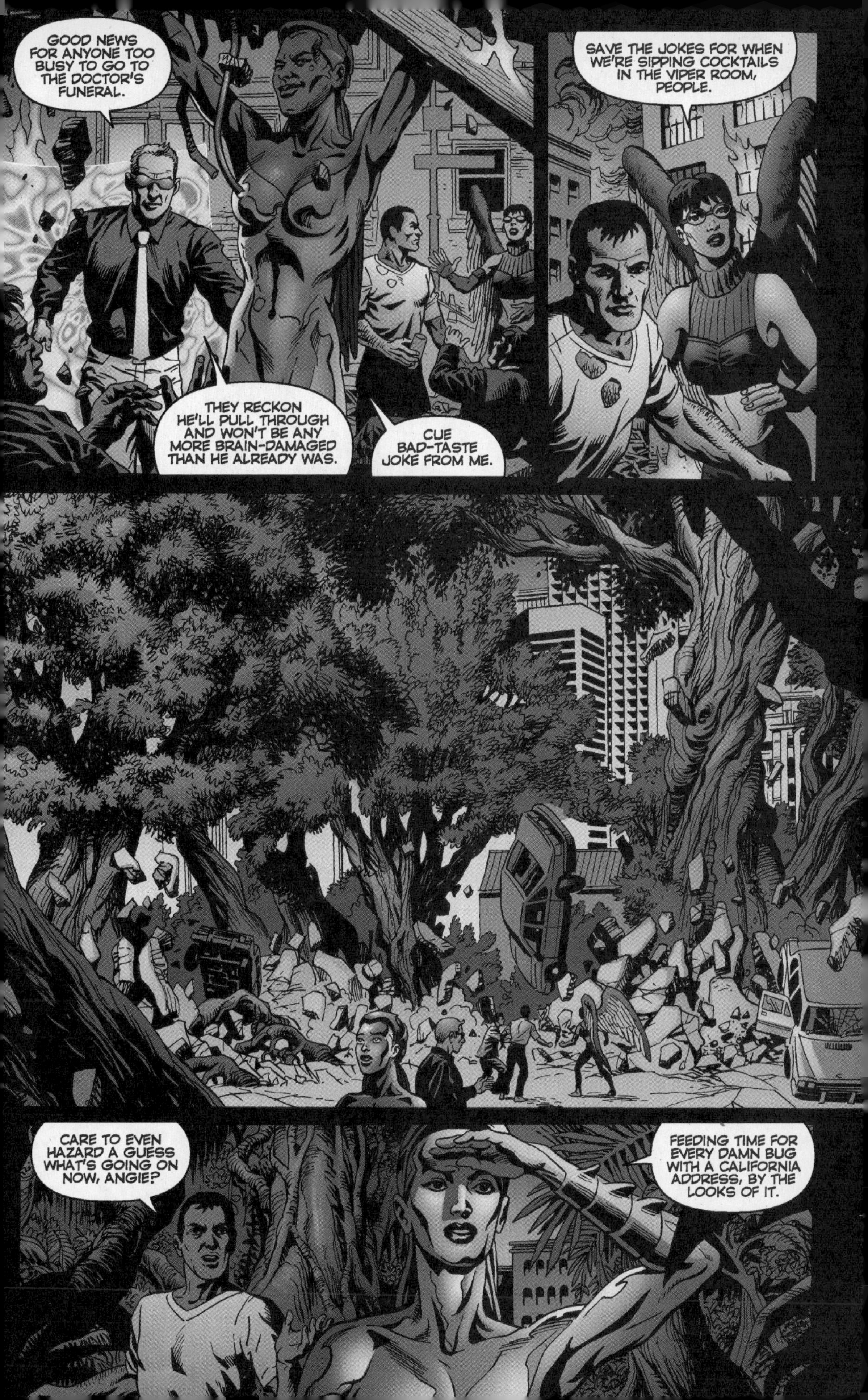
GOOD NEWS FOR ANYONE TOO BUSY TO GO TO THE DOCTOR'S FUNERAL.
THEY RECKON HE'LL PULL THROUGH AND WON'T BE ANY MORE BRAIN-DAMAGED THAN HE ALREADY WAS.
CUE BAD-TASTE JOKE FROM ME.
SAVE THE JOKES FOR WHEN WE'RE SIPPING COCKTAILS IN THE VIPER ROOM, PEOPLE.
CARE TO EVEN HAZARD A GUESS WHAT'S GOING ON NOW, ANGIE?
FEEDING TIME FOR EVERY DAMN BUG WITH A CALIFORNIA ADDRESS, BY THE LOOKS OF IT.

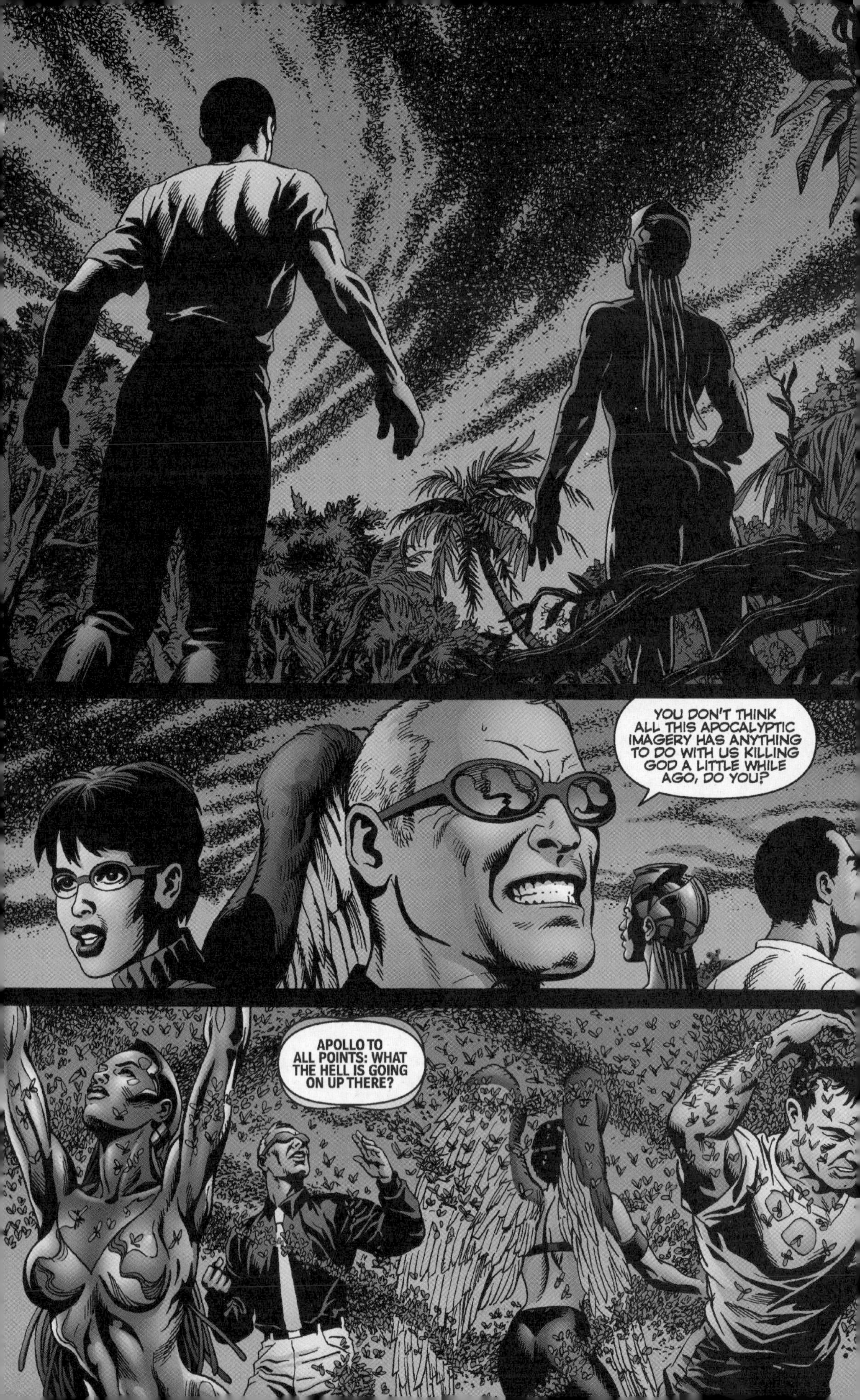
YOU DON'T THINK ALL THIS APOCALYPTIC IMAGERY HAS ANYTHING TO DO WITH US KILLING GOD A LITTLE WHILE AGO, DO YOU?
APOLLO TO ALL POINTS: WHAT THE HELL IS GOING ON UP THERE?

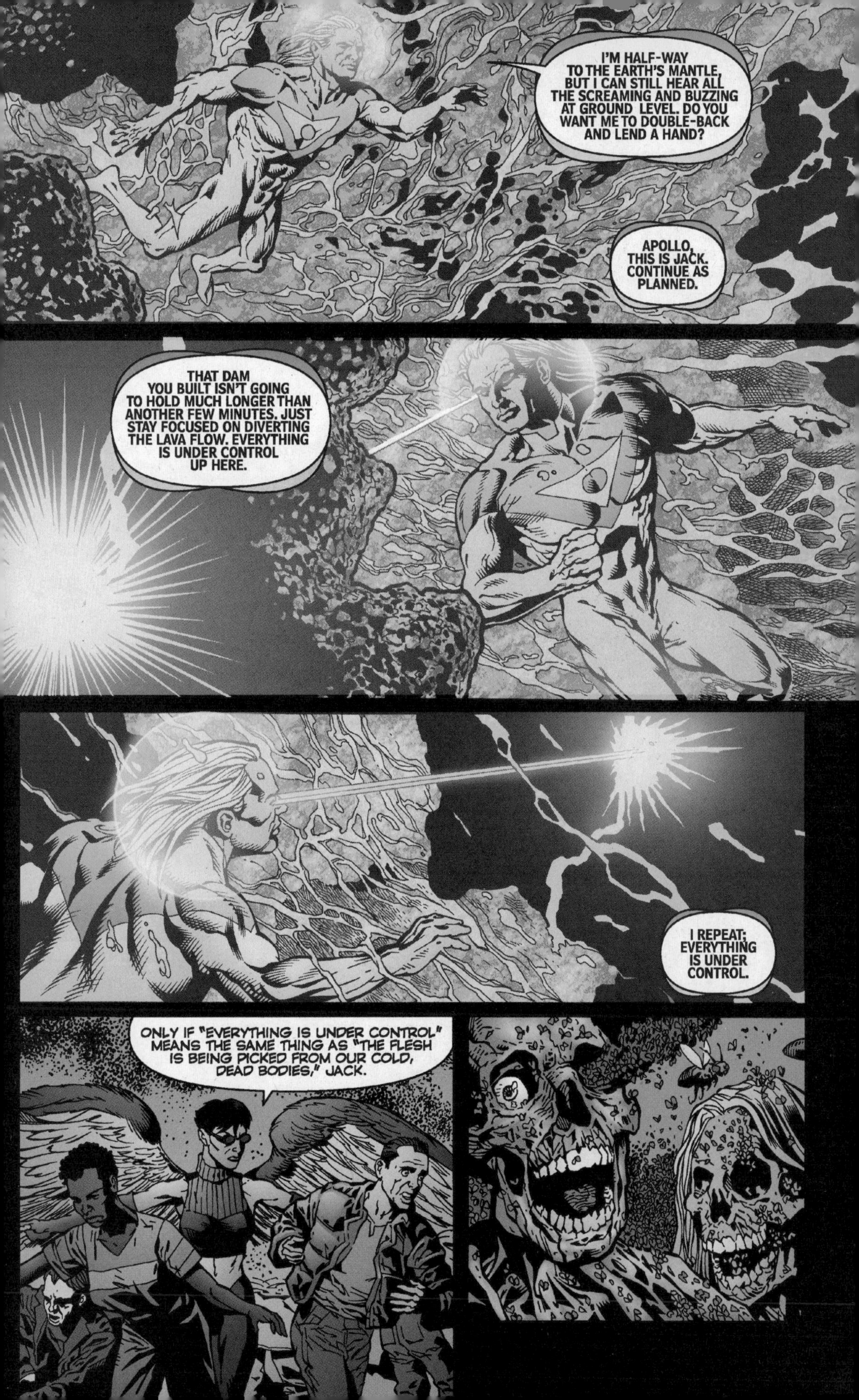
I'M HALF-WAY TO THE EARTH'S MANTLE, BUT I CAN STILL HEAR ALL THE SCREAMING AND BUZZING AT GROUND LEVEL. DO YOU WANT ME TO DOUBLE-BACK AND LEND A HAND?
APOLLO, THIS IS JACK. CONTINUE AS PLANNED.
THAT DAM YOU BUILT ISN'T GOING TO HOLD MUCH LONGER THAN ANOTHER FEW MINUTES. JUST STAY FOCUSED ON DIVERTING THE LAVA FLOW. EVERYTHING IS UNDER CONTROL UP HERE.
I REPEAT; EVERYTHING IS UNDER CONTROL.
ONLY IF "EVERYTHING IS UNDER CONTROL" MEANS THE SAME THING AS "THE FLESH IS BEING PICKED FROM OUR COLD, DEAD BODIES," JACK.

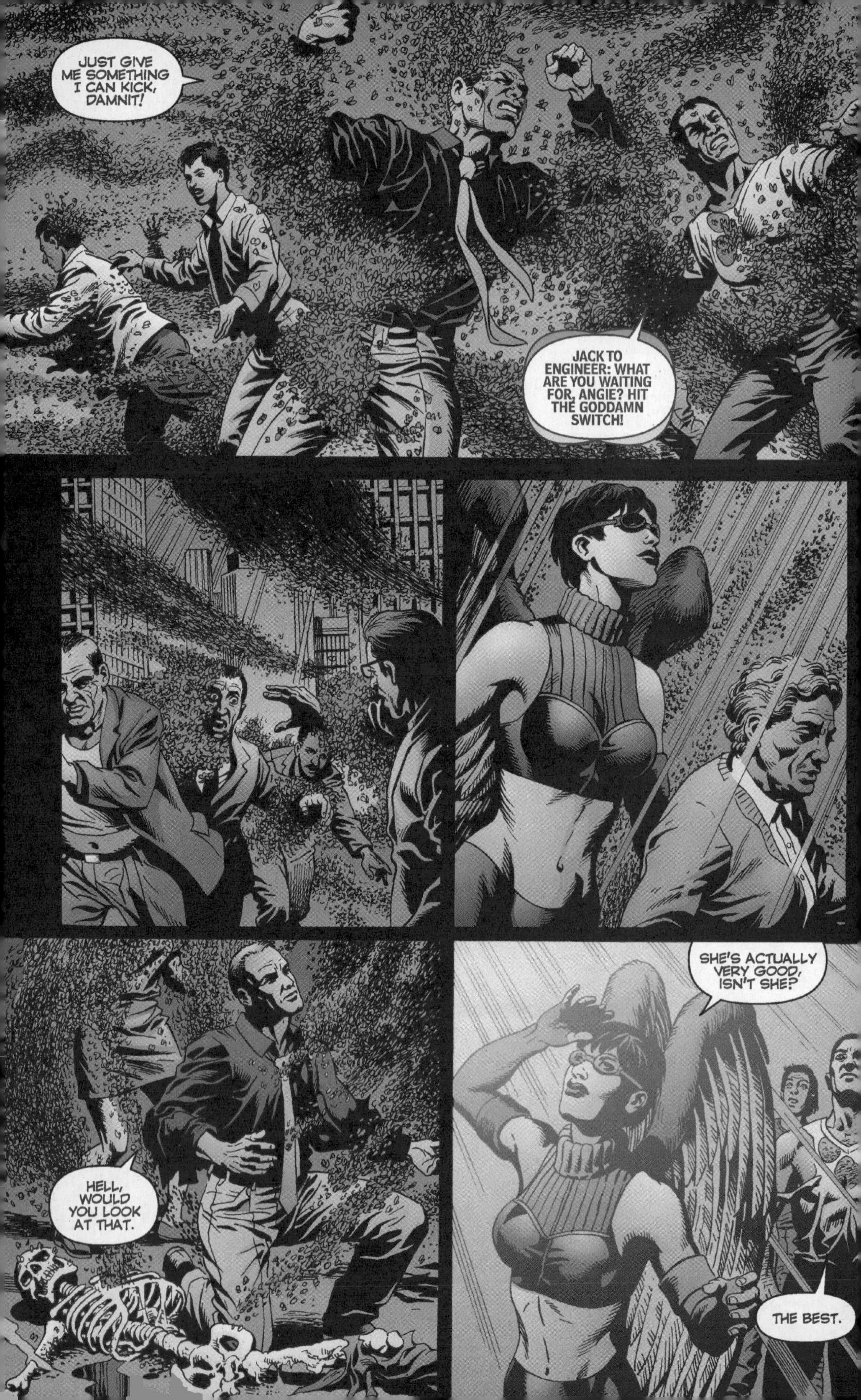
JUST GIVE ME SOMETHING I CAN KICK, DAMNIT!
JACK TO ENGINEER: WHAT ARE YOU WAITING FOR, ANGIE? HIT THE GODDAMN SWITCH!
HELL, WOULD YOU LOOK AT THAT.
SHE'S ACTUALLY VERY GOOD, ISN'T SHE?
THE BEST.

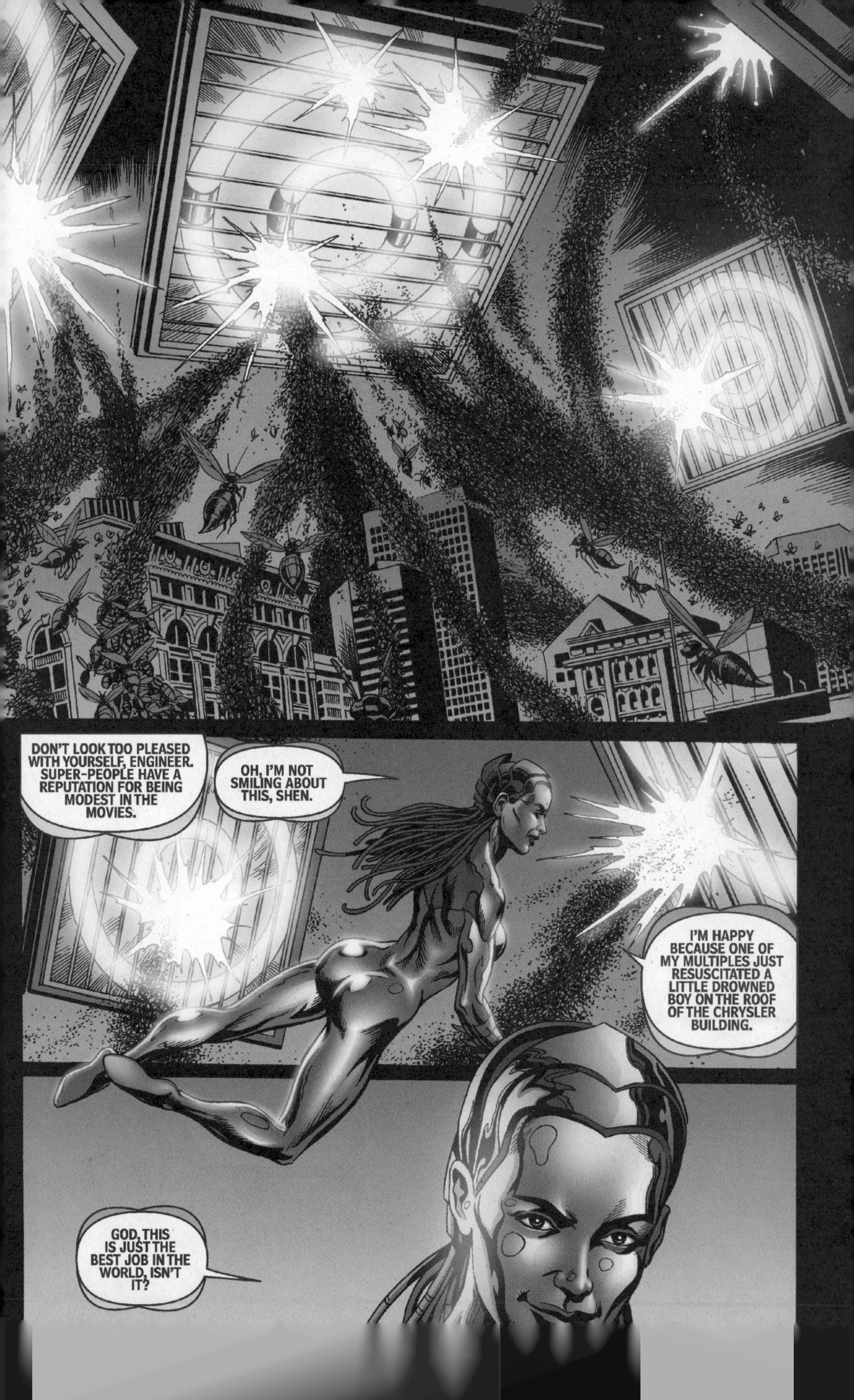
DON'T LOOK TOO PLEASED WITH YOURSELF, ENGINEER. SUPER-PEOPLE HAVE A REPUTATION FOR BEING MODEST IN THE MOVIES.
OH, I'M NOT SMILING ABOUT THIS, SHEN.
I'M HAPPY BECAUSE ONE OF MY MULTIPLES JUST RESUSCITATED A LITTLE DROWNED BOY ON THE ROOF OF THE CHRYSLER BUILDING.
GOD, THIS IS JUST THE BEST JOB IN THE WORLD, ISN'T IT?

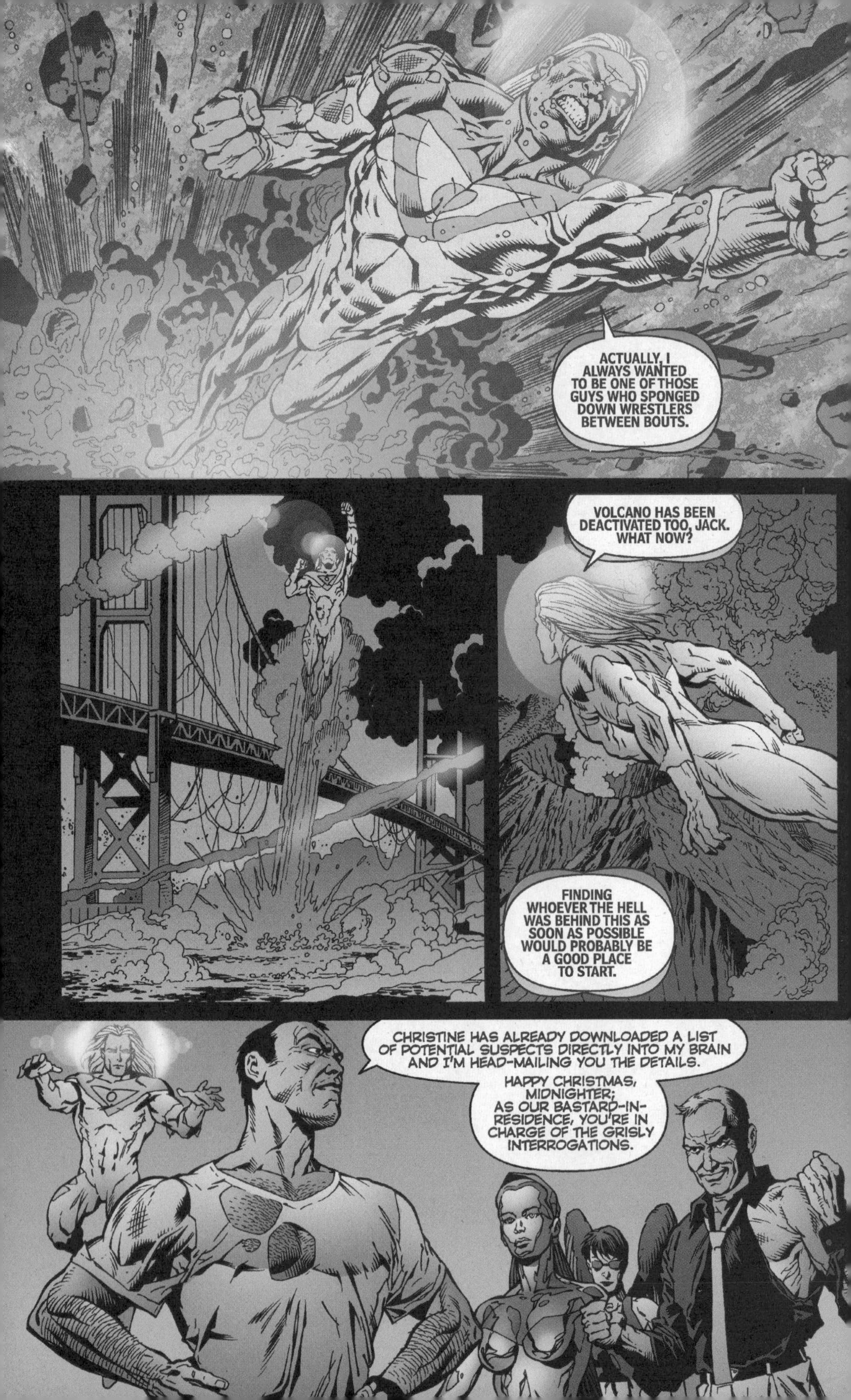
ACTUALLY, I ALWAYS WANTED TO BE ONE OF THOSE GUYS WHO SPONGED DOWN WRESTLERS BETWEEN BOUTS.
VOLCANO HAS BEEN DEACTIVATED TOO, JACK. WHAT NOW?
FINDING WHOEVER THE HELL WAS BEHIND THIS AS SOON AS POSSIBLE WOULD PROBABLY BE A GOOD PLACE TO START.
CHRISTINE HAS ALREADY DOWNLOADED A LIST OF POTENTIAL SUSPECTS DIRECTLY INTO MY BRAIN AND I'M HEAD-MAILING YOU THE DETAILS.
HAPPY CHRISTMAS, MIDNIGHTER; AS OUR BASTARD-IN-RESIDENCE, YOU'RE IN CHARGE OF THE GRISLY INTERROGATIONS.

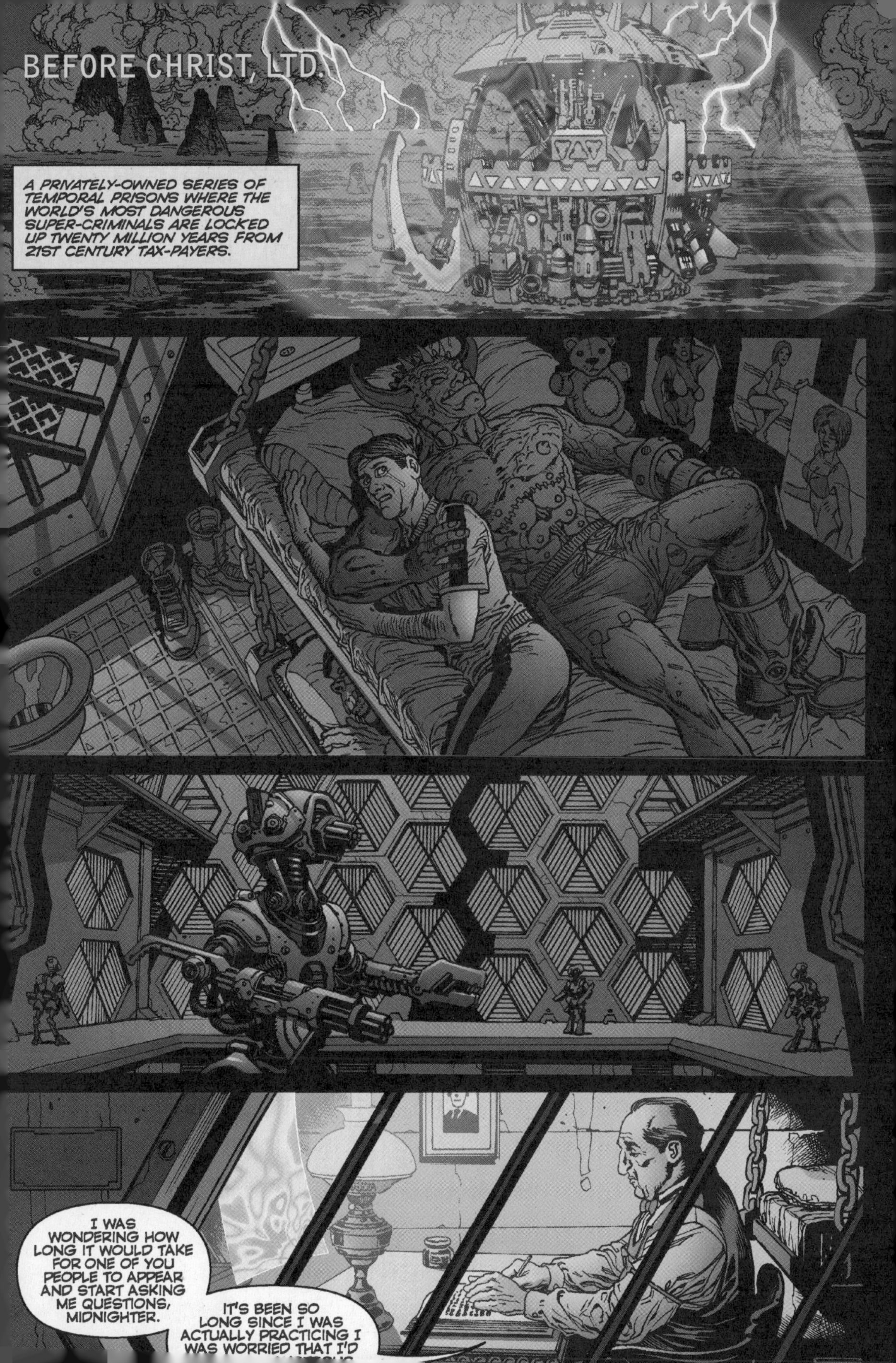
BEFORE CHRIST, LTD.
A PRIVATELY-OWNED SERIES OF TEMPORAL PRISONS WHERE THE WORLD'S MOST DANGEROUS SUPER-CRIMINALS ARE LOCKED UP TWENTY MILLION YEARS FROM 21ST CENTURY TAX-PAYERS.
I WAS WONDERING HOW LONG IT WOULD TAKE FOR ONE OF YOU PEOPLE TO APPEAR AND START ASKING ME QUESTIONS, MIDNIGHTER.
IT'S BEEN SO LONG SINCE I WAS ACTUALLY PRACTICING I WAS WORRIED THAT I'D

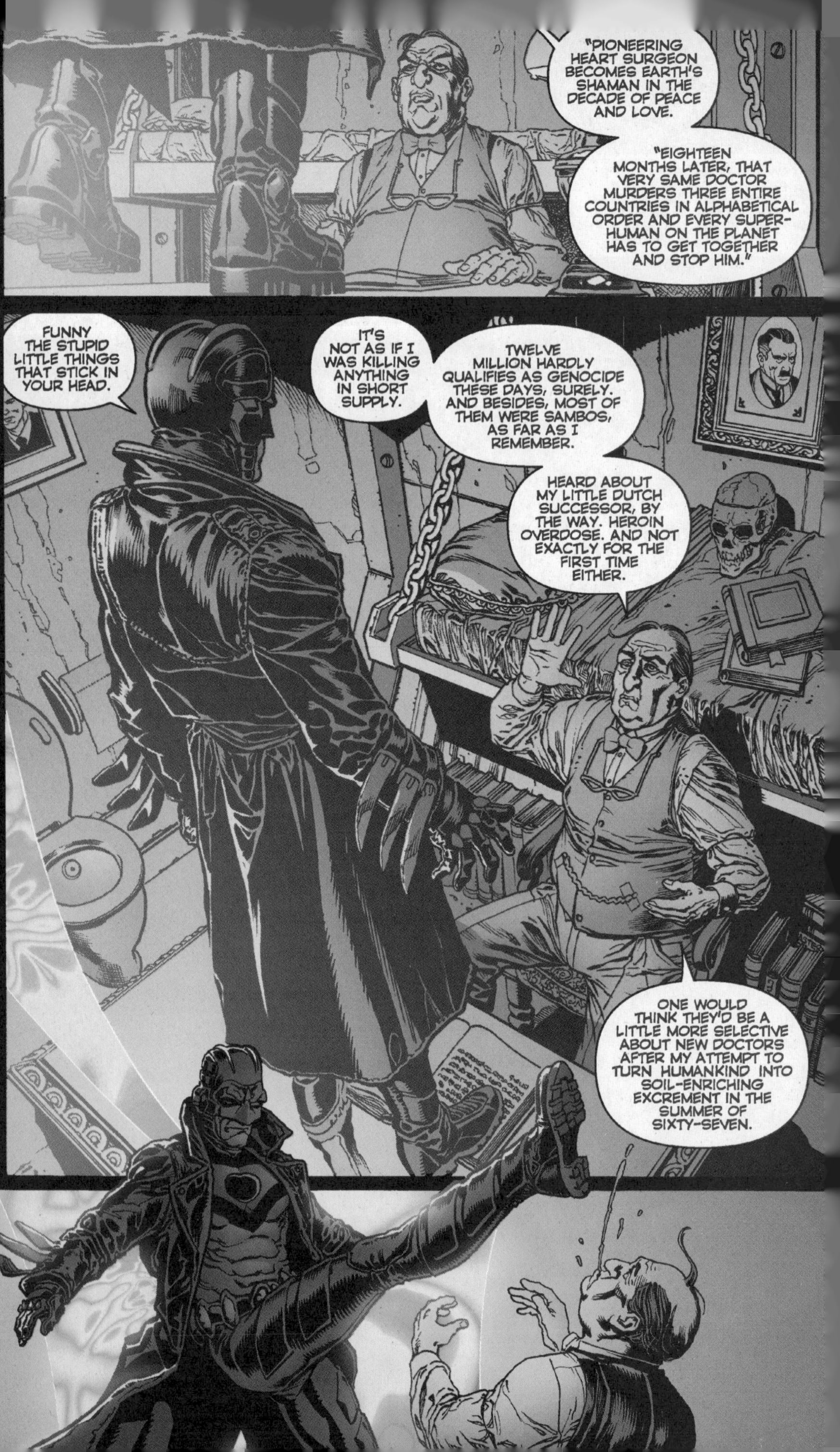
"PIONEERING HEART SURGEON BECOMES EARTH'S SHAMAN IN THE DECADE OF PEACE AND LOVE.
"EIGHTEEN MONTHS LATER, THAT VERY SAME DOCTOR MURDERS THREE ENTIRE COUNTRIES IN ALPHABETICAL ORDER AND EVERY SUPER-HUMAN ON THE PLANET HAS TO GET TOGETHER AND STOP HIM."
FUNNY THE STUPID LITTLE THINGS THAT STICK IN YOUR HEAD.
IT'S NOT AS IF I WAS KILLING ANYTHING IN SHORT SUPPLY.
TWELVE MILLION HARDLY QUALIFIES AS GENOCIDE THESE DAYS, SURELY. AND BESIDES, MOST OF THEM WERE SAMBOS, AS FAR AS I REMEMBER.
HEARD ABOUT MY LITTLE DUTCH SUCCESSOR, BY THE WAY. HEROIN OVERDOSE. AND NOT EXACTLY FOR THE FIRST TIME EITHER.
ONE WOULD THINK THEY'D BE A LITTLE MORE SELECTIVE ABOUT NEW DOCTORS AFTER MY ATTEMPT TO TURN HUMANKIND INTO SOIL-ENRICHING EXCREMENT IN THE SUMMER OF SIXTY-SEVEN.

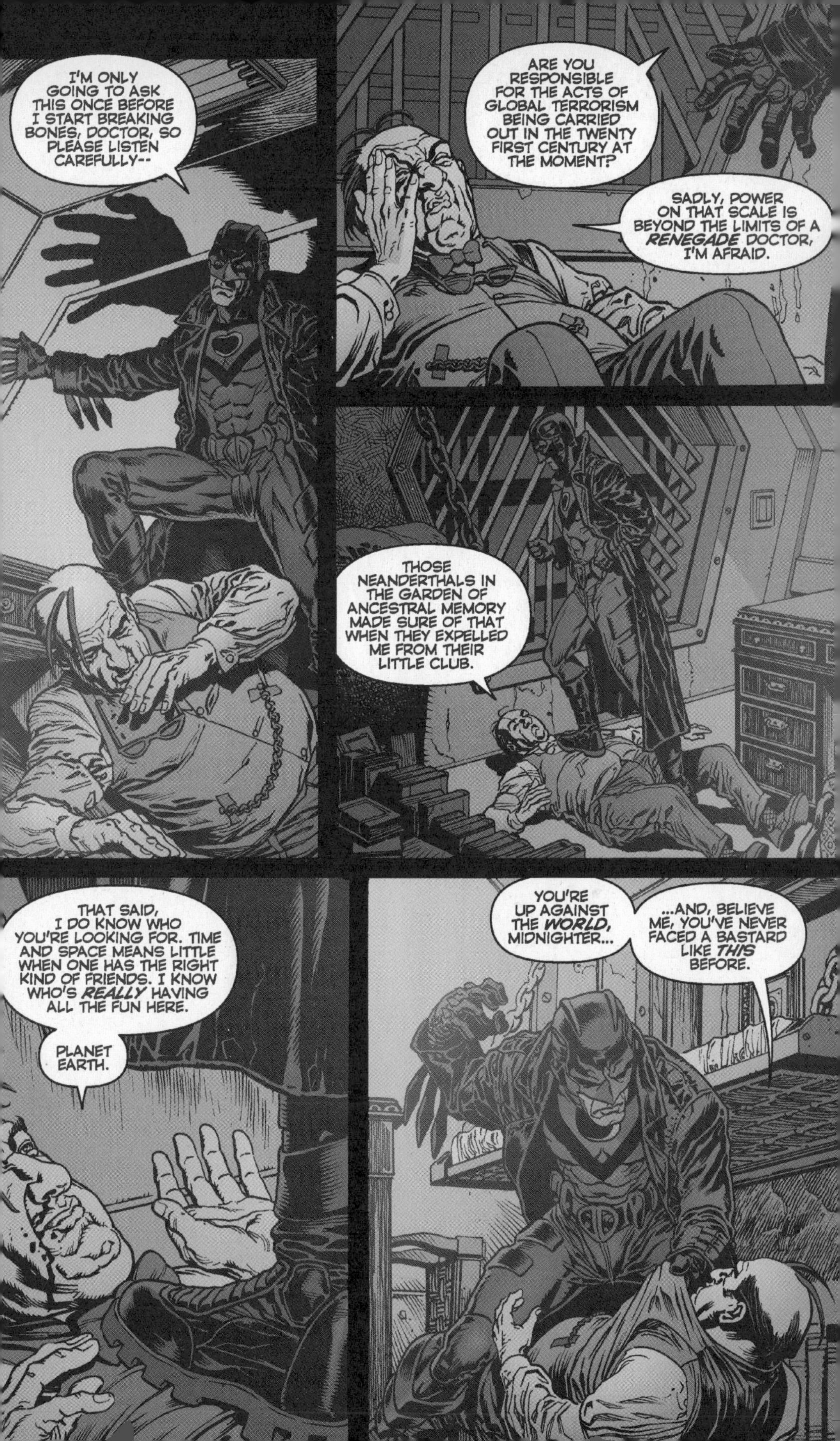
I'M ONLY GOING TO ASK THIS ONCE BEFORE I START BREAKING BONES, DOCTOR, SO PLEASE LISTEN CAREFULLY--
ARE YOU RESPONSIBLE FOR THE ACTS OF GLOBAL TERRORISM BEING CARRIED OUT IN THE TWENTY FIRST CENTURY AT THE MOMENT?
SADLY, POWER ON THAT SCALE IS BEYOND THE LIMITS OF A *RENEGADE* DOCTOR, I'M AFRAID.
THOSE NEANDERTHALS IN THE GARDEN OF ANCESTRAL MEMORY MADE SURE OF THAT WHEN THEY EXPELLED ME FROM THEIR LITTLE CLUB.
THAT SAID, I DO KNOW WHO YOU'RE LOOKING FOR. TIME AND SPACE MEANS LITTLE WHEN ONE HAS THE RIGHT KIND OF FRIENDS. I KNOW WHO'S *REALLY* HAVING ALL THE FUN HERE.
PLANET EARTH.
YOU'RE UP AGAINST THE *WORLD,* MIDNIGHTER...
...AND, BELIEVE ME, YOU'VE NEVER FACED A BASTARD LIKE *THIS* BEFORE.

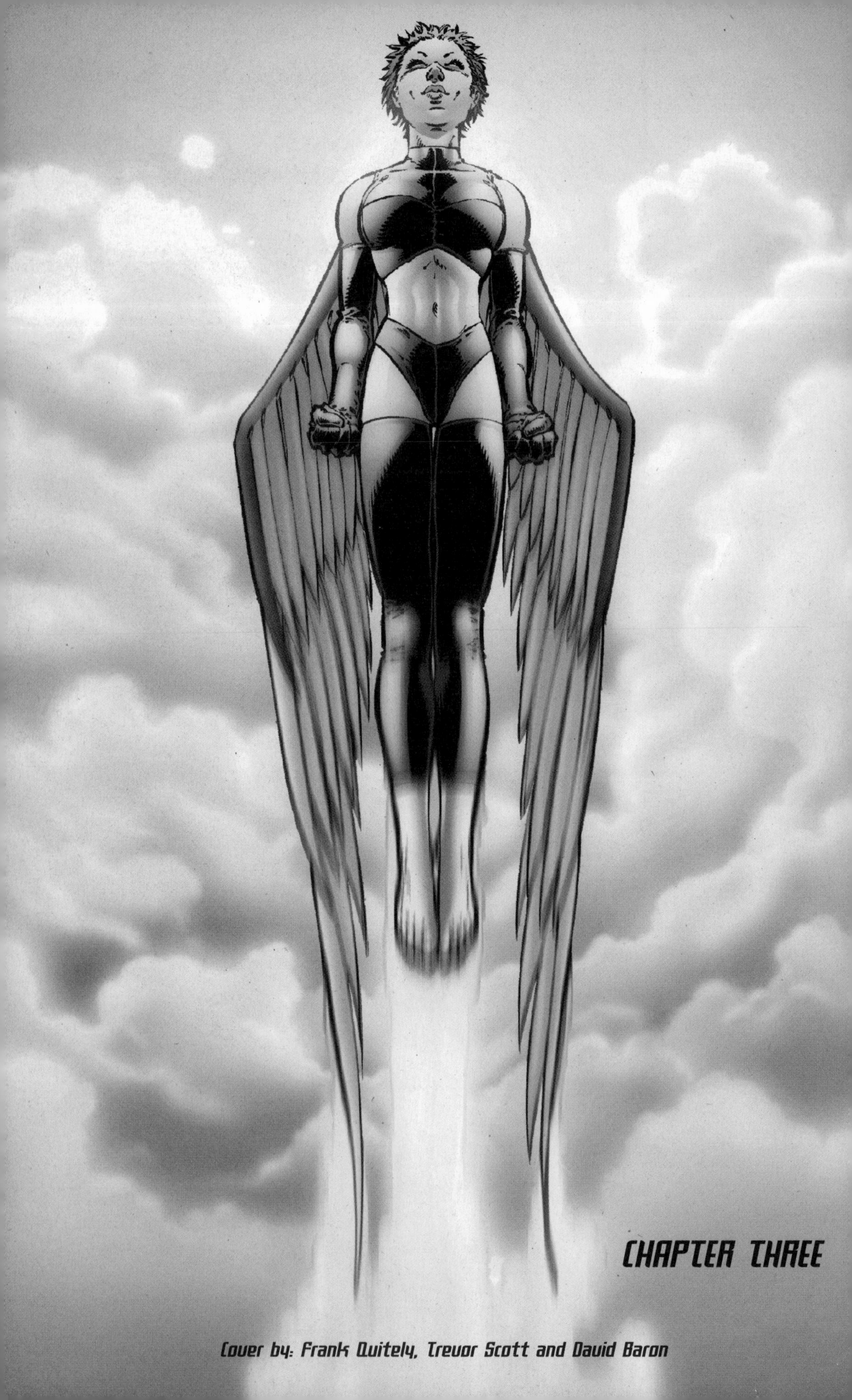

CHAPTER THREE

Cover by: Frank Quitely, Trevor Scott and David Baron

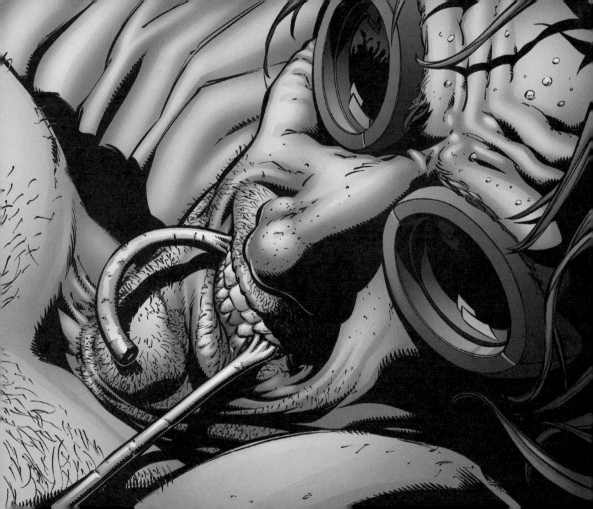

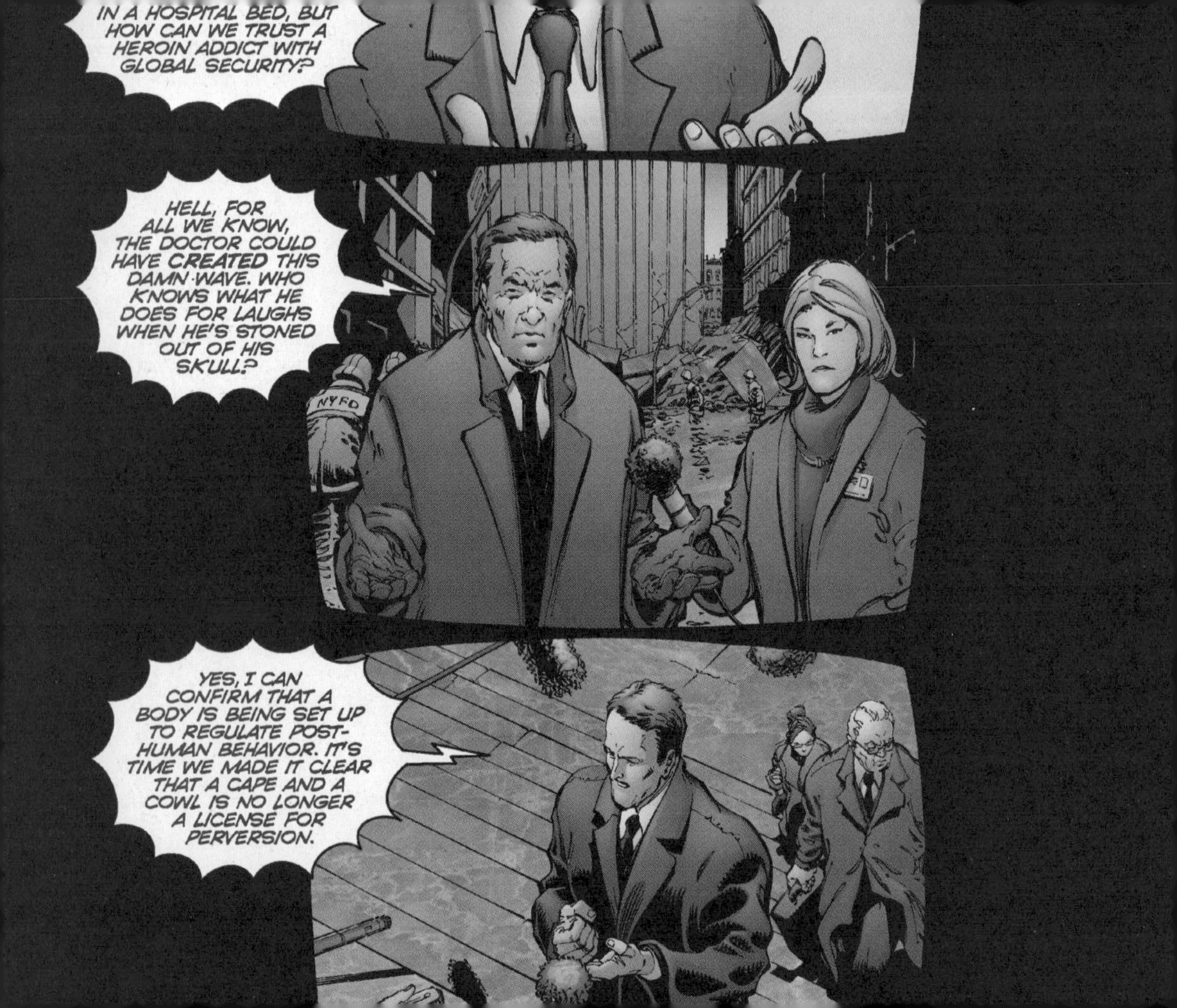
IN A HOSPITAL BED, BUT HOW CAN WE TRUST A HEROIN ADDICT WITH GLOBAL SECURITY?
HELL, FOR ALL WE KNOW, THE DOCTOR COULD HAVE CREATED THIS DAMN WAVE. WHO KNOWS WHAT HE DOES FOR LAUGHS WHEN HE'S STONED OUT OF HIS SKULL?
NYFD
YES, I CAN CONFIRM THAT A BODY IS BEING SET UP TO REGULATE POST-HUMAN BEHAVIOR. IT'S TIME WE MADE IT CLEAR THAT A CAPE AND A COWL IS NO LONGER A LICENSE FOR PERVERSION.

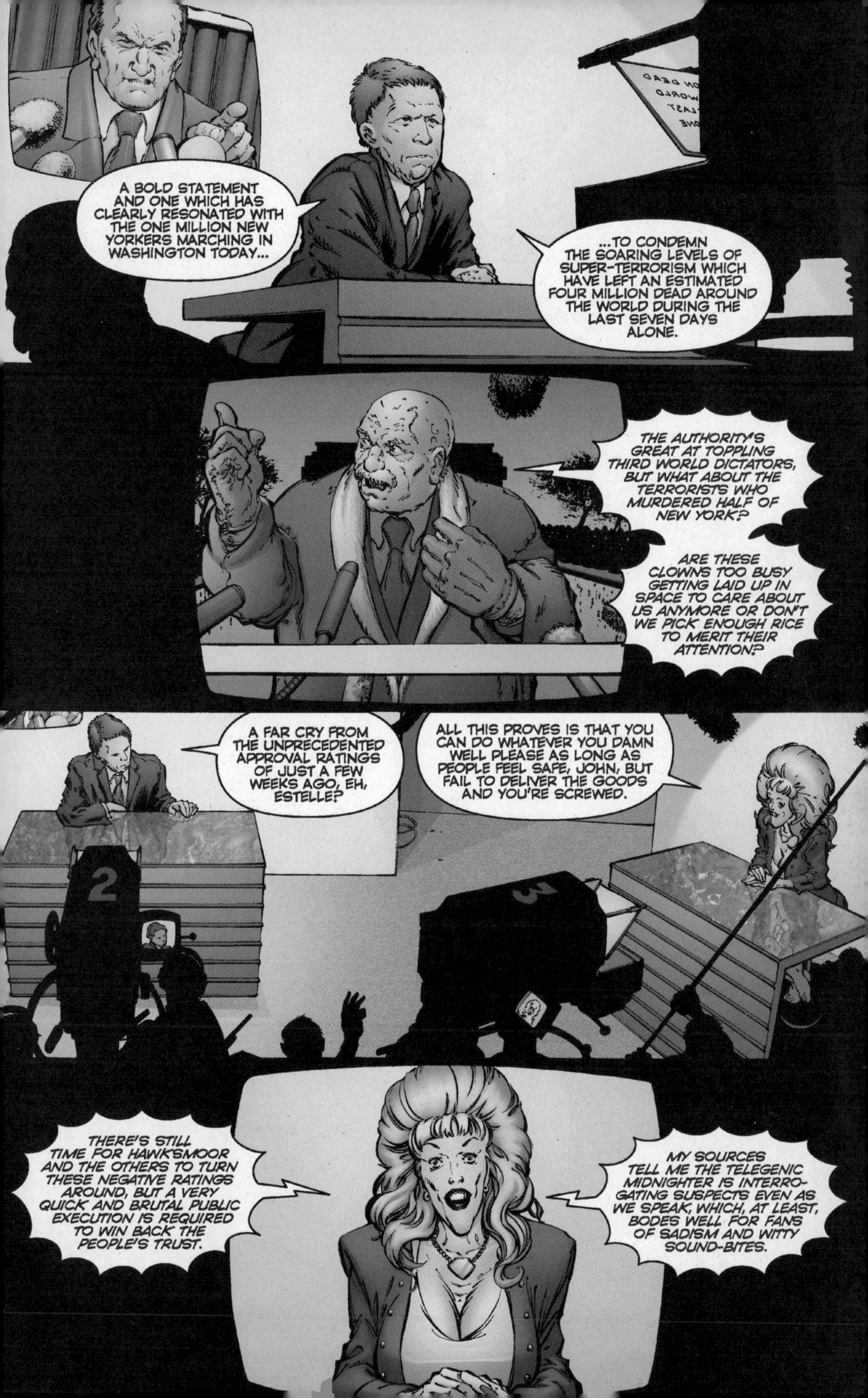
A BOLD STATEMENT AND ONE WHICH HAS CLEARLY RESONATED WITH THE ONE MILLION NEW YORKERS MARCHING IN WASHINGTON TODAY...
...TO CONDEMN THE SOARING LEVELS OF SUPER-TERRORISM WHICH HAVE LEFT AN ESTIMATED FOUR MILLION DEAD AROUND THE WORLD DURING THE LAST SEVEN DAYS ALONE.
THE AUTHORITY'S GREAT AT TOPPLING THIRD WORLD DICTATORS, BUT WHAT ABOUT THE TERRORISTS WHO MURDERED HALF OF NEW YORK?
ARE THESE CLOWNS TOO BUSY GETTING LAID UP IN SPACE TO CARE ABOUT US ANYMORE OR DON'T WE PICK ENOUGH RICE TO MERIT THEIR ATTENTION?
A FAR CRY FROM THE UNPRECEDENTED APPROVAL RATINGS OF JUST A FEW WEEKS AGO, EH, ESTELLE?
ALL THIS PROVES IS THAT YOU CAN DO WHATEVER YOU DAMN WELL PLEASE AS LONG AS PEOPLE FEEL SAFE, JOHN, BUT FAIL TO DELIVER THE GOODS AND YOU'RE SCREWED.
2
3
THERE'S STILL TIME FOR HAWKSMOOR AND THE OTHERS TO TURN THESE NEGATIVE RATINGS AROUND, BUT A VERY QUICK AND BRUTAL PUBLIC EXECUTION IS REQUIRED TO WIN BACK THE PEOPLE'S TRUST.
MY SOURCES TELL ME THE TELEGENIC MIDNIGHTER IS INTERROGATING SUSPECTS EVEN AS WE SPEAK, WHICH, AT LEAST, BODES WELL FOR FANS OF SADISM AND WITTY SOUND-BITES.

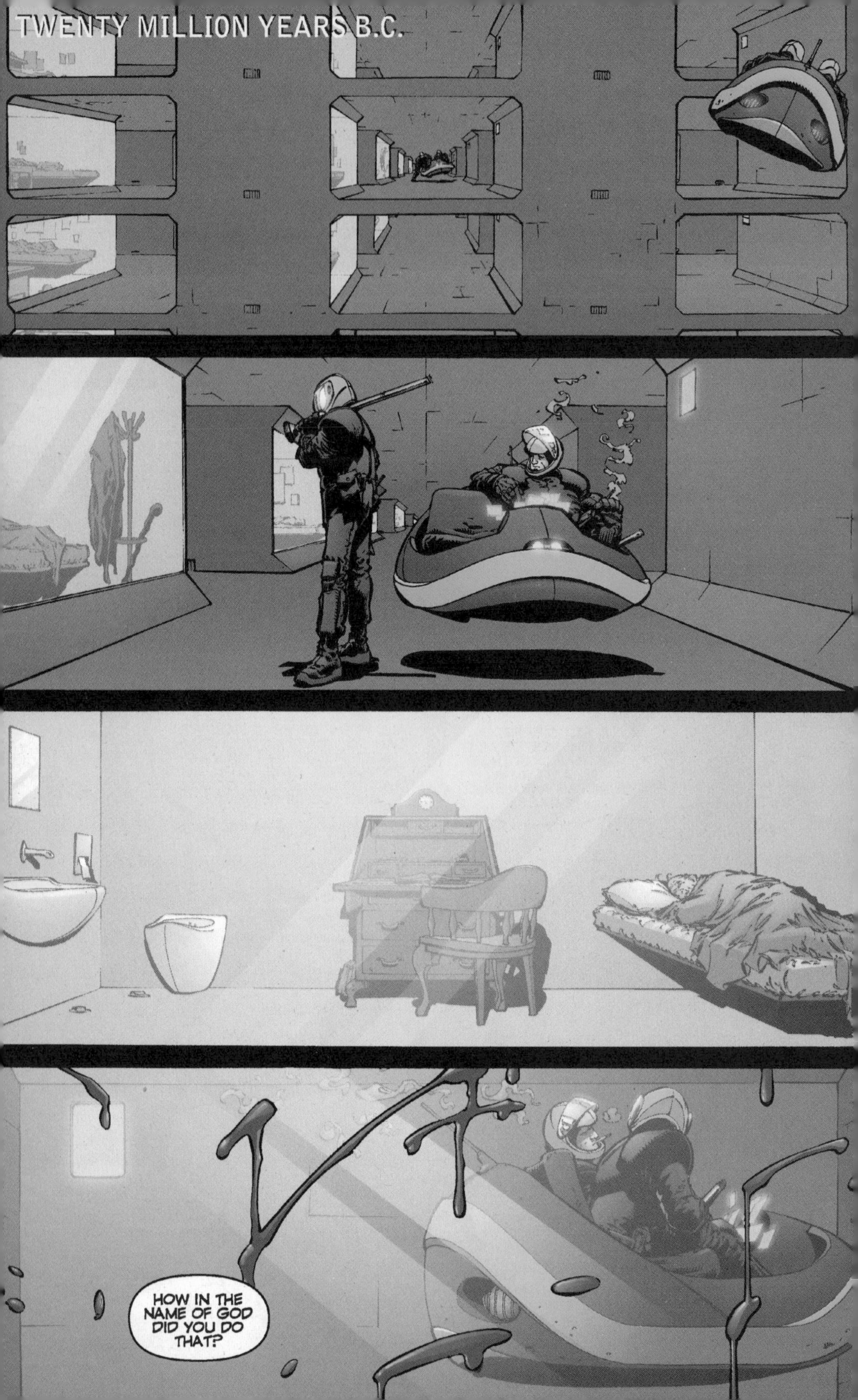
TWENTY MILLION YEARS B.C.
HOW IN THE NAME OF GOD DID YOU DO THAT?

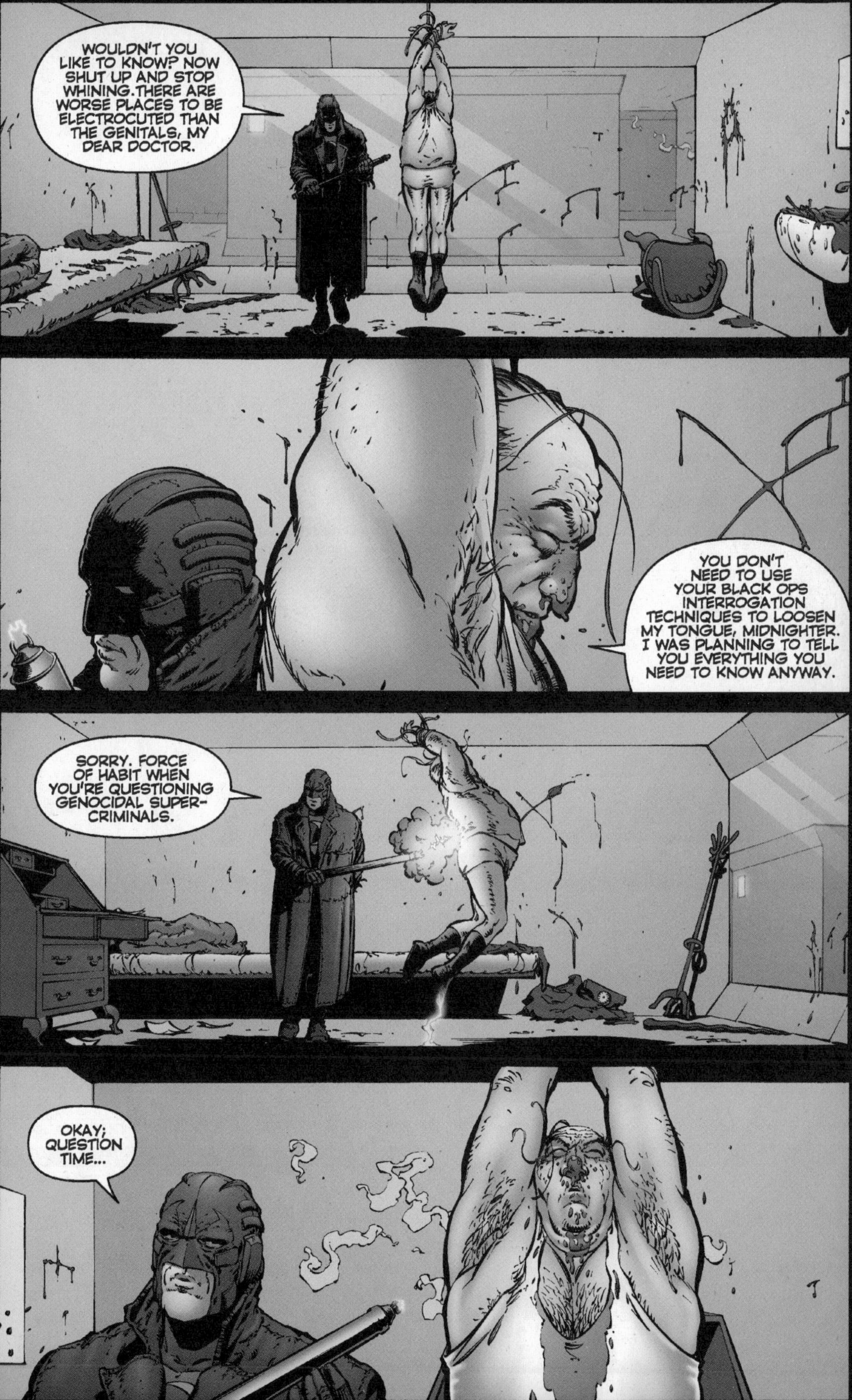
WOULDN'T YOU LIKE TO KNOW? NOW SHUT UP AND STOP WHINING. THERE ARE WORSE PLACES TO BE ELECTROCUTED THAN THE GENITALS, MY DEAR DOCTOR.
YOU DON'T NEED TO USE YOUR BLACK OPS INTERROGATION TECHNIQUES TO LOOSEN MY TONGUE, MIDNIGHTER. I WAS PLANNING TO TELL YOU EVERYTHING YOU NEED TO KNOW ANYWAY.
SORRY. FORCE OF HABIT WHEN YOU'RE QUESTIONING GENOCIDAL SUPER-CRIMINALS.
OKAY; QUESTION TIME...

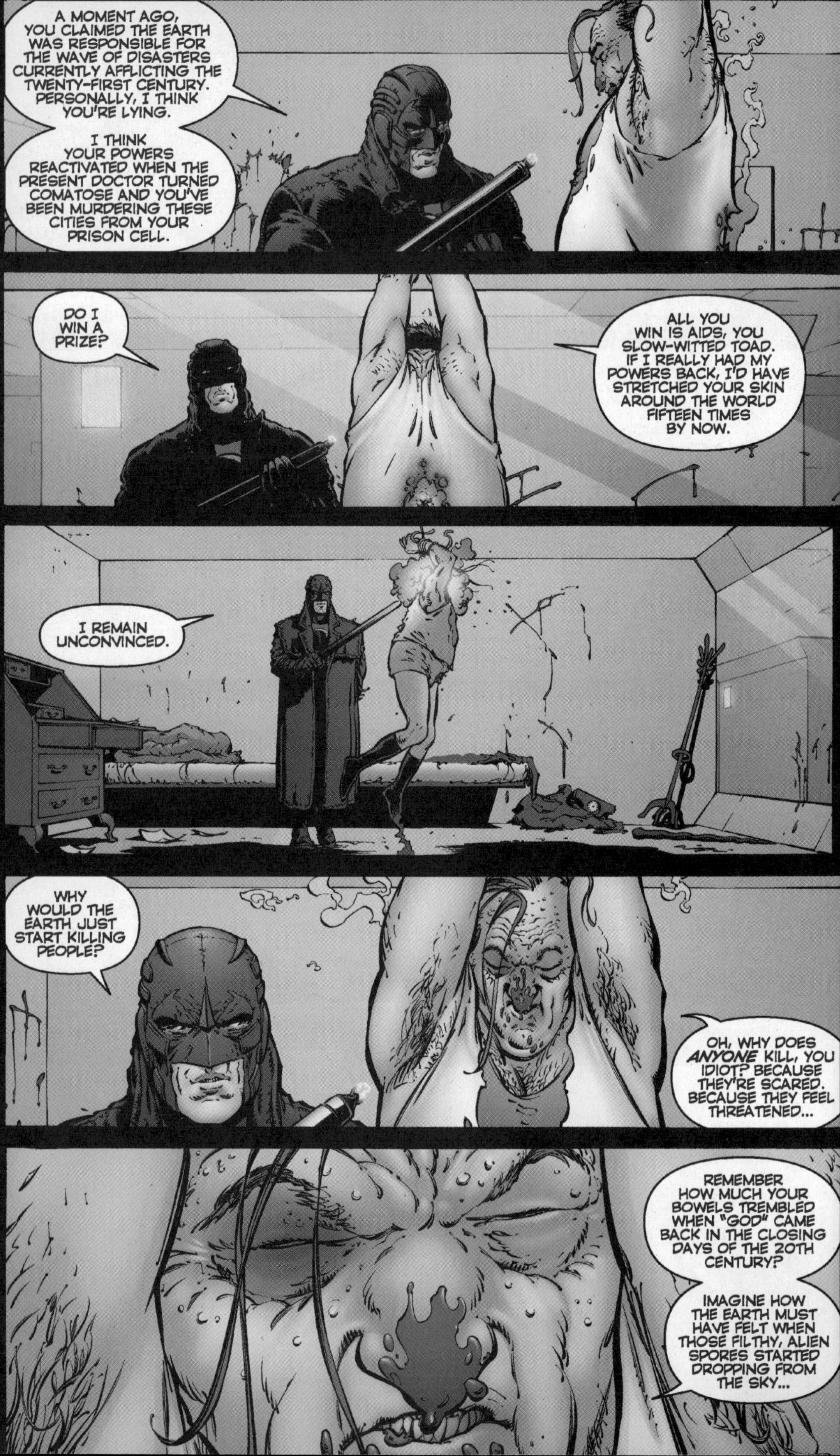

A MOMENT AGO, YOU CLAIMED THE EARTH WAS RESPONSIBLE FOR THE WAVE OF DISASTERS CURRENTLY AFFLICTING THE TWENTY-FIRST CENTURY. PERSONALLY, I THINK YOU'RE LYING.
I THINK YOUR POWERS REACTIVATED WHEN THE PRESENT DOCTOR TURNED COMATOSE AND YOU'VE BEEN MURDERING THESE CITIES FROM YOUR PRISON CELL.
DO I WIN A PRIZE?
ALL YOU WIN IS AIDS, YOU SLOW-WITTED TOAD. IF I REALLY HAD MY POWERS BACK, I'D HAVE STRETCHED YOUR SKIN AROUND THE WORLD FIFTEEN TIMES BY NOW.
I REMAIN UNCONVINCED.
WHY WOULD THE EARTH JUST START KILLING PEOPLE?
OH, WHY DOES ANYONE KILL, YOU IDIOT? BECAUSE THEY'RE SCARED. BECAUSE THEY FEEL THREATENED...
REMEMBER HOW MUCH YOUR BOWELS TREMBLED WHEN "GOD" CAME BACK IN THE CLOSING DAYS OF THE 20TH CENTURY?
IMAGINE HOW THE EARTH MUST HAVE FELT WHEN THOSE FILTHY, ALIEN SPORES STARTED DROPPING FROM THE SKY...

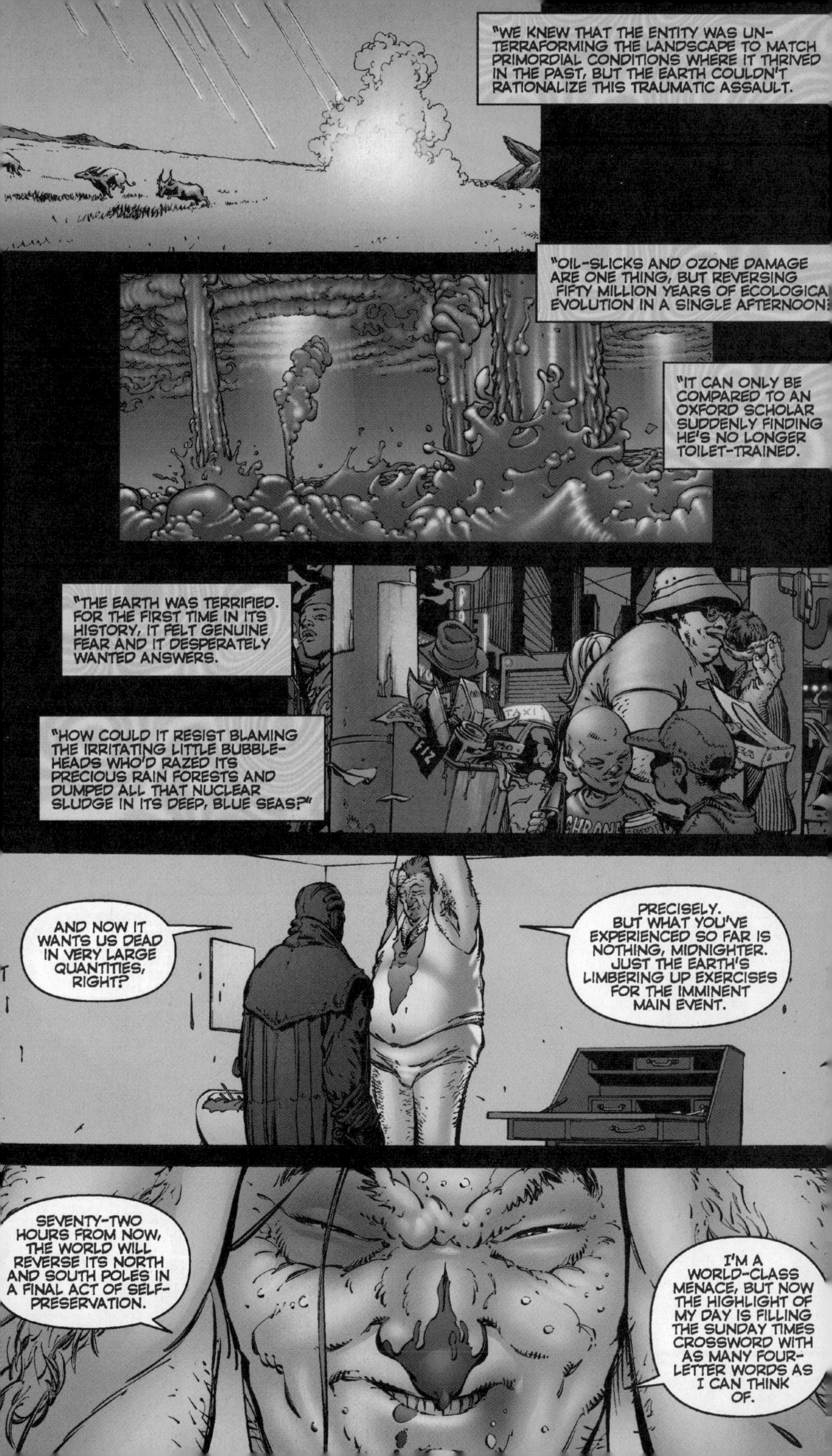
"WE KNEW THAT THE ENTITY WAS UN-TERRAFORMING THE LANDSCAPE TO MATCH PRIMORDIAL CONDITIONS WHERE IT THRIVED IN THE PAST, BUT THE EARTH COULDN'T RATIONALIZE THIS TRAUMATIC ASSAULT.
"OIL-SLICKS AND OZONE DAMAGE ARE ONE THING, BUT REVERSING FIFTY MILLION YEARS OF ECOLOGICAL EVOLUTION IN A SINGLE AFTERNOON?
"IT CAN ONLY BE COMPARED TO AN OXFORD SCHOLAR SUDDENLY FINDING HE'S NO LONGER TOILET-TRAINED.
"THE EARTH WAS TERRIFIED. FOR THE FIRST TIME IN ITS HISTORY, IT FELT GENUINE FEAR AND IT DESPERATELY WANTED ANSWERS.
"HOW COULD IT RESIST BLAMING THE IRRITATING LITTLE BUBBLE-HEADS WHO'D RAZED ITS PRECIOUS RAIN FORESTS AND DUMPED ALL THAT NUCLEAR SLUDGE IN ITS DEEP, BLUE SEAS?"
AND NOW IT WANTS US DEAD IN VERY LARGE QUANTITIES, RIGHT?
PRECISELY. BUT WHAT YOU'VE EXPERIENCED SO FAR IS NOTHING, MIDNIGHTER. JUST THE EARTH'S LIMBERING UP EXERCISES FOR THE IMMINENT MAIN EVENT.
SEVENTY-TWO HOURS FROM NOW, THE WORLD WILL REVERSE ITS NORTH AND SOUTH POLES IN A FINAL ACT OF SELF-PRESERVATION.
I'M A WORLD-CLASS MENACE, BUT NOW THE HIGHLIGHT OF MY DAY IS FILLING THE SUNDAY TIMES CROSSWORD WITH AS MANY FOUR-LETTER WORDS AS I CAN THINK OF.

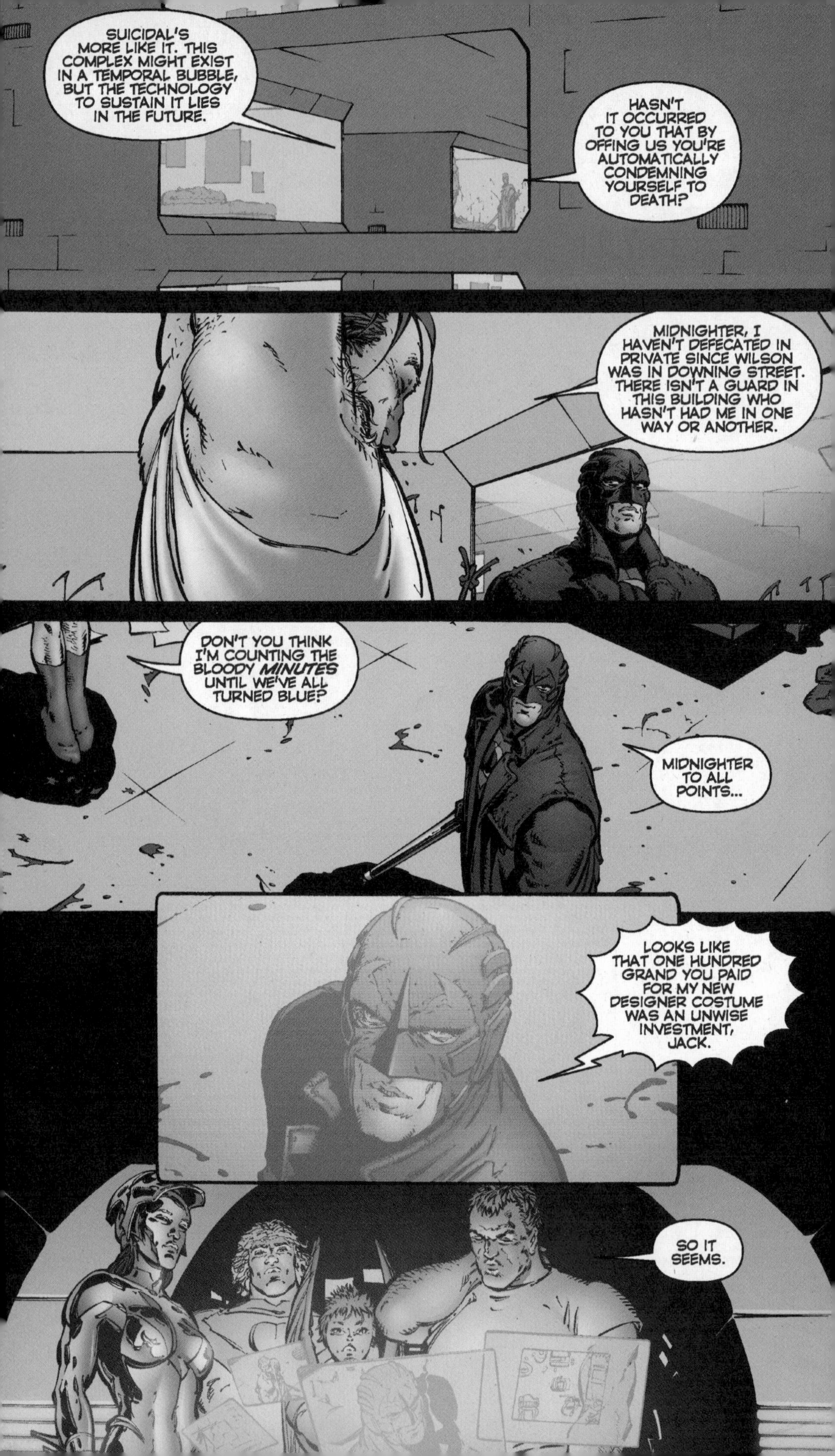
SUICIDAL'S MORE LIKE IT. THIS COMPLEX MIGHT EXIST IN A TEMPORAL BUBBLE, BUT THE TECHNOLOGY TO SUSTAIN IT LIES IN THE FUTURE.
HASN'T IT OCCURRED TO YOU THAT BY OFFING US YOU'RE AUTOMATICALLY CONDEMNING YOURSELF TO DEATH?
MIDNIGHTER, I HAVEN'T DEFECATED IN PRIVATE SINCE WILSON WAS IN DOWNING STREET. THERE ISN'T A GUARD IN THIS BUILDING WHO HASN'T HAD ME IN ONE WAY OR ANOTHER.
DON'T YOU THINK I'M COUNTING THE BLOODY *MINUTES* UNTIL WE'VE ALL TURNED BLUE?
MIDNIGHTER TO ALL POINTS...
LOOKS LIKE THAT ONE HUNDRED GRAND YOU PAID FOR MY NEW DESIGNER COSTUME WAS AN UNWISE INVESTMENT, JACK.
SO IT SEEMS.

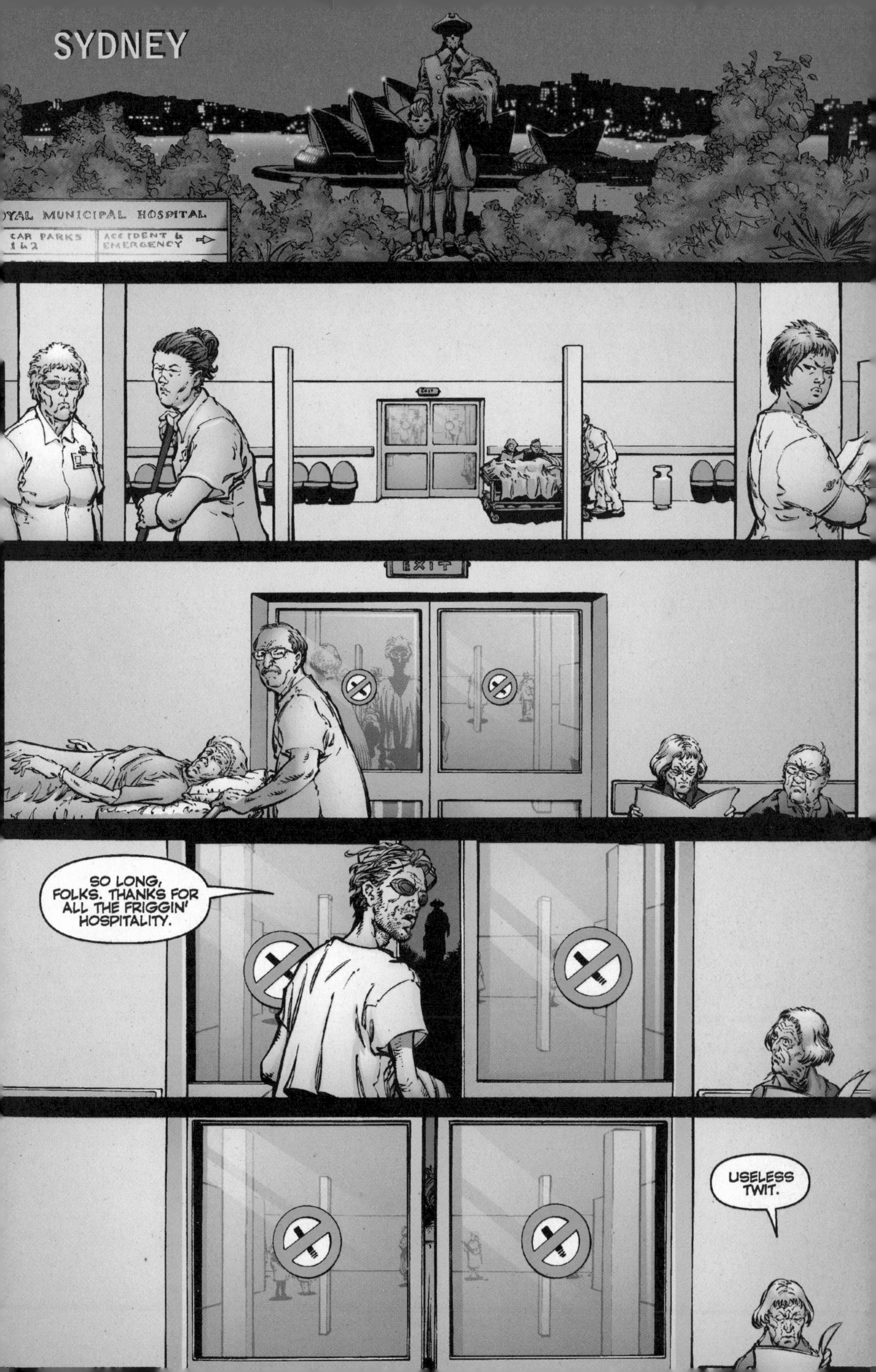
SYDNEY
OYAL MUNICIPAL HOSPITAL
CAR PARKS 1 & 2
ACCIDENT & EMERGENCY
EXIT
EXIT
SO LONG, FOLKS. THANKS FOR ALL THE FRIGGIN' HOSPITALITY.
USELESS TWIT.

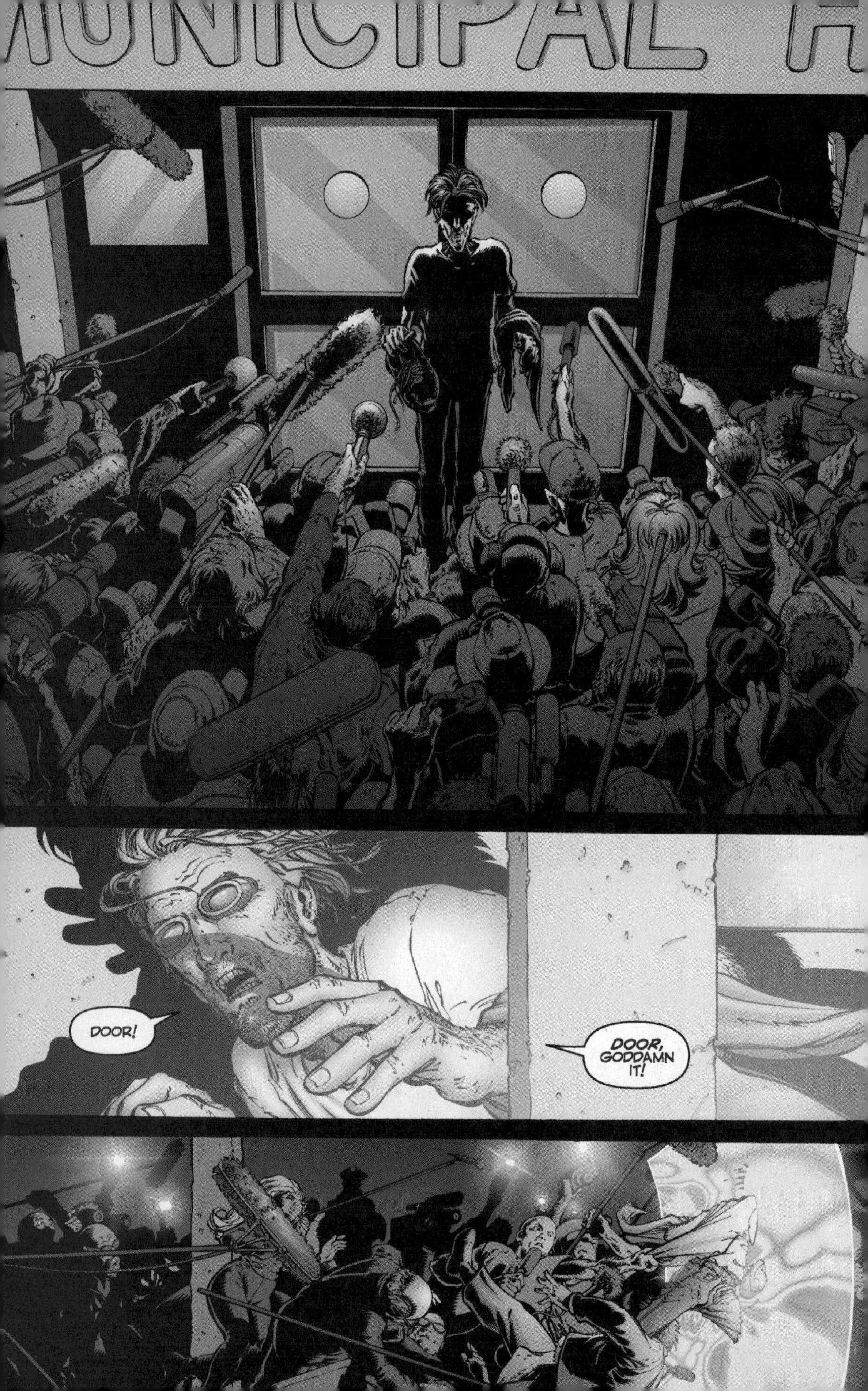
MUNICIPAL H
DOOR!
DOOR, GODDAMN IT!

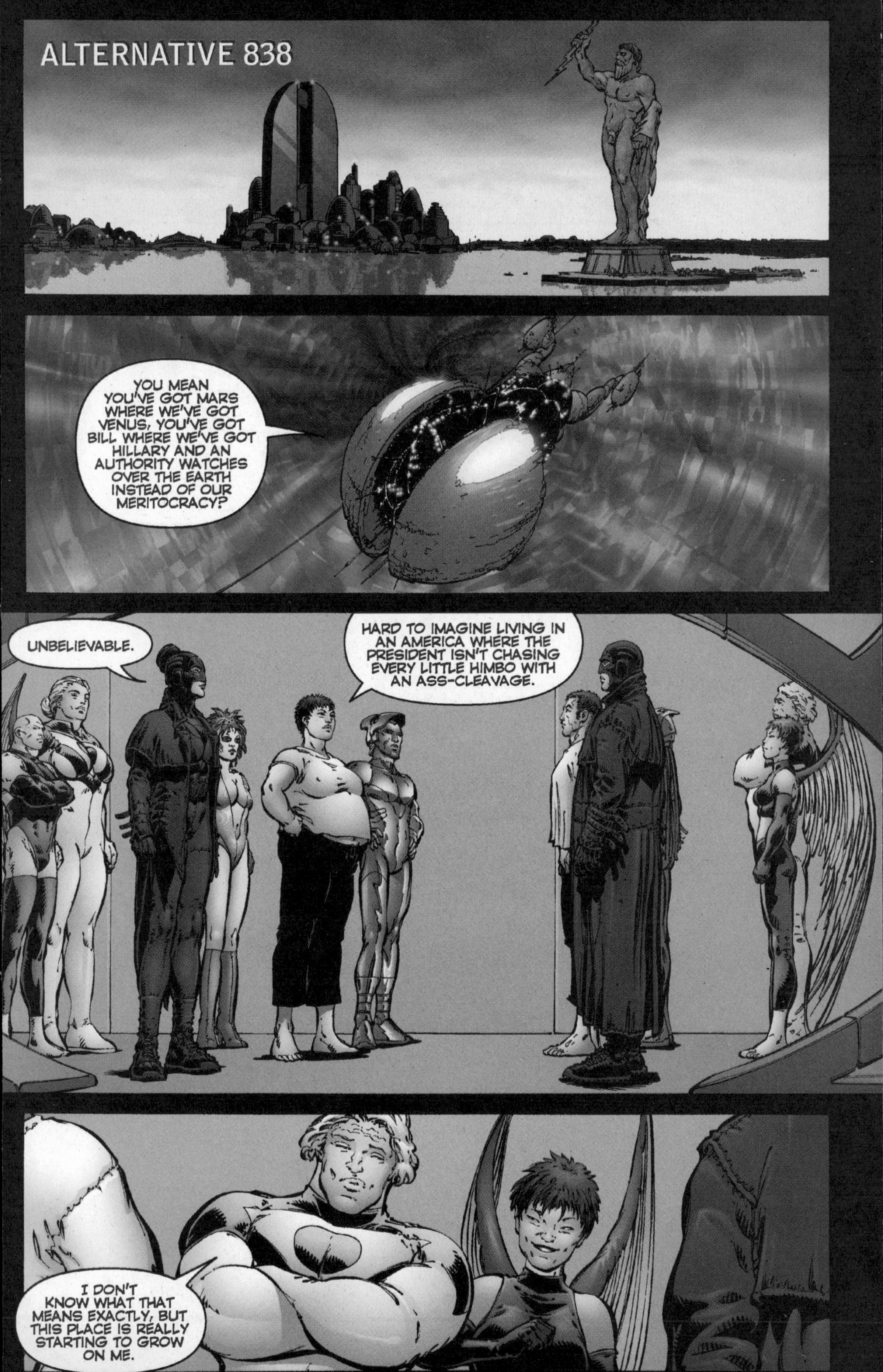
ALTERNATIVE 838
YOU MEAN YOU'VE GOT MARS WHERE WE'VE GOT VENUS, YOU'VE GOT BILL WHERE WE'VE GOT HILLARY AND AN AUTHORITY WATCHES OVER THE EARTH INSTEAD OF OUR MERITOCRACY?
UNBELIEVABLE.
HARD TO IMAGINE LIVING IN AN AMERICA WHERE THE PRESIDENT ISN'T CHASING EVERY LITTLE HIMBO WITH AN ASS-CLEAVAGE.
I DON'T KNOW WHAT THAT MEANS EXACTLY, BUT THIS PLACE IS REALLY STARTING TO GROW ON ME.

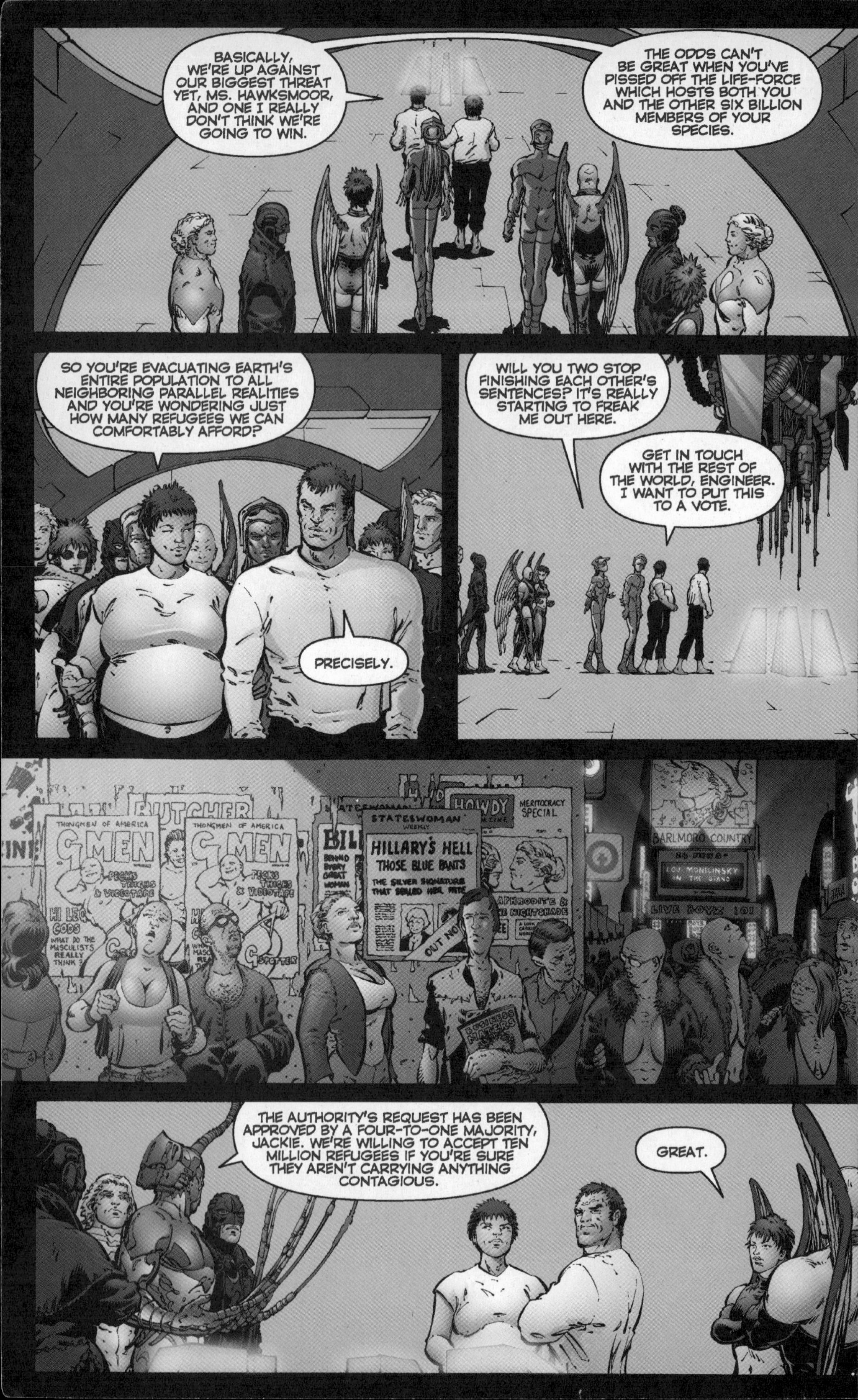

BASICALLY, WE'RE UP AGAINST OUR BIGGEST THREAT YET, MS. HAWKSMOOR, AND ONE I REALLY DON'T THINK WE'RE GOING TO WIN.
THE ODDS CAN'T BE GREAT WHEN YOU'VE PISSED OFF THE LIFE-FORCE WHICH HOSTS BOTH YOU AND THE OTHER SIX BILLION MEMBERS OF YOUR SPECIES.
SO YOU'RE EVACUATING EARTH'S ENTIRE POPULATION TO ALL NEIGHBORING PARALLEL REALITIES AND YOU'RE WONDERING JUST HOW MANY REFUGEES WE CAN COMFORTABLY AFFORD?
PRECISELY.
WILL YOU TWO STOP FINISHING EACH OTHER'S SENTENCES? IT'S REALLY STARTING TO FREAK ME OUT HERE.
GET IN TOUCH WITH THE REST OF THE WORLD, ENGINEER. I WANT TO PUT THIS TO A VOTE.
BUTCHER
THONGMEN OF AMERICA
G MEN
PECKS THIGHS & VIDEOTAPE
HI LEG GODS
WHAT DO THE MASCULISTS REALLY THINK?
THONGMEN OF AMERICA
G MEN
PECKS THIGHS & VIDEOTAPE
G SPOTTER
BEHIND EVERY GREAT WOMAN
STATESWOMAN WEEKLY
HILLARY'S HELL
THOSE BLUE PANTS
THE SILVER SIGNATURE THAT SEALED HER FATE
OUT NOW
HOWDY
MERITOCRACY SPECIAL
APHRODITE & THE NIGHTSHADE
BARLMORO COUNTRY
LOU MONILINSKY IN THE STAND
LIVE BOYZ 101
BUSINESS MATTERS
THE AUTHORITY'S REQUEST HAS BEEN APPROVED BY A FOUR-TO-ONE MAJORITY, JACKIE. WE'RE WILLING TO ACCEPT TEN MILLION REFUGEES IF YOU'RE SURE THEY AREN'T CARRYING ANYTHING CONTAGIOUS.
GREAT.

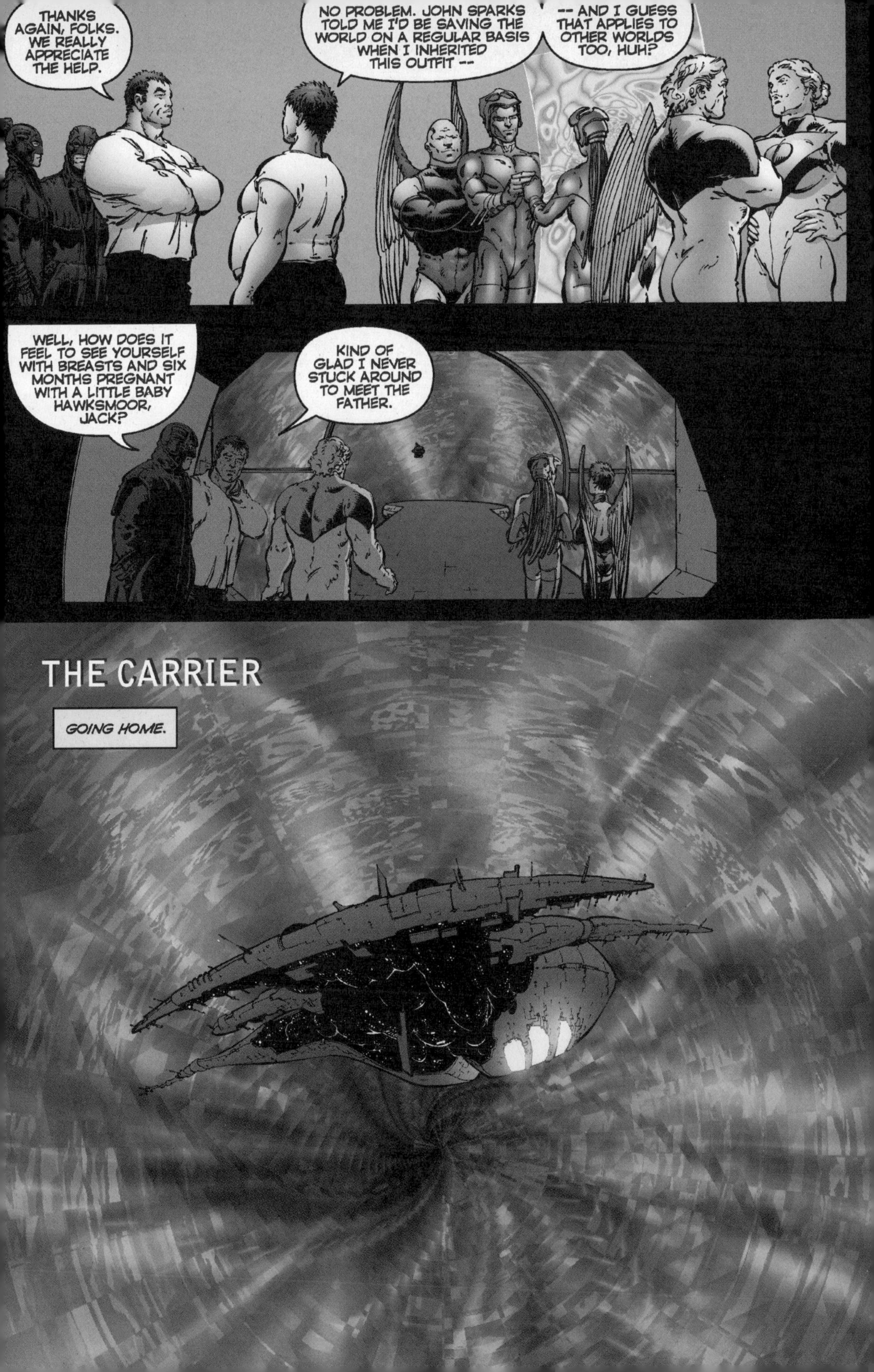
THANKS AGAIN, FOLKS. WE REALLY APPRECIATE THE HELP.
NO PROBLEM. JOHN SPARKS TOLD ME I'D BE SAVING THE WORLD ON A REGULAR BASIS WHEN I INHERITED THIS OUTFIT --
-- AND I GUESS THAT APPLIES TO OTHER WORLDS TOO, HUH?
WELL, HOW DOES IT FEEL TO SEE YOURSELF WITH BREASTS AND SIX MONTHS PREGNANT WITH A LITTLE BABY HAWKSMOOR, JACK?
KIND OF GLAD I NEVER STUCK AROUND TO MEET THE FATHER.
THE CARRIER
GOING HOME.

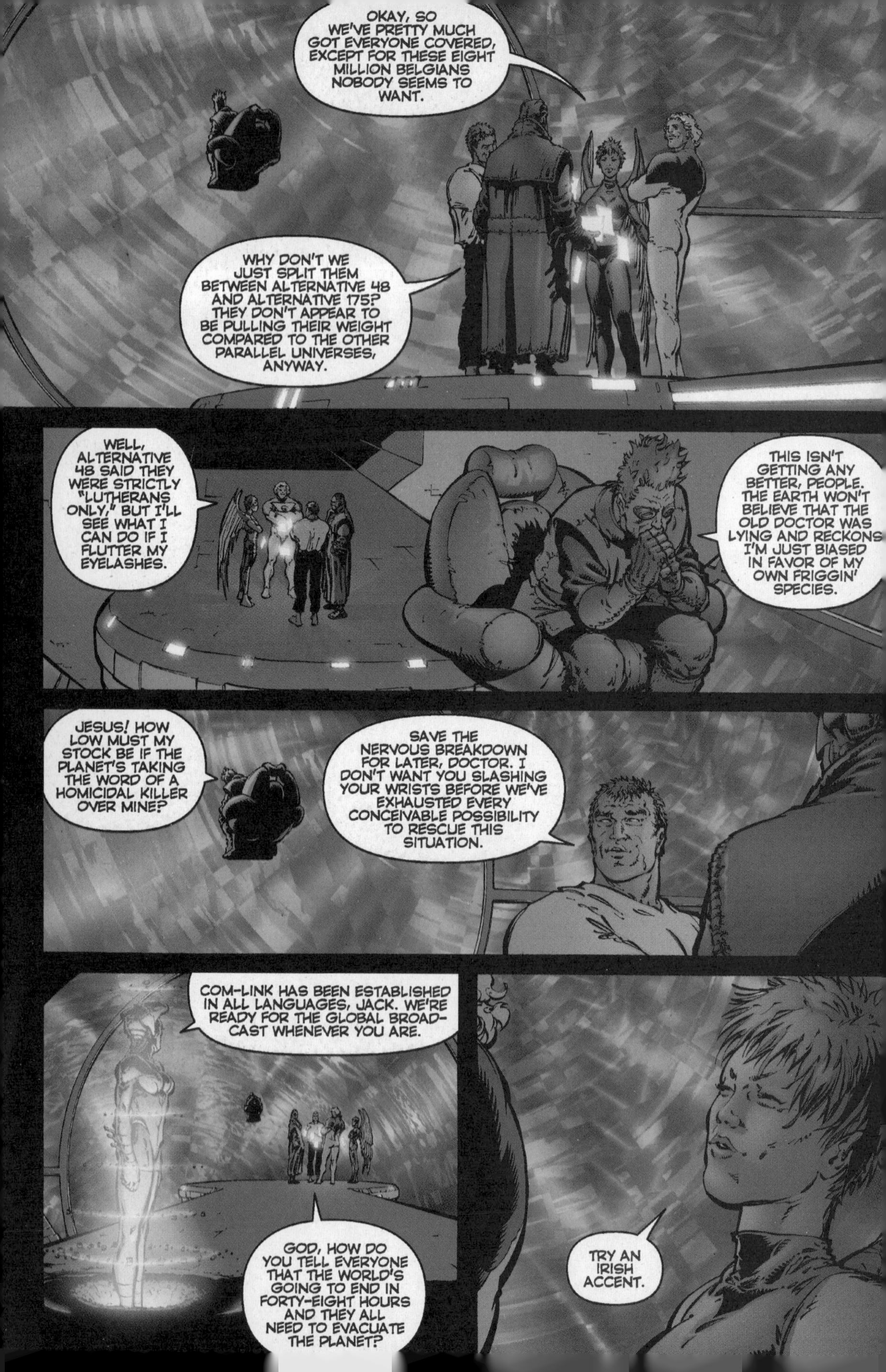
OKAY, SO WE'VE PRETTY MUCH GOT EVERYONE COVERED, EXCEPT FOR THESE EIGHT MILLION BELGIANS NOBODY SEEMS TO WANT.
WHY DON'T WE JUST SPLIT THEM BETWEEN ALTERNATIVE 48 AND ALTERNATIVE 175? THEY DON'T APPEAR TO BE PULLING THEIR WEIGHT COMPARED TO THE OTHER PARALLEL UNIVERSES, ANYWAY.
WELL, ALTERNATIVE 48 SAID THEY WERE STRICTLY "LUTHERANS ONLY," BUT I'LL SEE WHAT I CAN DO IF I FLUTTER MY EYELASHES.
THIS ISN'T GETTING ANY BETTER, PEOPLE. THE EARTH WON'T BELIEVE THAT THE OLD DOCTOR WAS LYING AND RECKONS I'M JUST BIASED IN FAVOR OF MY OWN FRIGGIN' SPECIES.
JESUS! HOW LOW MUST MY STOCK BE IF THE PLANET'S TAKING THE WORD OF A HOMICIDAL KILLER OVER MINE?
SAVE THE NERVOUS BREAKDOWN FOR LATER, DOCTOR. I DON'T WANT YOU SLASHING YOUR WRISTS BEFORE WE'VE EXHAUSTED EVERY CONCEIVABLE POSSIBILITY TO RESCUE THIS SITUATION.
COM-LINK HAS BEEN ESTABLISHED IN ALL LANGUAGES, JACK. WE'RE READY FOR THE GLOBAL BROAD-CAST WHENEVER YOU ARE.
GOD, HOW DO YOU TELL EVERYONE THAT THE WORLD'S GOING TO END IN FORTY-EIGHT HOURS AND THEY ALL NEED TO EVACUATE THE PLANET?
TRY AN IRISH ACCENT.

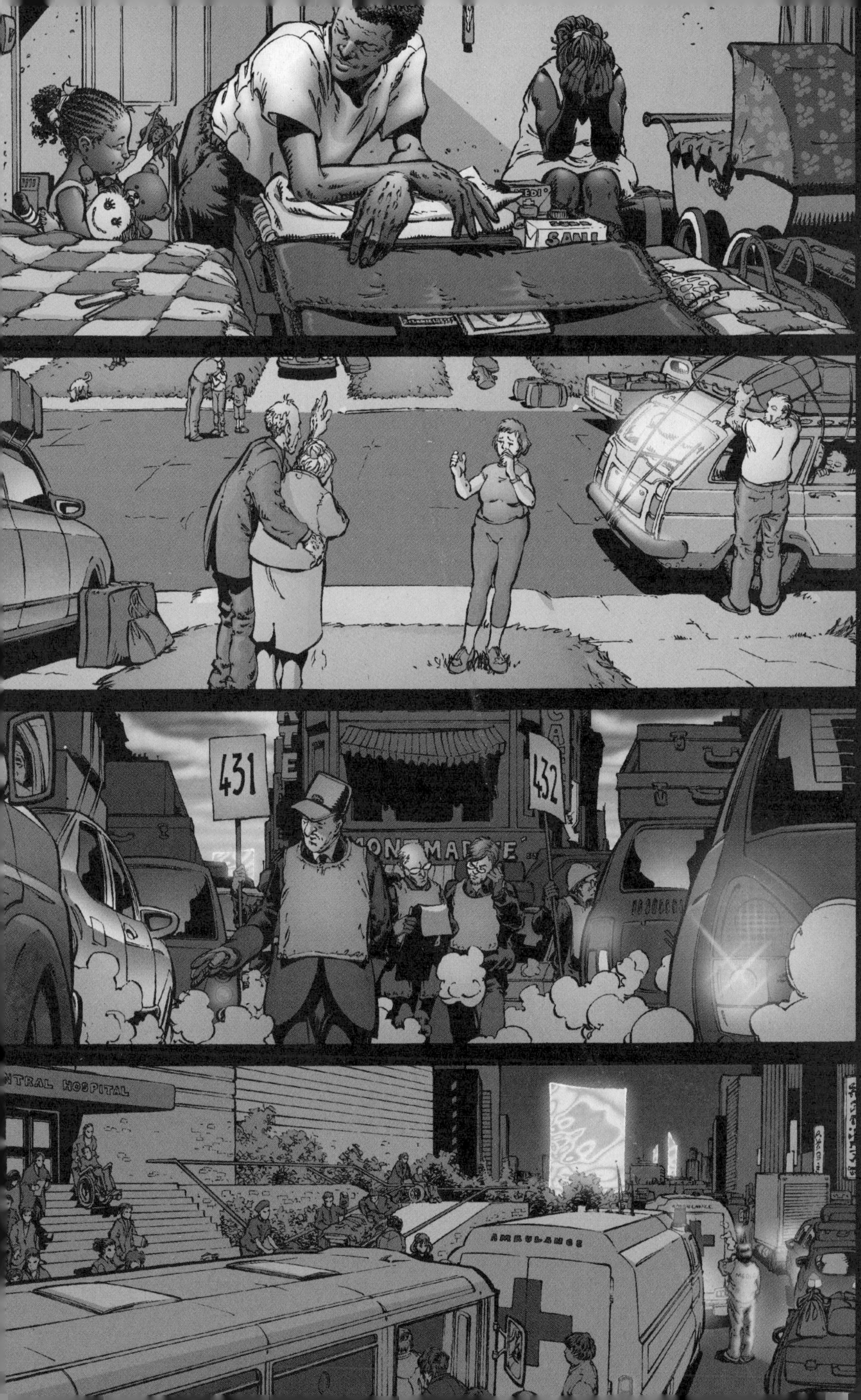
431
432
NTRAL HOSPITAL
AMBULANCE

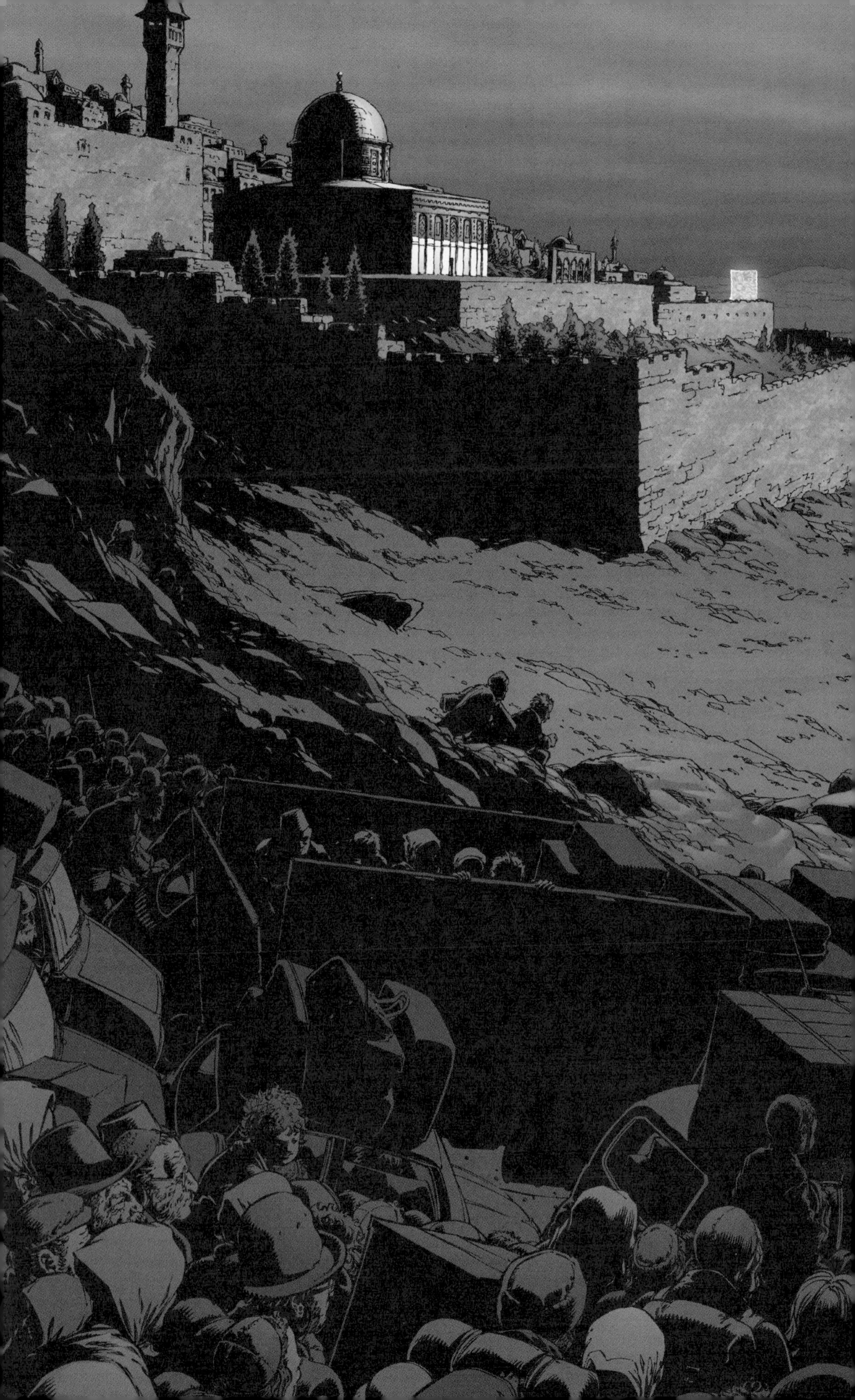

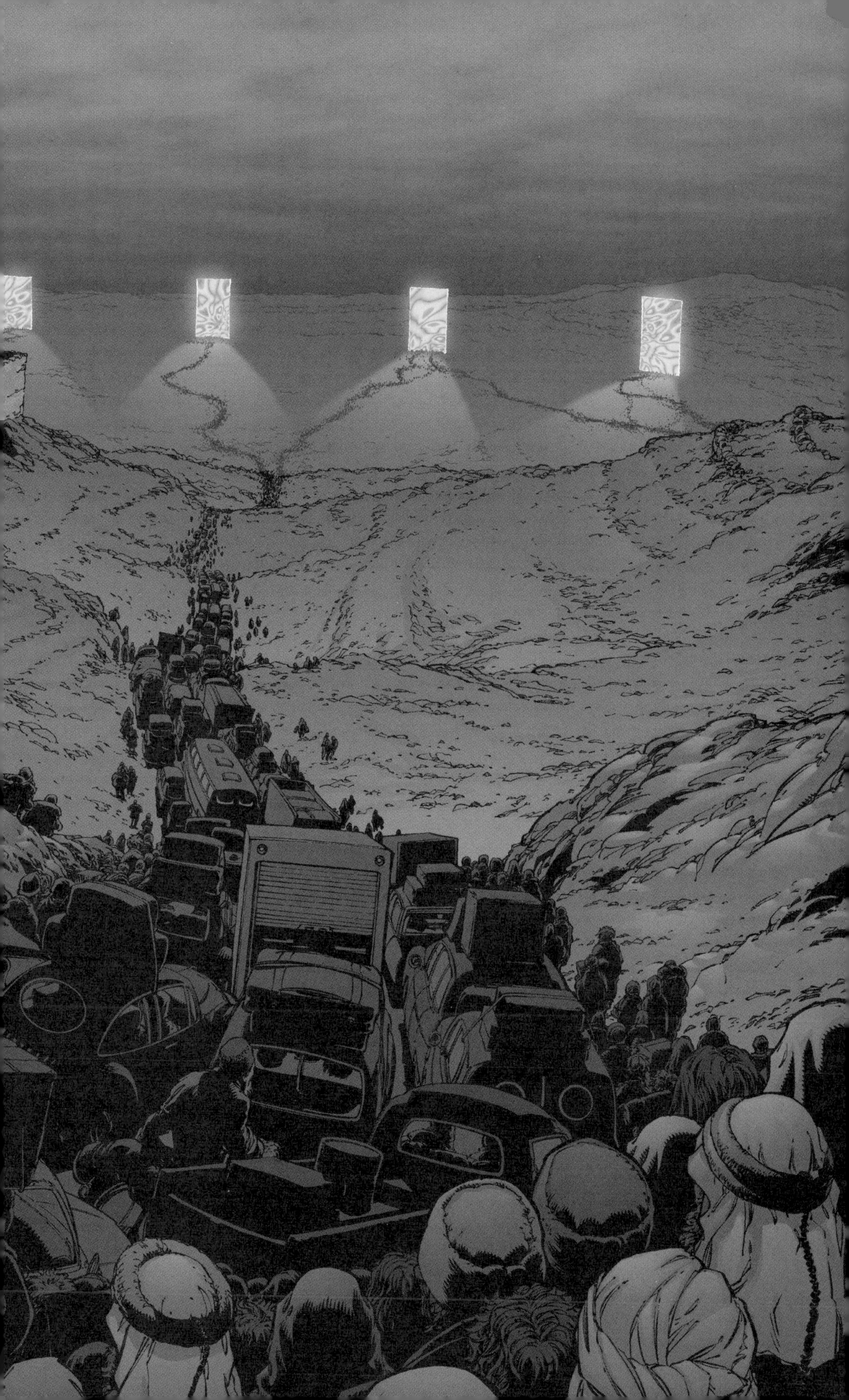

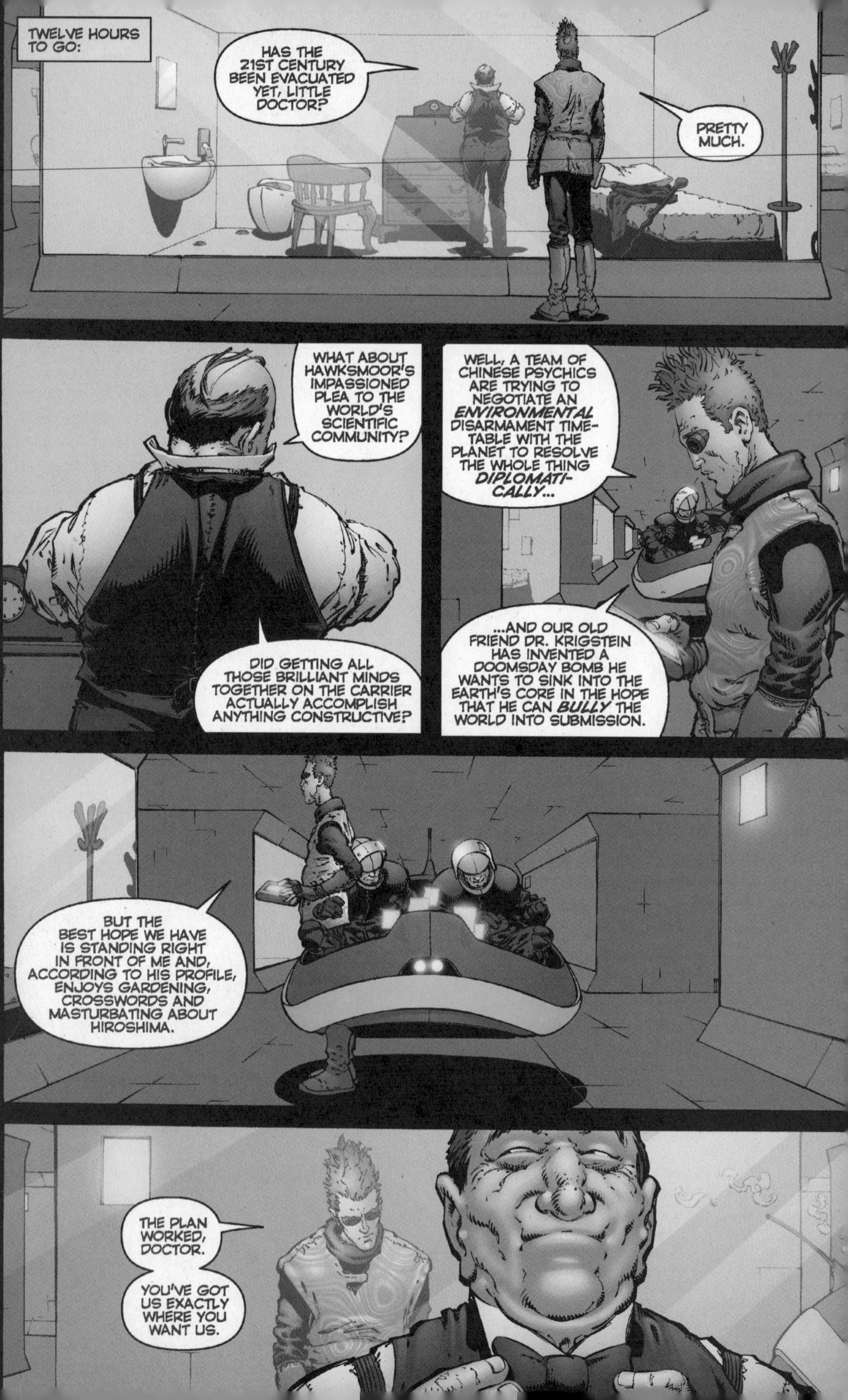
TWELVE HOURS TO GO:
HAS THE 21ST CENTURY BEEN EVACUATED YET, LITTLE DOCTOR?
PRETTY MUCH.
WHAT ABOUT HAWKSMOOR'S IMPASSIONED PLEA TO THE WORLD'S SCIENTIFIC COMMUNITY?
DID GETTING ALL THOSE BRILLIANT MINDS TOGETHER ON THE CARRIER ACTUALLY ACCOMPLISH ANYTHING CONSTRUCTIVE?
WELL, A TEAM OF CHINESE PSYCHICS ARE TRYING TO NEGOTIATE AN *ENVIRONMENTAL* DISARMAMENT TIME-TABLE WITH THE PLANET TO RESOLVE THE WHOLE THING *DIPLOMATI-CALLY*...
...AND OUR OLD FRIEND DR. KRIGSTEIN HAS INVENTED A DOOMSDAY BOMB HE WANTS TO SINK INTO THE EARTH'S CORE IN THE HOPE THAT HE CAN *BULLY* THE WORLD INTO SUBMISSION.
BUT THE BEST HOPE WE HAVE IS STANDING RIGHT IN FRONT OF ME AND, ACCORDING TO HIS PROFILE, ENJOYS GARDENING, CROSSWORDS AND MASTURBATING ABOUT HIROSHIMA.
THE PLAN WORKED, DOCTOR.
YOU'VE GOT US EXACTLY WHERE YOU WANT US.

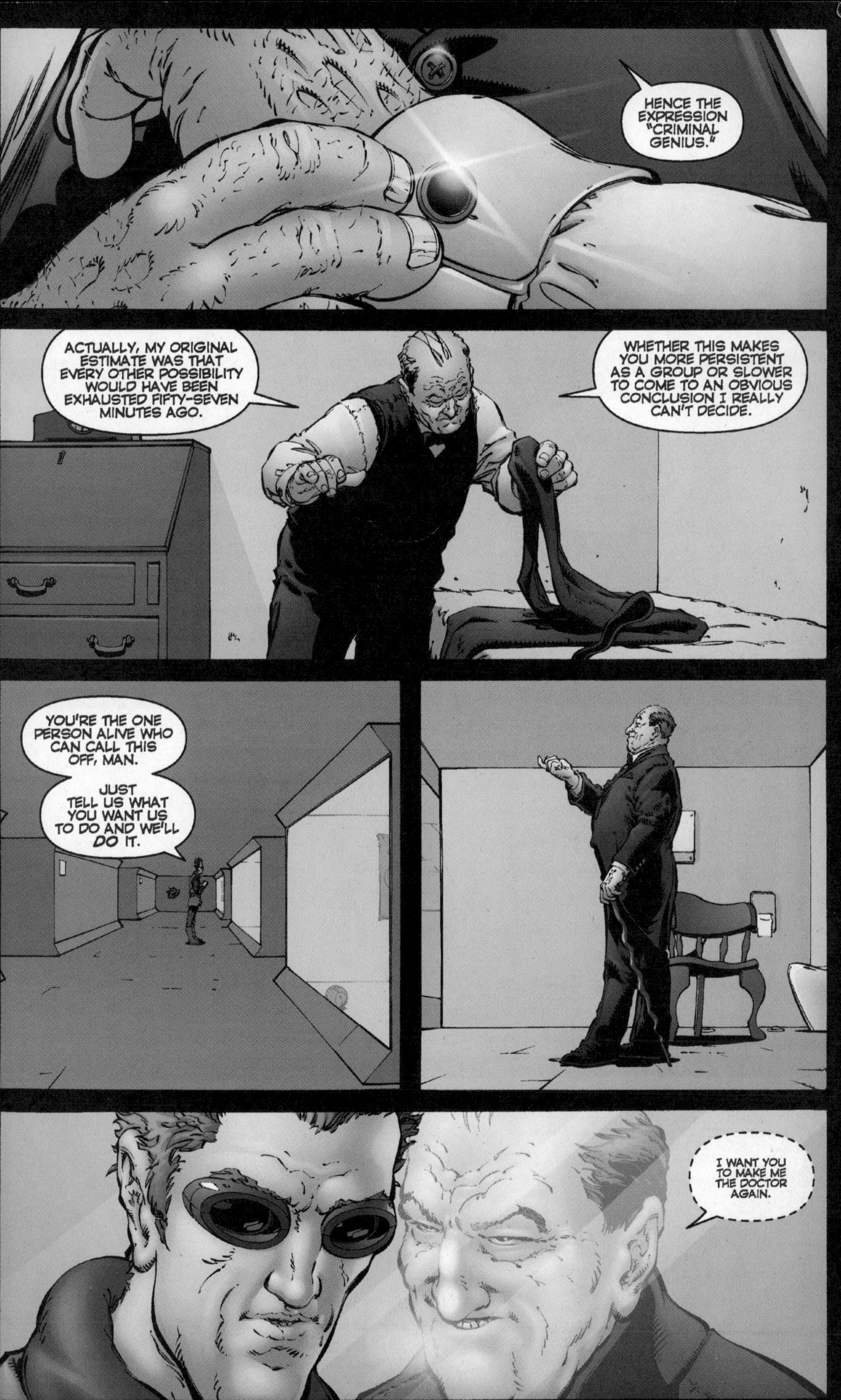
HENCE THE EXPRESSION "CRIMINAL GENIUS."
ACTUALLY, MY ORIGINAL ESTIMATE WAS THAT EVERY OTHER POSSIBILITY WOULD HAVE BEEN EXHAUSTED FIFTY-SEVEN MINUTES AGO.
WHETHER THIS MAKES YOU MORE PERSISTENT AS A GROUP OR SLOWER TO COME TO AN OBVIOUS CONCLUSION I REALLY CAN'T DECIDE.
YOU'RE THE ONE PERSON ALIVE WHO CAN CALL THIS OFF, MAN.
JUST TELL US WHAT YOU WANT US TO DO AND WE'LL *DO* IT.
I WANT YOU TO MAKE ME THE DOCTOR AGAIN.

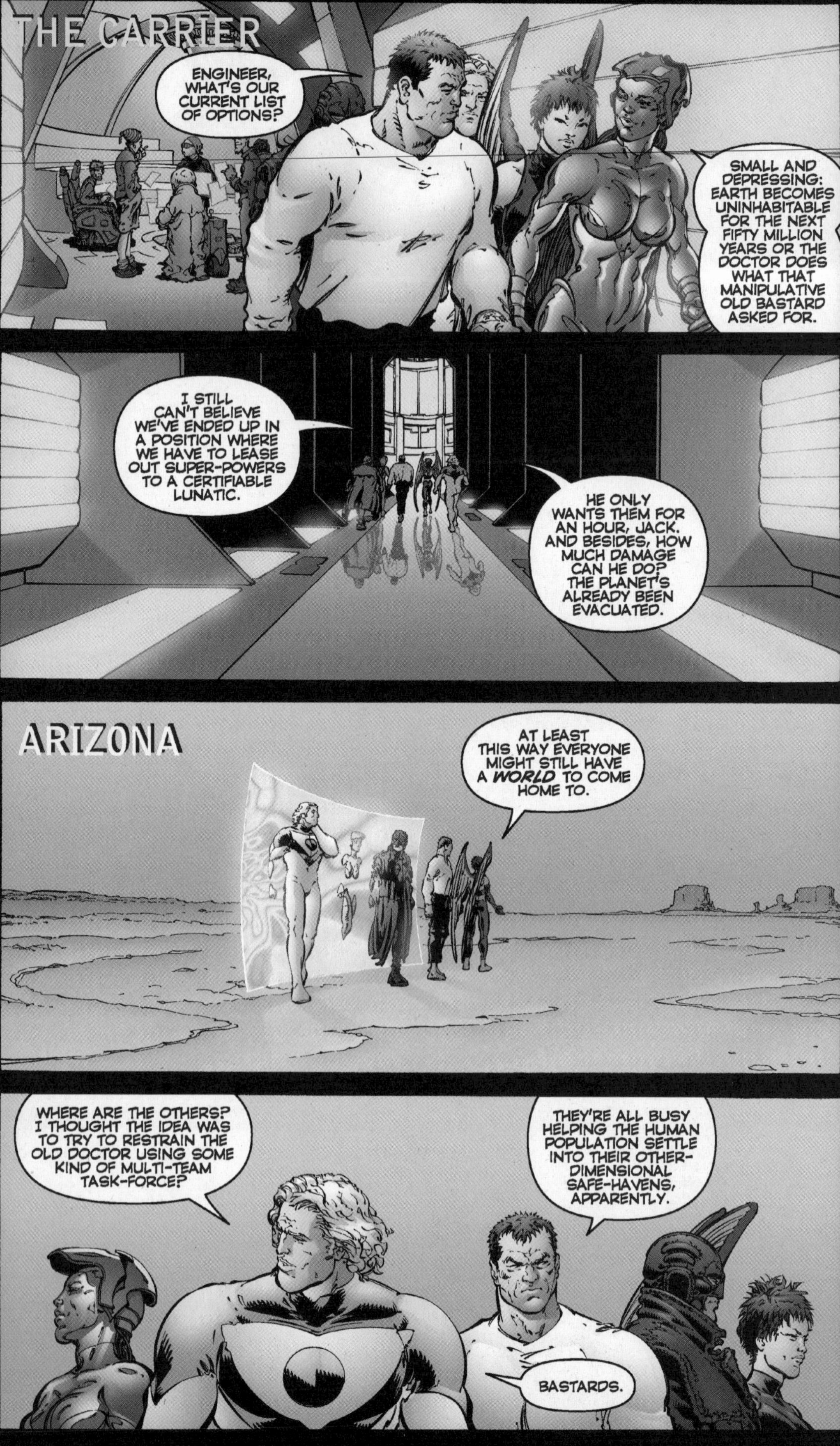
THE CARRIER
ENGINEER, WHAT'S OUR CURRENT LIST OF OPTIONS?
SMALL AND DEPRESSING: EARTH BECOMES UNINHABITABLE FOR THE NEXT FIFTY MILLION YEARS OR THE DOCTOR DOES WHAT THAT MANIPULATIVE OLD BASTARD ASKED FOR.
I STILL CAN'T BELIEVE WE'VE ENDED UP IN A POSITION WHERE WE HAVE TO LEASE OUT SUPER-POWERS TO A CERTIFIABLE LUNATIC.
HE ONLY WANTS THEM FOR AN HOUR, JACK. AND BESIDES, HOW MUCH DAMAGE CAN HE DO? THE PLANET'S ALREADY BEEN EVACUATED.
ARIZONA
AT LEAST THIS WAY EVERYONE MIGHT STILL HAVE A *WORLD* TO COME HOME TO.
WHERE ARE THE OTHERS? I THOUGHT THE IDEA WAS TO TRY TO RESTRAIN THE OLD DOCTOR USING SOME KIND OF MULTI-TEAM TASK-FORCE?
THEY'RE ALL BUSY HELPING THE HUMAN POPULATION SETTLE INTO THEIR OTHER-DIMENSIONAL SAFE-HAVENS, APPARENTLY.
BASTARDS.

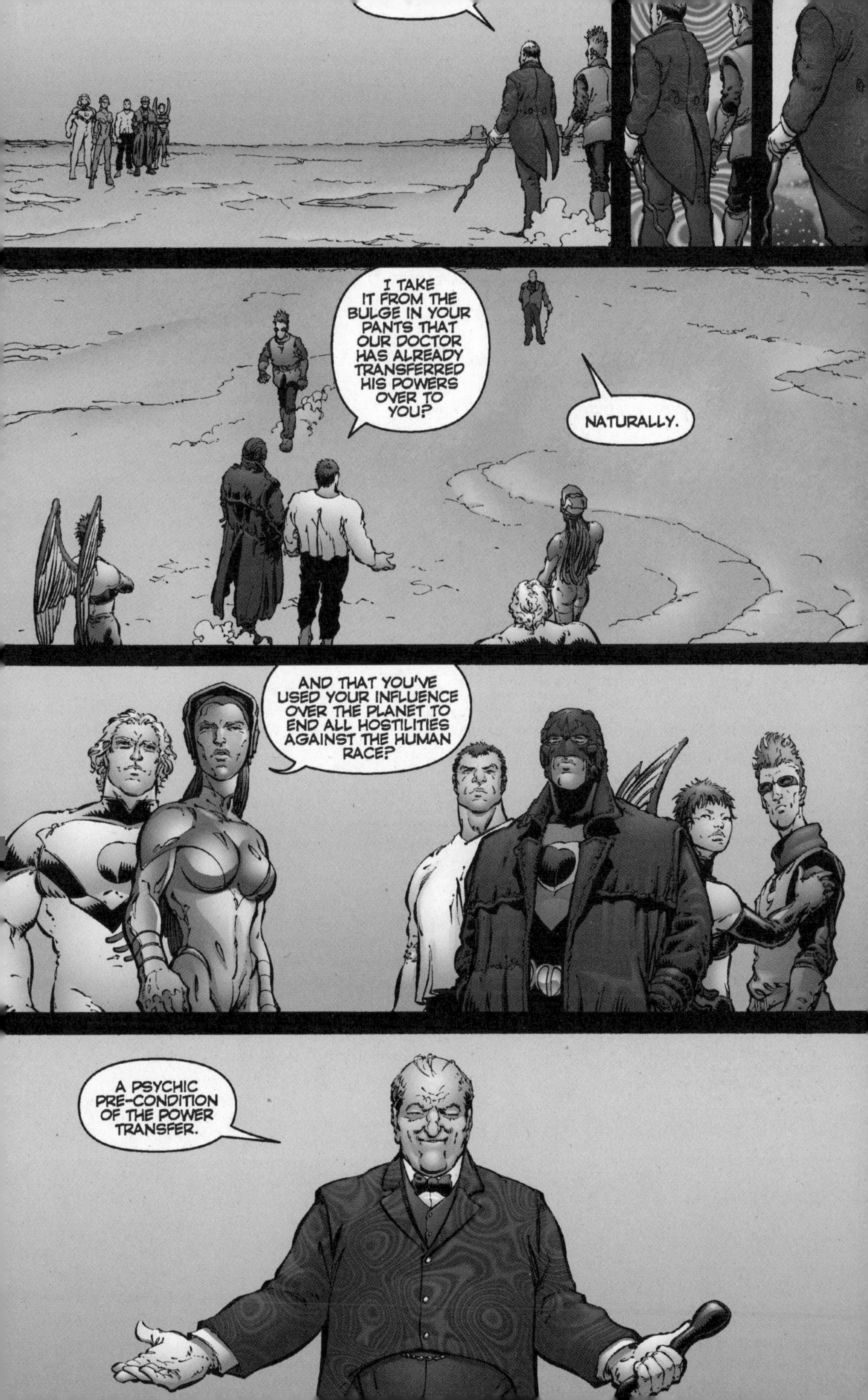
I TAKE IT FROM THE BULGE IN YOUR PANTS THAT OUR DOCTOR HAS ALREADY TRANSFERRED HIS POWERS OVER TO YOU?
NATURALLY.
AND THAT YOU'VE USED YOUR INFLUENCE OVER THE PLANET TO END ALL HOSTILITIES AGAINST THE HUMAN RACE?
A PSYCHIC PRE-CONDITION OF THE POWER TRANSFER.

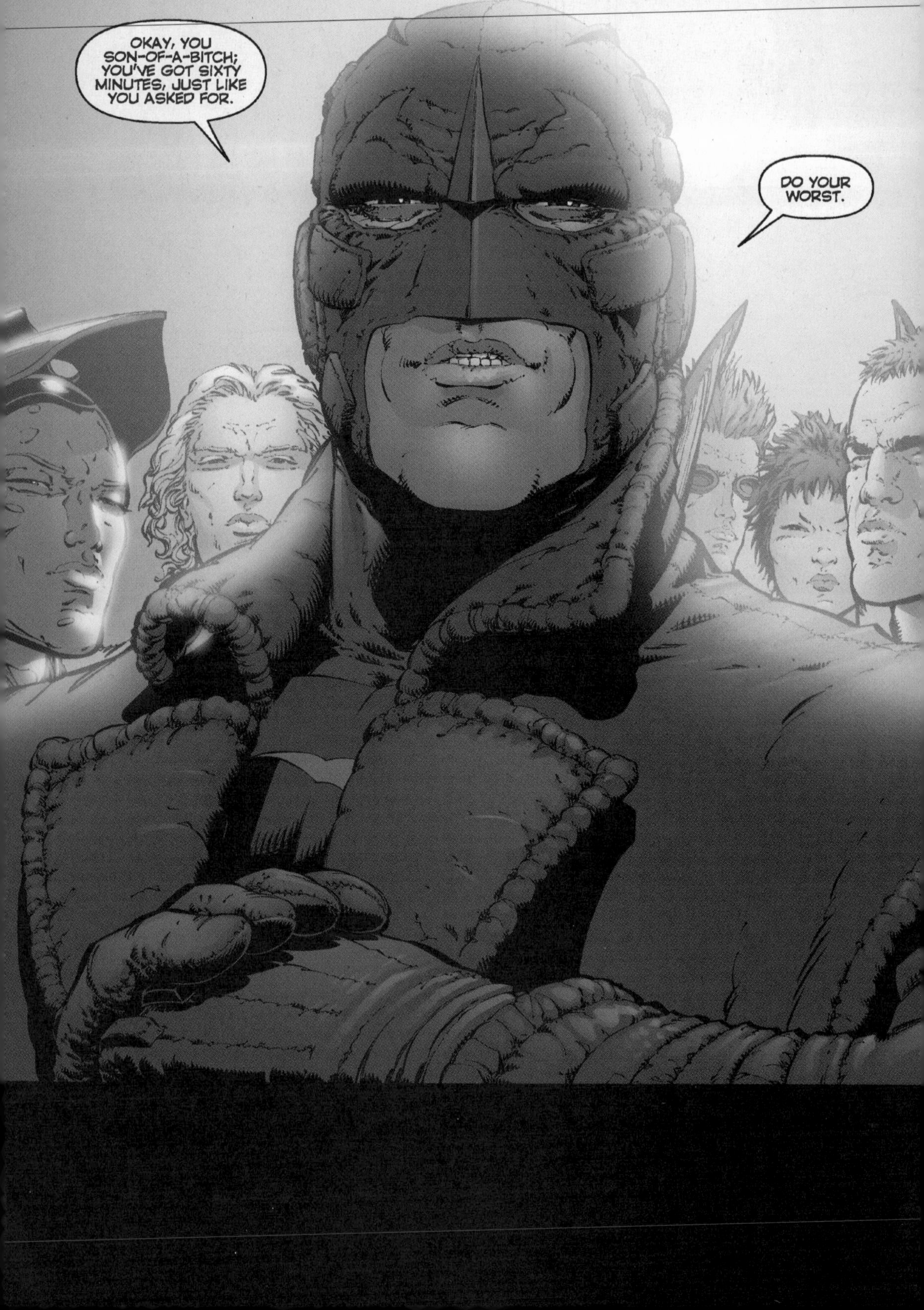
OKAY, YOU SON-OF-A-BITCH; YOU'VE GOT SIXTY MINUTES, JUST LIKE YOU ASKED FOR.
DO YOUR WORST.

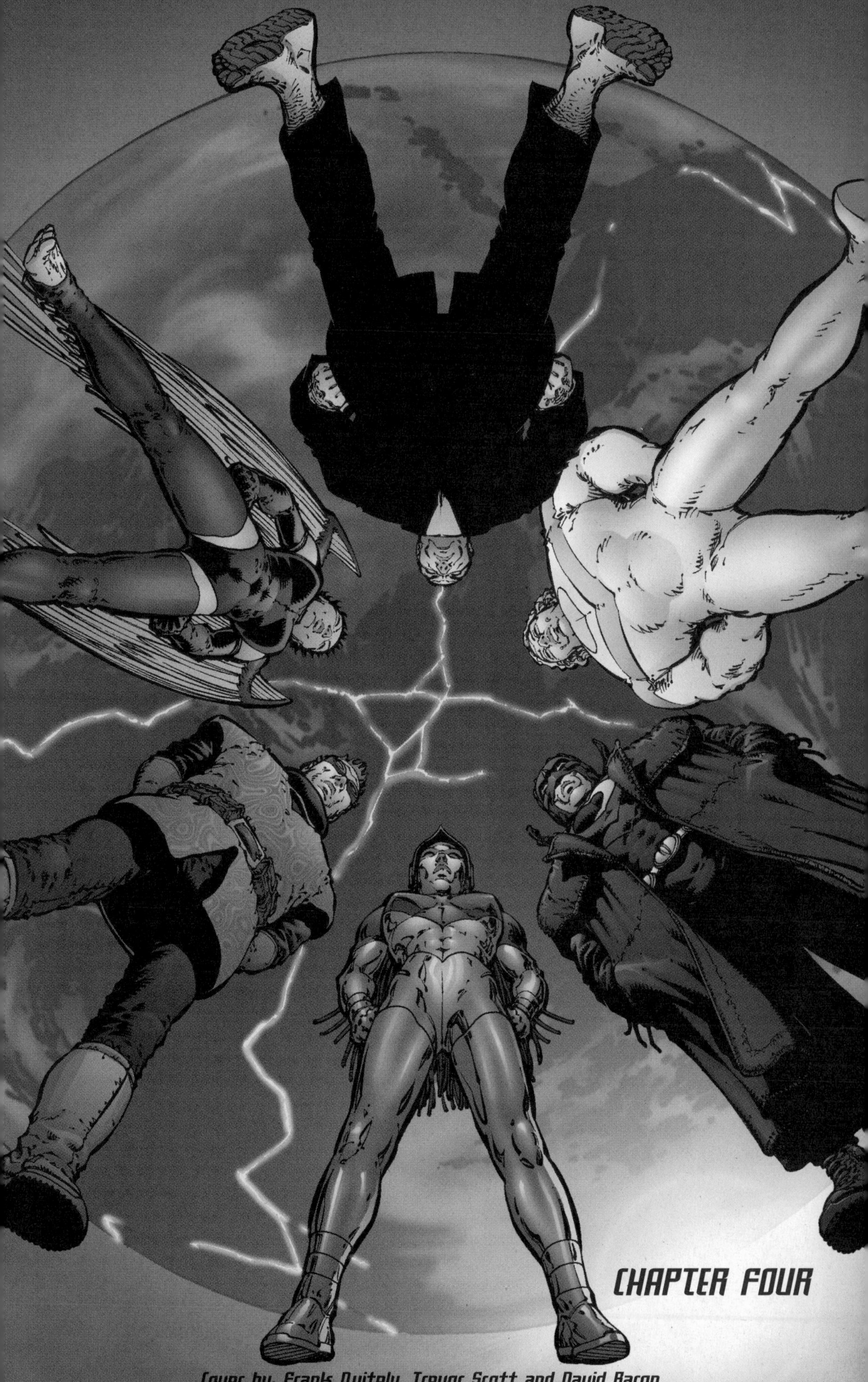
CHAPTER FOUR

Cover by: Frank Quitely, Trevor Scott and David Baron

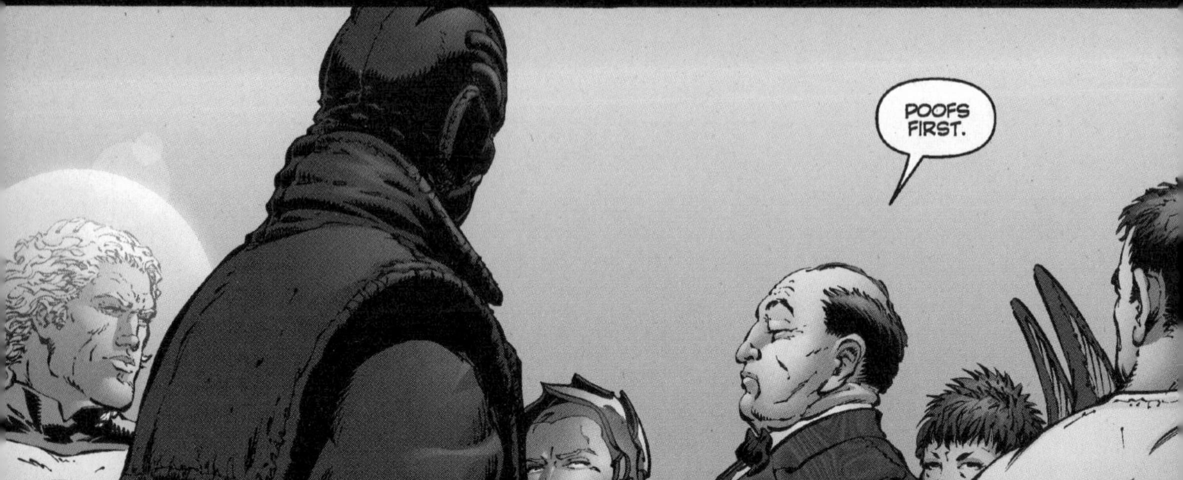
POOFS FIRST.

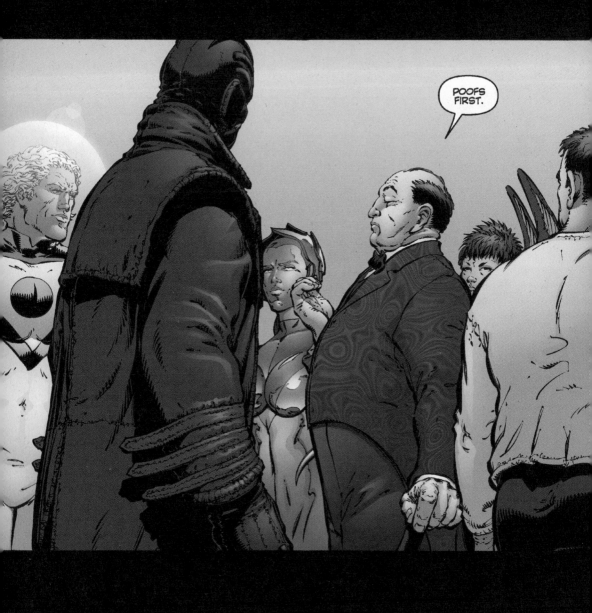

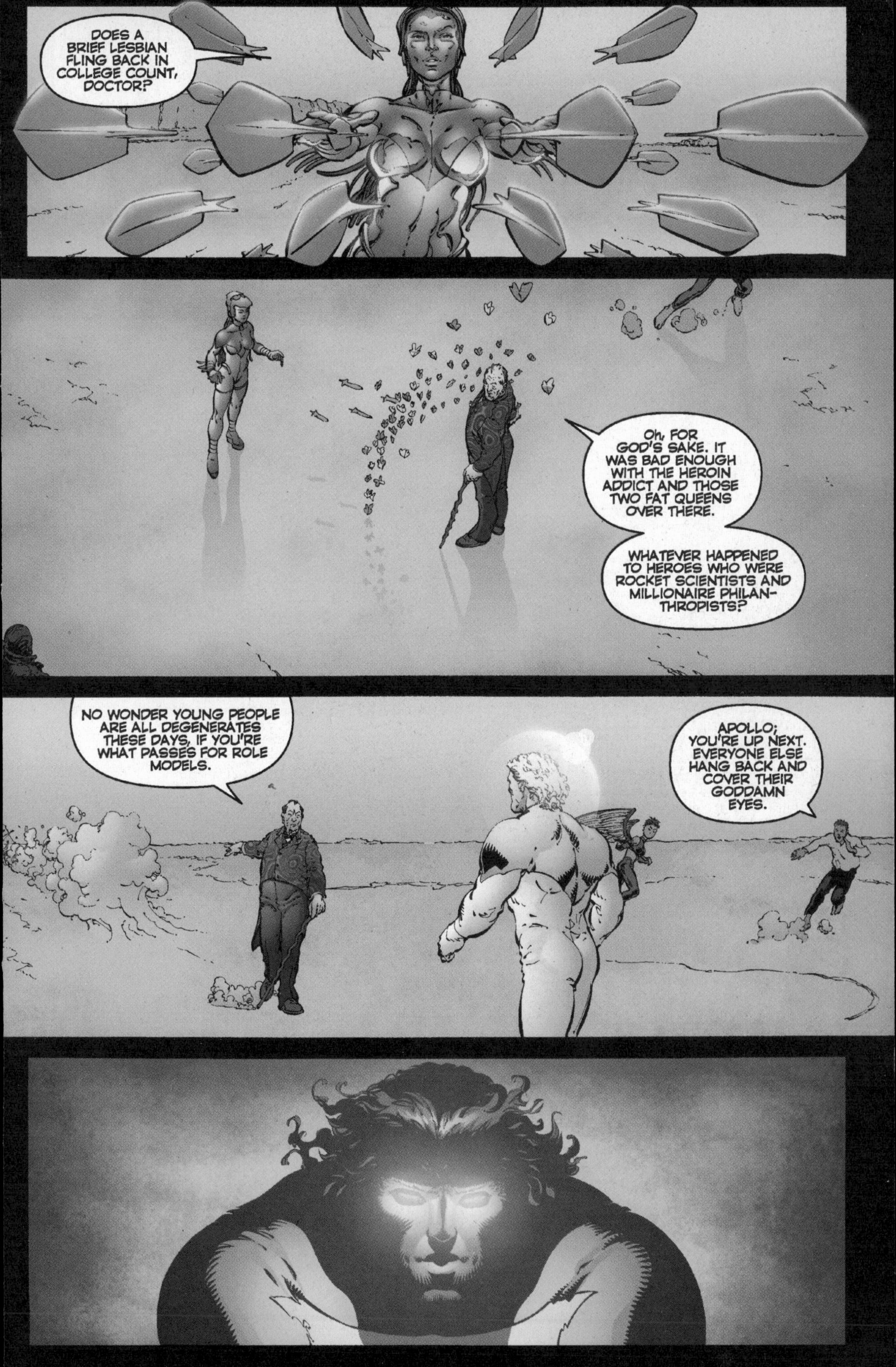
DOES A BRIEF LESBIAN FLING BACK IN COLLEGE COUNT, DOCTOR?
Oh, FOR GOD'S SAKE. IT WAS BAD ENOUGH WITH THE HEROIN ADDICT AND THOSE TWO FAT QUEENS OVER THERE.
WHATEVER HAPPENED TO HEROES WHO WERE ROCKET SCIENTISTS AND MILLIONAIRE PHILAN-THROPISTS?
NO WONDER YOUNG PEOPLE ARE ALL DEGENERATES THESE DAYS, IF YOU'RE WHAT PASSES FOR ROLE MODELS.
APOLLO; YOU'RE UP NEXT. EVERYONE ELSE HANG BACK AND COVER THEIR GODDAMN EYES.

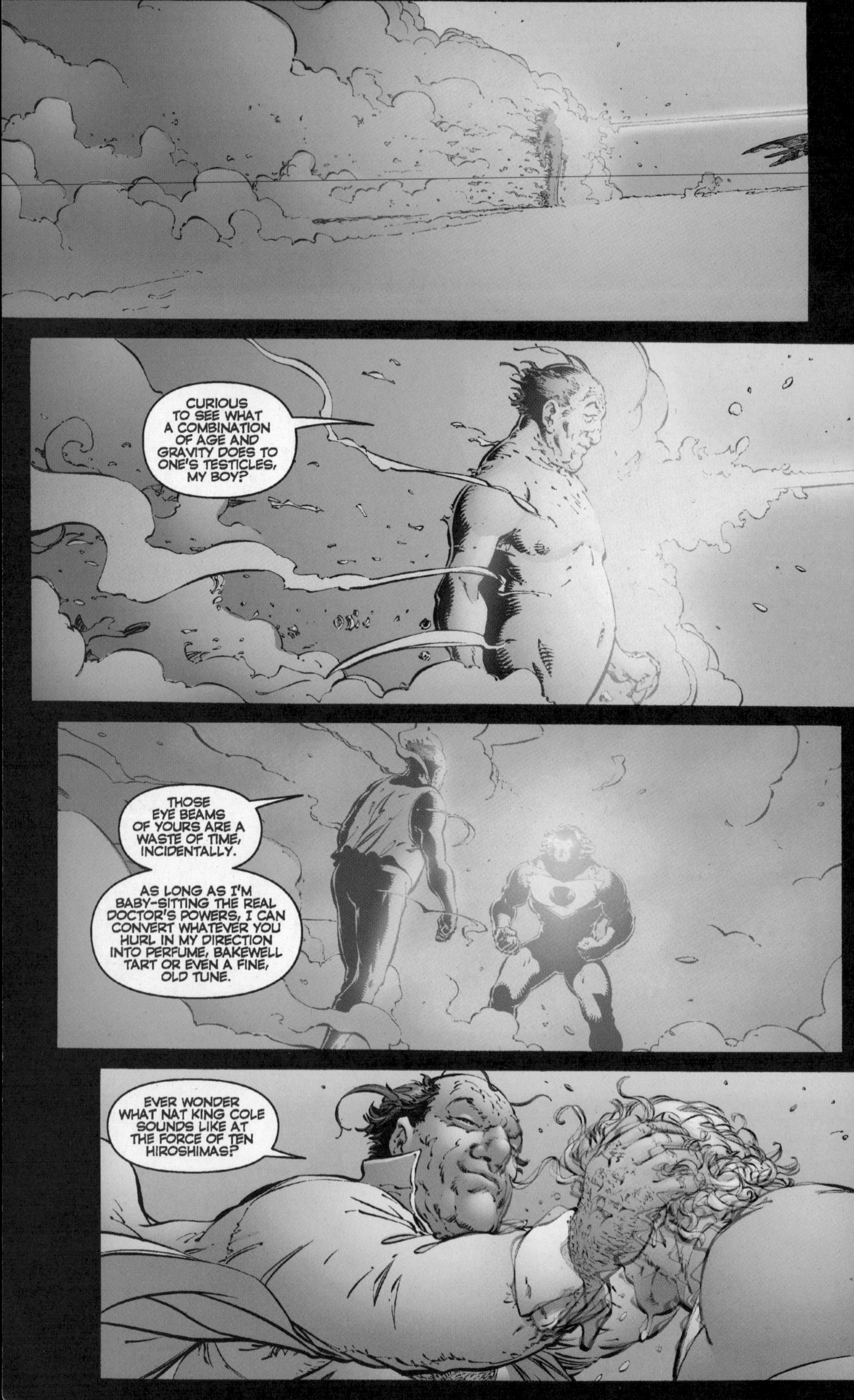
CURIOUS TO SEE WHAT A COMBINATION OF AGE AND GRAVITY DOES TO ONE'S TESTICLES, MY BOY?
THOSE EYE BEAMS OF YOURS ARE A WASTE OF TIME, INCIDENTALLY.
AS LONG AS I'M BABY-SITTING THE REAL DOCTOR'S POWERS, I CAN CONVERT WHATEVER YOU HURL IN MY DIRECTION INTO PERFUME, BAKEWELL TART OR EVEN A FINE, OLD TUNE.
EVER WONDER WHAT NAT KING COLE SOUNDS LIKE AT THE FORCE OF TEN HIROSHIMAS?

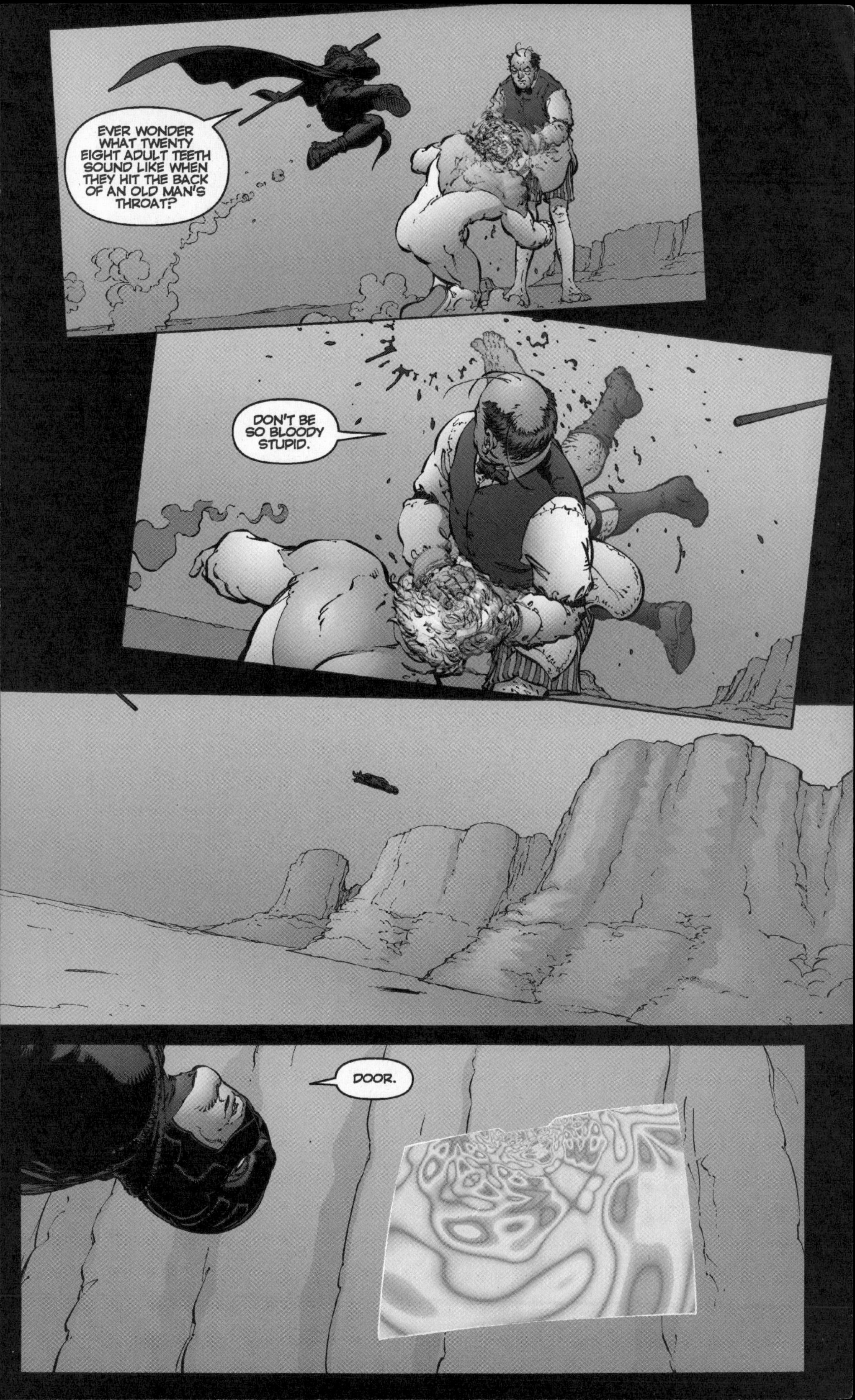
EVER WONDER WHAT TWENTY EIGHT ADULT TEETH SOUND LIKE WHEN THEY HIT THE BACK OF AN OLD MAN'S THROAT?
DON'T BE SO BLOODY STUPID.
DOOR.

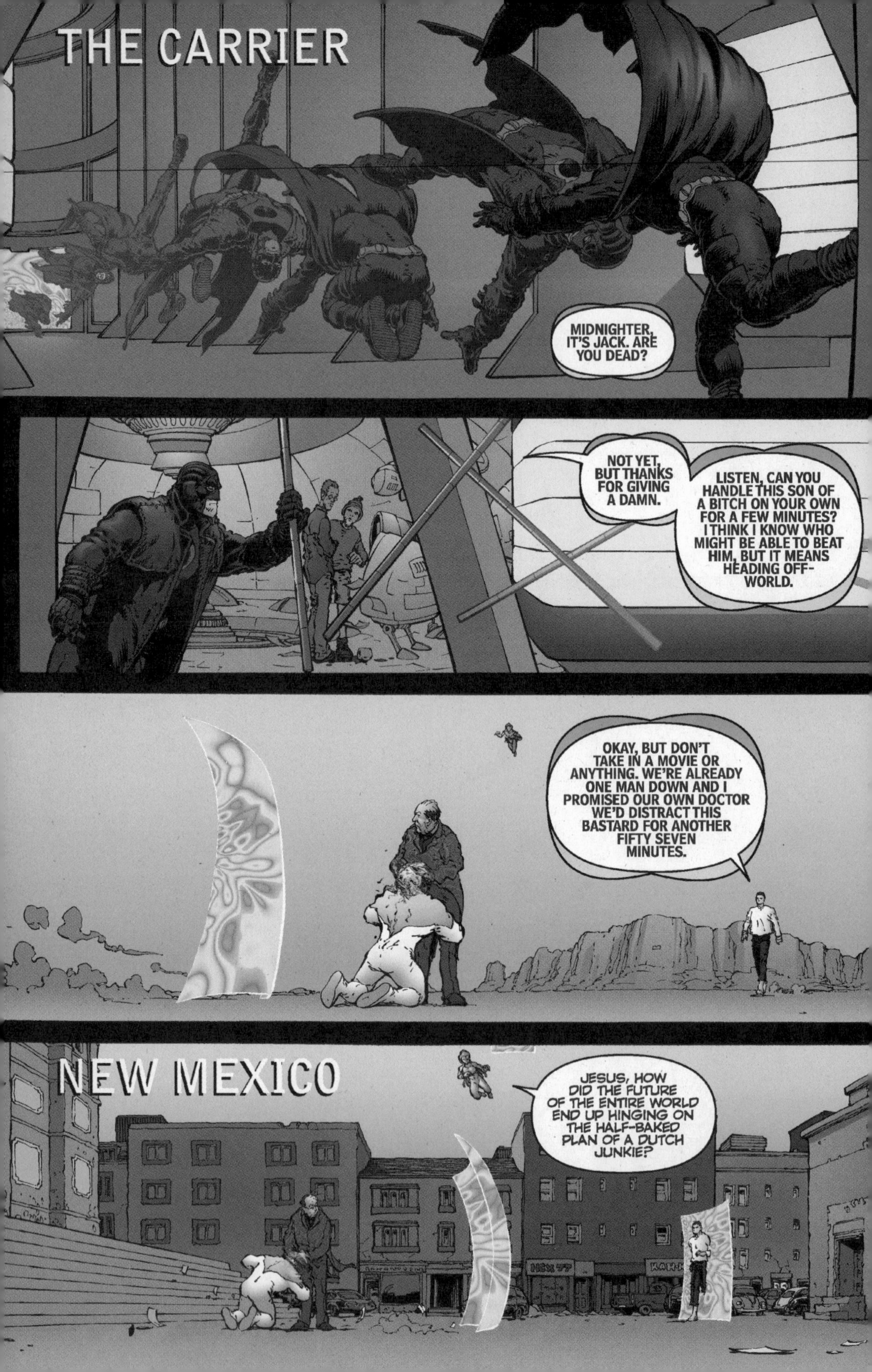
THE CARRIER
MIDNIGHTER, IT'S JACK. ARE YOU DEAD?
NOT YET, BUT THANKS FOR GIVING A DAMN.
LISTEN, CAN YOU HANDLE THIS SON OF A BITCH ON YOUR OWN FOR A FEW MINUTES? I THINK I KNOW WHO MIGHT BE ABLE TO BEAT HIM, BUT IT MEANS HEADING OFF-WORLD.
OKAY, BUT DON'T TAKE IN A MOVIE OR ANYTHING. WE'RE ALREADY ONE MAN DOWN AND I PROMISED OUR OWN DOCTOR WE'D DISTRACT THIS BASTARD FOR ANOTHER FIFTY SEVEN MINUTES.
NEW MEXICO
JESUS, HOW DID THE FUTURE OF THE ENTIRE WORLD END UP HINGING ON THE HALF-BAKED PLAN OF A DUTCH JUNKIE?

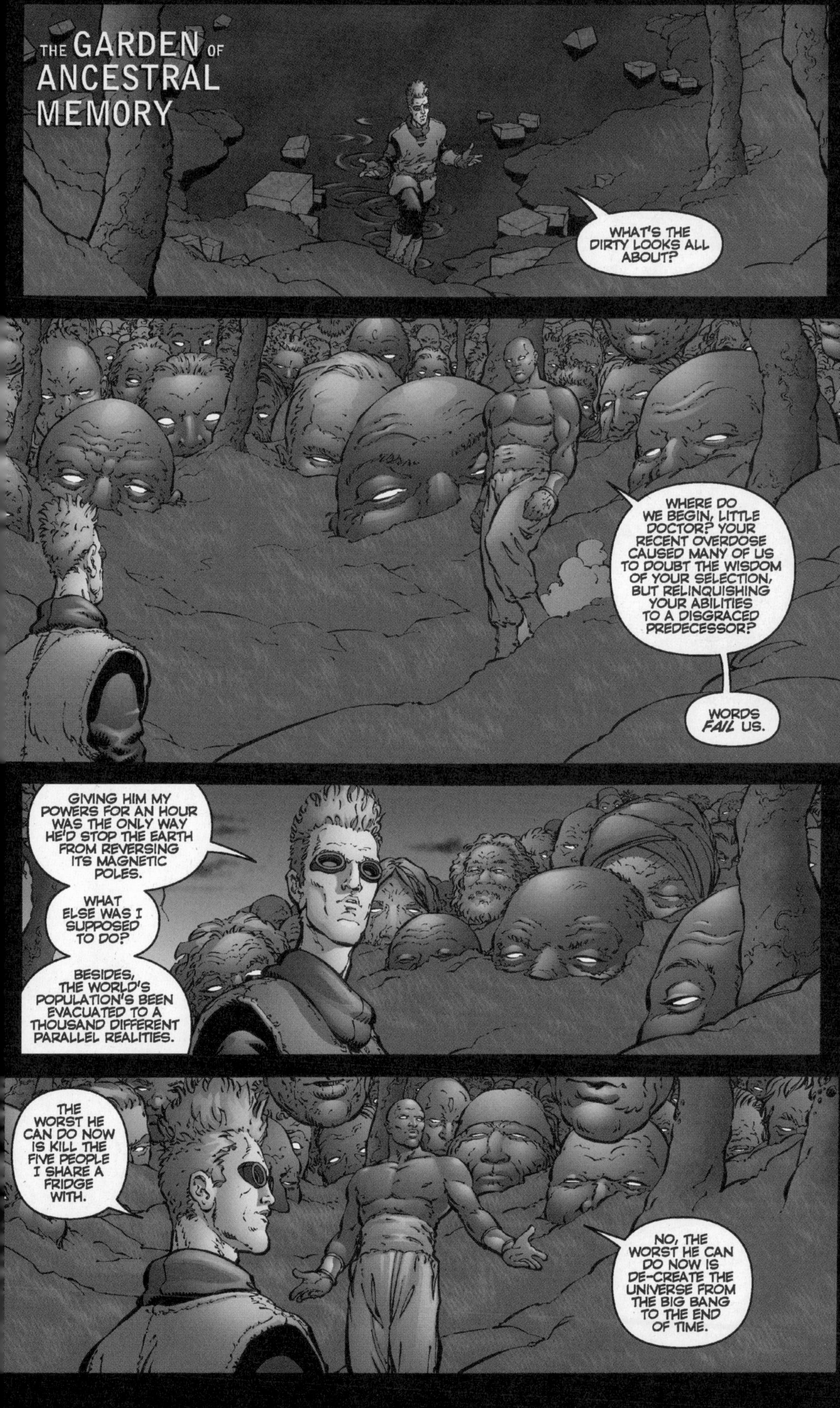

THE GARDEN OF ANCESTRAL MEMORY

WHAT'S THE DIRTY LOOKS ALL ABOUT?

WHERE DO WE BEGIN, LITTLE DOCTOR? YOUR RECENT OVERDOSE CAUSED MANY OF US TO DOUBT THE WISDOM OF YOUR SELECTION, BUT RELINQUISHING YOUR ABILITIES TO A DISGRACED PREDECESSOR?

WORDS *FAIL* US.

GIVING HIM MY POWERS FOR AN HOUR WAS THE ONLY WAY HE'D STOP THE EARTH FROM REVERSING ITS MAGNETIC POLES.

WHAT ELSE WAS I SUPPOSED TO DO?

BESIDES, THE WORLD'S POPULATION'S BEEN EVACUATED TO A THOUSAND DIFFERENT PARALLEL REALITIES.

THE WORST HE CAN DO NOW IS KILL THE FIVE PEOPLE I SHARE A FRIDGE WITH.

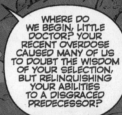

NO, THE WORST HE CAN DO NOW IS DE-CREATE THE UNIVERSE FROM THE BIG BANG TO THE END OF TIME.

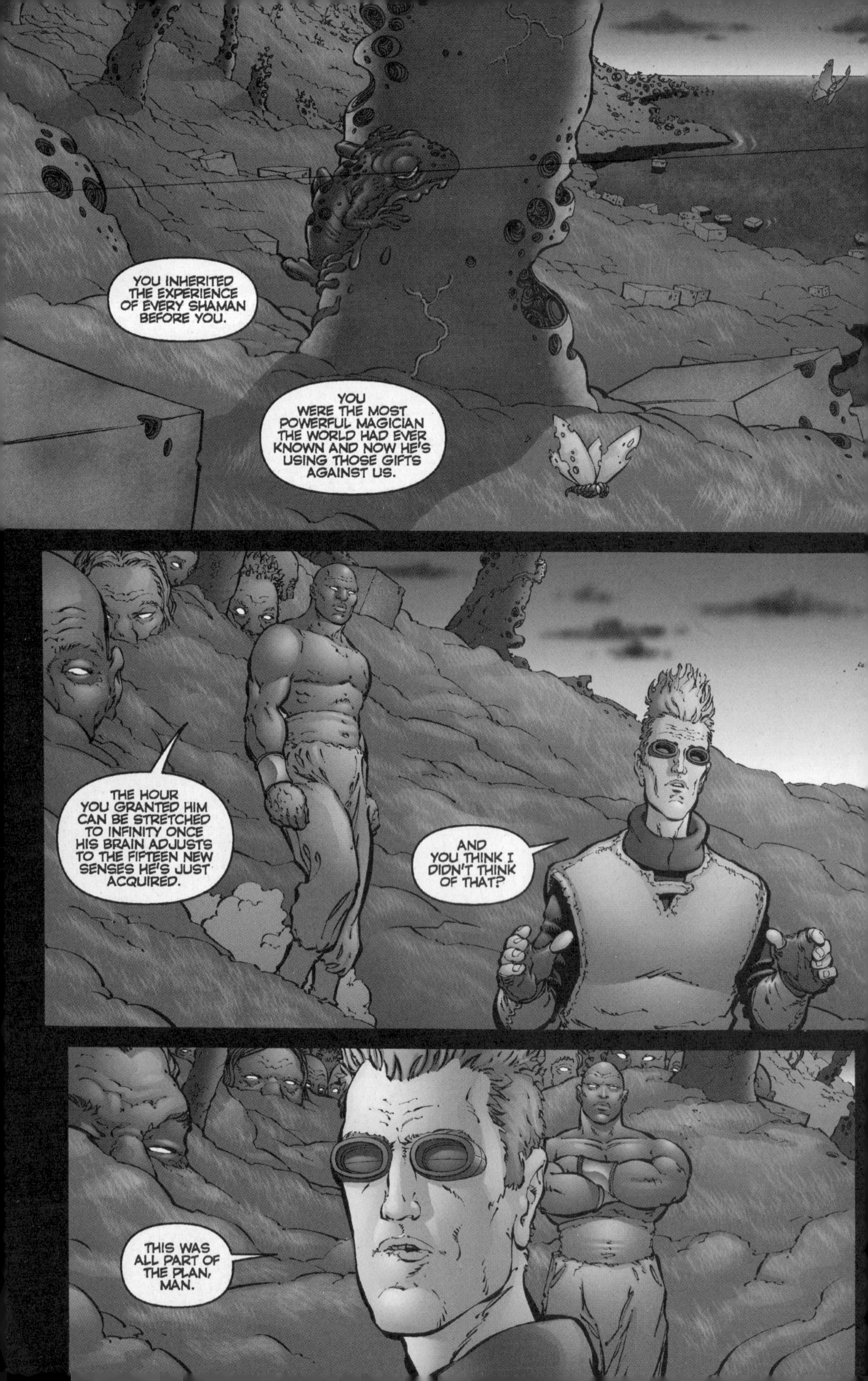
YOU INHERITED THE EXPERIENCE OF EVERY SHAMAN BEFORE YOU.
YOU WERE THE MOST POWERFUL MAGICIAN THE WORLD HAD EVER KNOWN AND NOW HE'S USING THOSE GIFTS AGAINST US.
THE HOUR YOU GRANTED HIM CAN BE STRETCHED TO INFINITY ONCE HIS BRAIN ADJUSTS TO THE FIFTEEN NEW SENSES HE'S JUST ACQUIRED.
AND YOU THINK I DIDN'T THINK OF THAT?
THIS WAS ALL PART OF THE PLAN, MAN.

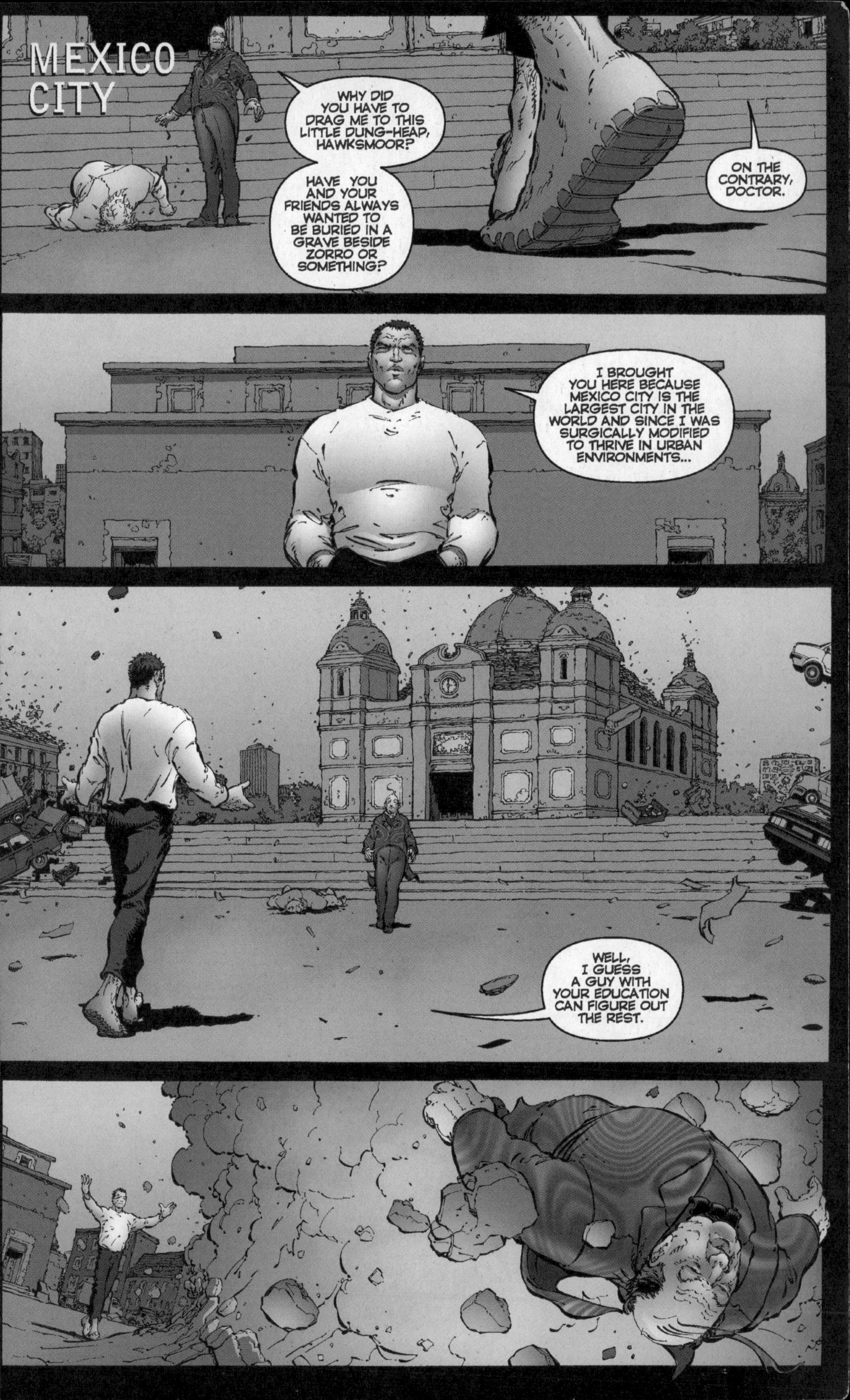
MEXICO CITY
WHY DID YOU HAVE TO DRAG ME TO THIS LITTLE DUNG-HEAP, HAWKSMOOR?
HAVE YOU AND YOUR FRIENDS ALWAYS WANTED TO BE BURIED IN A GRAVE BESIDE ZORRO OR SOMETHING?
ON THE CONTRARY, DOCTOR.
I BROUGHT YOU HERE BECAUSE MEXICO CITY IS THE LARGEST CITY IN THE WORLD AND SINCE I WAS SURGICALLY MODIFIED TO THRIVE IN URBAN ENVIRONMENTS...
WELL, I GUESS A GUY WITH YOUR EDUCATION CAN FIGURE OUT THE REST.

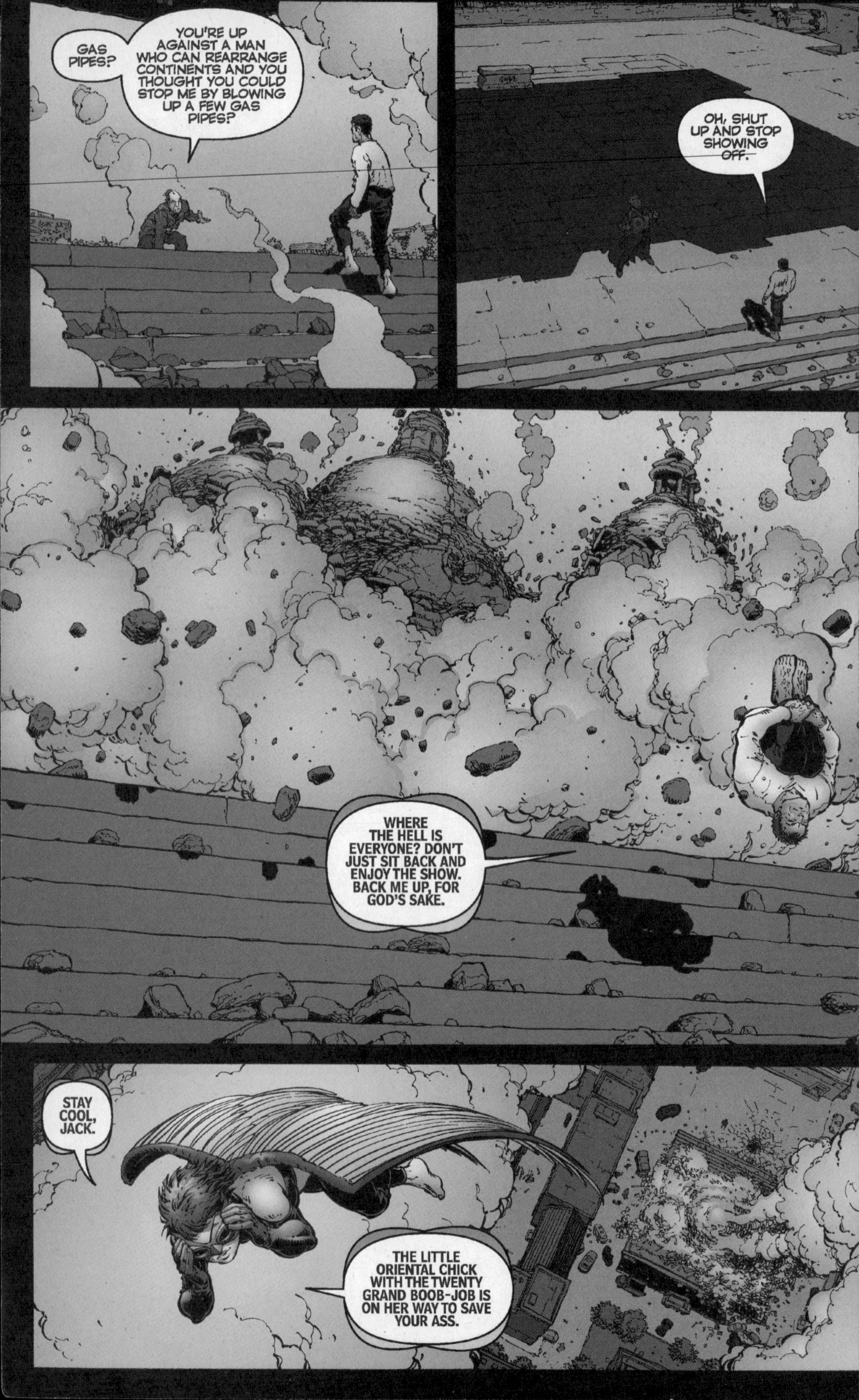
GAS PIPES?
YOU'RE UP AGAINST A MAN WHO CAN REARRANGE CONTINENTS AND YOU THOUGHT YOU COULD STOP ME BY BLOWING UP A FEW GAS PIPES?
OH, SHUT UP AND STOP SHOWING OFF.
WHERE THE HELL IS EVERYONE? DON'T JUST SIT BACK AND ENJOY THE SHOW. BACK ME UP, FOR GOD'S SAKE.
STAY COOL, JACK.
THE LITTLE ORIENTAL CHICK WITH THE TWENTY GRAND BOOB-JOB IS ON HER WAY TO SAVE YOUR ASS.

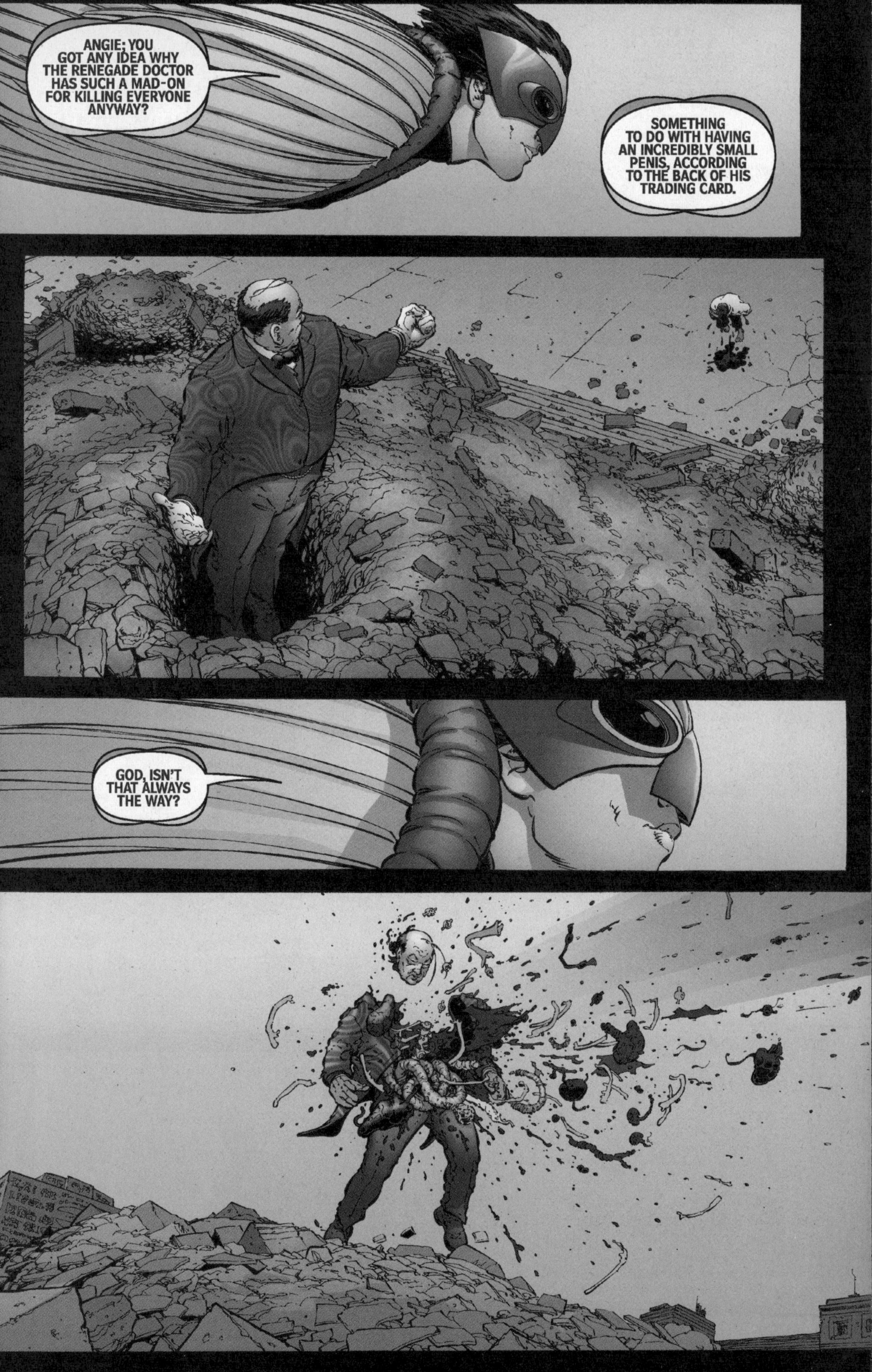
ANGIE; YOU GOT ANY IDEA WHY THE RENEGADE DOCTOR HAS SUCH A MAD-ON FOR KILLING EVERYONE ANYWAY?
SOMETHING TO DO WITH HAVING AN INCREDIBLY SMALL PENIS, ACCORDING TO THE BACK OF HIS TRADING CARD.
GOD, ISN'T THAT ALWAYS THE WAY?

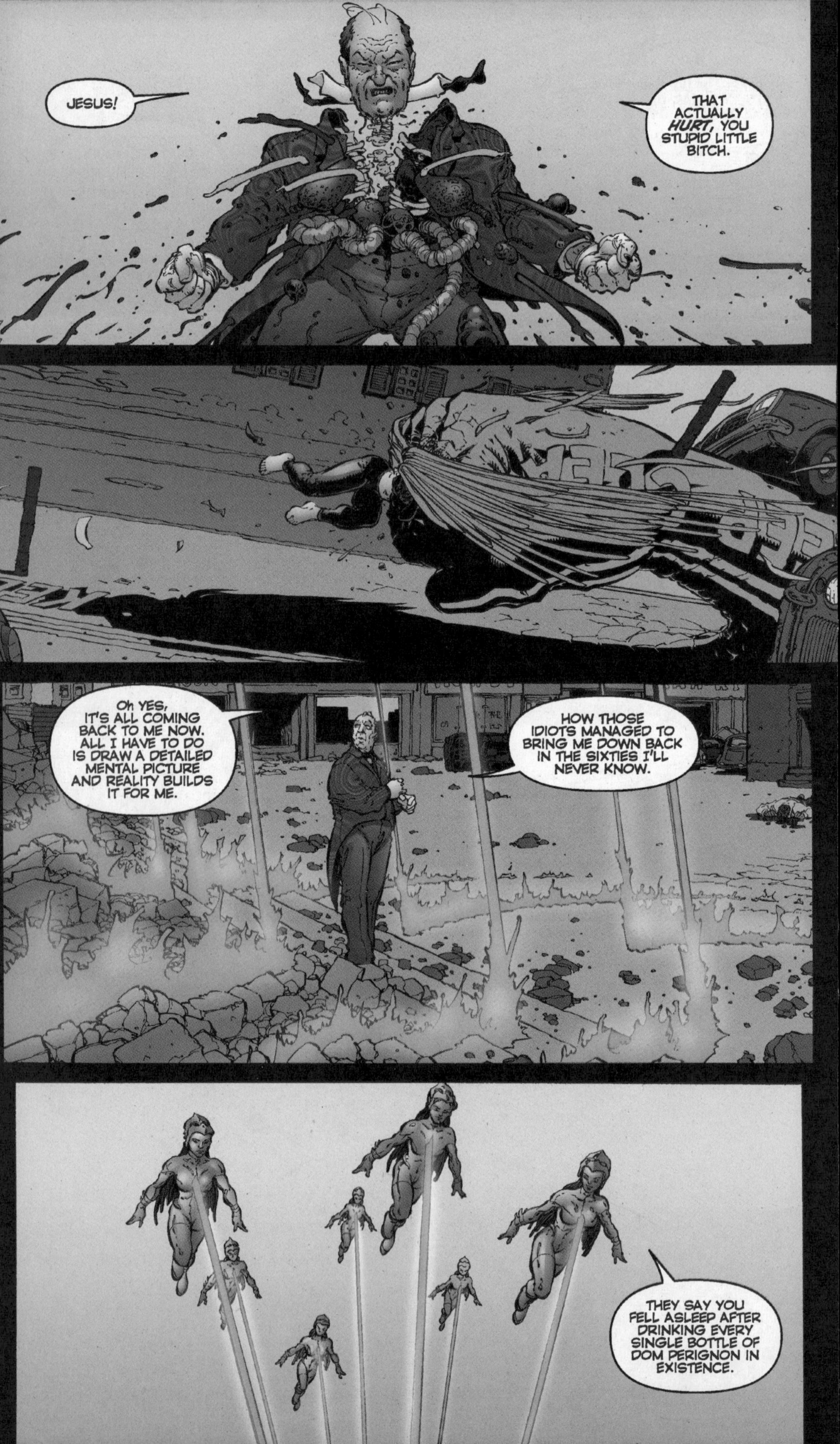
JESUS!
THAT ACTUALLY HURT, YOU STUPID LITTLE BITCH.
Oh YES, IT'S ALL COMING BACK TO ME NOW. ALL I HAVE TO DO IS DRAW A DETAILED MENTAL PICTURE AND REALITY BUILDS IT FOR ME.
HOW THOSE IDIOTS MANAGED TO BRING ME DOWN BACK IN THE SIXTIES I'LL NEVER KNOW.
THEY SAY YOU FELL ASLEEP AFTER DRINKING EVERY SINGLE BOTTLE OF DOM PERIGNON IN EXISTENCE.

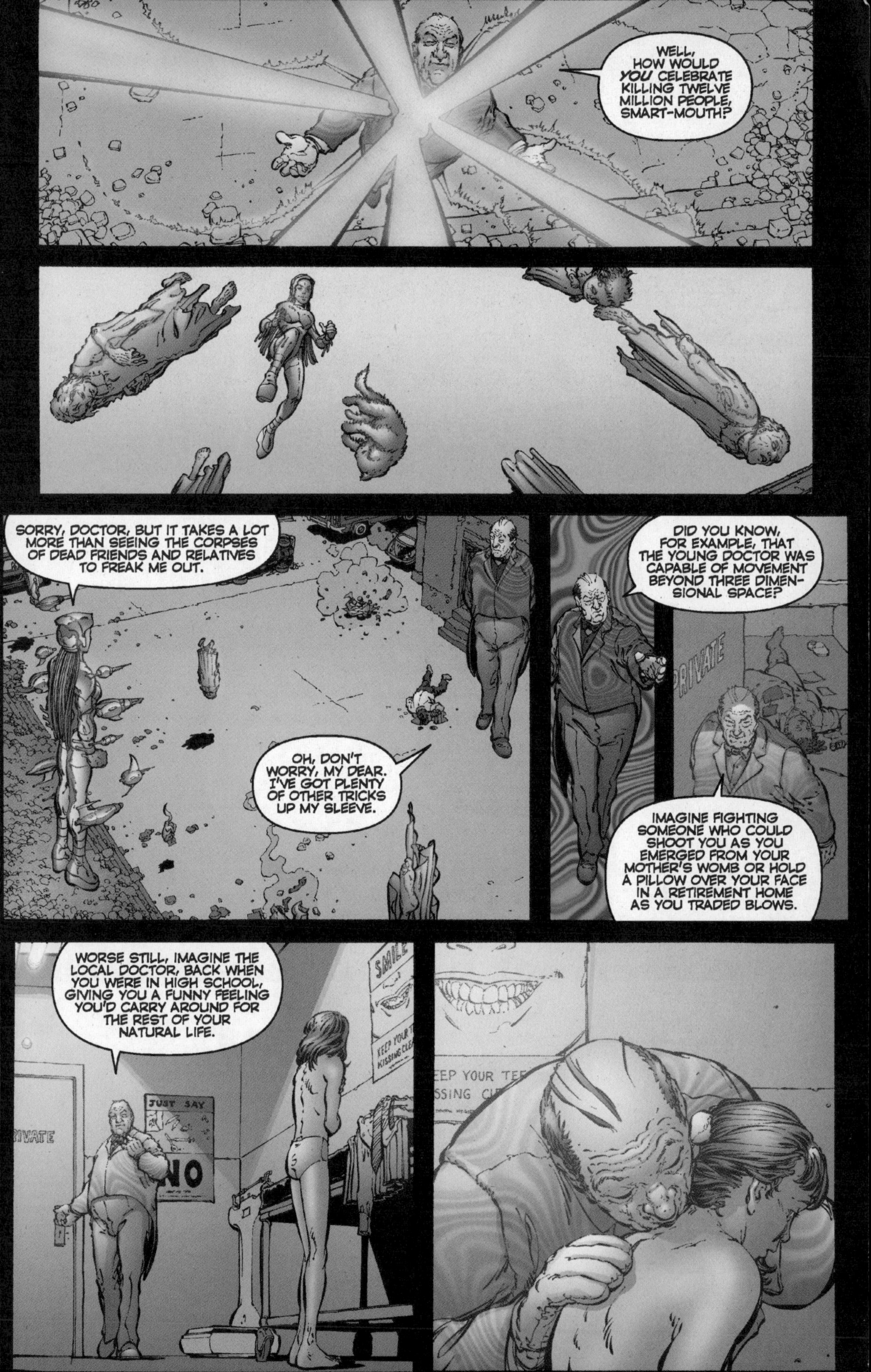
WELL, HOW WOULD *YOU* CELEBRATE KILLING TWELVE MILLION PEOPLE, SMART-MOUTH?
SORRY, DOCTOR, BUT IT TAKES A LOT MORE THAN SEEING THE CORPSES OF DEAD FRIENDS AND RELATIVES TO FREAK ME OUT.
OH, DON'T WORRY, MY DEAR. I'VE GOT PLENTY OF OTHER TRICKS UP MY SLEEVE.
DID YOU KNOW, FOR EXAMPLE, THAT THE YOUNG DOCTOR WAS CAPABLE OF MOVEMENT BEYOND THREE DIMEN-SIONAL SPACE?
PRIVATE
IMAGINE FIGHTING SOMEONE WHO COULD SHOOT YOU AS YOU EMERGED FROM YOUR MOTHER'S WOMB OR HOLD A PILLOW OVER YOUR FACE IN A RETIREMENT HOME AS YOU TRADED BLOWS.
WORSE STILL, IMAGINE THE LOCAL DOCTOR, BACK WHEN YOU WERE IN HIGH SCHOOL, GIVING YOU A FUNNY FEELING YOU'D CARRY AROUND FOR THE REST OF YOUR NATURAL LIFE.
JUST SAY
NO
RIVATE
EP YOUR TE
SSING CL

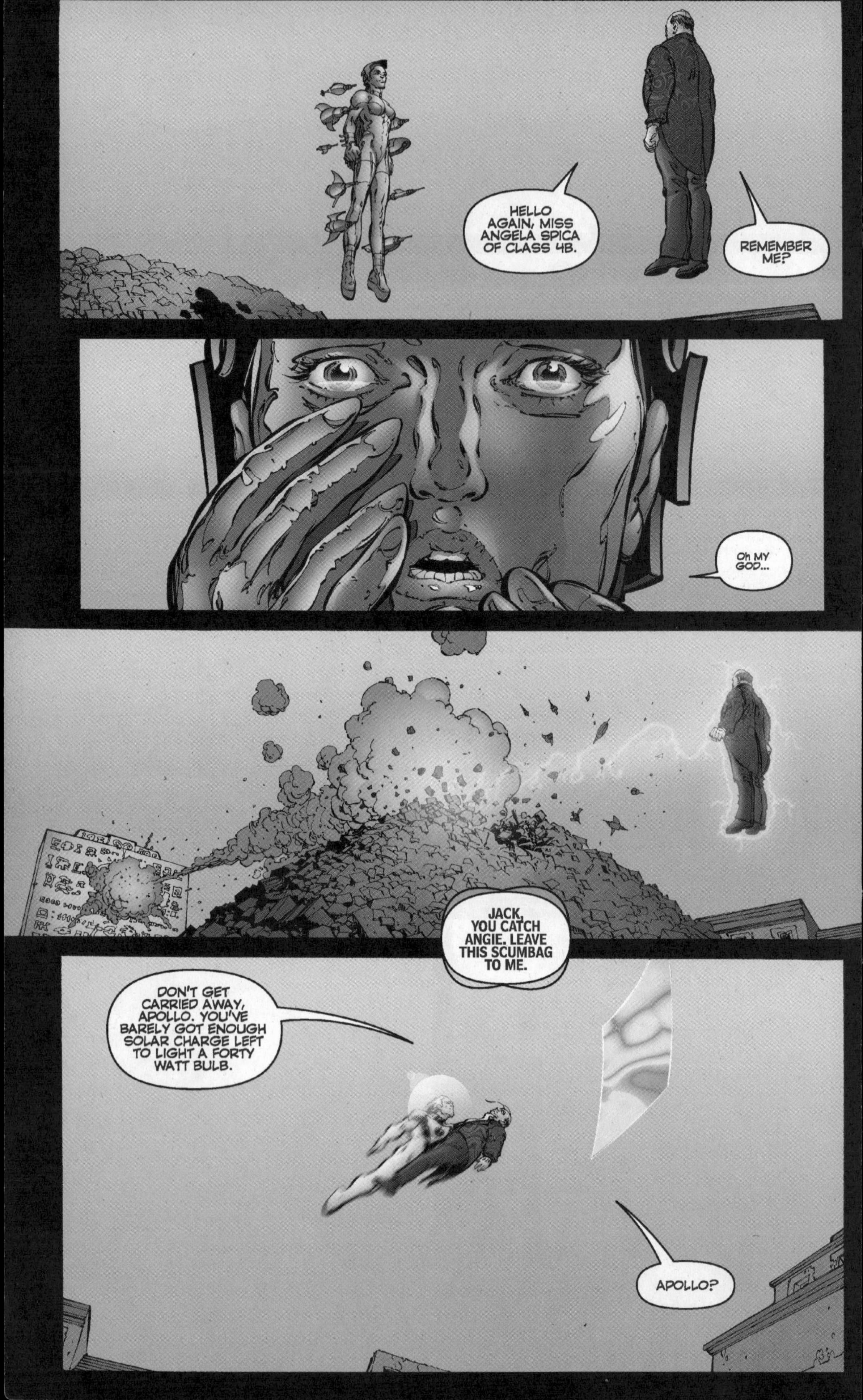

HELLO AGAIN, MISS ANGELA SPICA OF CLASS 4B.
REMEMBER ME?
Oh MY GOD...
JACK, YOU CATCH ANGIE. LEAVE THIS SCUMBAG TO ME.
DON'T GET CARRIED AWAY, APOLLO. YOU'VE BARELY GOT ENOUGH SOLAR CHARGE LEFT TO LIGHT A FORTY WATT BULB.
APOLLO?

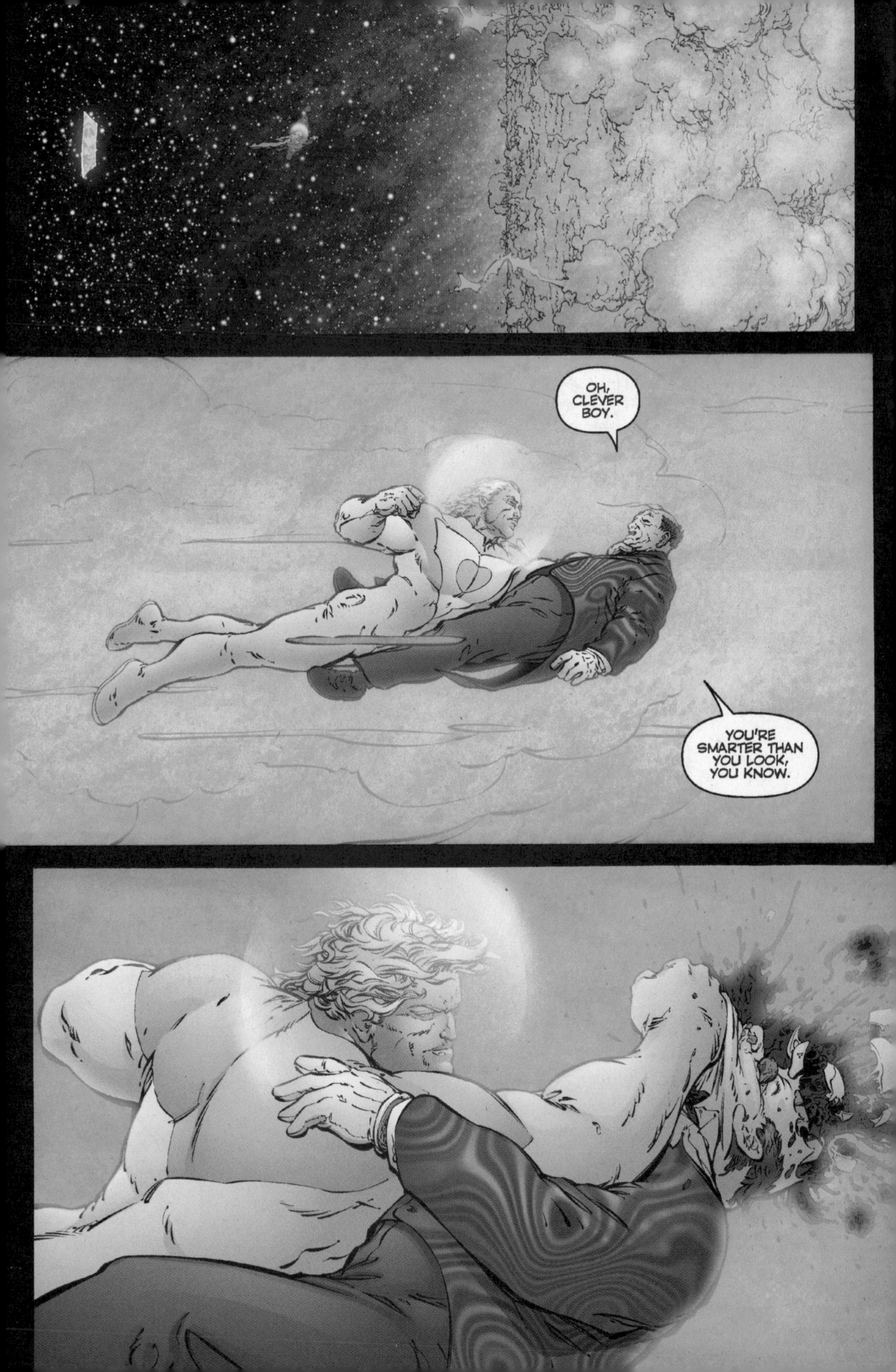
OH, CLEVER BOY.
YOU'RE SMARTER THAN YOU LOOK, YOU KNOW.

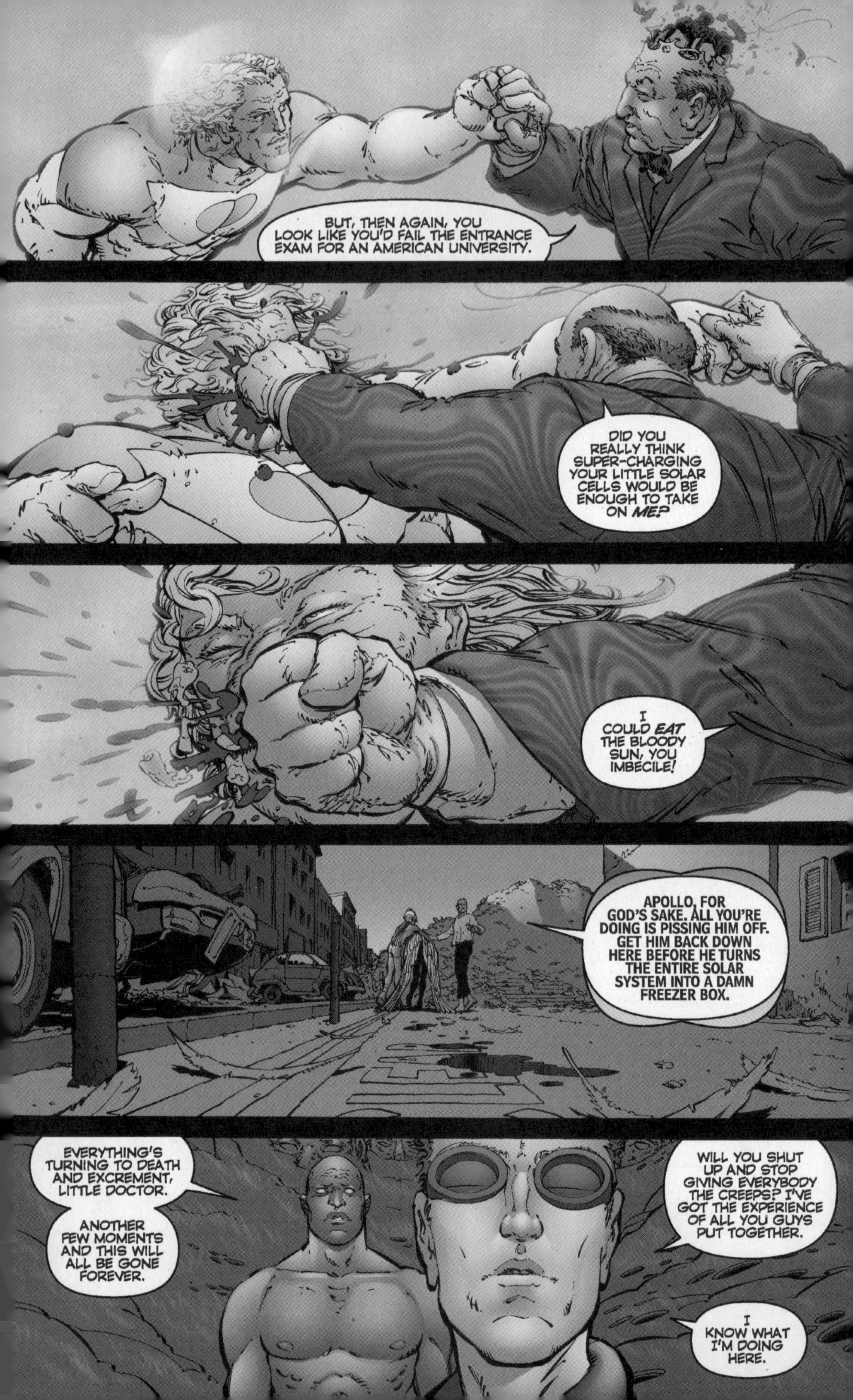
BUT, THEN AGAIN, YOU LOOK LIKE YOU'D FAIL THE ENTRANCE EXAM FOR AN AMERICAN UNIVERSITY.
DID YOU REALLY THINK SUPER-CHARGING YOUR LITTLE SOLAR CELLS WOULD BE ENOUGH TO TAKE ON *ME?*
I COULD *EAT* THE BLOODY SUN, YOU IMBECILE!
APOLLO, FOR GOD'S SAKE. ALL YOU'RE DOING IS PISSING HIM OFF. GET HIM BACK DOWN HERE BEFORE HE TURNS THE ENTIRE SOLAR SYSTEM INTO A DAMN FREEZER BOX.
EVERYTHING'S TURNING TO DEATH AND EXCREMENT, LITTLE DOCTOR.
ANOTHER FEW MOMENTS AND THIS WILL ALL BE GONE FOREVER.
WILL YOU SHUT UP AND STOP GIVING EVERYBODY THE CREEPS? I'VE GOT THE EXPERIENCE OF ALL YOU GUYS PUT TOGETHER.
I KNOW WHAT I'M DOING HERE.

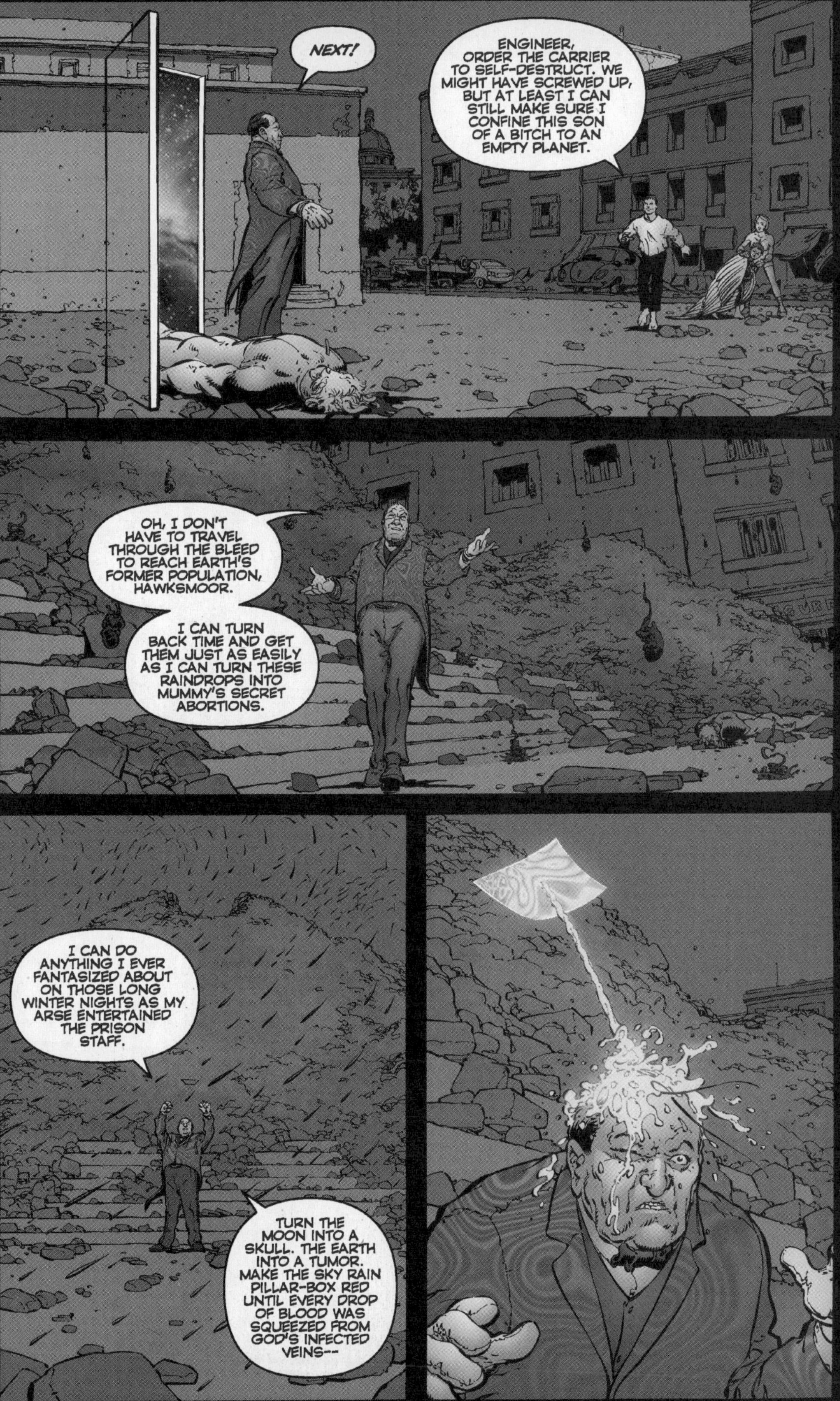
NEXT!
ENGINEER, ORDER THE CARRIER TO SELF-DESTRUCT. WE MIGHT HAVE SCREWED UP, BUT AT LEAST I CAN STILL MAKE SURE I CONFINE THIS SON OF A BITCH TO AN EMPTY PLANET.
OH, I DON'T HAVE TO TRAVEL THROUGH THE BLEED TO REACH EARTH'S FORMER POPULATION, HAWKSMOOR.
I CAN TURN BACK TIME AND GET THEM JUST AS EASILY AS I CAN TURN THESE RAINDROPS INTO MUMMY'S SECRET ABORTIONS.
I CAN DO ANYTHING I EVER FANTASIZED ABOUT ON THOSE LONG WINTER NIGHTS AS MY ARSE ENTERTAINED THE PRISON STAFF.
TURN THE MOON INTO A SKULL. THE EARTH INTO A TUMOR. MAKE THE SKY RAIN PILLAR-BOX RED UNTIL EVERY DROP OF BLOOD WAS SQUEEZED FROM GOD'S INFECTED VEINS--

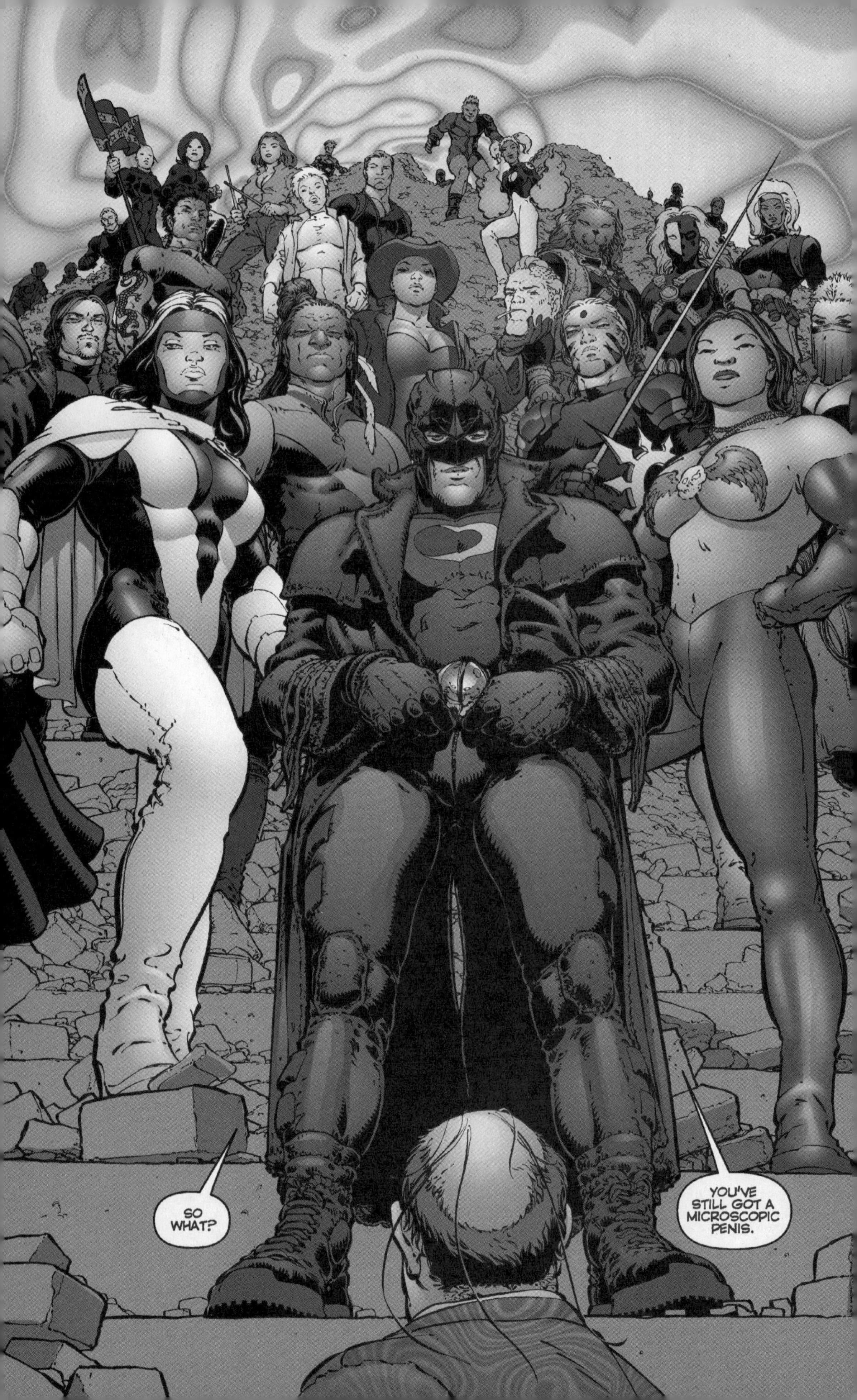

SO WHAT?
YOU'VE STILL GOT A MICROSCOPIC PENIS.

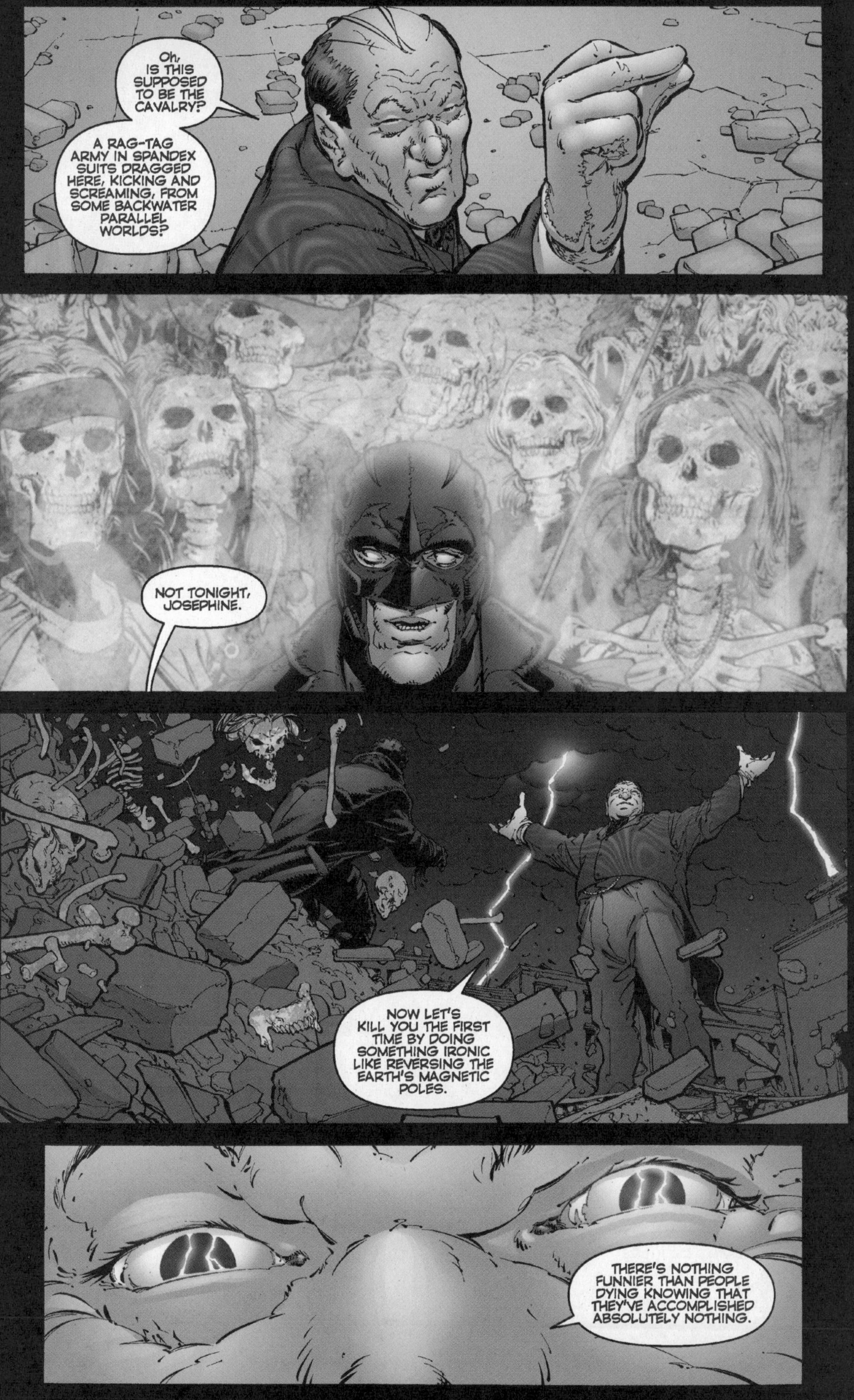
Oh, IS THIS SUPPOSED TO BE THE CAVALRY?
A RAG-TAG ARMY IN SPANDEX SUITS DRAGGED HERE, KICKING AND SCREAMING, FROM SOME BACKWATER PARALLEL WORLDS?
NOT TONIGHT, JOSEPHINE.
NOW LET'S KILL YOU THE FIRST TIME BY DOING SOMETHING IRONIC LIKE REVERSING THE EARTH'S MAGNETIC POLES.
THERE'S NOTHING FUNNIER THAN PEOPLE DYING KNOWING THAT THEY'VE ACCOMPLISHED ABSOLUTELY NOTHING.

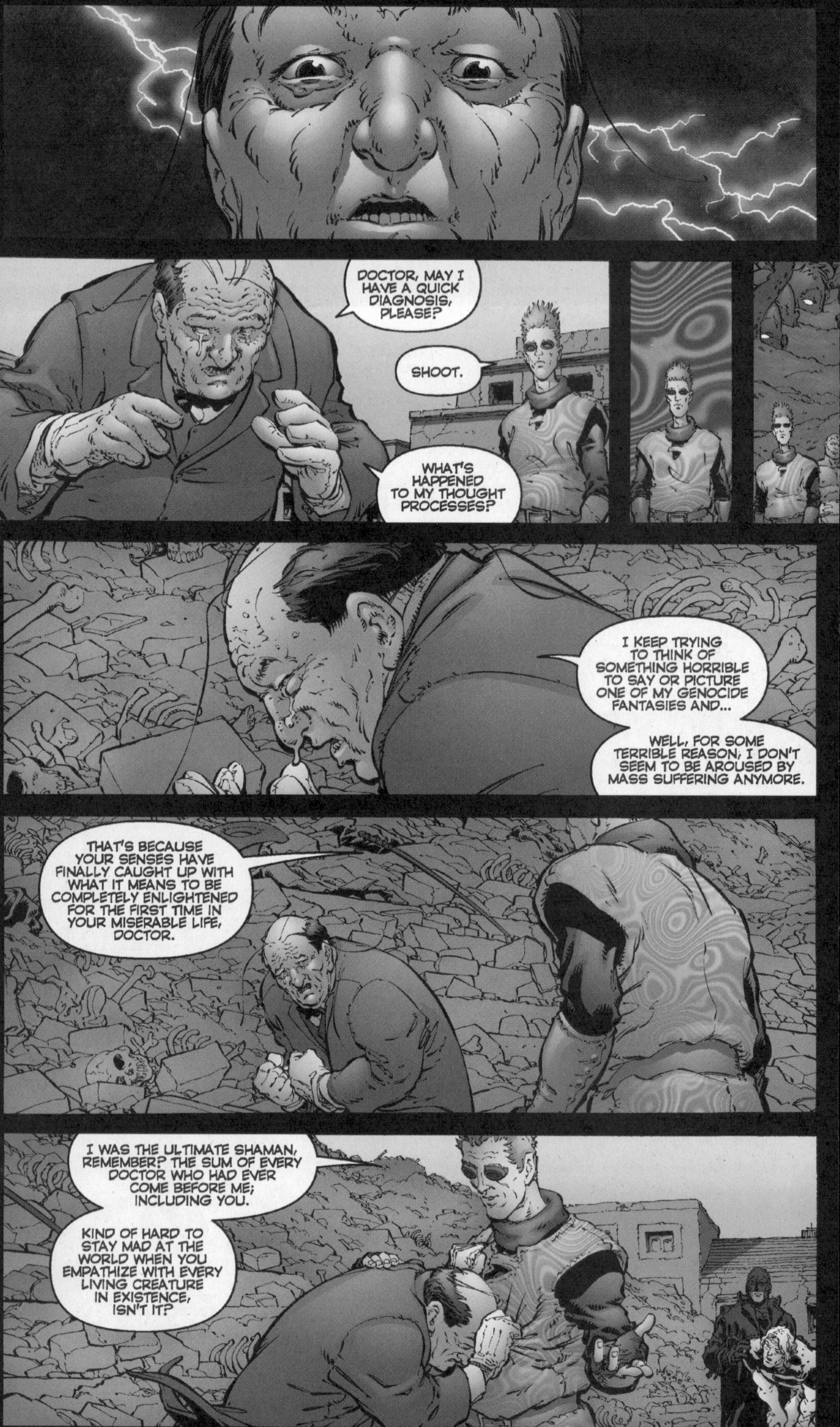
DOCTOR, MAY I HAVE A QUICK DIAGNOSIS, PLEASE?
SHOOT.
WHAT'S HAPPENED TO MY THOUGHT PROCESSES?
I KEEP TRYING TO THINK OF SOMETHING HORRIBLE TO SAY OR PICTURE ONE OF MY GENOCIDE FANTASIES AND...
WELL, FOR SOME TERRIBLE REASON, I DON'T SEEM TO BE AROUSED BY MASS SUFFERING ANYMORE.
THAT'S BECAUSE YOUR SENSES HAVE FINALLY CAUGHT UP WITH WHAT IT MEANS TO BE COMPLETELY ENLIGHTENED FOR THE FIRST TIME IN YOUR MISERABLE LIFE, DOCTOR.
I WAS THE ULTIMATE SHAMAN, REMEMBER? THE SUM OF EVERY DOCTOR WHO HAD EVER COME BEFORE ME; INCLUDING YOU.
KIND OF HARD TO STAY MAD AT THE WORLD WHEN YOU EMPATHIZE WITH EVERY LIVING CREATURE IN EXISTENCE, ISN'T IT?

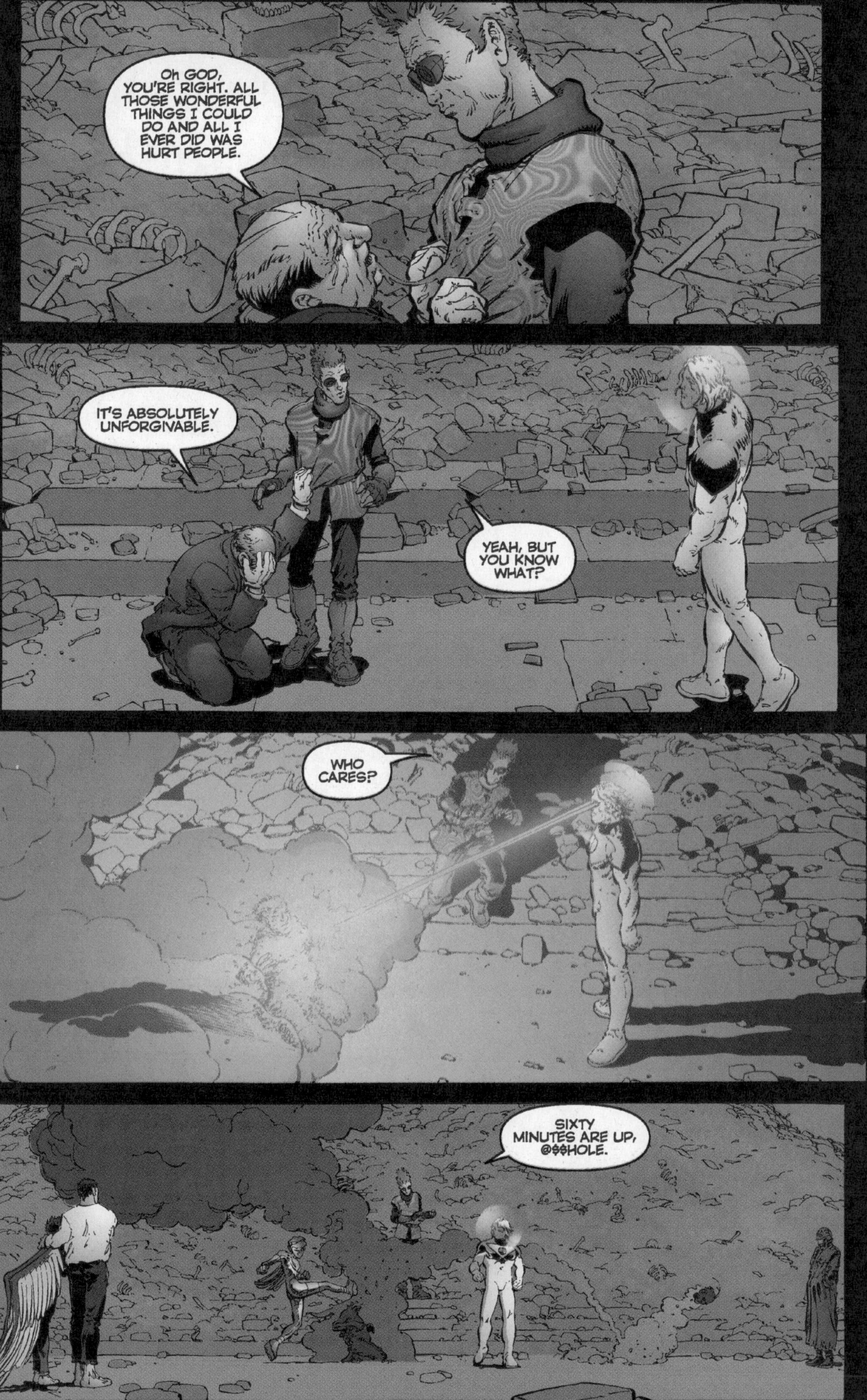
Oh GOD, YOU'RE RIGHT. ALL THOSE WONDERFUL THINGS I COULD DO AND ALL I EVER DID WAS HURT PEOPLE.
IT'S ABSOLUTELY UNFORGIVABLE.
YEAH, BUT YOU KNOW WHAT?
WHO CARES?
SIXTY MINUTES ARE UP, @$$HOLE.

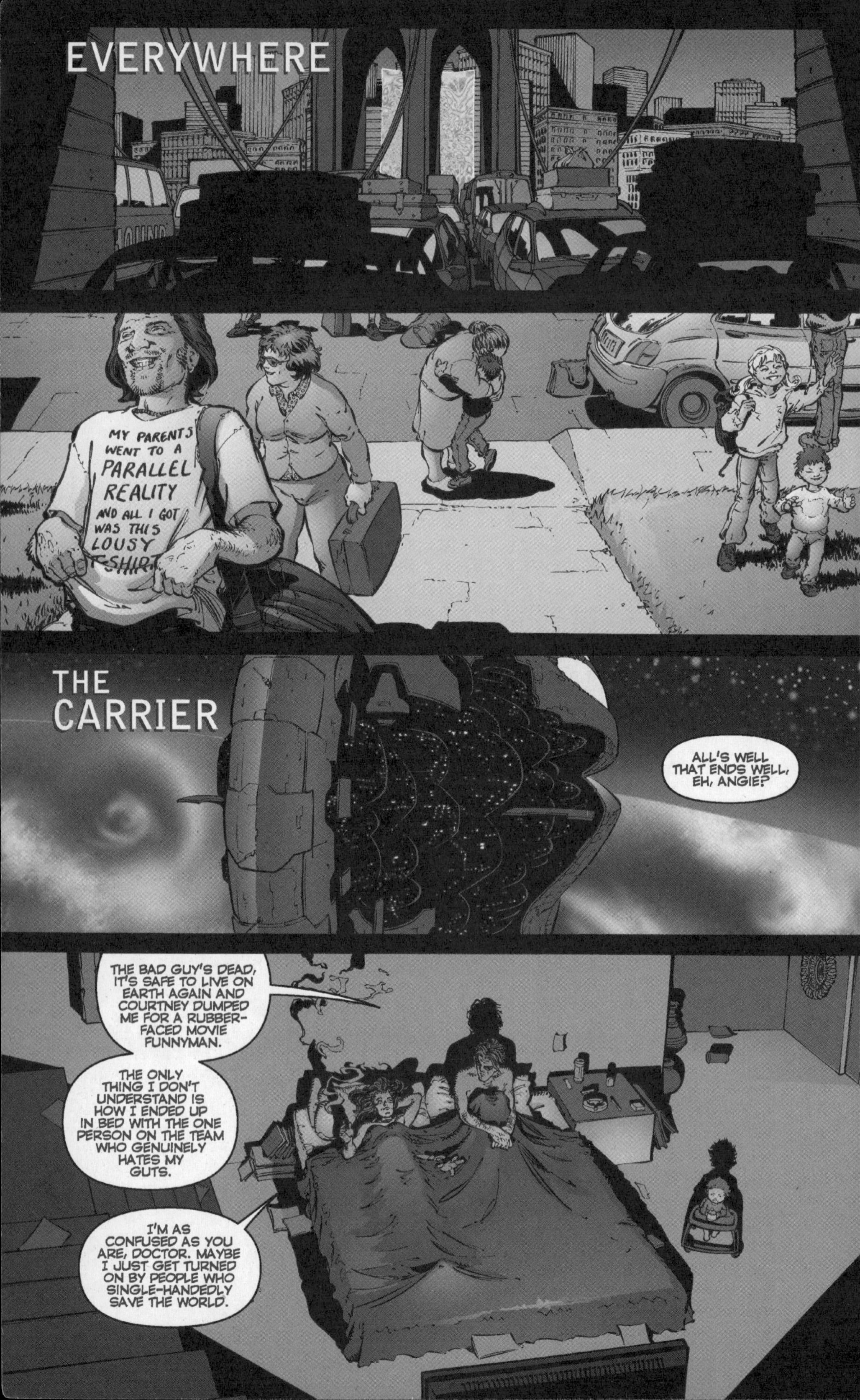
EVERYWHERE
MY PARENTS WENT TO A PARALLEL REALITY AND ALL I GOT WAS THIS LOUSY T-SHIRT
THE CARRIER
ALL'S WELL THAT ENDS WELL, EH, ANGIE?
THE BAD GUY'S DEAD, IT'S SAFE TO LIVE ON EARTH AGAIN AND COURTNEY DUMPED ME FOR A RUBBER-FACED MOVIE FUNNYMAN.
THE ONLY THING I DON'T UNDERSTAND IS HOW I ENDED UP IN BED WITH THE ONE PERSON ON THE TEAM WHO GENUINELY HATES MY GUTS.
I'M AS CONFUSED AS YOU ARE, DOCTOR. MAYBE I JUST GET TURNED ON BY PEOPLE WHO SINGLE-HANDEDLY SAVE THE WORLD.

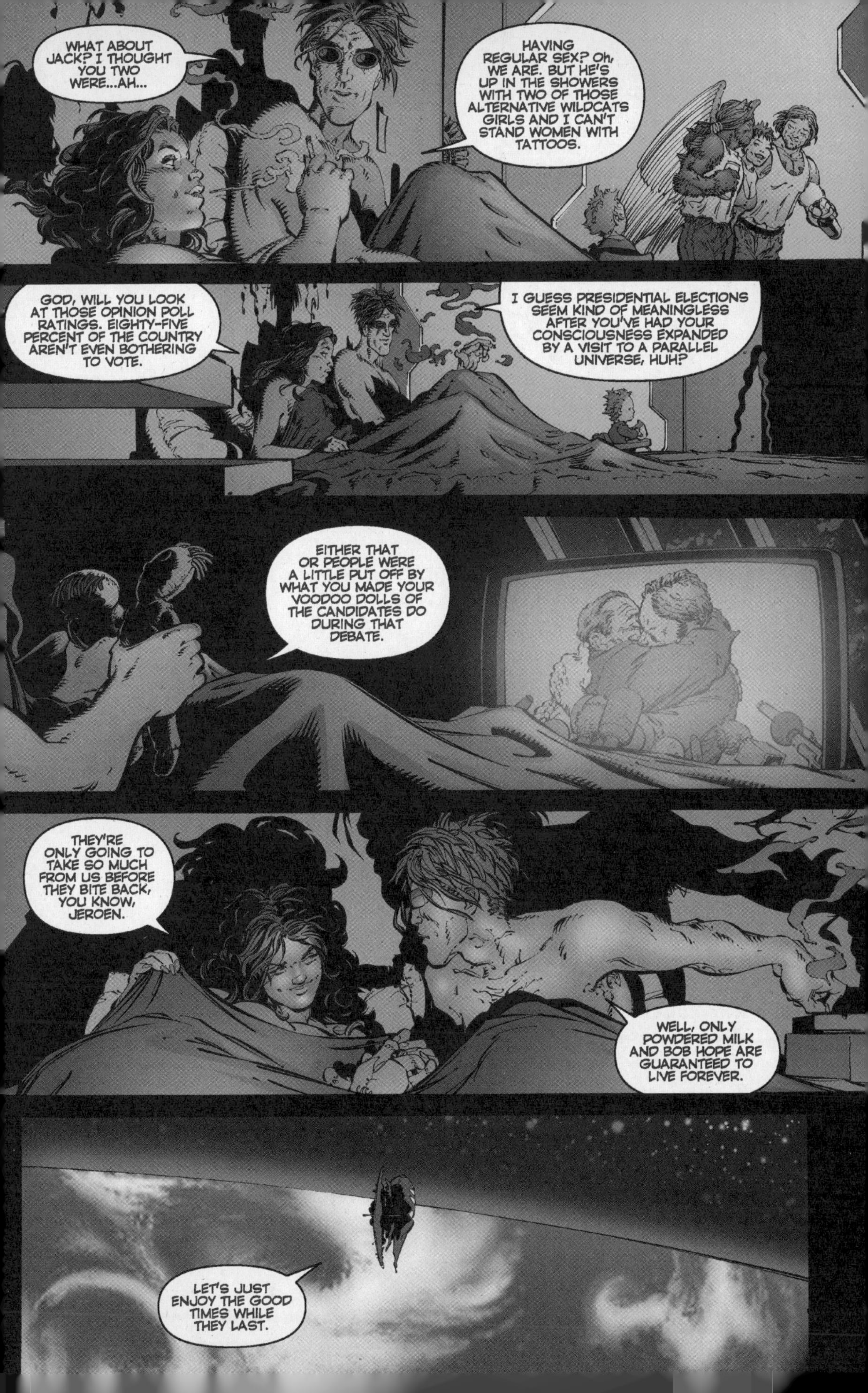
WHAT ABOUT JACK? I THOUGHT YOU TWO WERE...AH...
HAVING REGULAR SEX? Oh, WE ARE. BUT HE'S UP IN THE SHOWERS WITH TWO OF THOSE ALTERNATIVE WILDCATS GIRLS AND I CAN'T STAND WOMEN WITH TATTOOS.
GOD, WILL YOU LOOK AT THOSE OPINION POLL RATINGS. EIGHTY-FIVE PERCENT OF THE COUNTRY AREN'T EVEN BOTHERING TO VOTE.
I GUESS PRESIDENTIAL ELECTIONS SEEM KIND OF MEANINGLESS AFTER YOU'VE HAD YOUR CONSCIOUSNESS EXPANDED BY A VISIT TO A PARALLEL UNIVERSE, HUH?
EITHER THAT OR PEOPLE WERE A LITTLE PUT OFF BY WHAT YOU MADE YOUR VOODOO DOLLS OF THE CANDIDATES DO DURING THAT DEBATE.
THEY'RE ONLY GOING TO TAKE SO MUCH FROM US BEFORE THEY BITE BACK, YOU KNOW, JEROEN.
WELL, ONLY POWDERED MILK AND BOB HOPE ARE GUARANTEED TO LIVE FOREVER.
LET'S JUST ENJOY THE GOOD TIMES WHILE THEY LAST.

AUTHORITY

2000 ANNUAL

DEVIL'S NIGHT

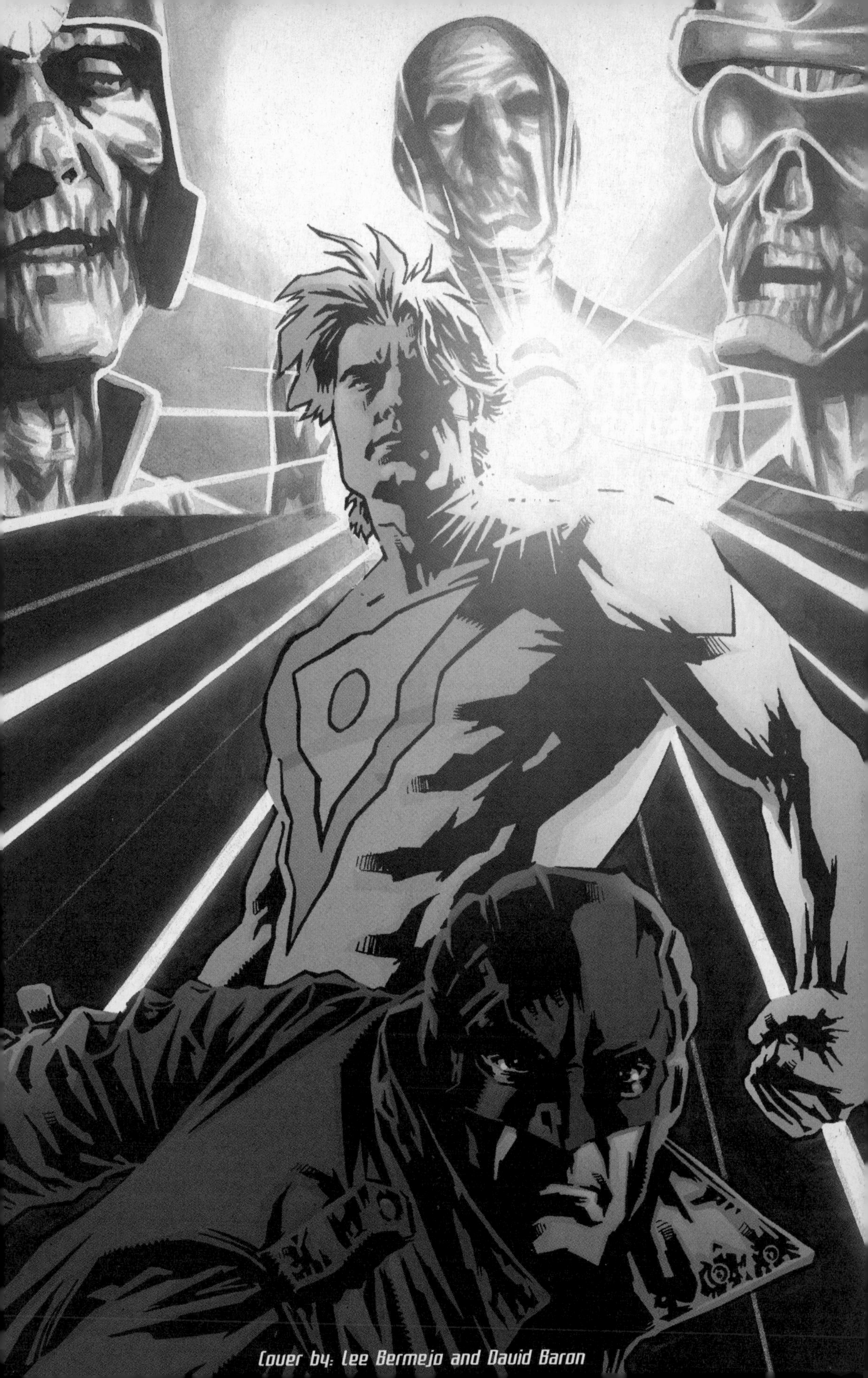

Cover by: Lee Bermejo and David Baron

The AUTHORITY
"THE BREAKS"
ONE of ONE

JOE CASEY
writer

CULLY HAMNER
artist

RAY SNYDER with CULLY HAMNER & MARK IRWIN
inkers

DAVID BARON
colorist

NAGHMEH ZAND
letterer

JOHN LAYMAN
editor

The Authority created by Warren Ellis and Bryan Hitch.

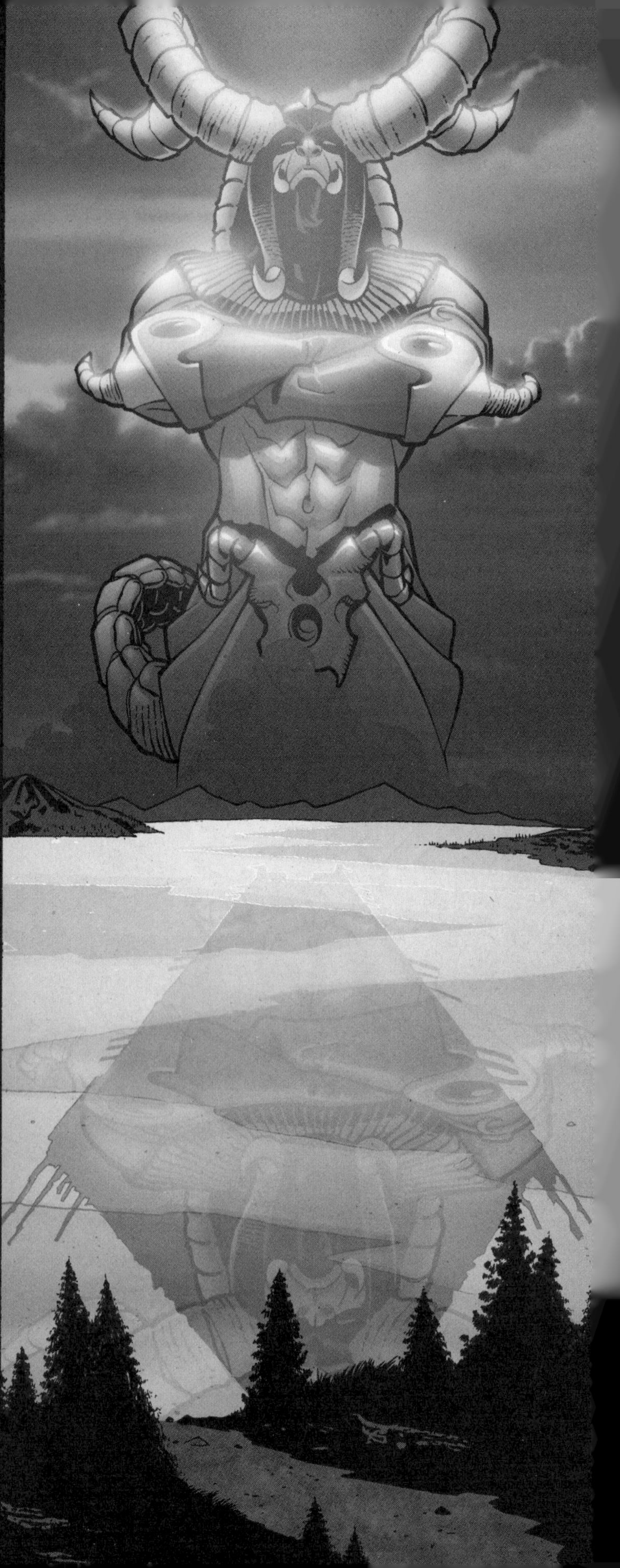

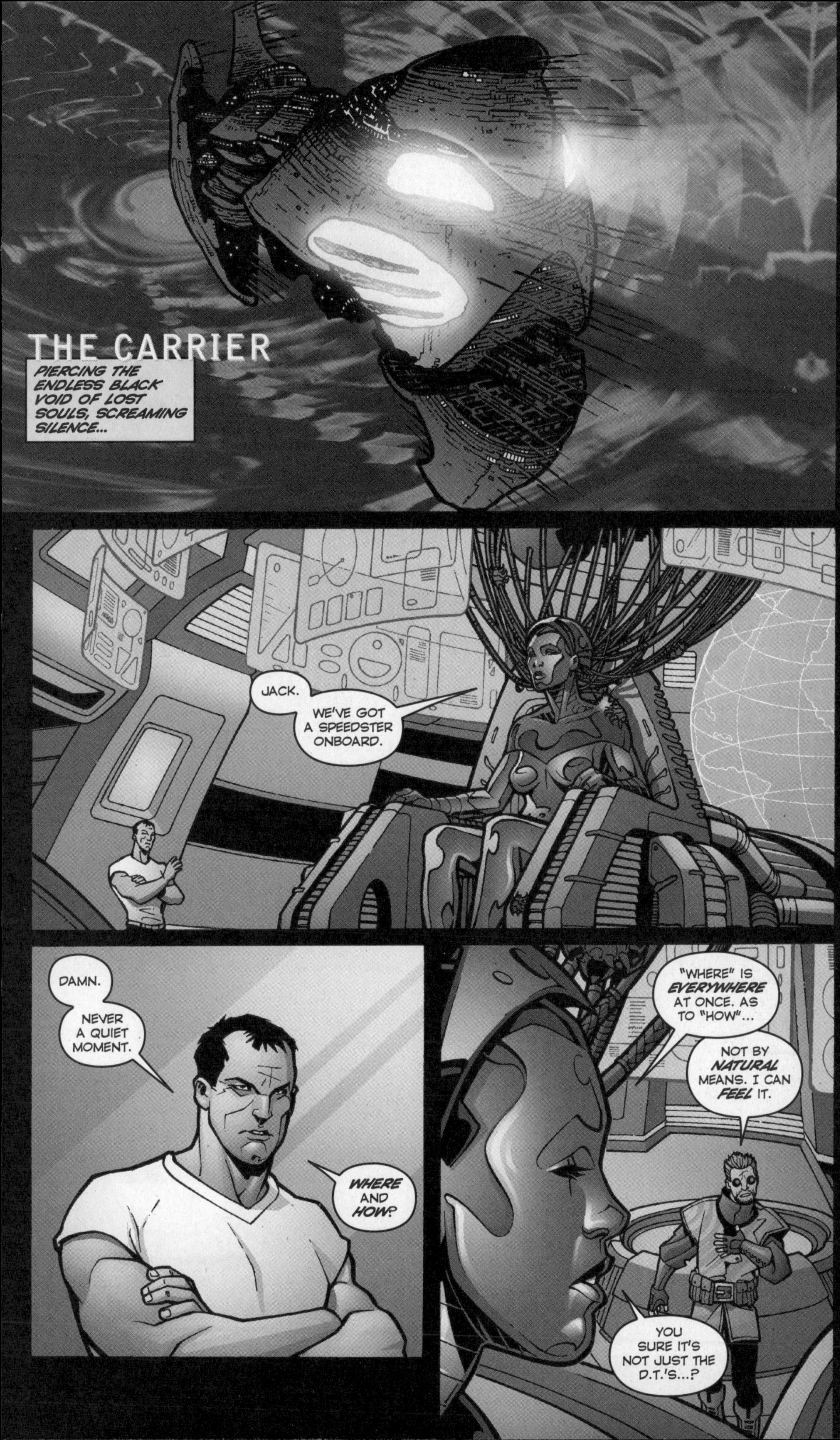
THE CARRIER
PIERCING THE ENDLESS BLACK VOID OF LOST SOULS, SCREAMING SILENCE...
JACK.
WE'VE GOT A SPEEDSTER ONBOARD.
DAMN.
NEVER A QUIET MOMENT.
WHERE AND HOW?
"WHERE" IS EVERYWHERE AT ONCE. AS TO "HOW"...
NOT BY NATURAL MEANS. I CAN FEEL IT.
YOU SURE IT'S NOT JUST THE D.T.'S...?

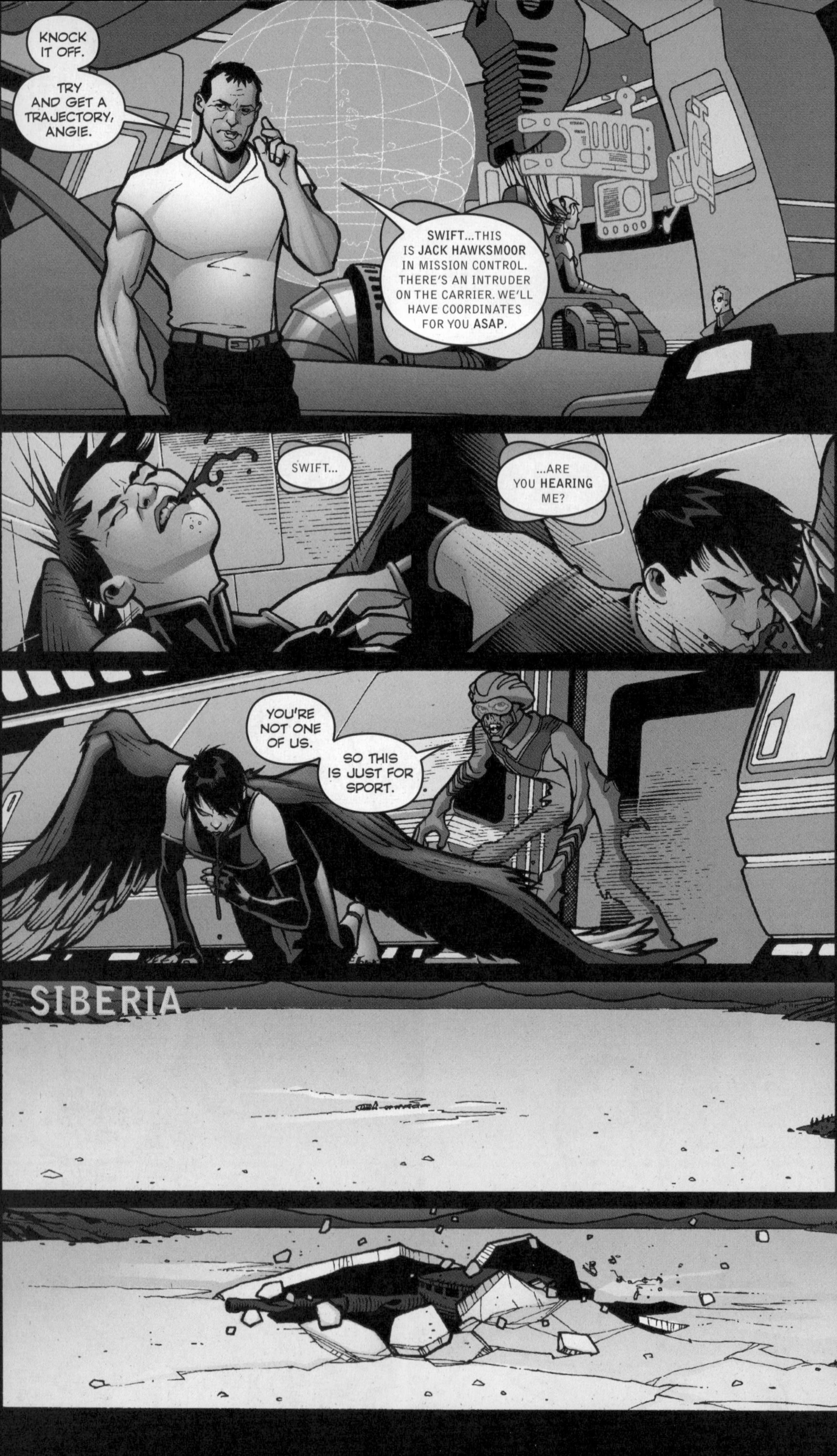
KNOCK IT OFF.
TRY AND GET A TRAJECTORY, ANGIE.
SWIFT...THIS IS JACK HAWKSMOOR IN MISSION CONTROL. THERE'S AN INTRUDER ON THE CARRIER. WE'LL HAVE COORDINATES FOR YOU ASAP.
SWIFT...
...ARE YOU HEARING ME?
YOU'RE NOT ONE OF US.
SO THIS IS JUST FOR SPORT.
SIBERIA

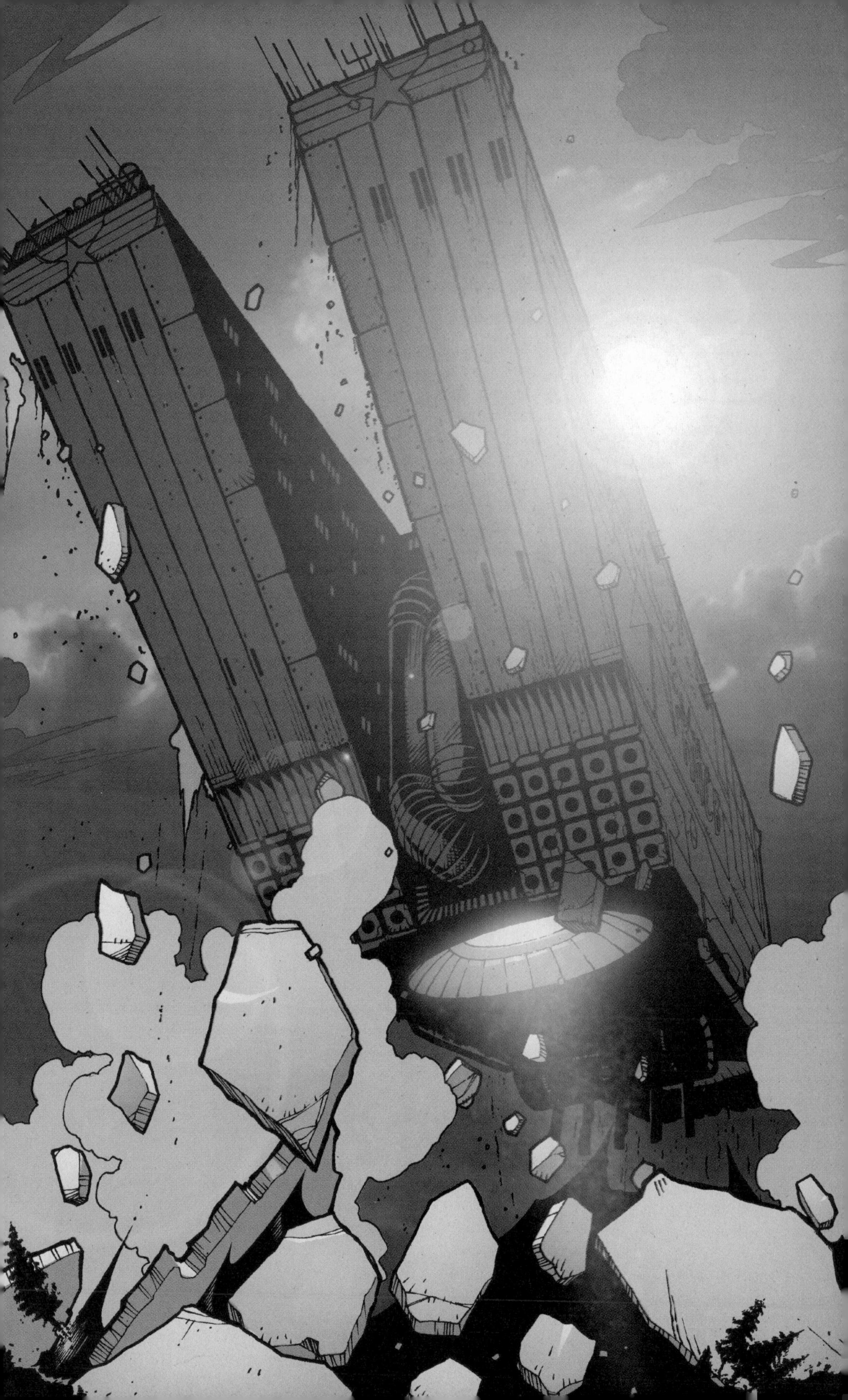

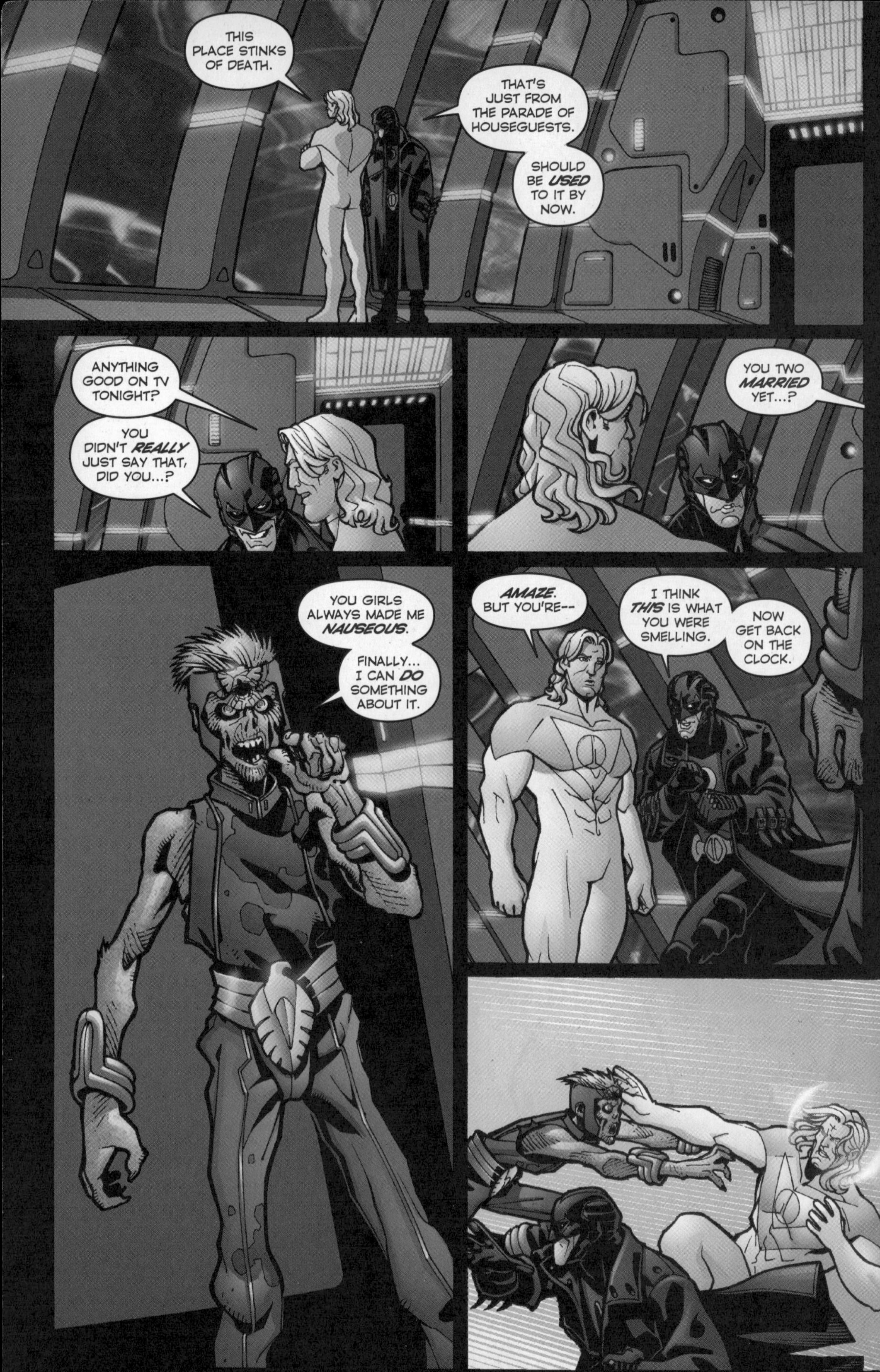
THIS PLACE STINKS OF DEATH.
THAT'S JUST FROM THE PARADE OF HOUSEGUESTS.
SHOULD BE USED TO IT BY NOW.
ANYTHING GOOD ON TV TONIGHT?
YOU DIDN'T REALLY JUST SAY THAT, DID YOU...?
YOU TWO MARRIED YET...?
YOU GIRLS ALWAYS MADE ME NAUSEOUS.
FINALLY... I CAN DO SOMETHING ABOUT IT.
AMAZE. BUT YOU'RE--
I THINK THIS IS WHAT YOU WERE SMELLING.
NOW GET BACK ON THE CLOCK.

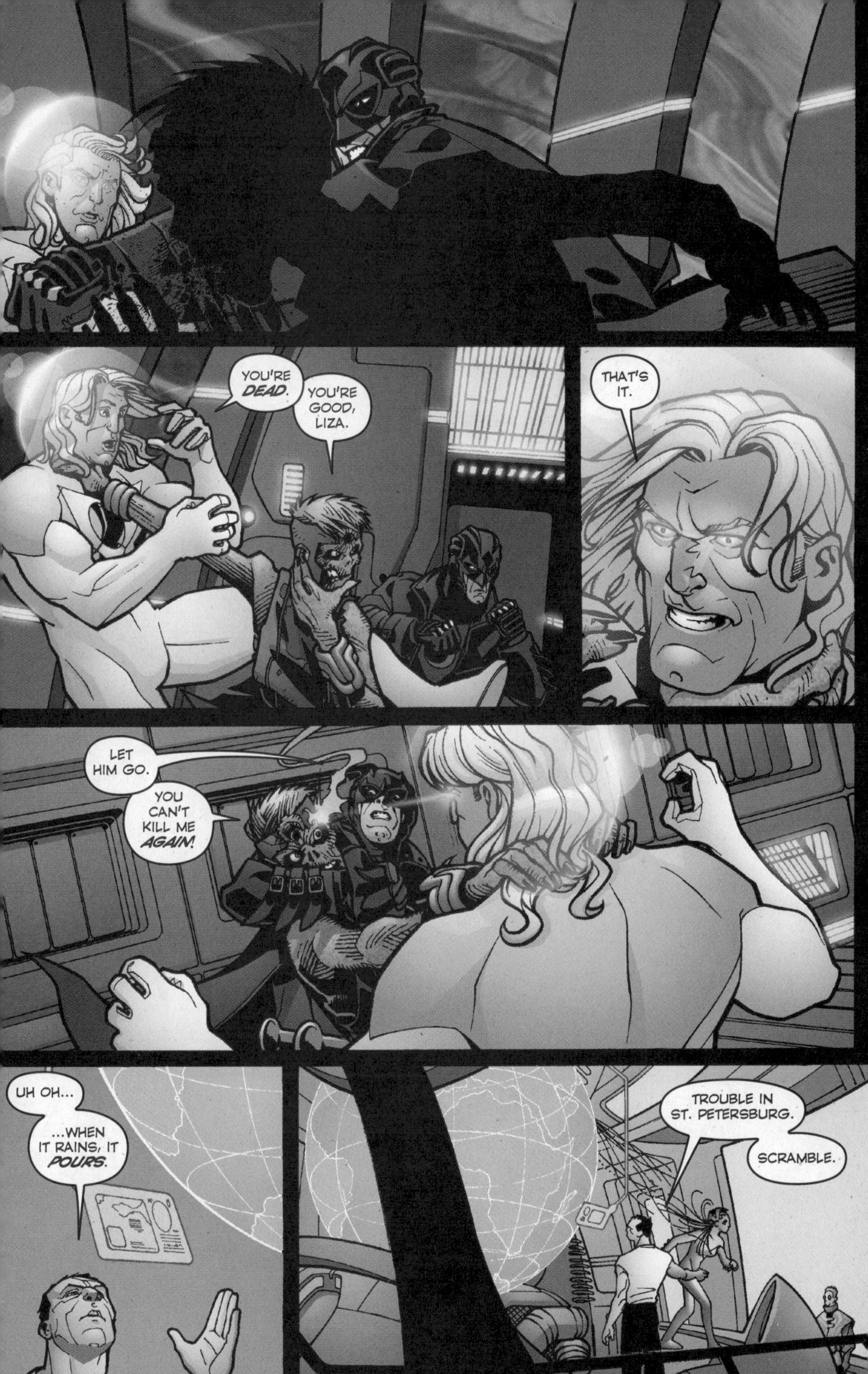
YOU'RE DEAD.
YOU'RE GOOD, LIZA.
THAT'S IT.
LET HIM GO.
YOU CAN'T KILL ME AGAIN!
UH OH...
...WHEN IT RAINS, IT POURS.
TROUBLE IN ST. PETERSBURG.
SCRAMBLE.

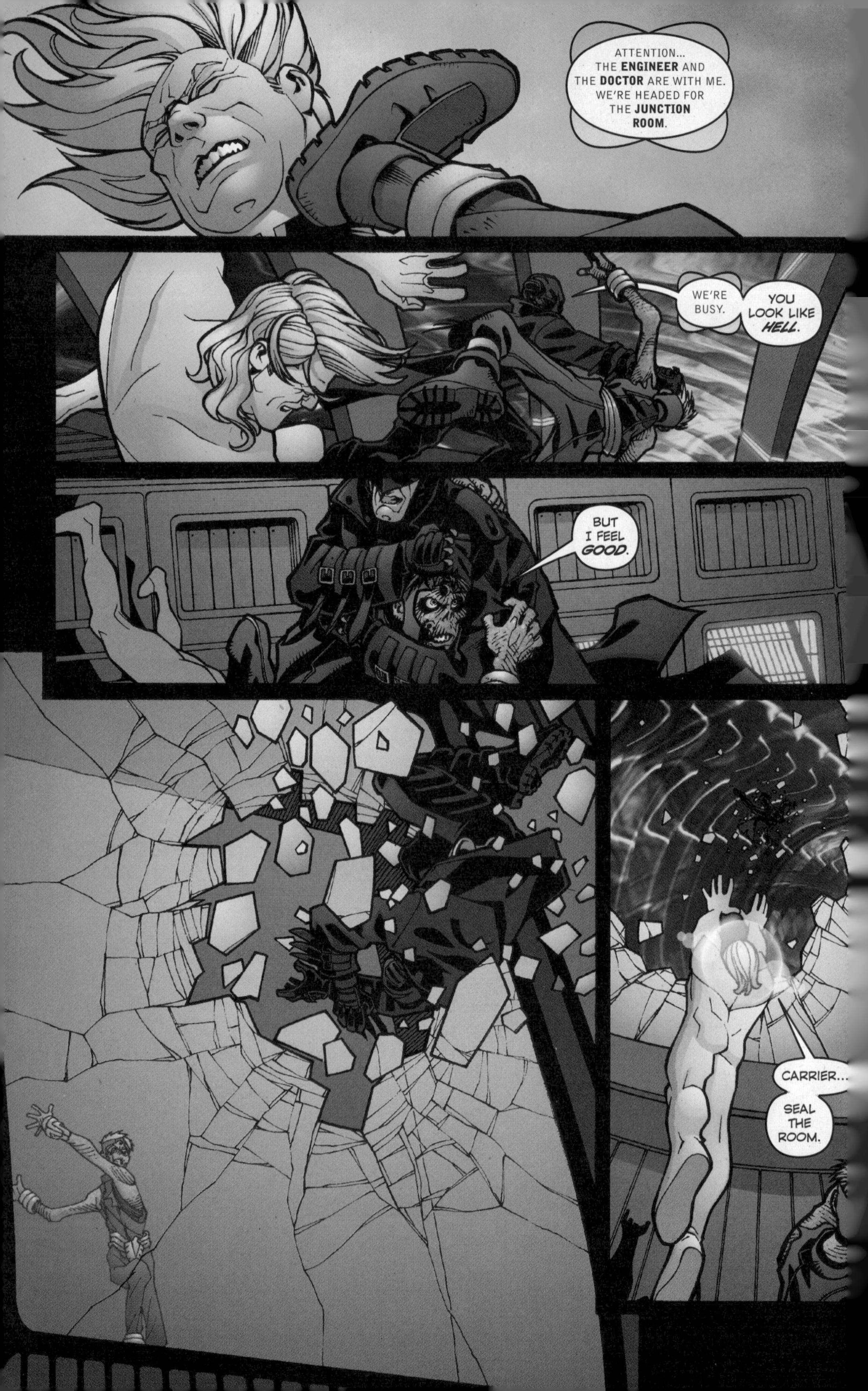
ATTENTION... THE **ENGINEER** AND THE **DOCTOR** ARE WITH ME. WE'RE HEADED FOR THE **JUNCTION ROOM**.
WE'RE BUSY.
YOU LOOK LIKE *HELL*.
BUT I FEEL *GOOD*.
CARRIER...
SEAL THE ROOM.

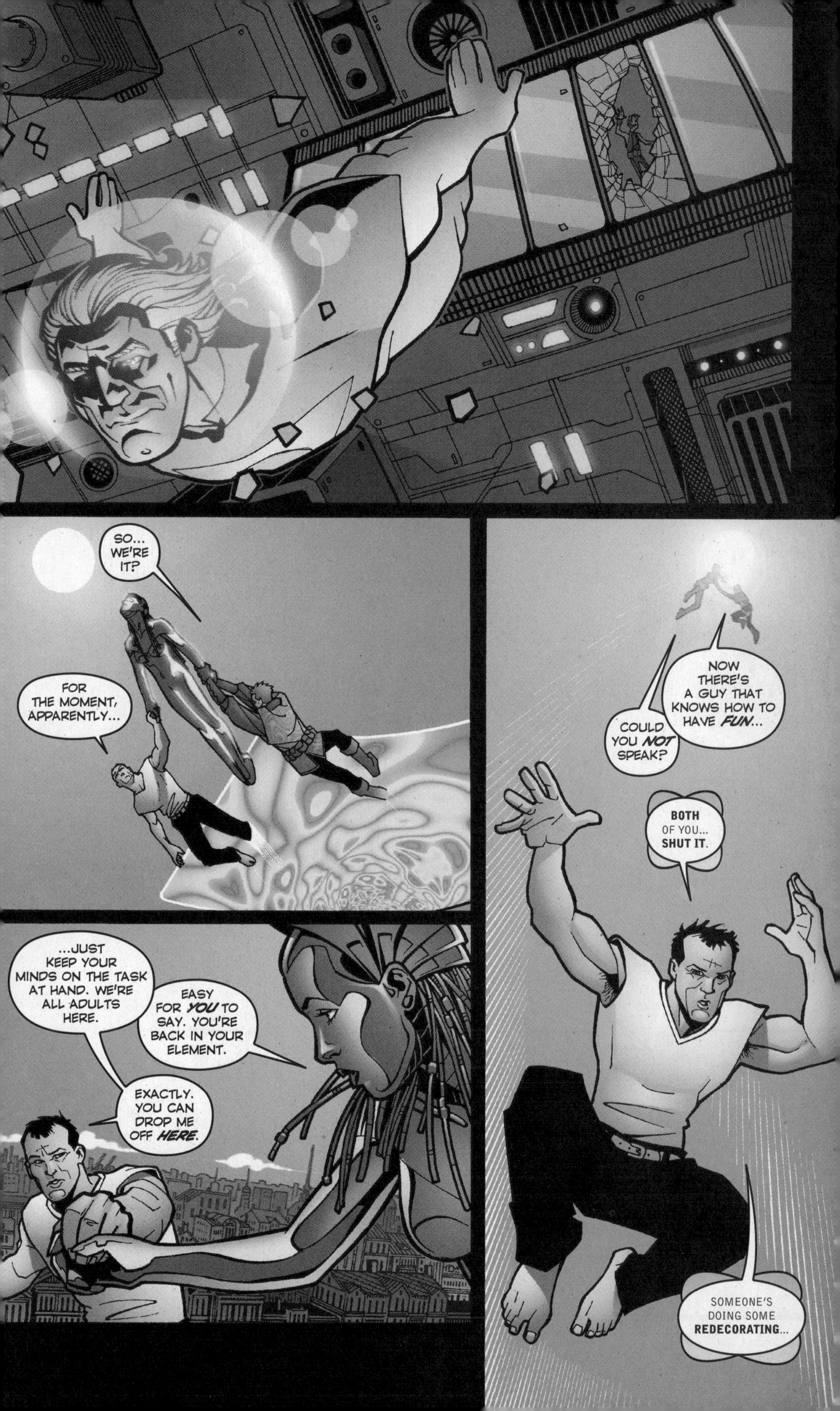
SO... WE'RE IT?
FOR THE MOMENT, APPARENTLY...
...JUST KEEP YOUR MINDS ON THE TASK AT HAND. WE'RE ALL ADULTS HERE.
EASY FOR YOU TO SAY. YOU'RE BACK IN YOUR ELEMENT.
EXACTLY. YOU CAN DROP ME OFF HERE.
NOW THERE'S A GUY THAT KNOWS HOW TO HAVE FUN...
COULD YOU NOT SPEAK?
BOTH OF YOU... SHUT IT.
SOMEONE'S DOING SOME REDECORATING...

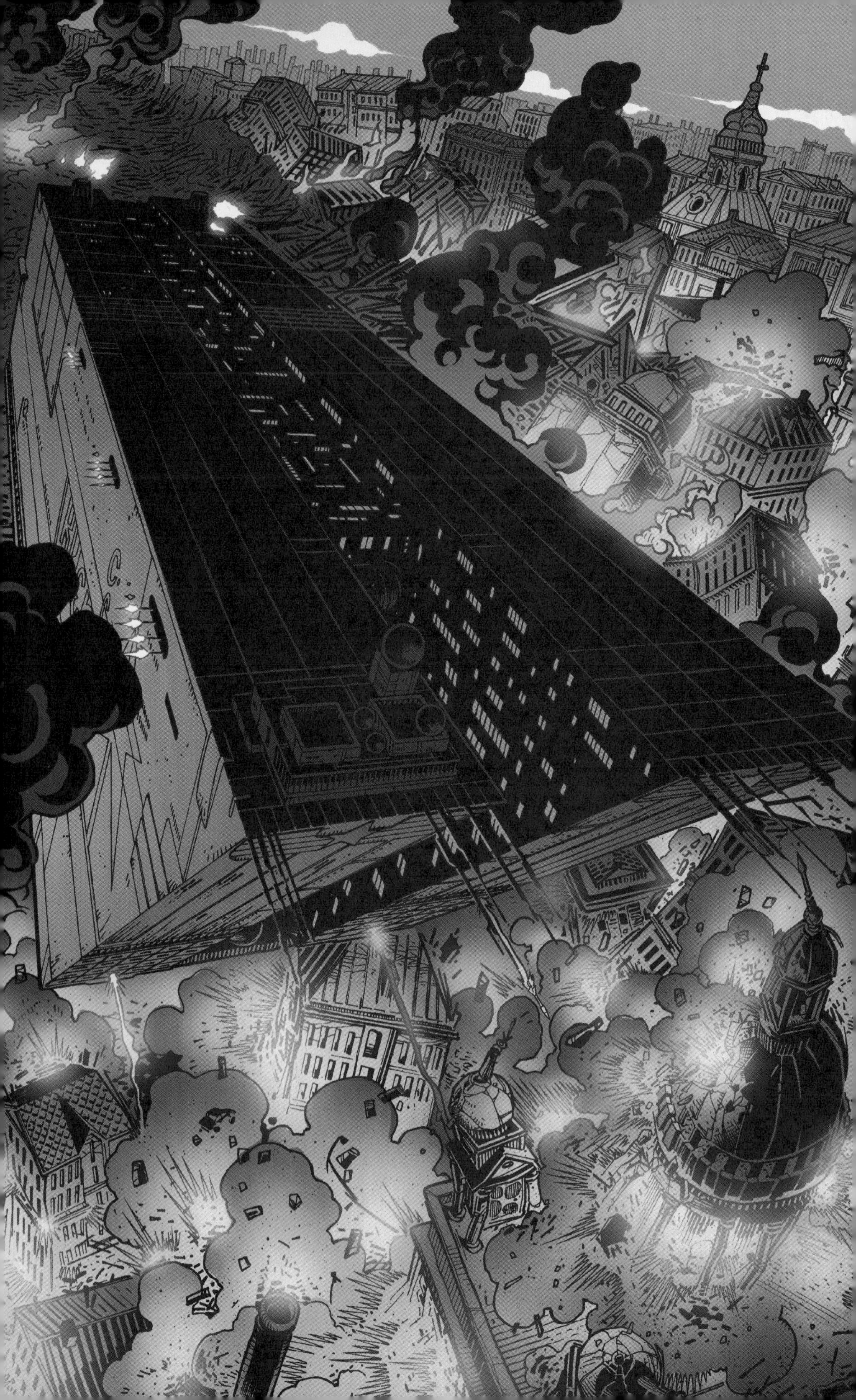

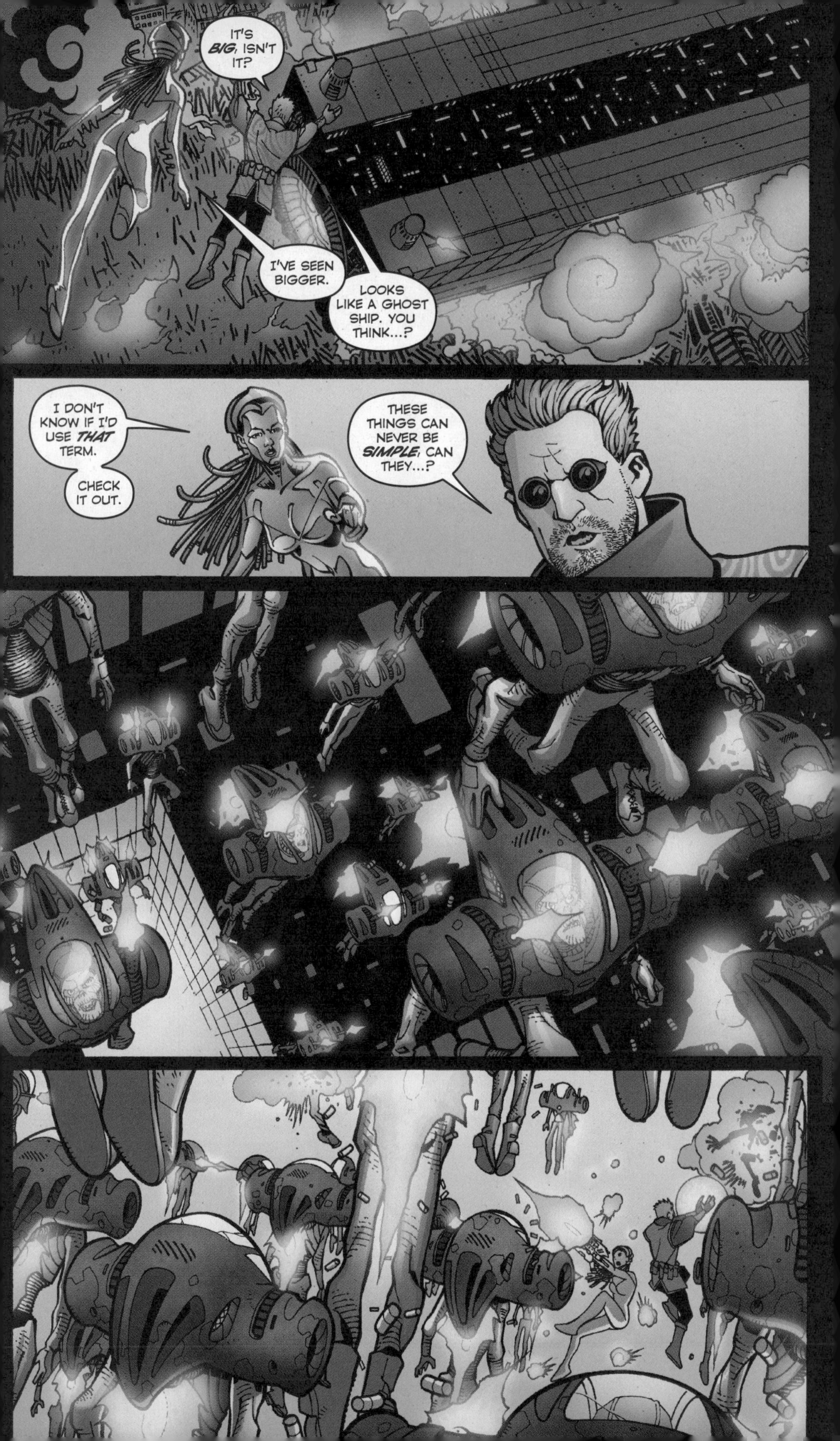
IT'S *BIG*, ISN'T IT?
I'VE SEEN BIGGER.
LOOKS LIKE A GHOST SHIP. YOU THINK...?
I DON'T KNOW IF I'D USE *THAT* TERM.
CHECK IT OUT.
THESE THINGS CAN NEVER BE *SIMPLE*, CAN THEY...?

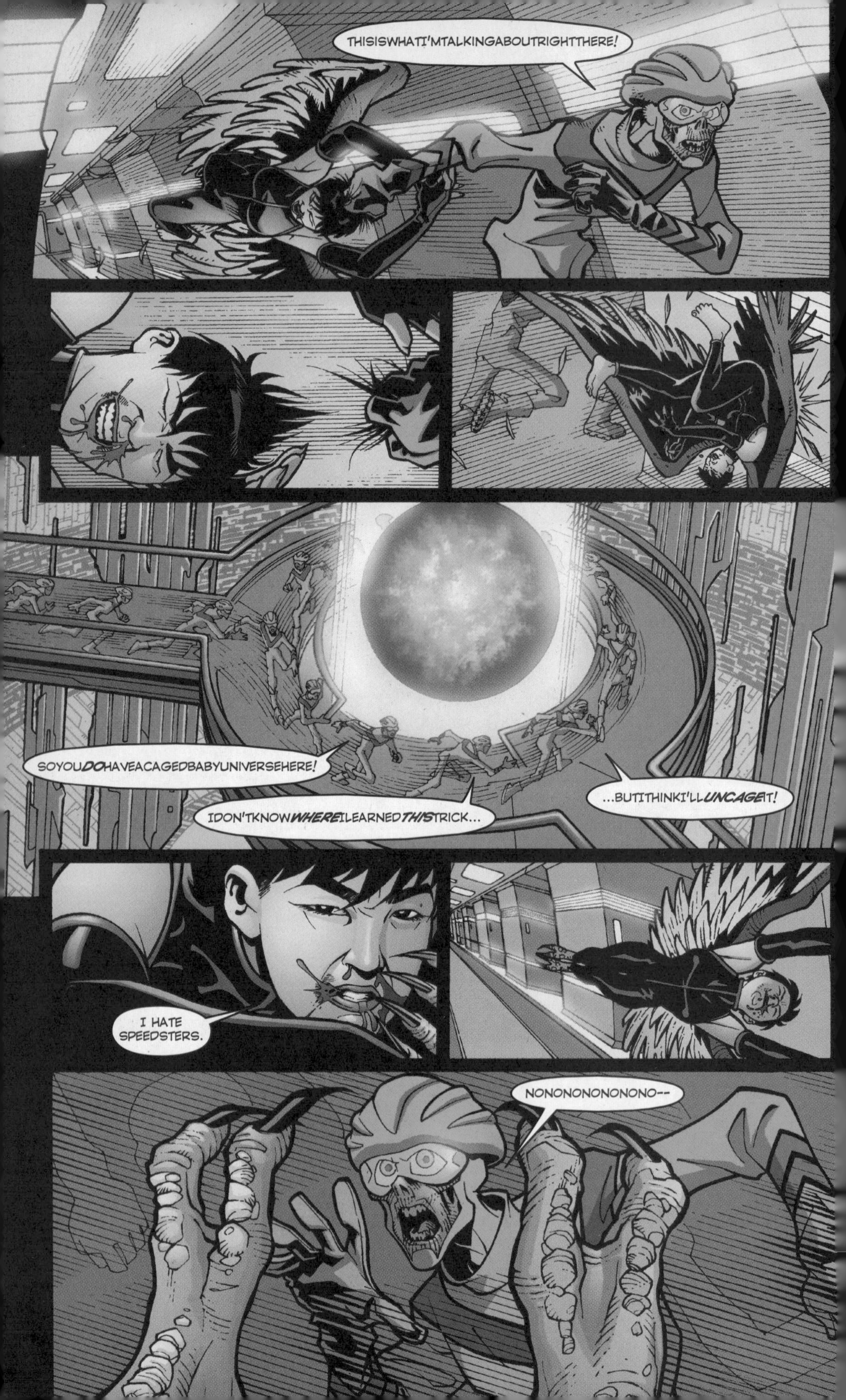
THISISWHATI'MTALKINGABOUTRIGHTTHERE!
SOYOU**DO**HAVEACAGEDBABYUNIVERSEHERE!
IDON'TKNOW**WHERE**ILEARNED**THIS**TRICK...
...BUTITHINKI'LL**UNCAGE**IT!
I HATE SPEEDSTERS.
NONONONONONONO--

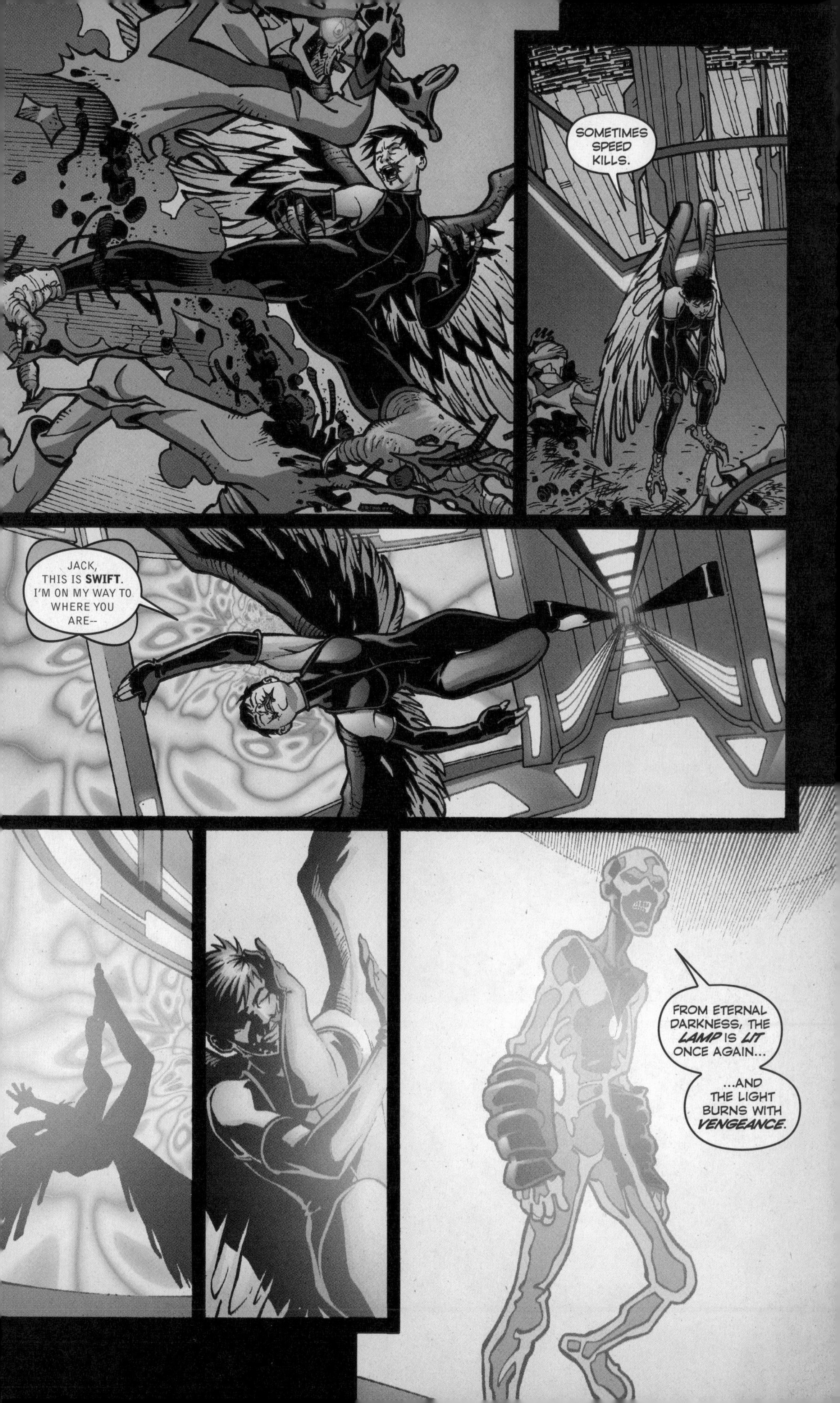
SOMETIMES SPEED KILLS.
JACK, THIS IS **SWIFT**. I'M ON MY WAY TO WHERE YOU ARE--
FROM ETERNAL DARKNESS, THE ***LAMP*** IS ***LIT*** ONCE AGAIN...
...AND THE LIGHT BURNS WITH ***VENGEANCE***.

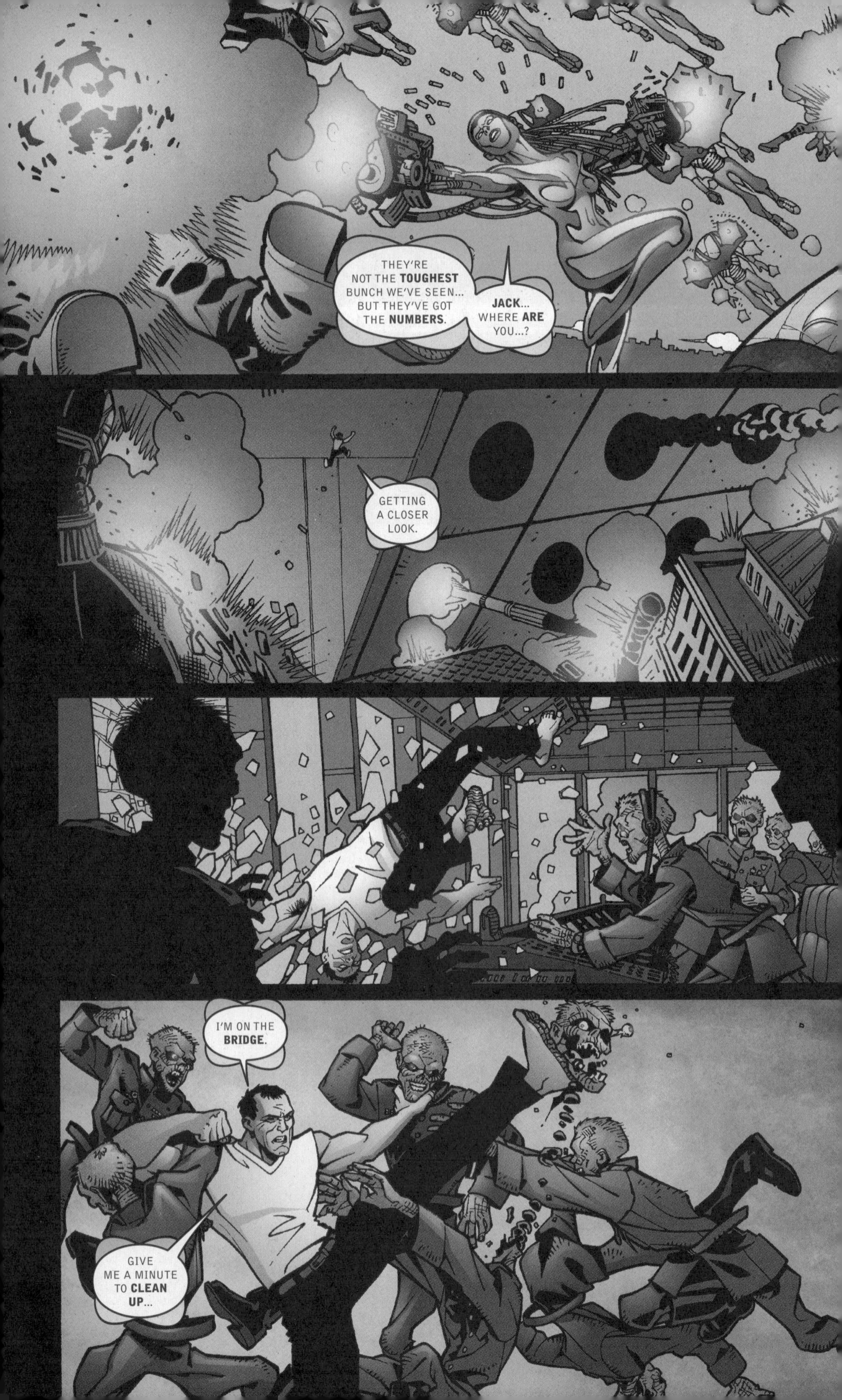
THEY'RE NOT THE **TOUGHEST** BUNCH WE'VE SEEN... BUT THEY'VE GOT THE **NUMBERS**.
JACK... WHERE **ARE** YOU...?
GETTING A CLOSER LOOK.
I'M ON THE **BRIDGE**.
GIVE ME A MINUTE TO **CLEAN UP**...

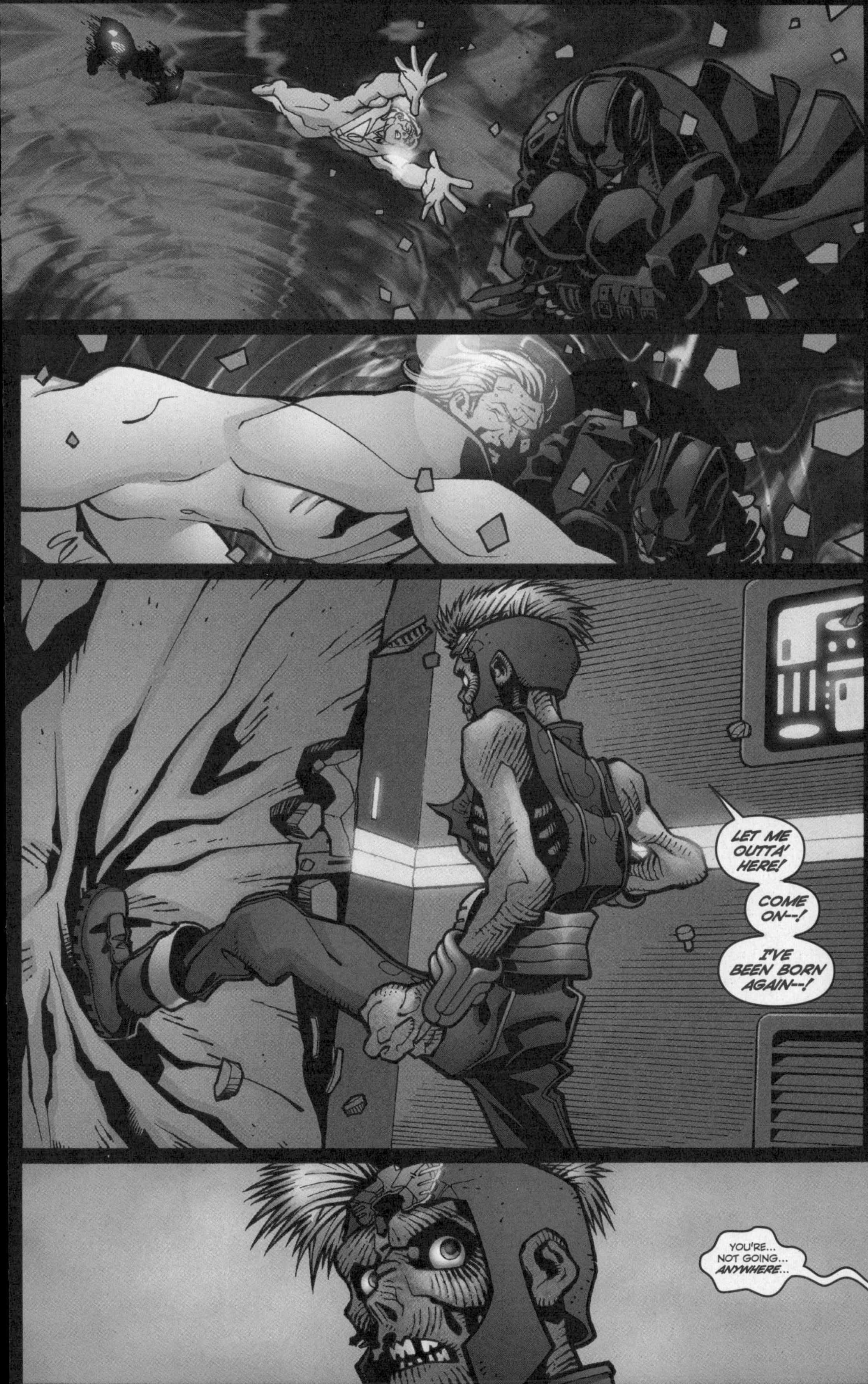

LET ME OUTTA' HERE!
COME ON--!
I'VE BEEN BORN AGAIN--!
YOU'RE... NOT GOING... ANYWHERE...

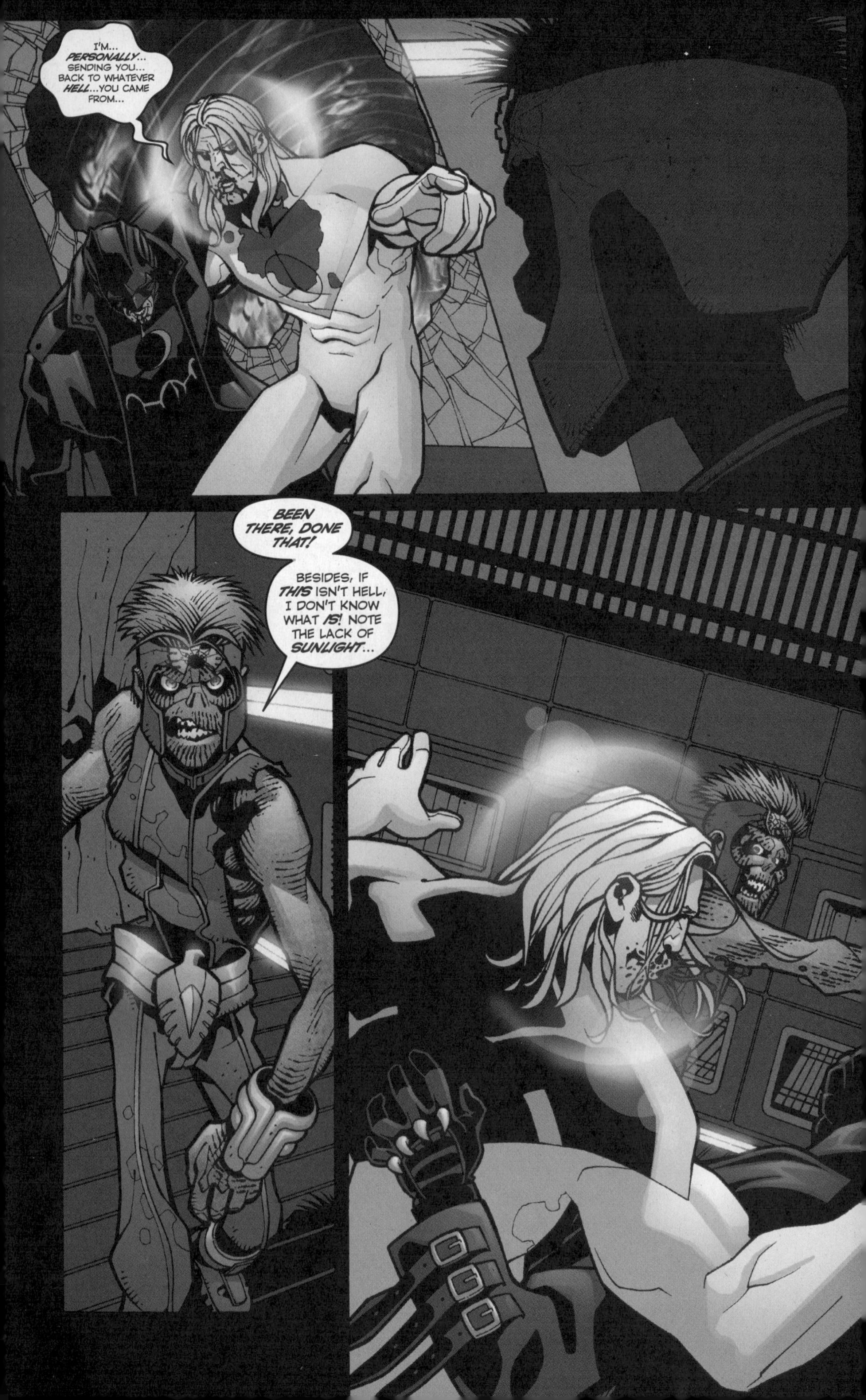
I'M... PERSONALLY... SENDING YOU... BACK TO WHATEVER HELL...YOU CAME FROM...
BEEN THERE, DONE THAT!
BESIDES, IF THIS ISN'T HELL, I DON'T KNOW WHAT IS! NOTE THE LACK OF SUNLIGHT...

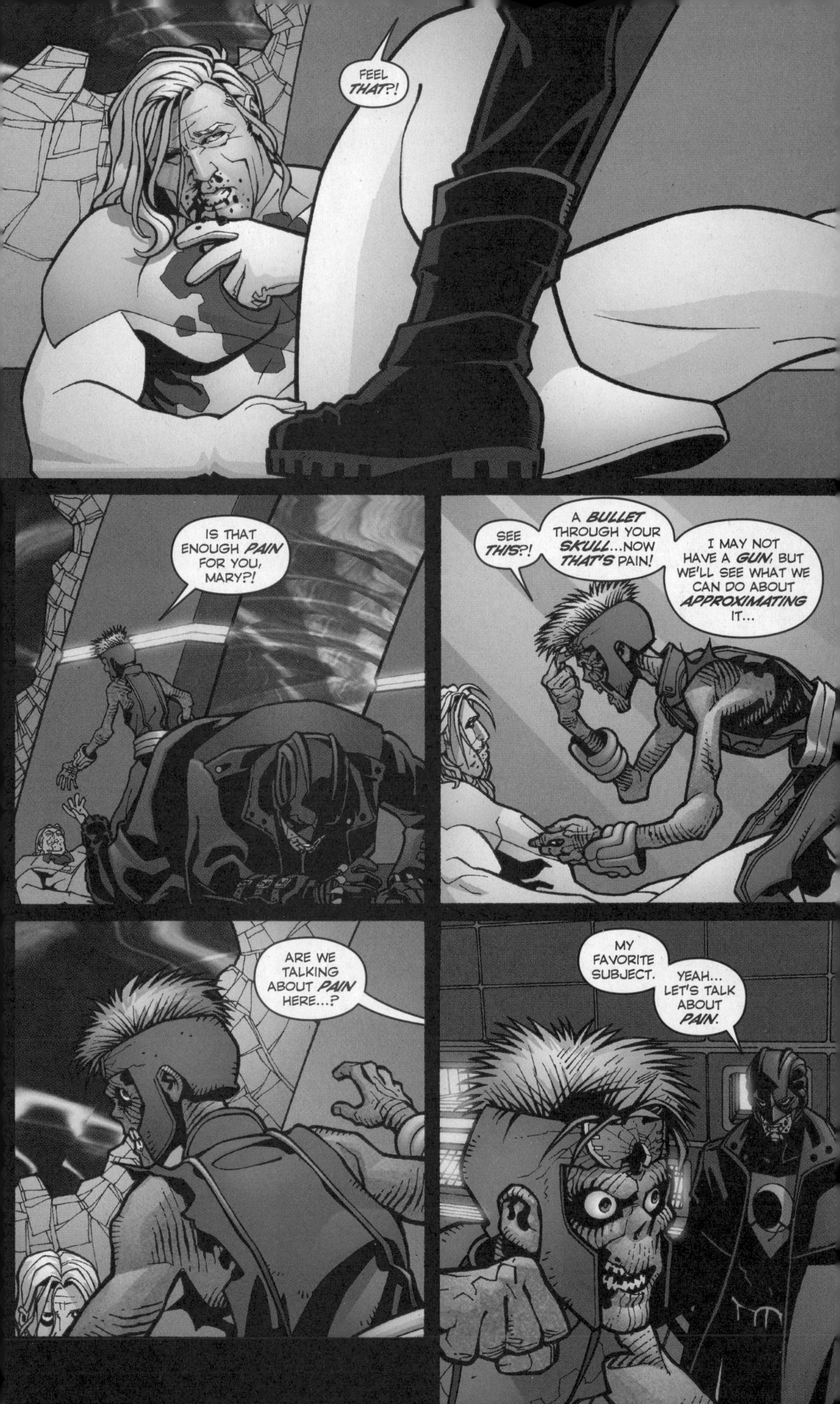
FEEL THAT?!
IS THAT ENOUGH PAIN FOR YOU, MARY?!
SEE THIS?!
A BULLET THROUGH YOUR SKULL...NOW THAT'S PAIN!
I MAY NOT HAVE A GUN, BUT WE'LL SEE WHAT WE CAN DO ABOUT APPROXIMATING IT...
ARE WE TALKING ABOUT PAIN HERE...?
MY FAVORITE SUBJECT.
YEAH... LET'S TALK ABOUT PAIN.

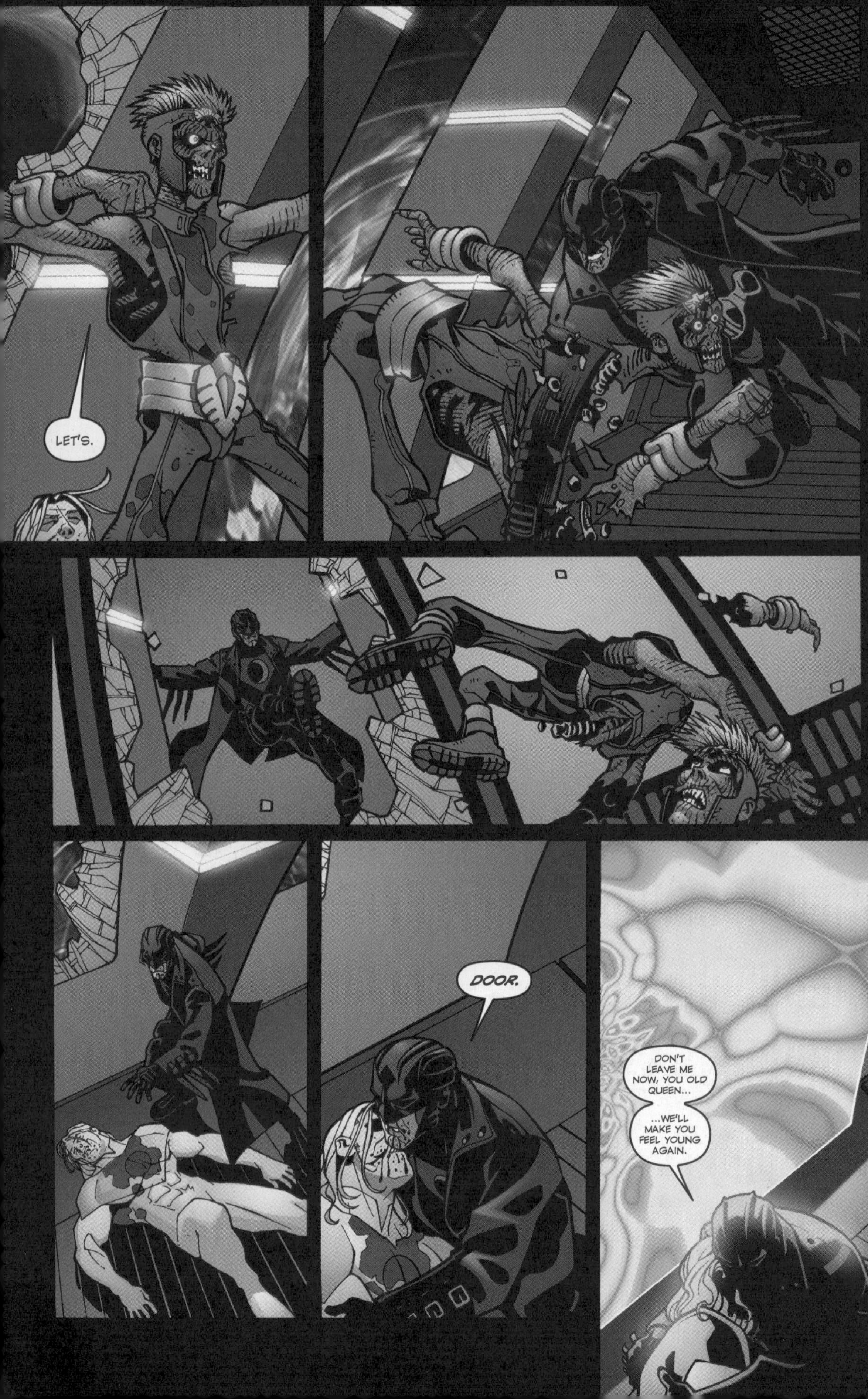
LET'S.
DOOR.
DON'T LEAVE ME NOW, YOU OLD QUEEN...
...WE'LL MAKE YOU FEEL YOUNG AGAIN.

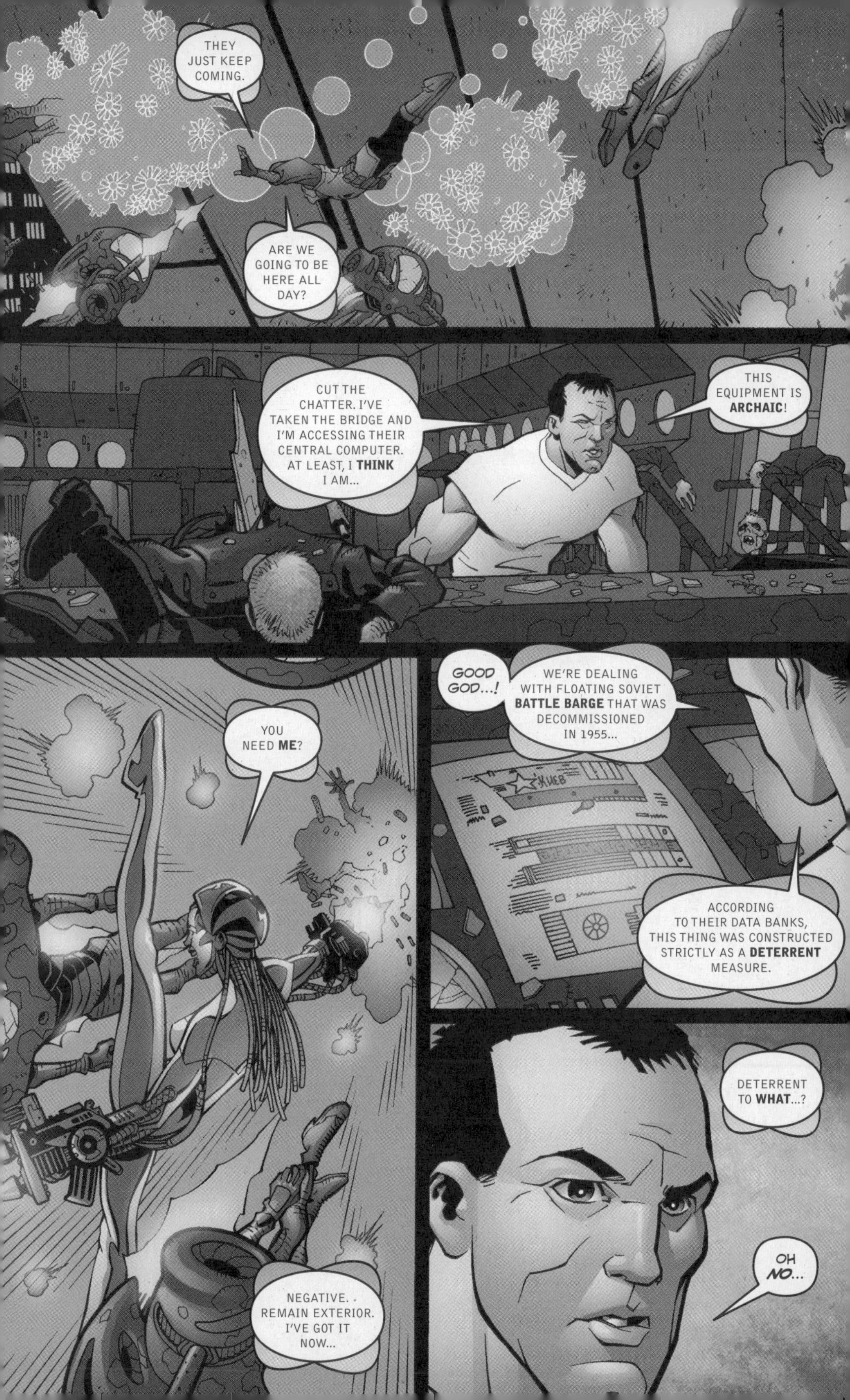
THEY JUST KEEP COMING.
ARE WE GOING TO BE HERE ALL DAY?
CUT THE CHATTER. I'VE TAKEN THE BRIDGE AND I'M ACCESSING THEIR CENTRAL COMPUTER. AT LEAST, I THINK I AM...
THIS EQUIPMENT IS ARCHAIC!
YOU NEED ME?
NEGATIVE. REMAIN EXTERIOR. I'VE GOT IT NOW...
GOOD GOD...!
WE'RE DEALING WITH FLOATING SOVIET BATTLE BARGE THAT WAS DECOMMISSIONED IN 1955...
ACCORDING TO THEIR DATA BANKS, THIS THING WAS CONSTRUCTED STRICTLY AS A DETERRENT MEASURE.
DETERRENT TO WHAT...?
OH NO...

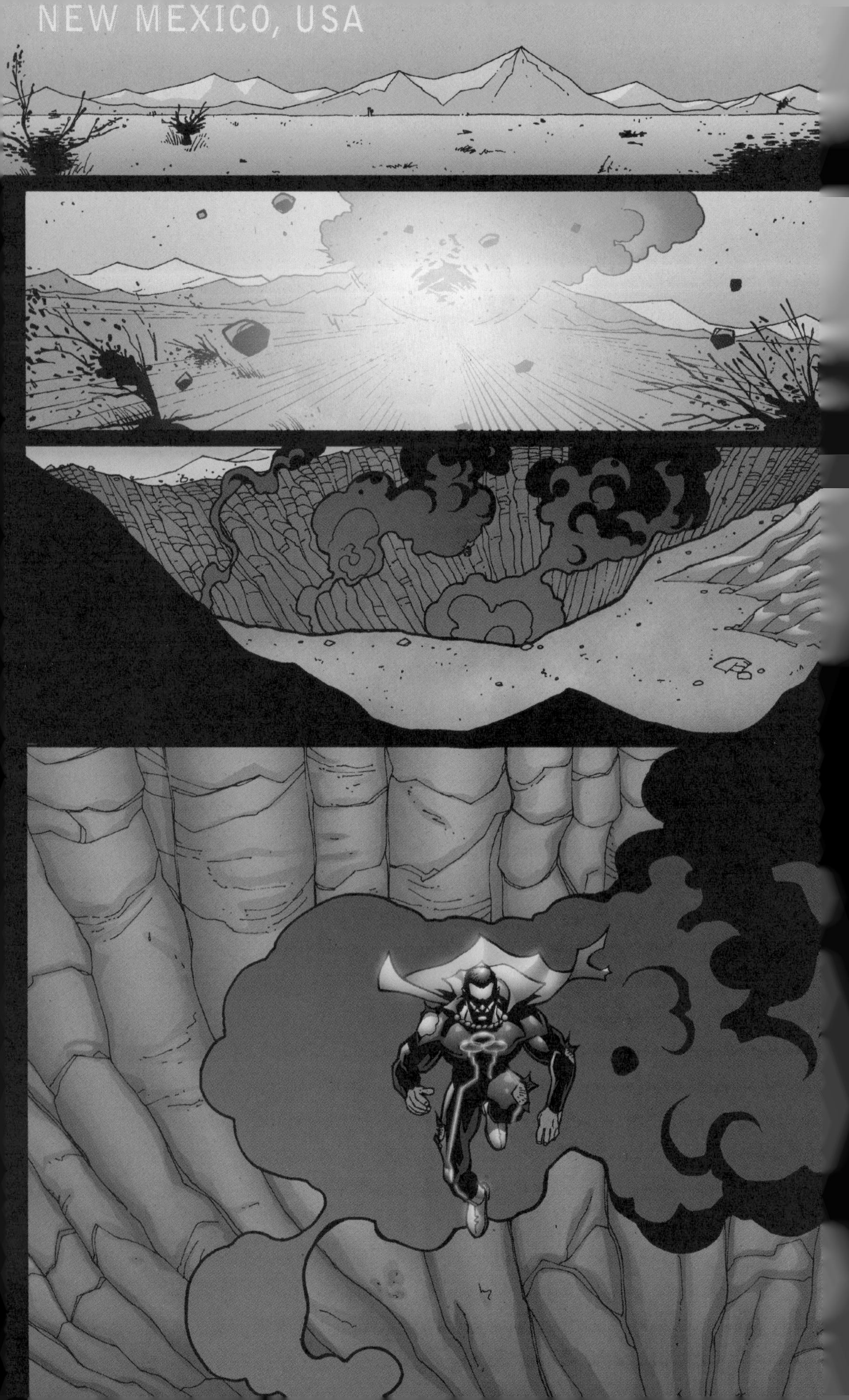
NEW MEXICO, USA

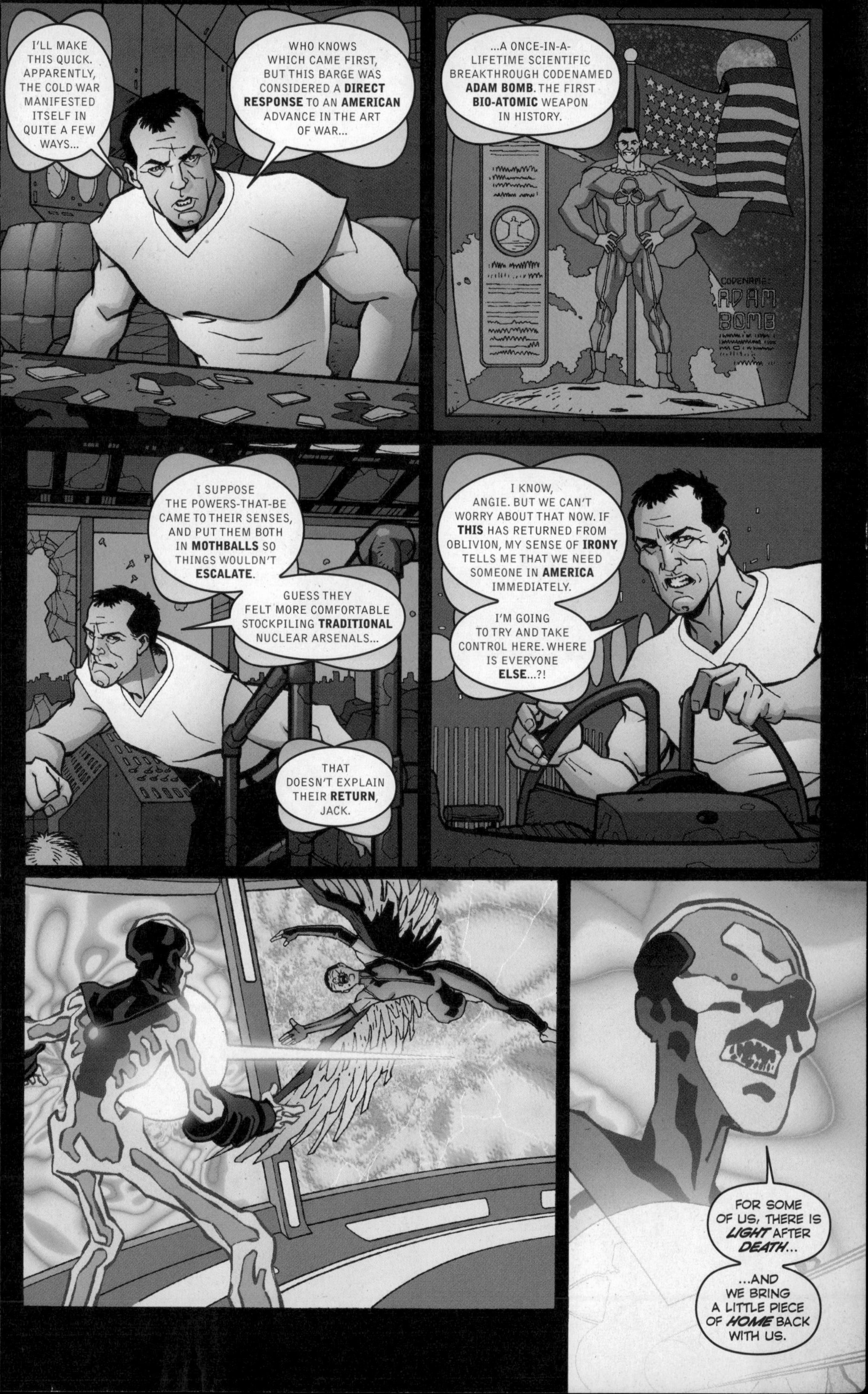
I'LL MAKE THIS QUICK. APPARENTLY, THE COLD WAR MANIFESTED ITSELF IN QUITE A FEW WAYS...
WHO KNOWS WHICH CAME FIRST, BUT THIS BARGE WAS CONSIDERED A **DIRECT RESPONSE** TO AN **AMERICAN** ADVANCE IN THE ART OF WAR...
...A ONCE-IN-A-LIFETIME SCIENTIFIC BREAKTHROUGH CODENAMED **ADAM BOMB**. THE FIRST **BIO-ATOMIC** WEAPON IN HISTORY.
CODENAME:
ADAM BOMB
I SUPPOSE THE POWERS-THAT-BE CAME TO THEIR SENSES, AND PUT THEM BOTH IN **MOTHBALLS** SO THINGS WOULDN'T **ESCALATE**.
GUESS THEY FELT MORE COMFORTABLE STOCKPILING **TRADITIONAL** NUCLEAR ARSENALS...
THAT DOESN'T EXPLAIN THEIR **RETURN**, JACK.
I KNOW, ANGIE. BUT WE CAN'T WORRY ABOUT THAT NOW. IF **THIS** HAS RETURNED FROM OBLIVION, MY SENSE OF **IRONY** TELLS ME THAT WE NEED SOMEONE IN **AMERICA** IMMEDIATELY.
I'M GOING TO TRY AND TAKE CONTROL HERE. WHERE IS EVERYONE **ELSE**...?!
FOR SOME OF US, THERE IS ***LIGHT*** AFTER ***DEATH***...
...AND WE BRING A LITTLE PIECE OF ***HOME*** BACK WITH US.

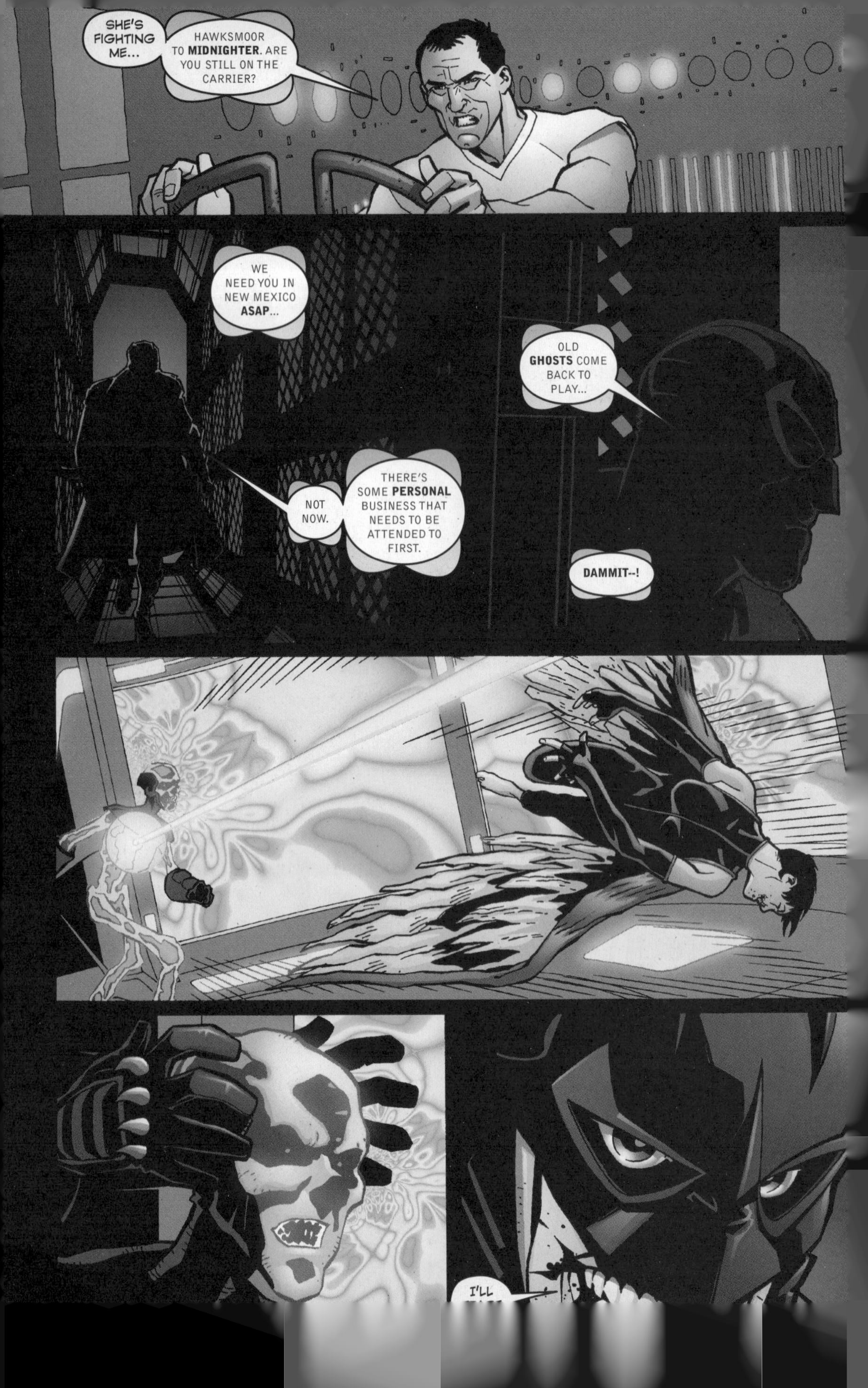
SHE'S FIGHTING ME...
HAWKSMOOR TO MIDNIGHTER. ARE YOU STILL ON THE CARRIER?
WE NEED YOU IN NEW MEXICO ASAP...
OLD GHOSTS COME BACK TO PLAY...
NOT NOW.
THERE'S SOME PERSONAL BUSINESS THAT NEEDS TO BE ATTENDED TO FIRST.
DAMMIT--!
I'LL

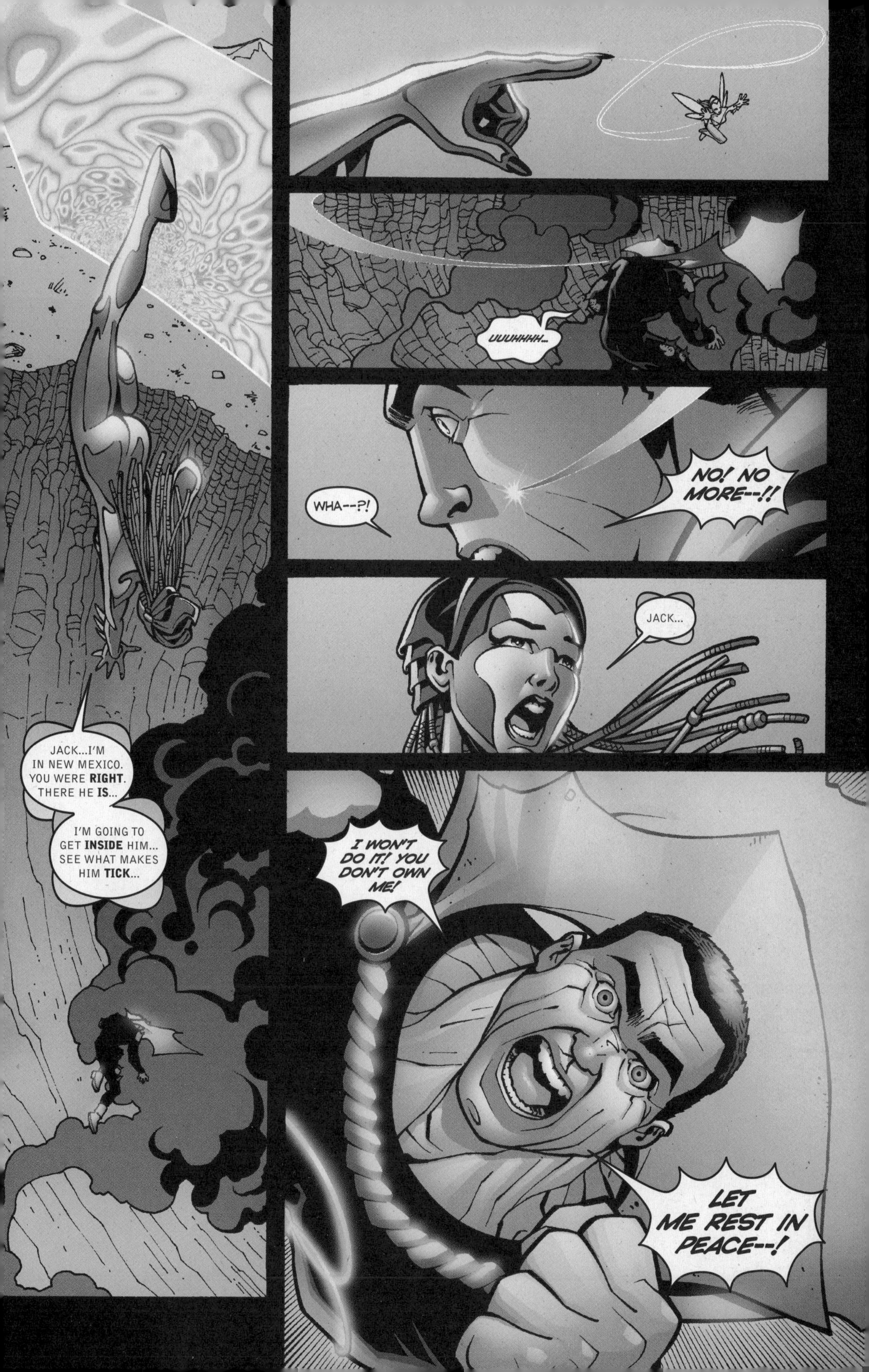
UUUHHHH...
WHA--?!
NO! NO MORE--!!
JACK...
JACK...I'M IN NEW MEXICO. YOU WERE **RIGHT**. THERE HE **IS**...
I'M GOING TO GET **INSIDE** HIM... SEE WHAT MAKES HIM **TICK**...
I WON'T DO IT! YOU DON'T OWN ME!
LET ME REST IN PEACE--!

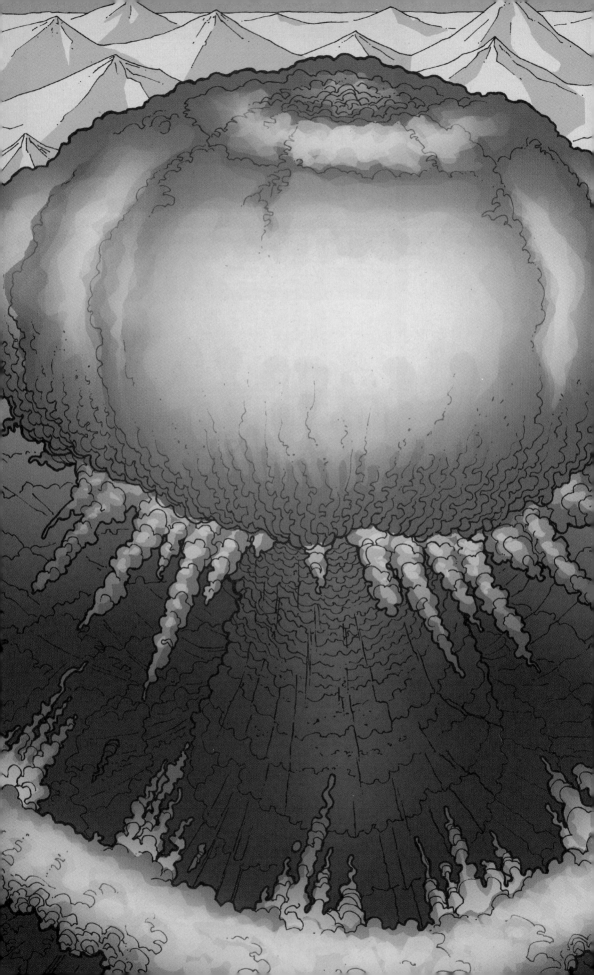

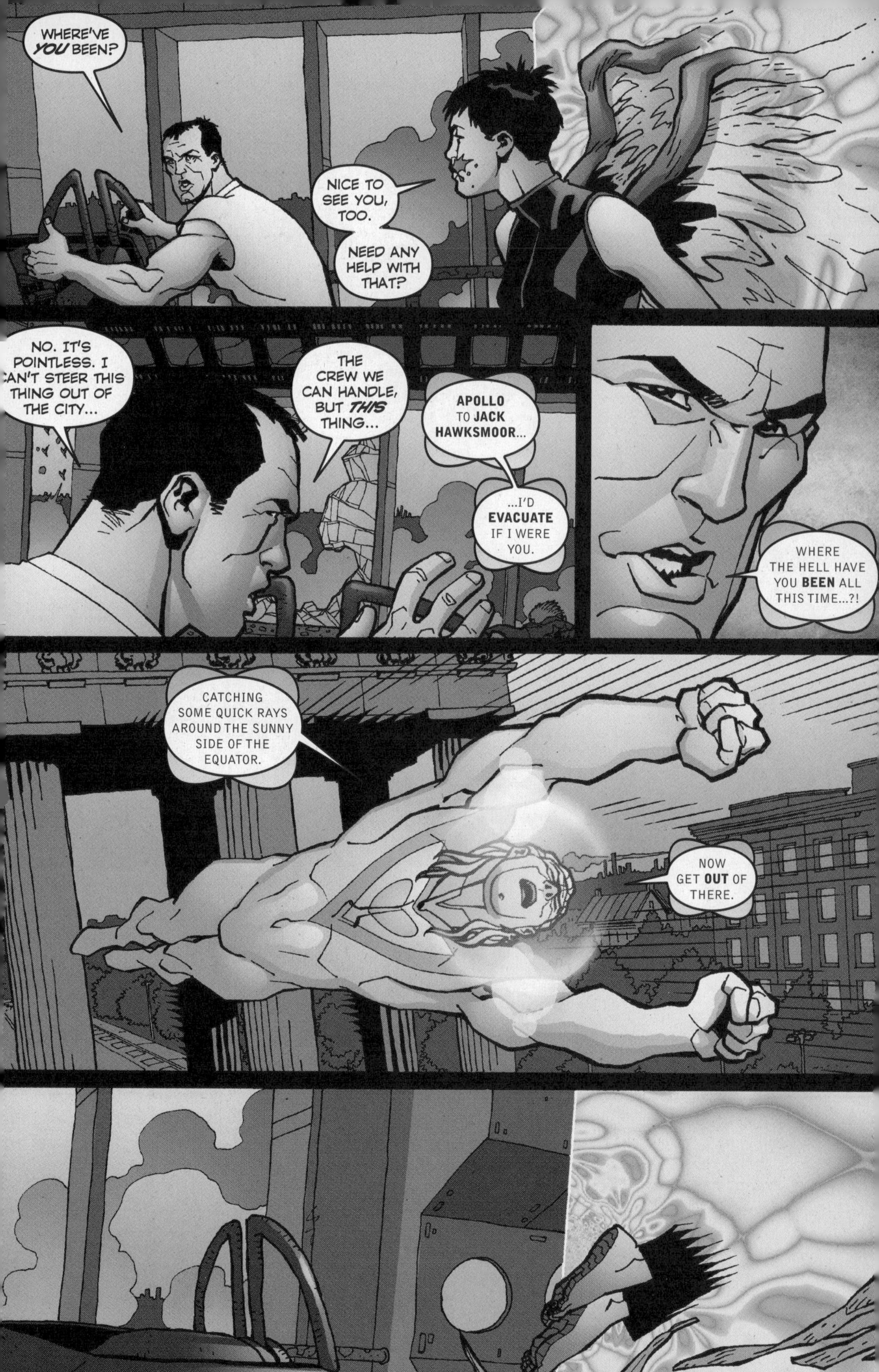
WHERE'VE *YOU* BEEN?
NICE TO SEE YOU, TOO.
NEED ANY HELP WITH THAT?
NO. IT'S POINTLESS. I CAN'T STEER THIS THING OUT OF THE CITY...
THE CREW WE CAN HANDLE, BUT *THIS* THING...
APOLLO TO **JACK HAWKSMOOR**...
...I'D **EVACUATE** IF I WERE YOU.
WHERE THE HELL HAVE YOU **BEEN** ALL THIS TIME...?!
CATCHING SOME QUICK RAYS AROUND THE SUNNY SIDE OF THE EQUATOR.
NOW GET **OUT** OF THERE.

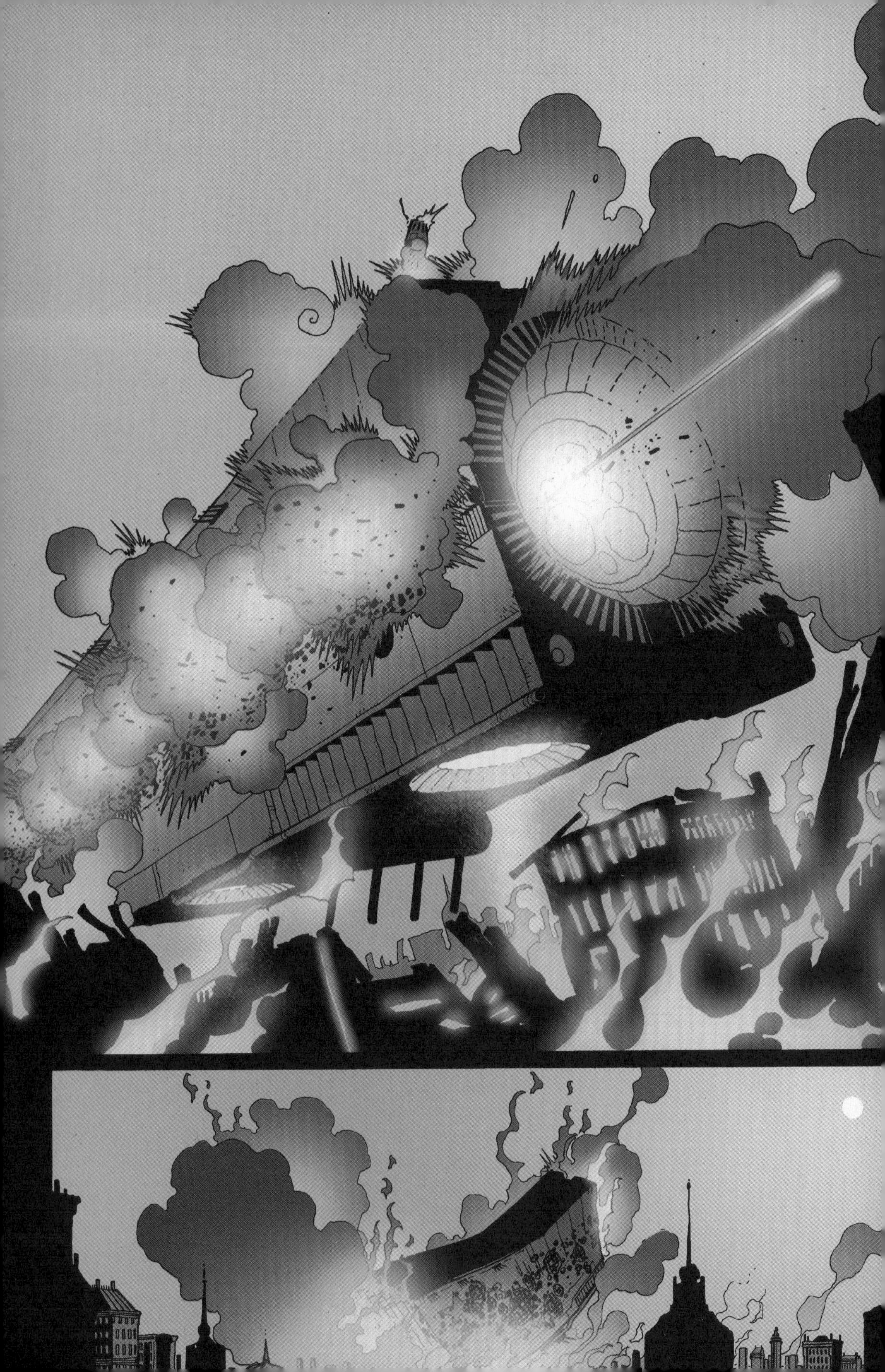

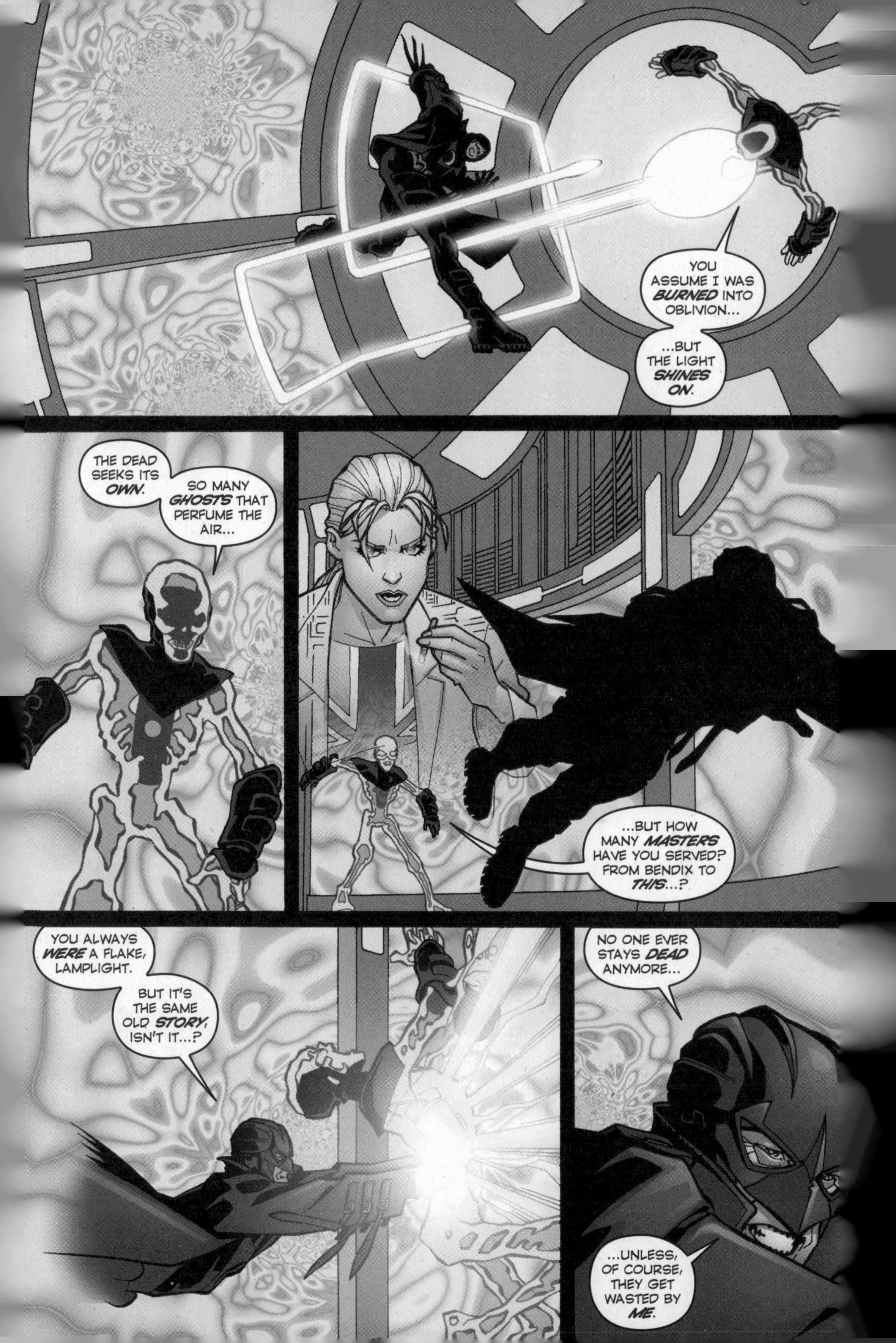
YOU ASSUME I WAS BURNED INTO OBLIVION...
...BUT THE LIGHT SHINES ON.
THE DEAD SEEKS ITS OWN.
SO MANY GHOSTS THAT PERFUME THE AIR...
...BUT HOW MANY MASTERS HAVE YOU SERVED? FROM BENDIX TO THIS...?
YOU ALWAYS WERE A FLAKE, LAMPLIGHT.
BUT IT'S THE SAME OLD STORY, ISN'T IT...?
NO ONE EVER STAYS DEAD ANYMORE...
...UNLESS, OF COURSE, THEY GET WASTED BY ME.

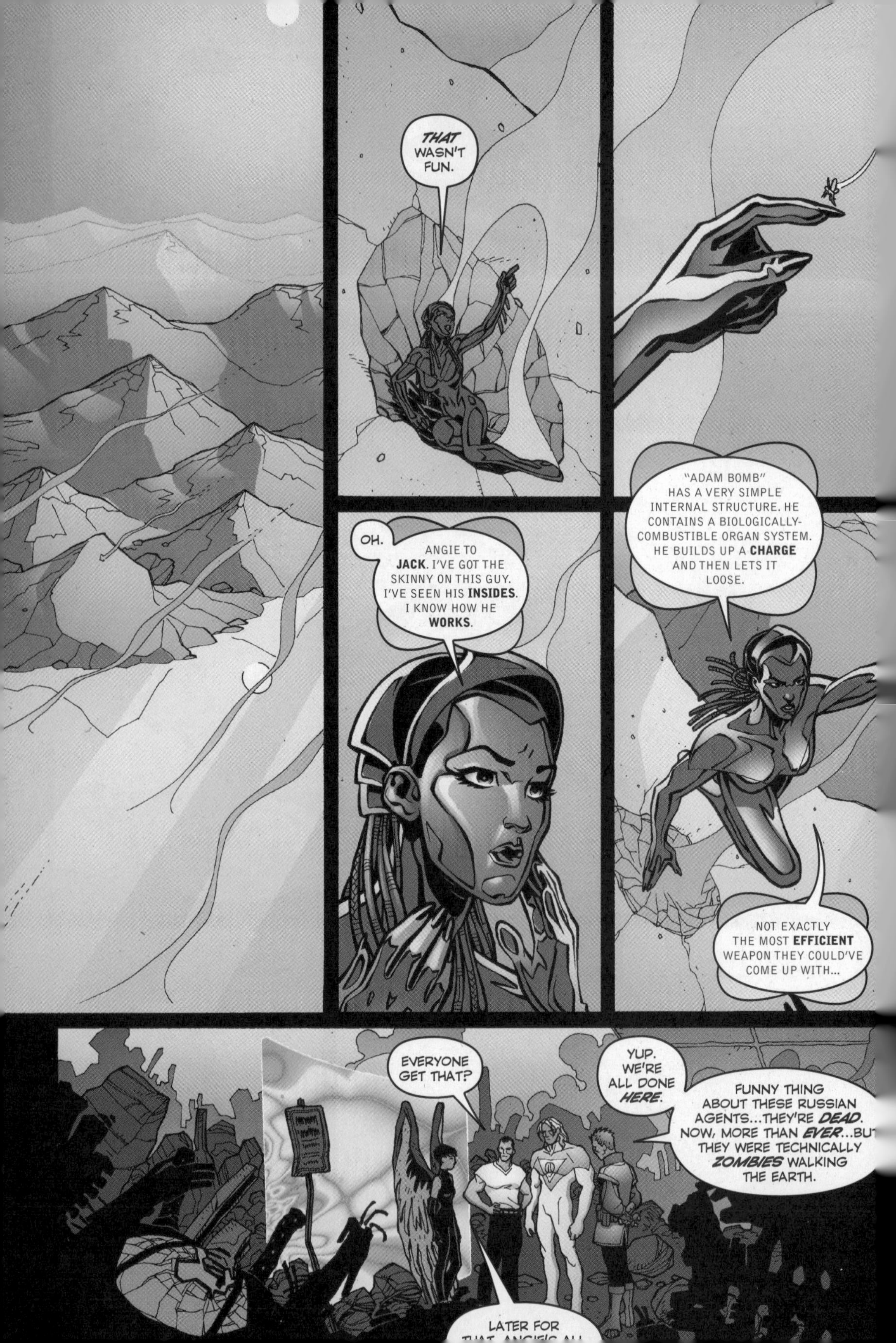
THAT WASN'T FUN.
OH.
ANGIE TO JACK. I'VE GOT THE SKINNY ON THIS GUY. I'VE SEEN HIS INSIDES. I KNOW HOW HE WORKS.
"ADAM BOMB" HAS A VERY SIMPLE INTERNAL STRUCTURE. HE CONTAINS A BIOLOGICALLY-COMBUSTIBLE ORGAN SYSTEM. HE BUILDS UP A CHARGE AND THEN LETS IT LOOSE.
NOT EXACTLY THE MOST EFFICIENT WEAPON THEY COULD'VE COME UP WITH...
EVERYONE GET THAT?
YUP. WE'RE ALL DONE HERE.
FUNNY THING ABOUT THESE RUSSIAN AGENTS...THEY'RE DEAD. NOW, MORE THAN EVER...BUT THEY WERE TECHNICALLY ZOMBIES WALKING THE EARTH.
LATER FOR

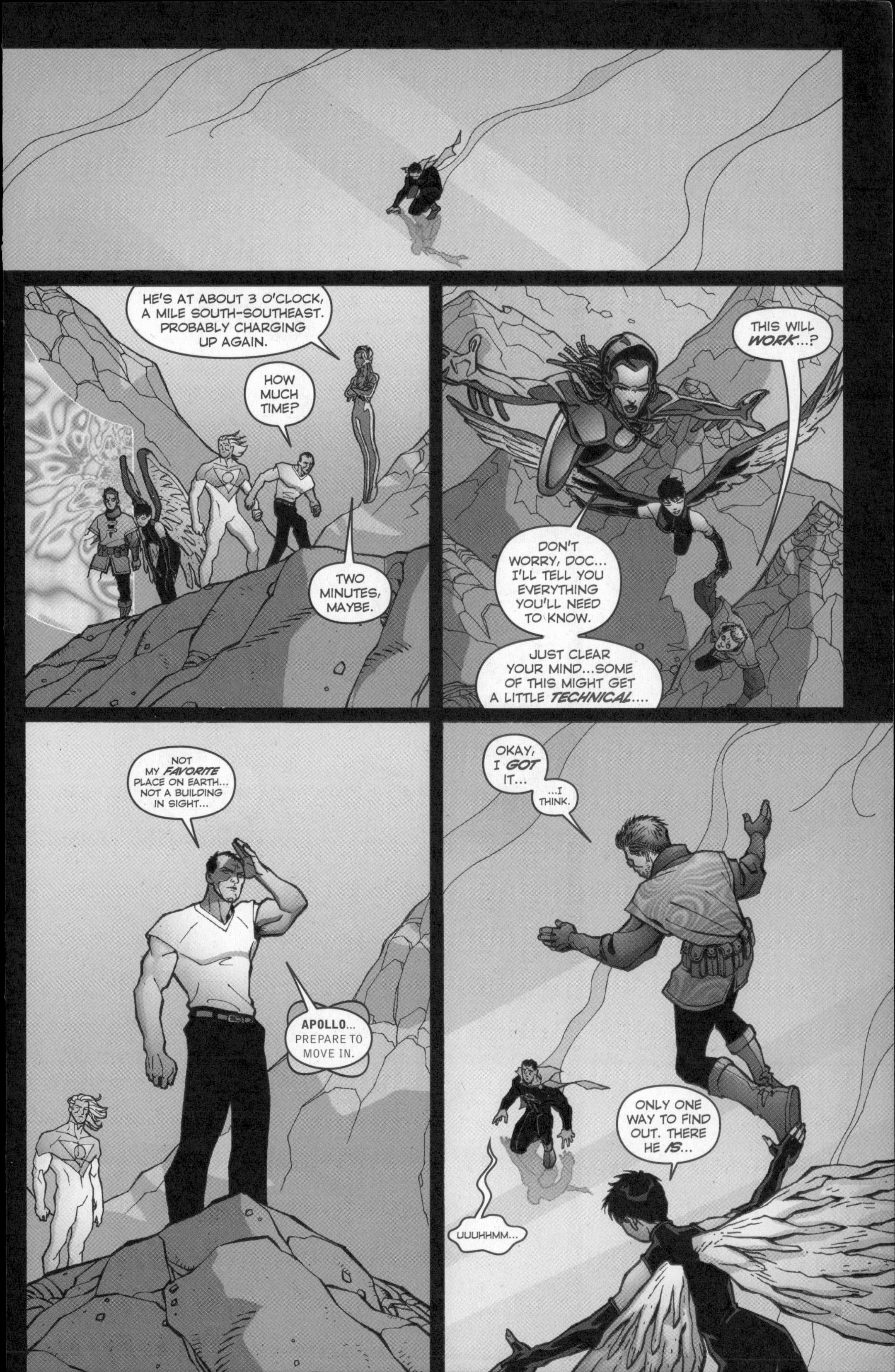

HE'S AT ABOUT 3 O'CLOCK, A MILE SOUTH-SOUTHEAST. PROBABLY CHARGING UP AGAIN.
HOW MUCH TIME?
TWO MINUTES, MAYBE.
THIS WILL WORK...?
DON'T WORRY, DOC... I'LL TELL YOU EVERYTHING YOU'LL NEED TO KNOW.
JUST CLEAR YOUR MIND...SOME OF THIS MIGHT GET A LITTLE TECHNICAL....
NOT MY FAVORITE PLACE ON EARTH... NOT A BUILDING IN SIGHT...
APOLLO... PREPARE TO MOVE IN.
OKAY, I GOT IT...
...I THINK.
ONLY ONE WAY TO FIND OUT. THERE HE IS...
UUUHHMM...

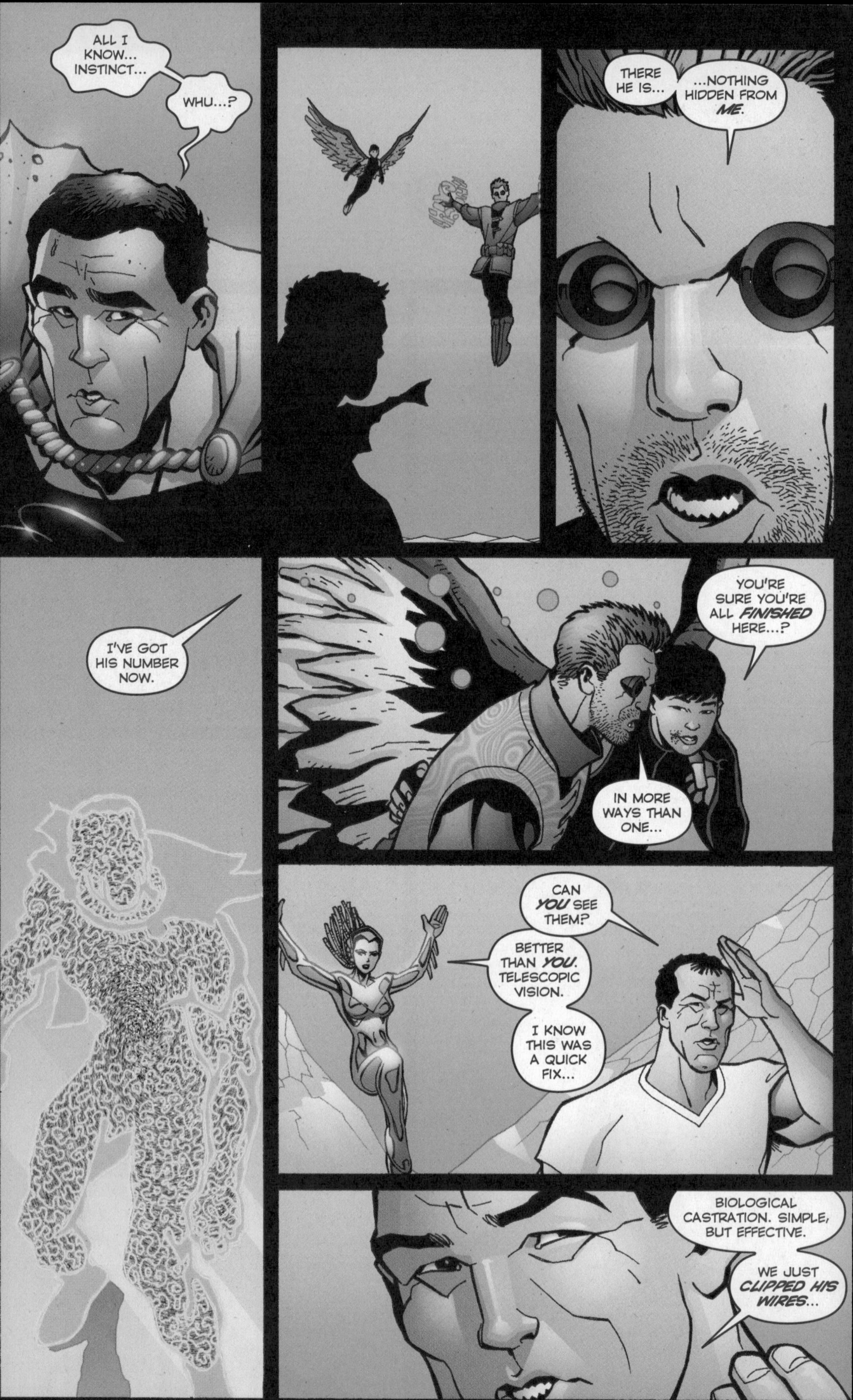
ALL I KNOW... INSTINCT...
WHU...?
THERE HE IS...
...NOTHING HIDDEN FROM ME.
I'VE GOT HIS NUMBER NOW.
YOU'RE SURE YOU'RE ALL FINISHED HERE...?
IN MORE WAYS THAN ONE...
CAN YOU SEE THEM?
BETTER THAN YOU. TELESCOPIC VISION.
I KNOW THIS WAS A QUICK FIX...
BIOLOGICAL CASTRATION. SIMPLE, BUT EFFECTIVE.
WE JUST CLIPPED HIS WIRES...

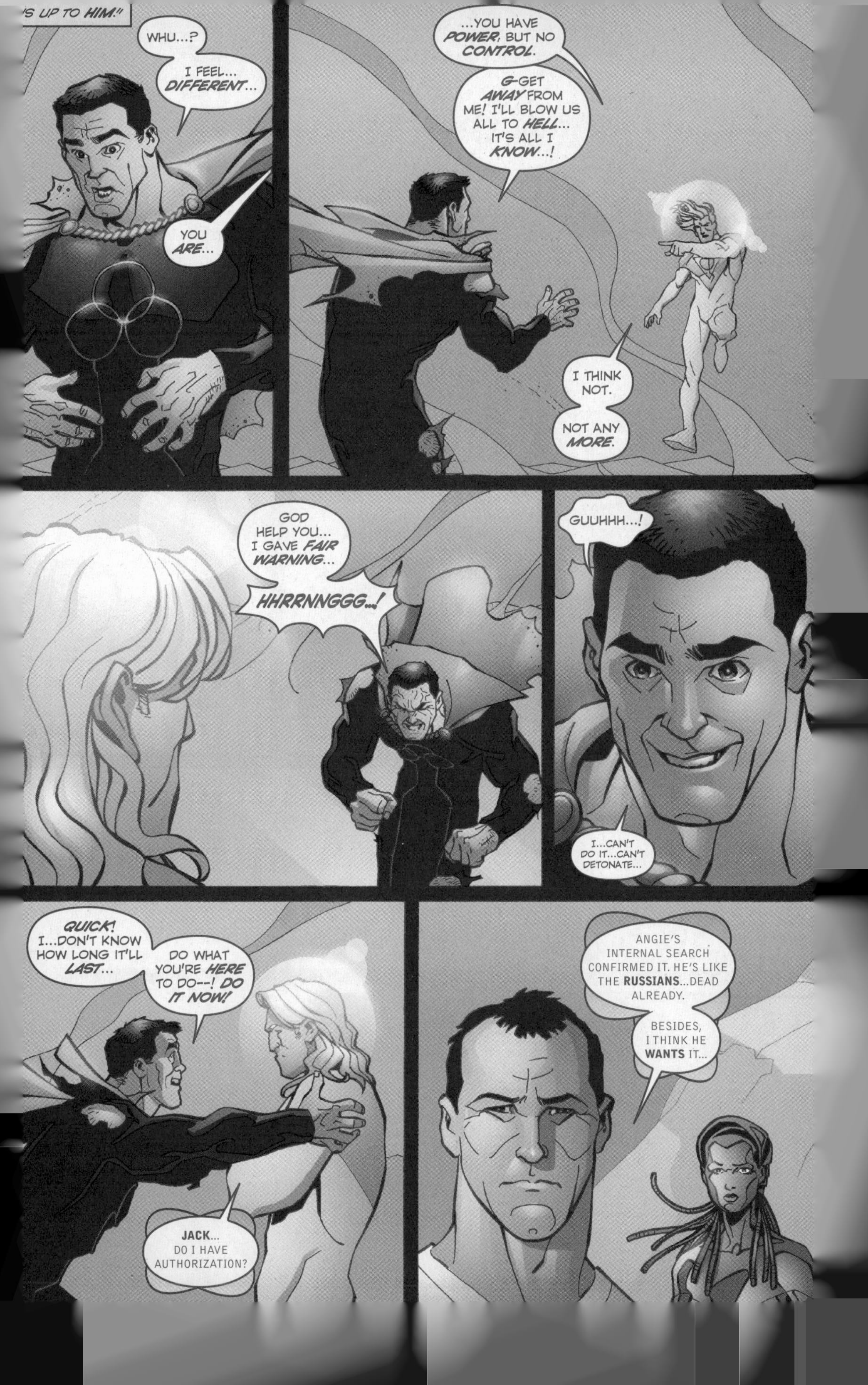

'S UP TO HIM."
WHU...?
I FEEL... DIFFERENT...
YOU ARE...
...YOU HAVE POWER, BUT NO CONTROL.
G-GET AWAY FROM ME! I'LL BLOW US ALL TO HELL... IT'S ALL I KNOW...!
I THINK NOT.
NOT ANY MORE.
GOD HELP YOU... I GAVE FAIR WARNING...
HHRRNNGGG...!
GUUHHH...!
I...CAN'T DO IT...CAN'T DETONATE...
QUICK! I...DON'T KNOW HOW LONG IT'LL LAST...
DO WHAT YOU'RE HERE TO DO--! DO IT NOW!
JACK... DO I HAVE AUTHORIZATION?
ANGIE'S INTERNAL SEARCH CONFIRMED IT. HE'S LIKE THE RUSSIANS...DEAD ALREADY.
BESIDES, I THINK HE WANTS IT...

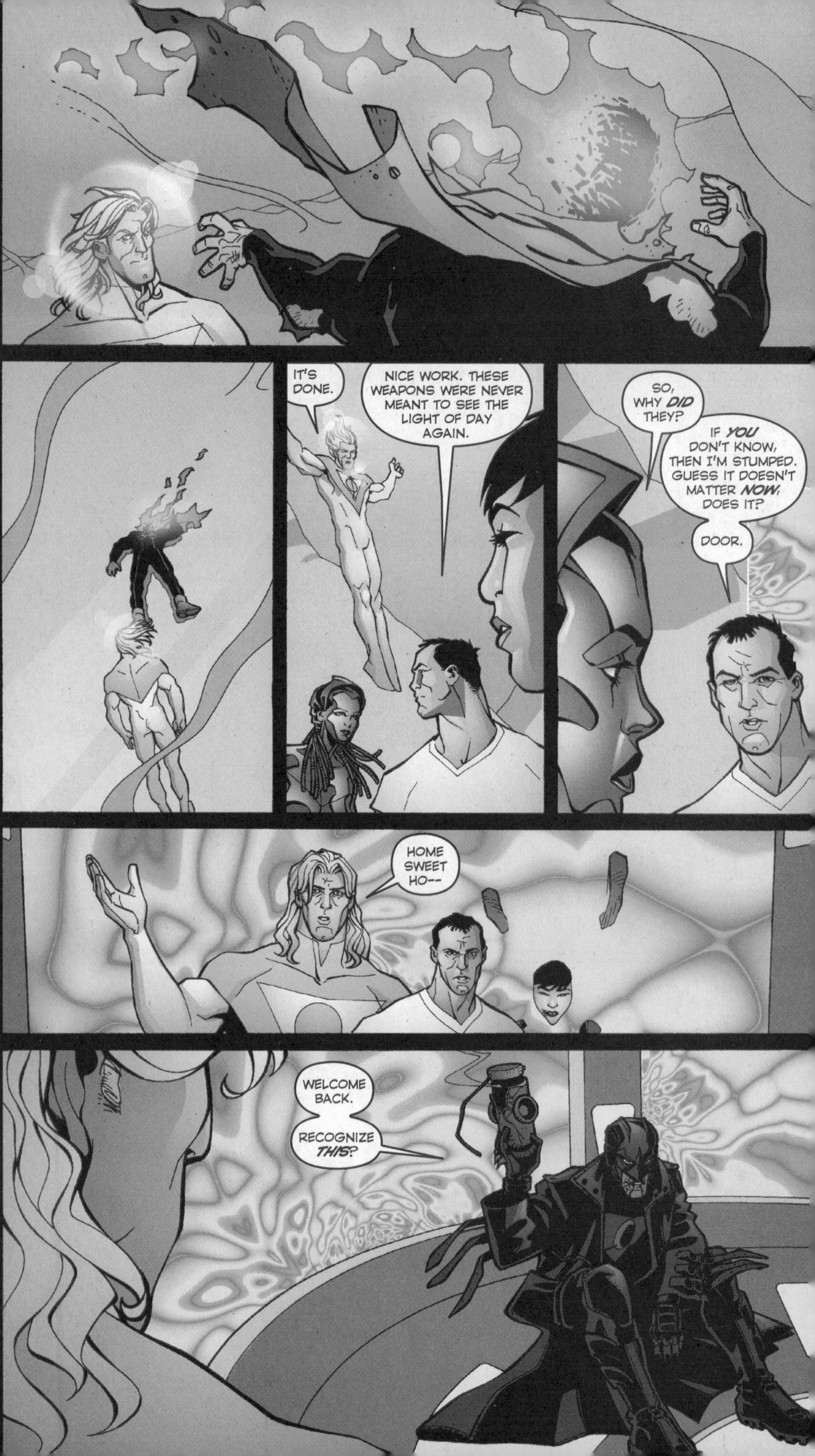
IT'S DONE.
NICE WORK. THESE WEAPONS WERE NEVER MEANT TO SEE THE LIGHT OF DAY AGAIN.
SO, WHY *DID* THEY?
IF *YOU* DON'T KNOW, THEN I'M STUMPED. GUESS IT DOESN'T MATTER *NOW*, DOES IT?
DOOR.
HOME SWEET HO--
WELCOME BACK.
RECOGNIZE *THIS*?

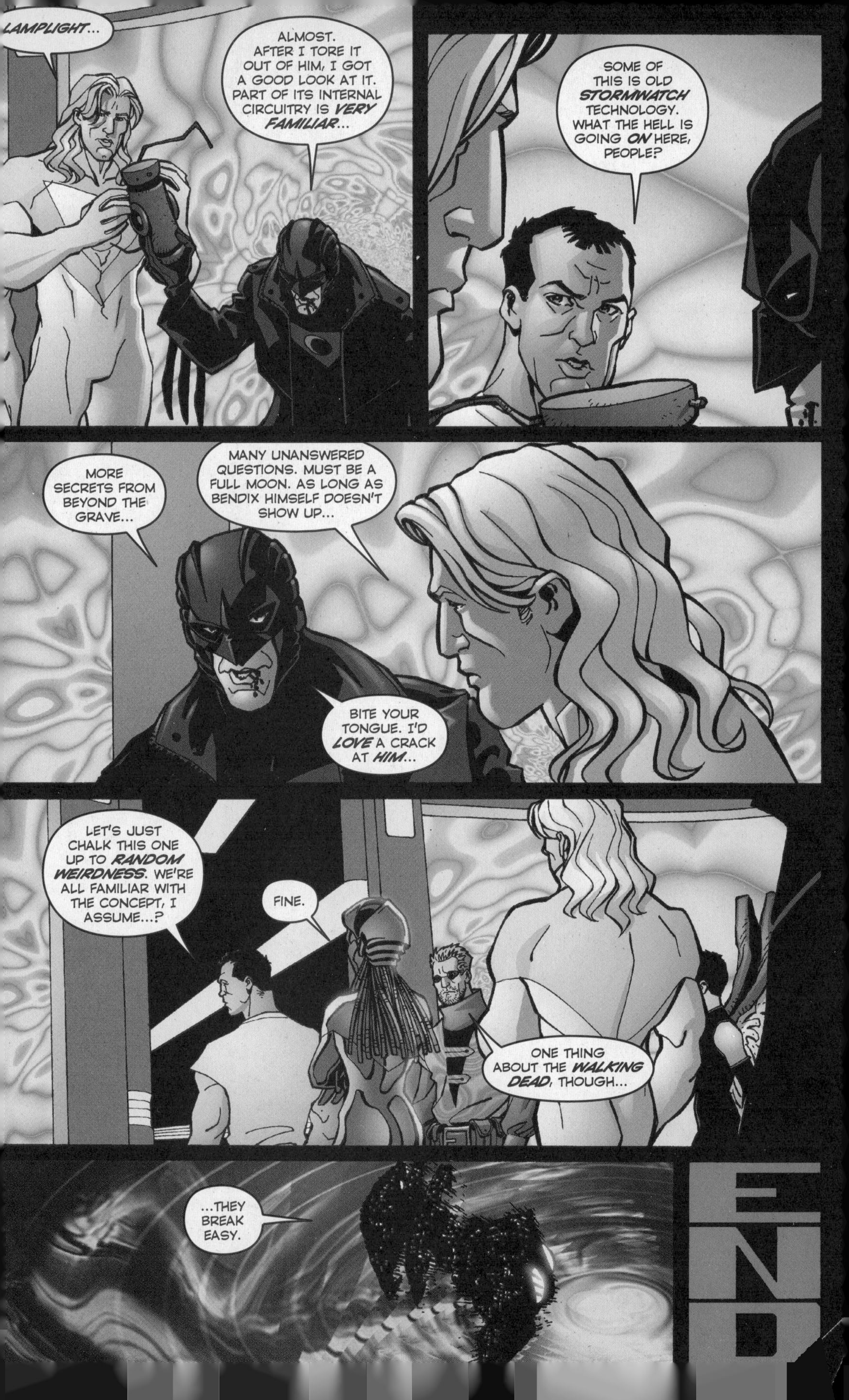
LAMPLIGHT...
ALMOST. AFTER I TORE IT OUT OF HIM, I GOT A GOOD LOOK AT IT. PART OF ITS INTERNAL CIRCUITRY IS VERY FAMILIAR...
SOME OF THIS IS OLD STORMWATCH TECHNOLOGY. WHAT THE HELL IS GOING ON HERE, PEOPLE?
MORE SECRETS FROM BEYOND THE GRAVE...
MANY UNANSWERED QUESTIONS. MUST BE A FULL MOON. AS LONG AS BENDIX HIMSELF DOESN'T SHOW UP...
BITE YOUR TONGUE. I'D LOVE A CRACK AT HIM...
LET'S JUST CHALK THIS ONE UP TO RANDOM WEIRDNESS. WE'RE ALL FAMILIAR WITH THE CONCEPT, I ASSUME...?
FINE.
ONE THING ABOUT THE WALKING DEAD, THOUGH...
...THEY BREAK EASY.
END

THE AUTHORITY
SUMMER SPECIAL

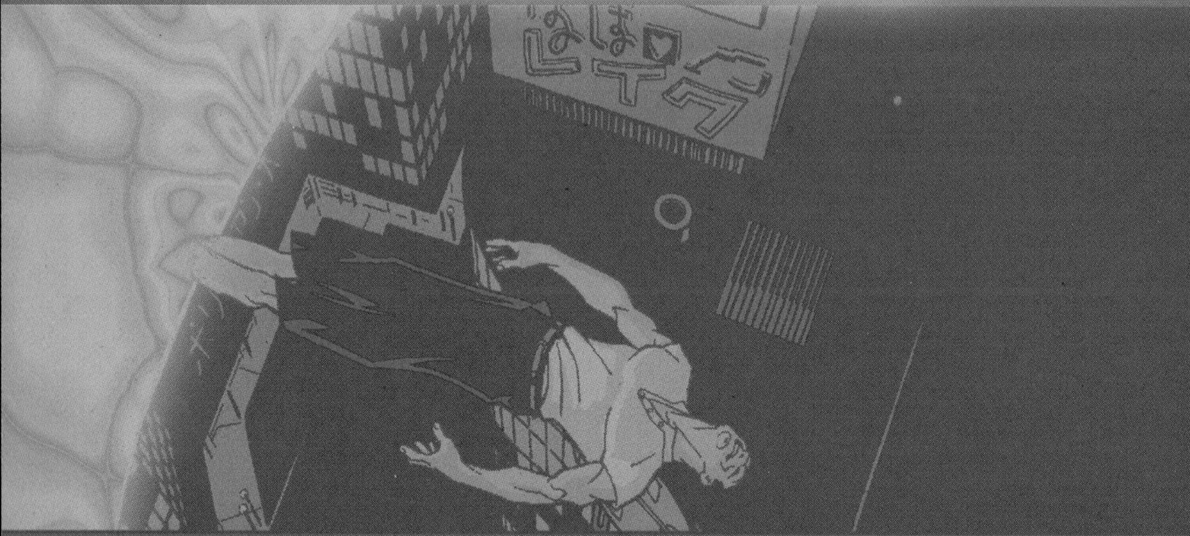

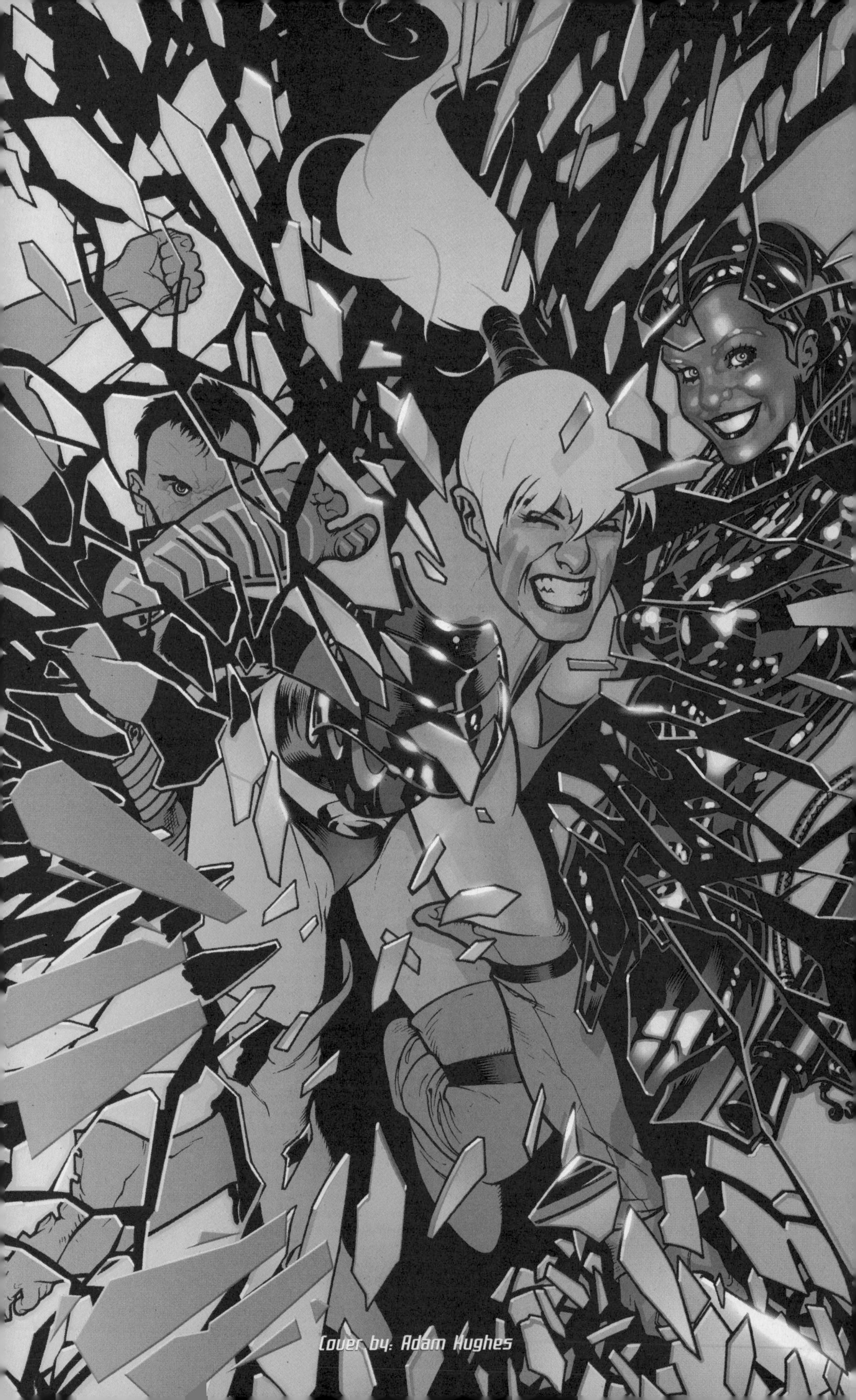

Cover by: Adam Hughes

THE AUTHORITY

ISOLATION

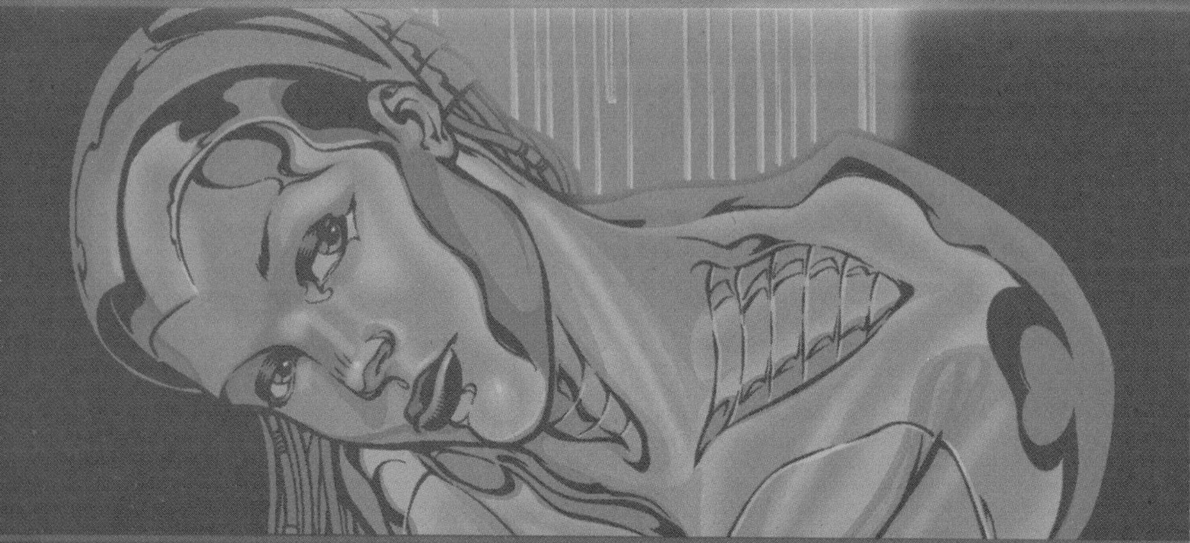

I'M A *LEGEND*.

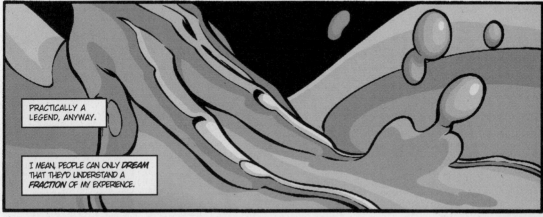

PRACTICALLY A LEGEND, ANYWAY.

I MEAN, PEOPLE CAN ONLY *DREAM* THAT THEY'D UNDERSTAND A *FRACTION* OF MY EXPERIENCE.

I'M THE ENGINEER. LIVING METAL IN FLUX.

I CAN MEASURE THE MAGNETON RESONANCE OF AN ENTIRE PLANET. I CAN NUCLEOSYNTHESIZE DIAMONDS FROM THE REMAINS OF MY CORNFLAKES, USING A CIGARETTE LIGHTER.

THERE'S NOTHING-- *NOTHING*--I CAN'T DO...

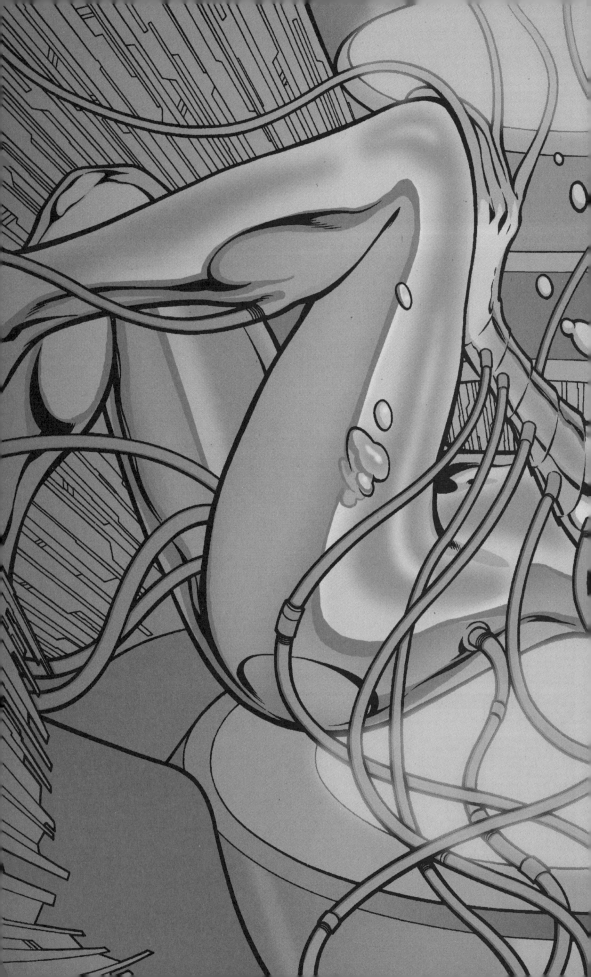

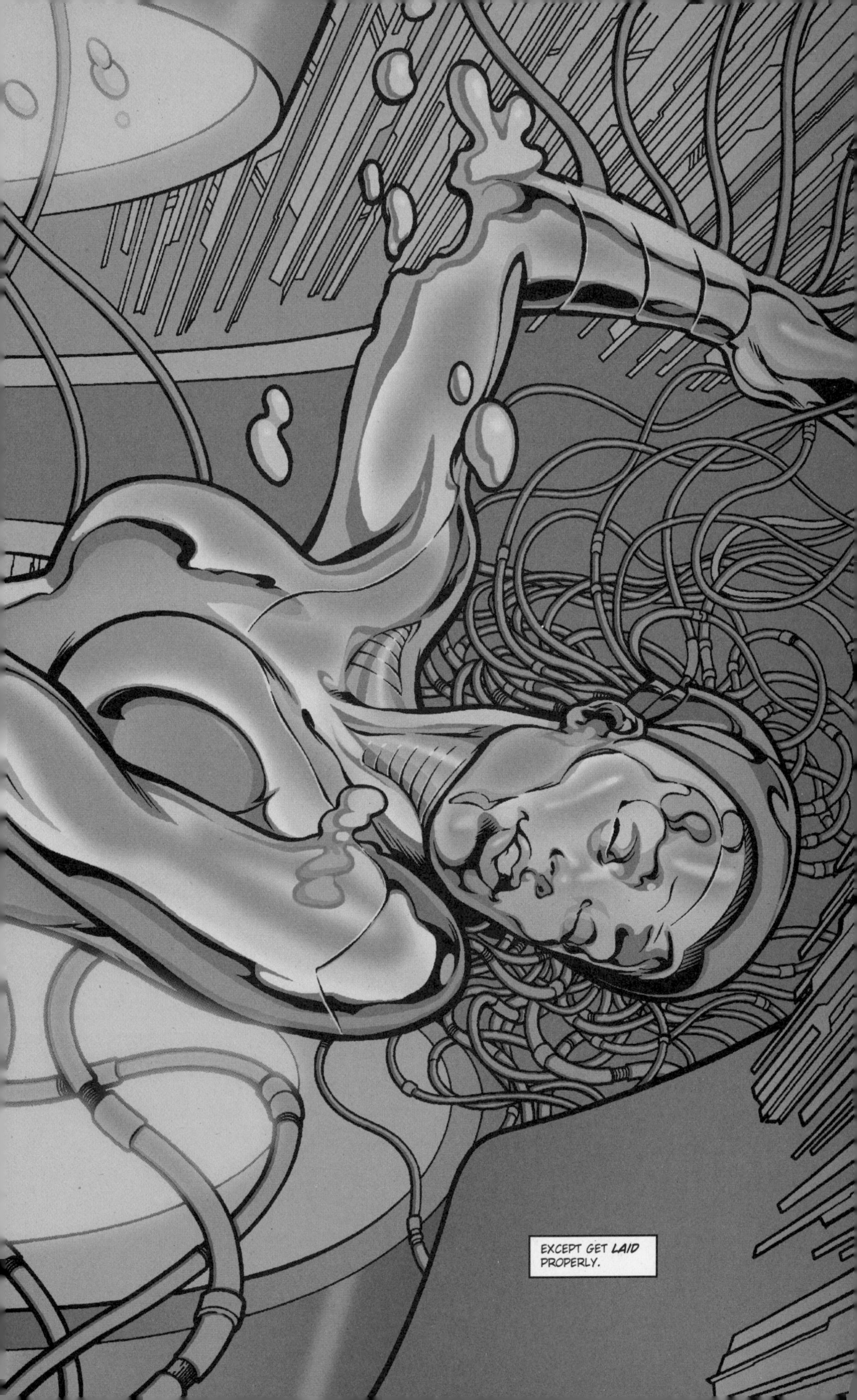
EXCEPT GET LAID PROPERLY.

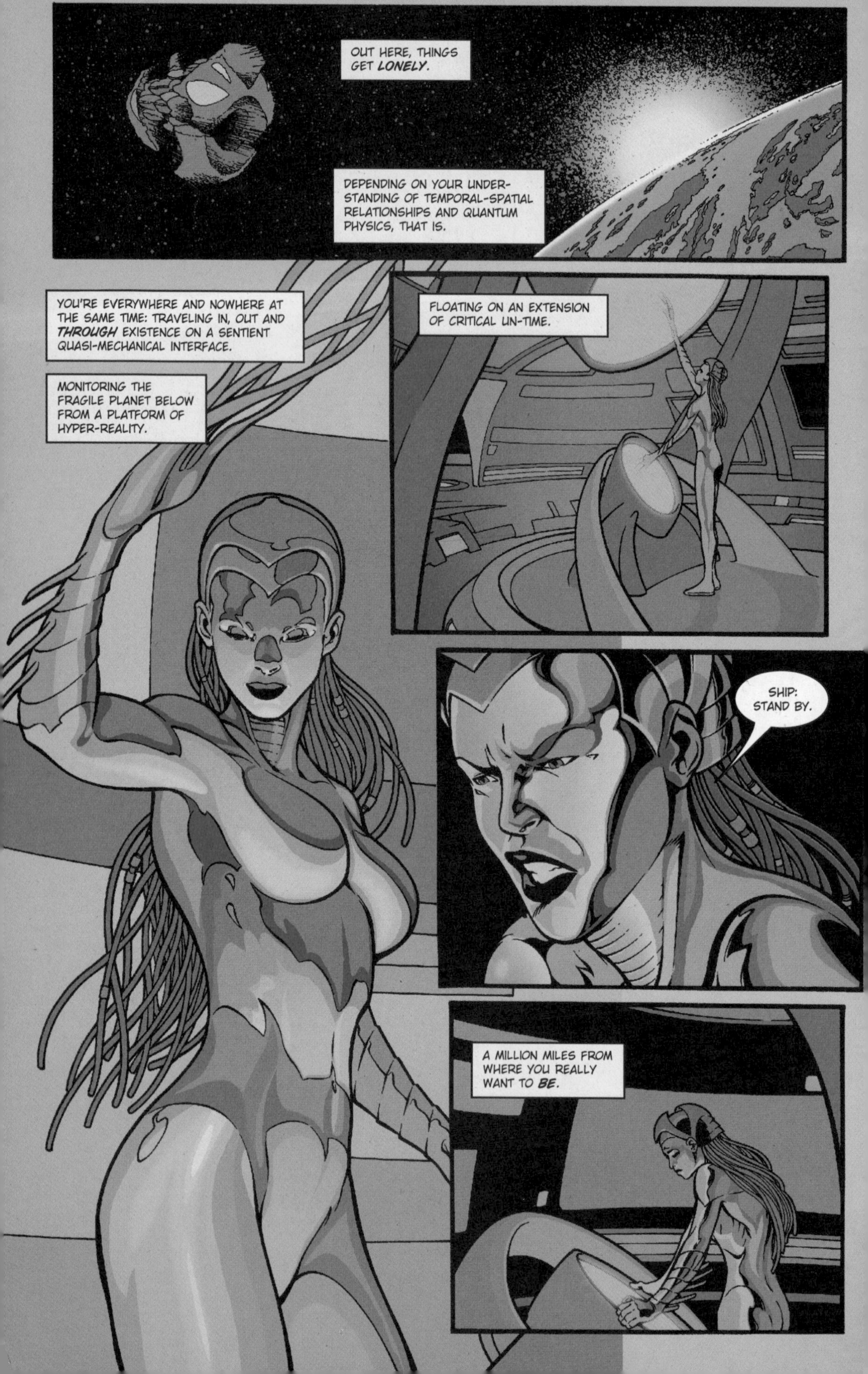
OUT HERE, THINGS GET *LONELY*.
DEPENDING ON YOUR UNDER-STANDING OF TEMPORAL-SPATIAL RELATIONSHIPS AND QUANTUM PHYSICS, THAT IS.
YOU'RE EVERYWHERE AND NOWHERE AT THE SAME TIME: TRAVELING IN, OUT AND *THROUGH* EXISTENCE ON A SENTIENT QUASI-MECHANICAL INTERFACE.
MONITORING THE FRAGILE PLANET BELOW FROM A PLATFORM OF HYPER-REALITY.
FLOATING ON AN EXTENSION OF CRITICAL UN-TIME.
SHIP: STAND BY.
A MILLION MILES FROM WHERE YOU REALLY WANT TO *BE*.

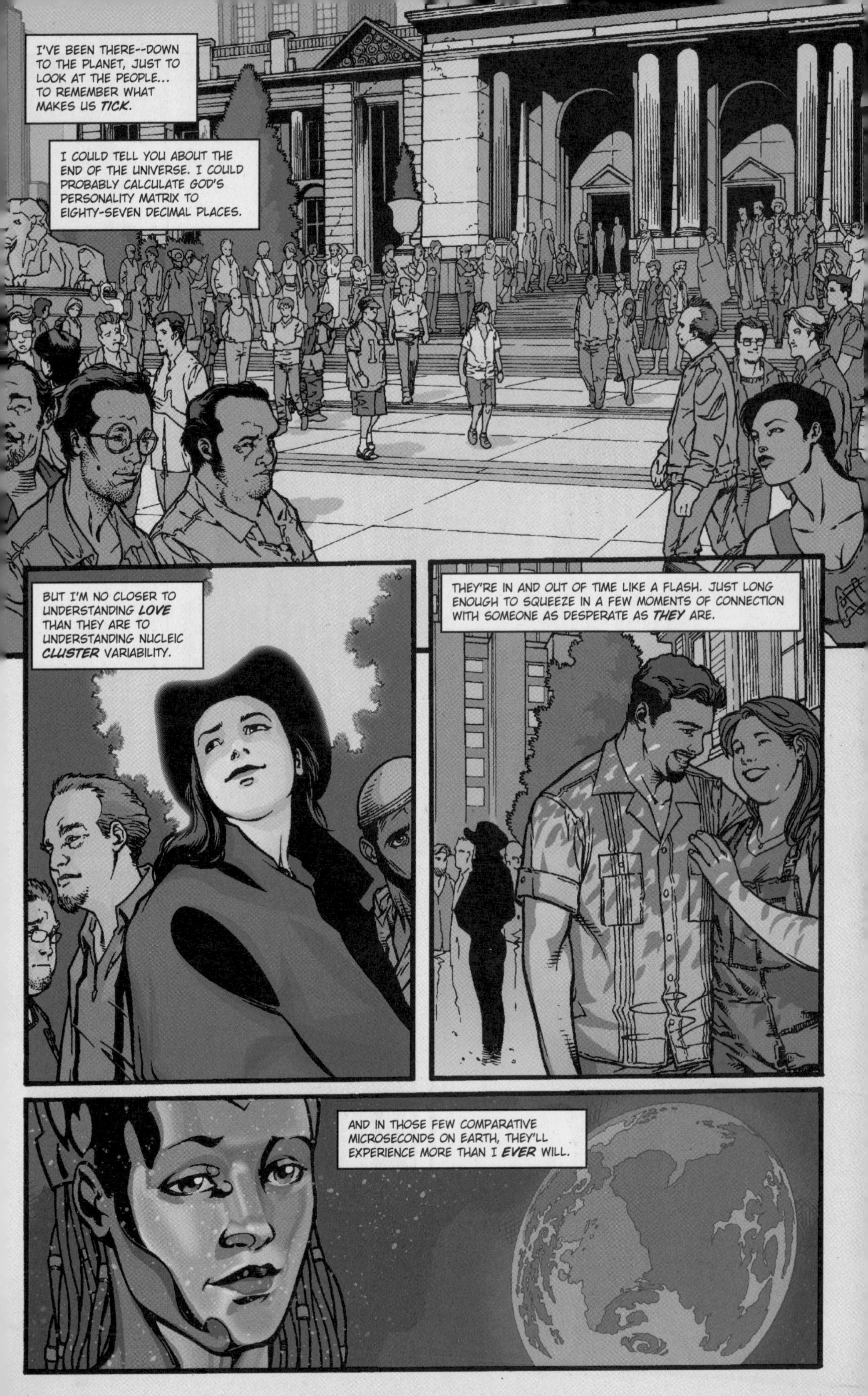
I'VE BEEN THERE--DOWN TO THE PLANET, JUST TO LOOK AT THE PEOPLE... TO REMEMBER WHAT MAKES US TICK.
I COULD TELL YOU ABOUT THE END OF THE UNIVERSE. I COULD PROBABLY CALCULATE GOD'S PERSONALITY MATRIX TO EIGHTY-SEVEN DECIMAL PLACES.
BUT I'M NO CLOSER TO UNDERSTANDING LOVE THAN THEY ARE TO UNDERSTANDING NUCLEIC CLUSTER VARIABILITY.
THEY'RE IN AND OUT OF TIME LIKE A FLASH. JUST LONG ENOUGH TO SQUEEZE IN A FEW MOMENTS OF CONNECTION WITH SOMEONE AS DESPERATE AS THEY ARE.
AND IN THOSE FEW COMPARATIVE MICROSECONDS ON EARTH, THEY'LL EXPERIENCE MORE THAN I EVER WILL.

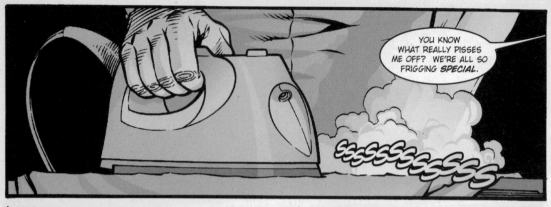

YOU KNOW WHAT REALLY PISSES ME OFF? WE'RE ALL SO FRIGGING *SPECIAL*.

SSSSSSSSSSSS

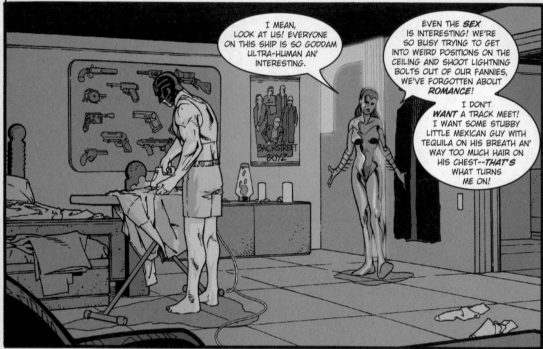

I MEAN, LOOK AT US! EVERYONE ON THIS SHIP IS SO GODDAM ULTRA-HUMAN AN' INTERESTING.

EVEN THE *SEX* IS INTERESTING! WE'RE SO BUSY TRYING TO GET INTO WEIRD POSITIONS ON THE CEILING AND SHOOT LIGHTNING BOLTS OUT OF OUR FANNIES, WE'VE FORGOTTEN ABOUT *ROMANCE*!

I DON'T *WANT* A TRACK MEET! I WANT SOME STUBBY LITTLE MEXICAN GUY WITH TEQUILA ON HIS BREATH AN' WAY TOO MUCH HAIR ON HIS CHEST--*THAT'S* WHAT TURNS ME ON!

BACKSTREET BOYZ

OH, WHAT'S THE POINT? *YOU* CERTAINLY WOULDN'T UNDERSTAND.

I MEAN, YOU'RE A SWEET GUY, MIDNIGHTER, BUT YOU'RE AS BENT AS A THREE-DOLLAR *BILL*--

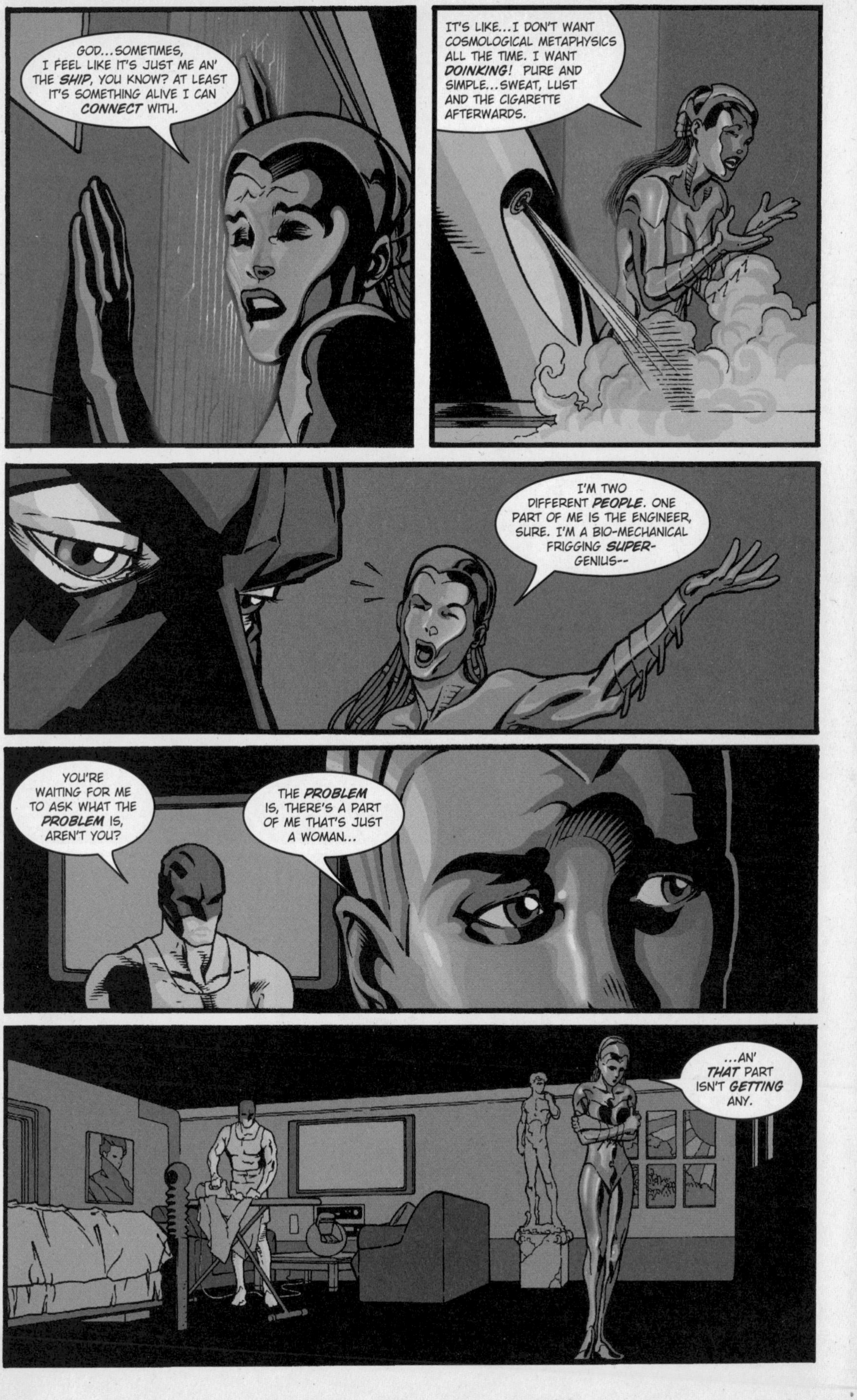
GOD...SOMETIMES, I FEEL LIKE IT'S JUST ME AN' THE *SHIP*, YOU KNOW? AT LEAST IT'S SOMETHING ALIVE I CAN *CONNECT* WITH.
IT'S LIKE...I DON'T WANT COSMOLOGICAL METAPHYSICS ALL THE TIME. I WANT *DOINKING!* PURE AND SIMPLE...SWEAT, LUST AND THE CIGARETTE AFTERWARDS.
I'M TWO DIFFERENT *PEOPLE*. ONE PART OF ME IS THE ENGINEER, SURE. I'M A BIO-MECHANICAL FRIGGING *SUPER*-GENIUS--
YOU'RE WAITING FOR ME TO ASK WHAT THE *PROBLEM* IS, AREN'T YOU?
THE *PROBLEM* IS, THERE'S A PART OF ME THAT'S JUST A WOMAN...
...AN' *THAT* PART ISN'T *GETTING* ANY.

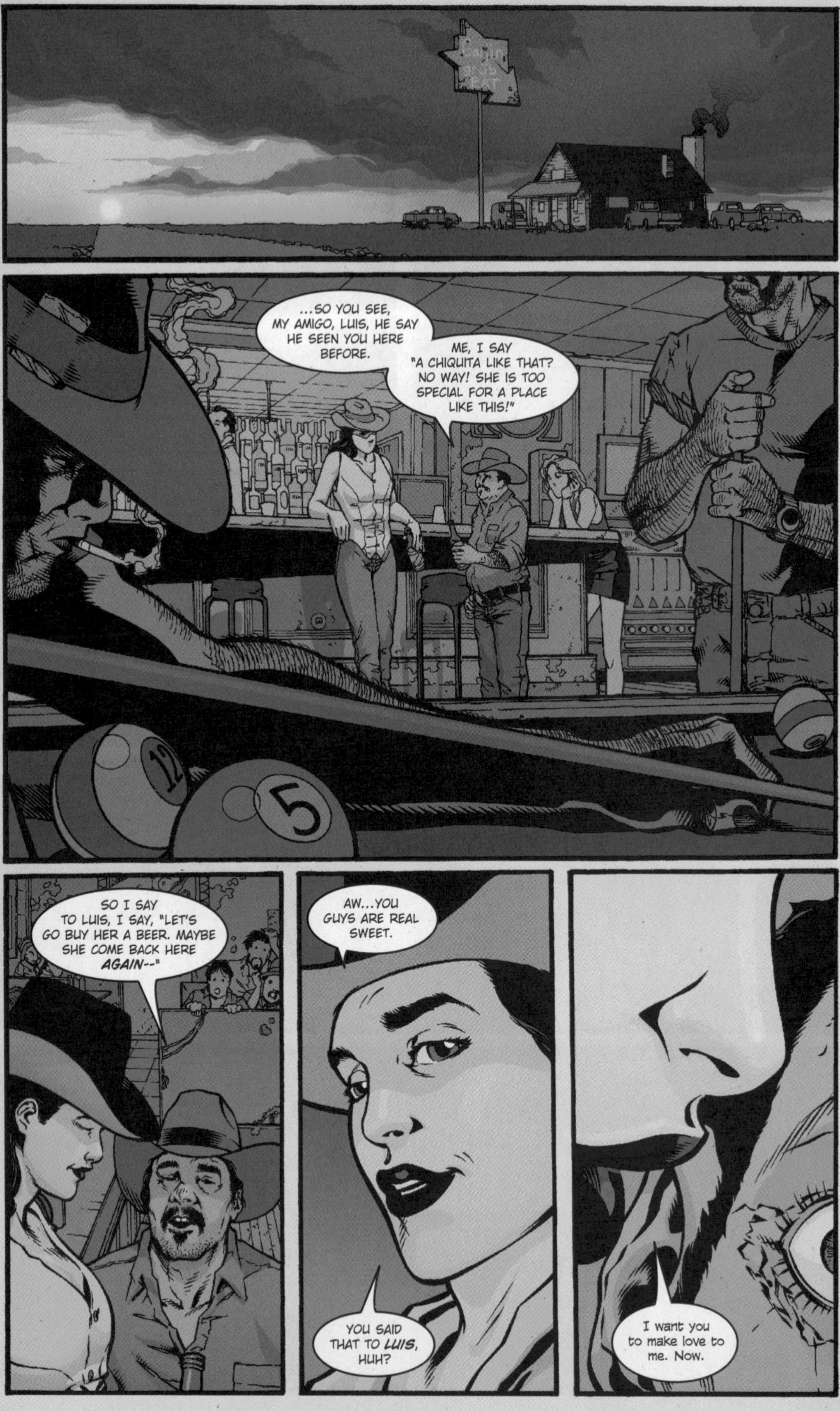
...SO YOU SEE, MY AMIGO, LUIS, HE SAY HE SEEN YOU HERE BEFORE.
ME, I SAY "A CHIQUITA LIKE THAT? NO WAY! SHE IS TOO SPECIAL FOR A PLACE LIKE THIS!"
SO I SAY TO LUIS, I SAY, "LET'S GO BUY HER A BEER. MAYBE SHE COME BACK HERE *AGAIN*--"
AW...YOU GUYS ARE REAL SWEET.
YOU SAID THAT TO *LUIS*, HUH?
I want you to make love to me. Now.

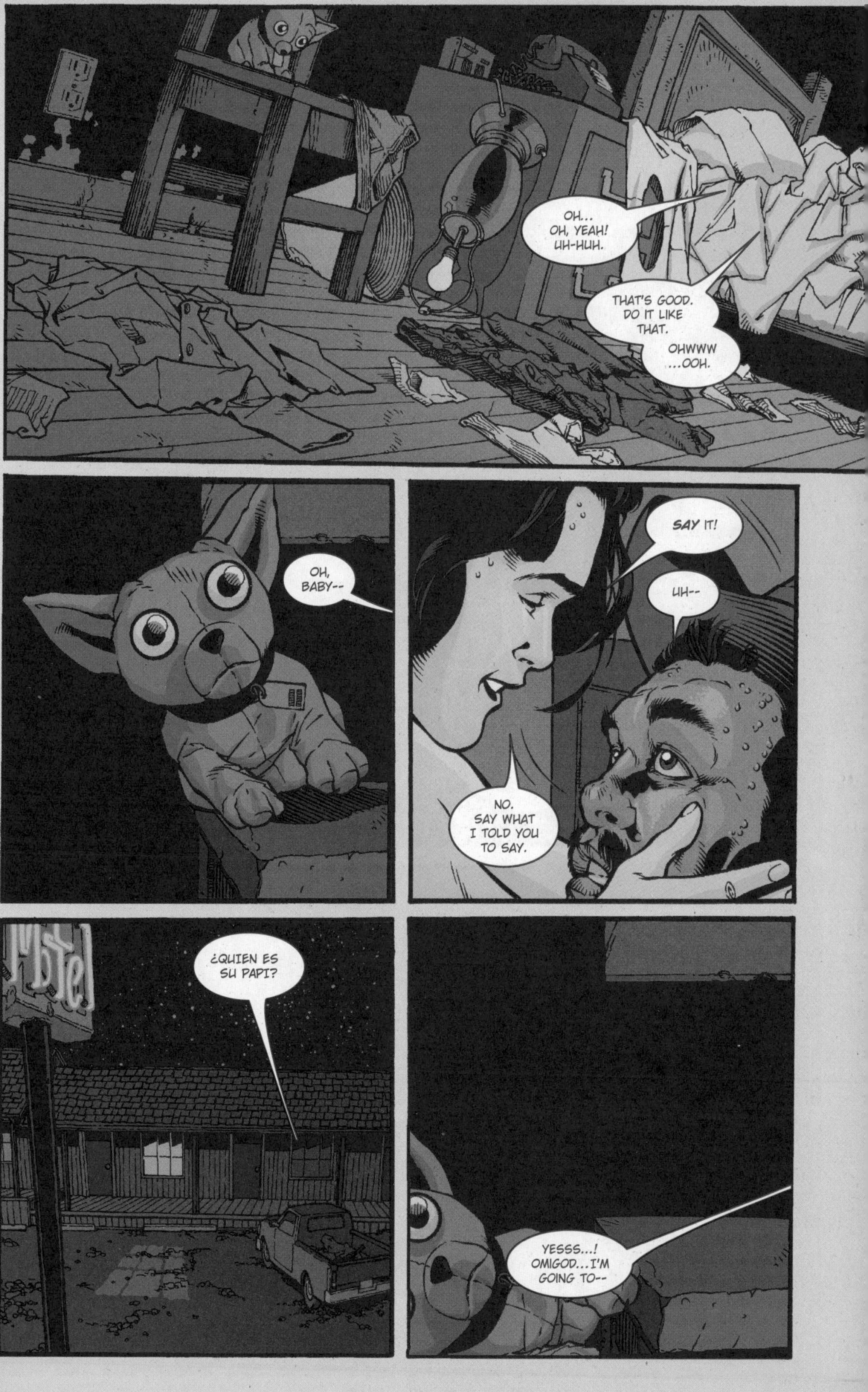
OH...
OH, YEAH!
UH-HUH.
THAT'S GOOD.
DO IT LIKE
THAT.
OHWWW
...OOH.
OH,
BABY--
SAY IT!
UH--
NO.
SAY WHAT
I TOLD YOU
TO SAY.
¿QUIEN ES
SU PAPI?
YESSS...!
OMIGOD...I'M
GOING TO--

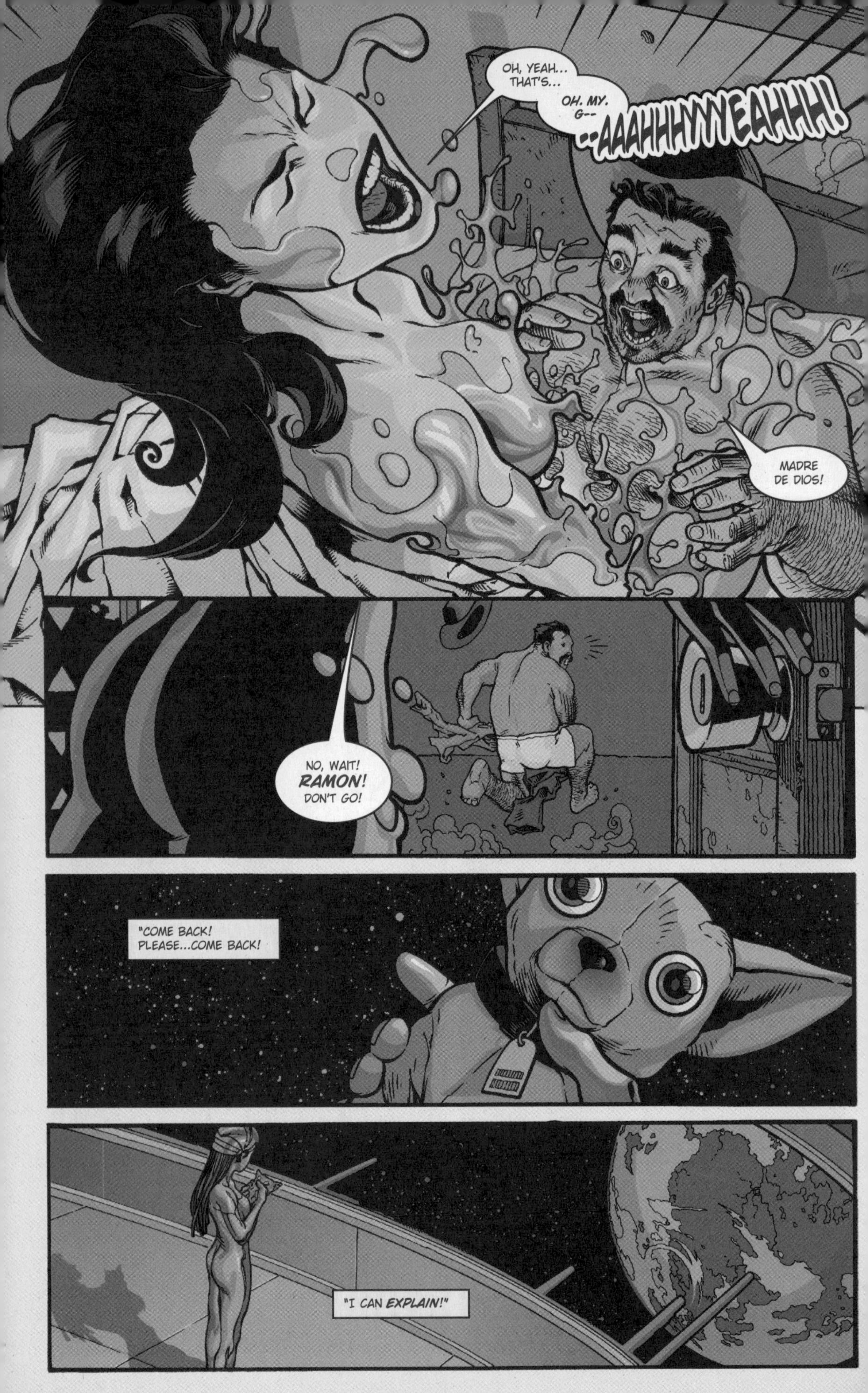

OH, YEAH... THAT'S...
OH. MY. G--
--AAAHHHYYYEAHHH!
MADRE DE DIOS!
NO, WAIT! RAMON! DON'T GO!
"COME BACK! PLEASE...COME BACK!
"I CAN EXPLAIN!"

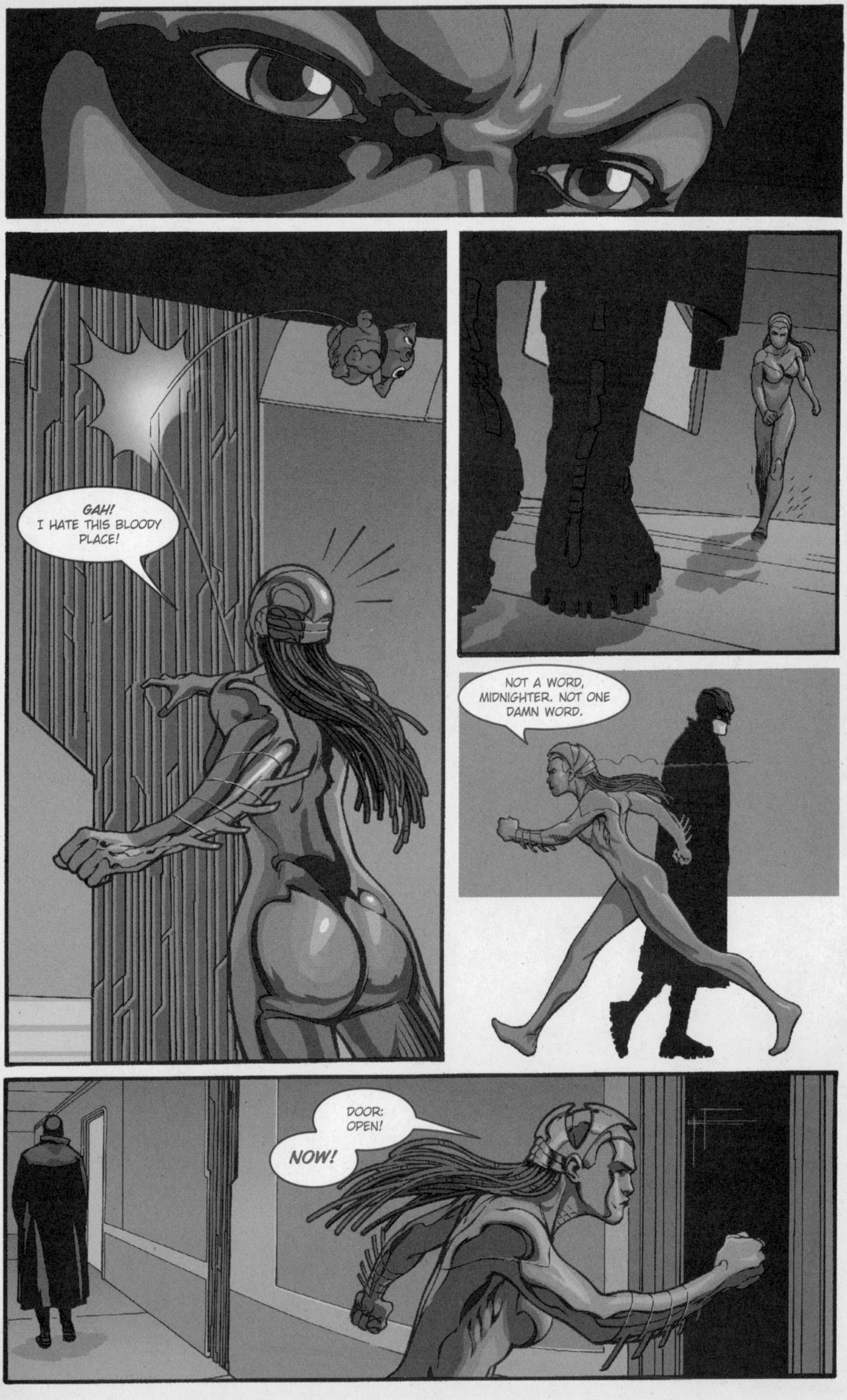
GAH! I HATE THIS BLOODY PLACE!
NOT A WORD, MIDNIGHTER. NOT ONE DAMN WORD.
DOOR: OPEN!
NOW!

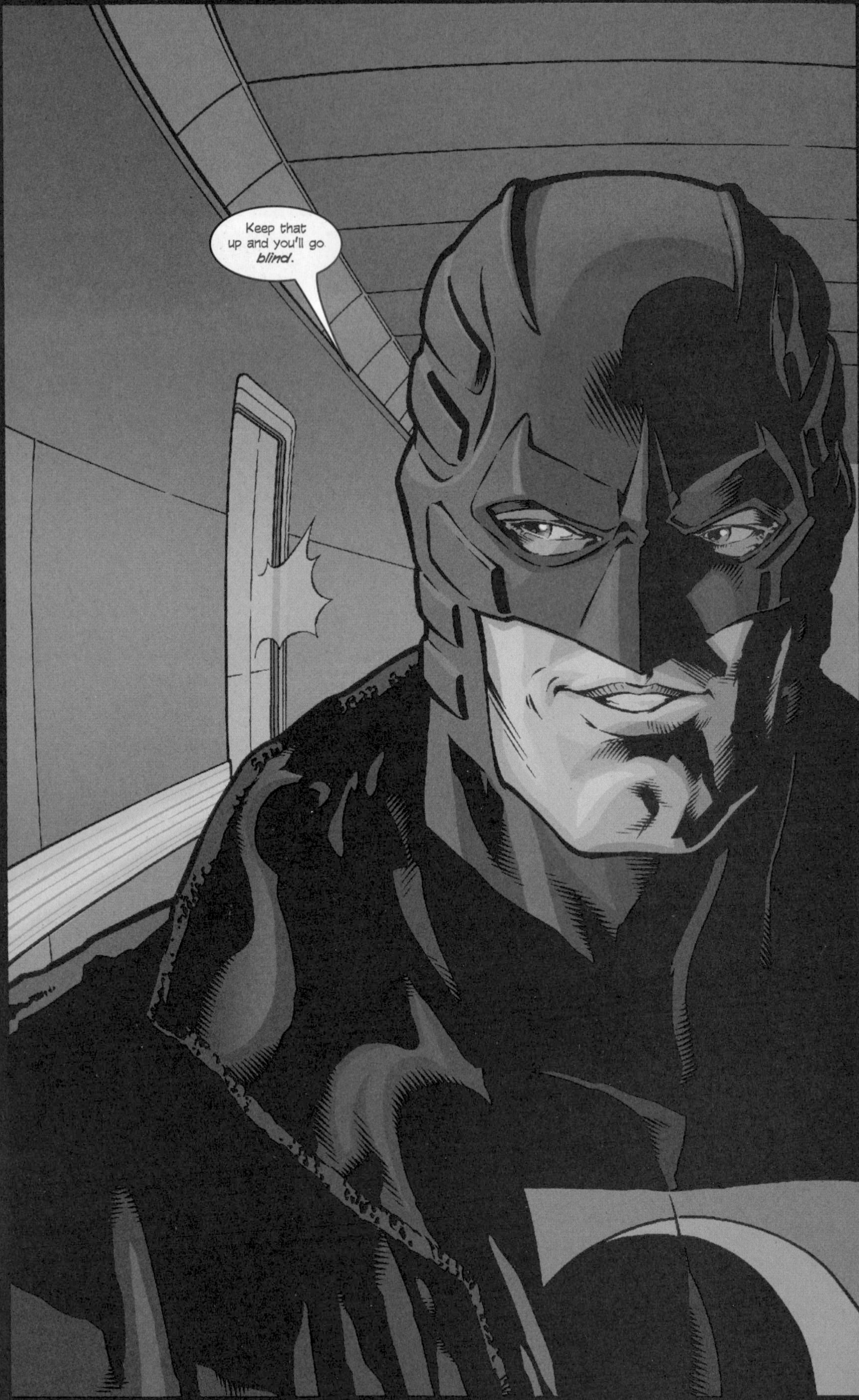
Keep that up and you'll go *blind*.

THE AUTHORITY

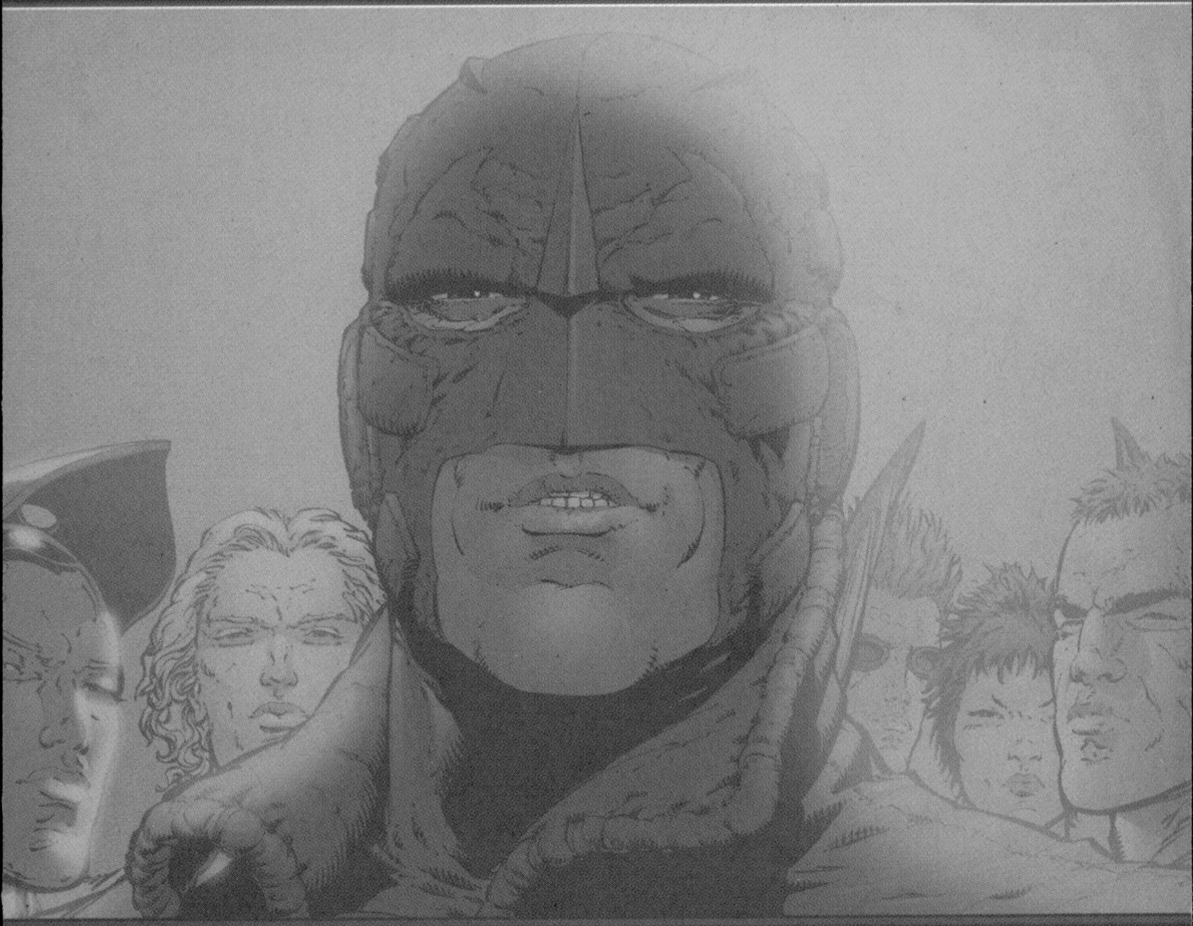

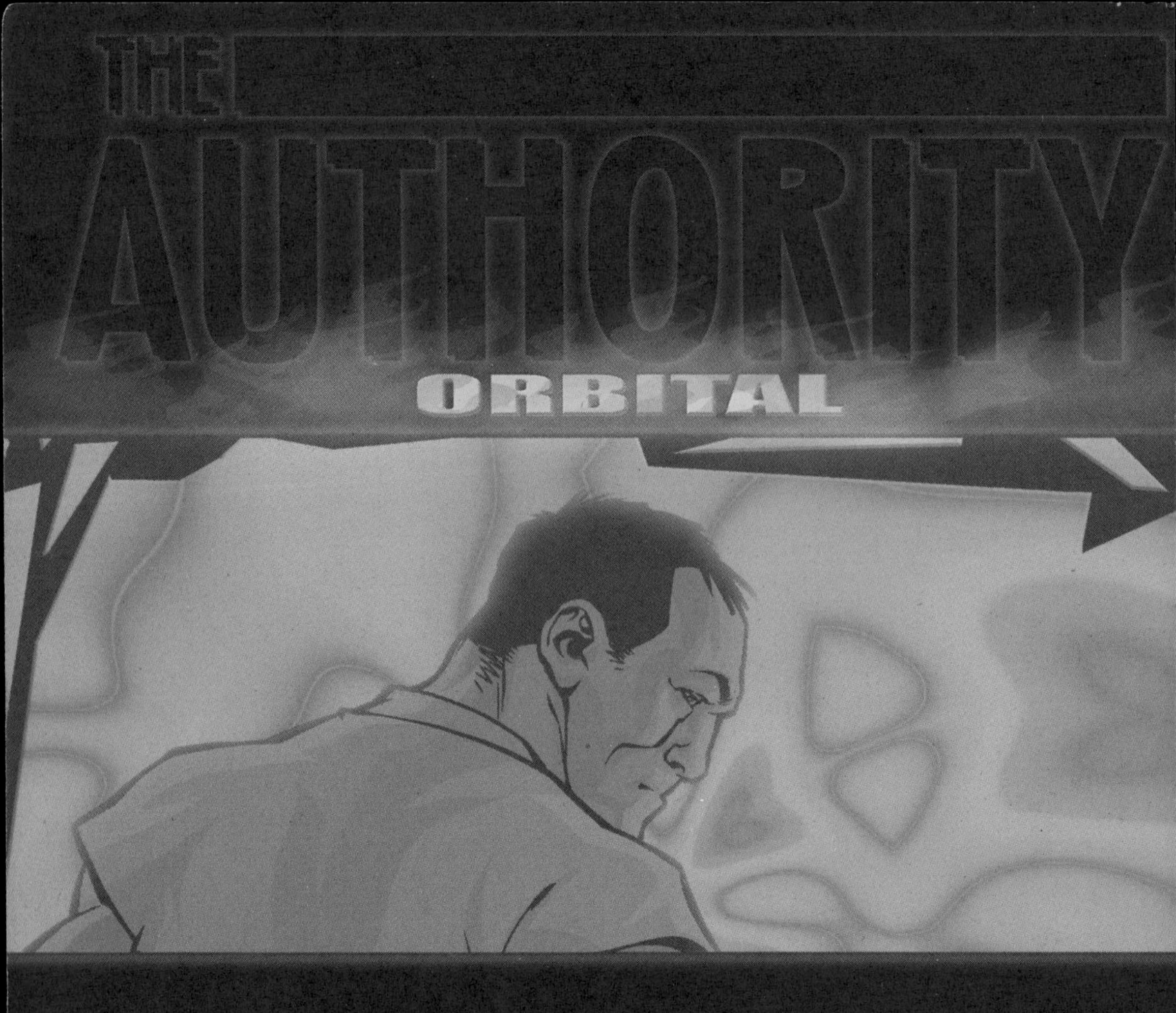
THE
AUTHORITY
ORBITAL

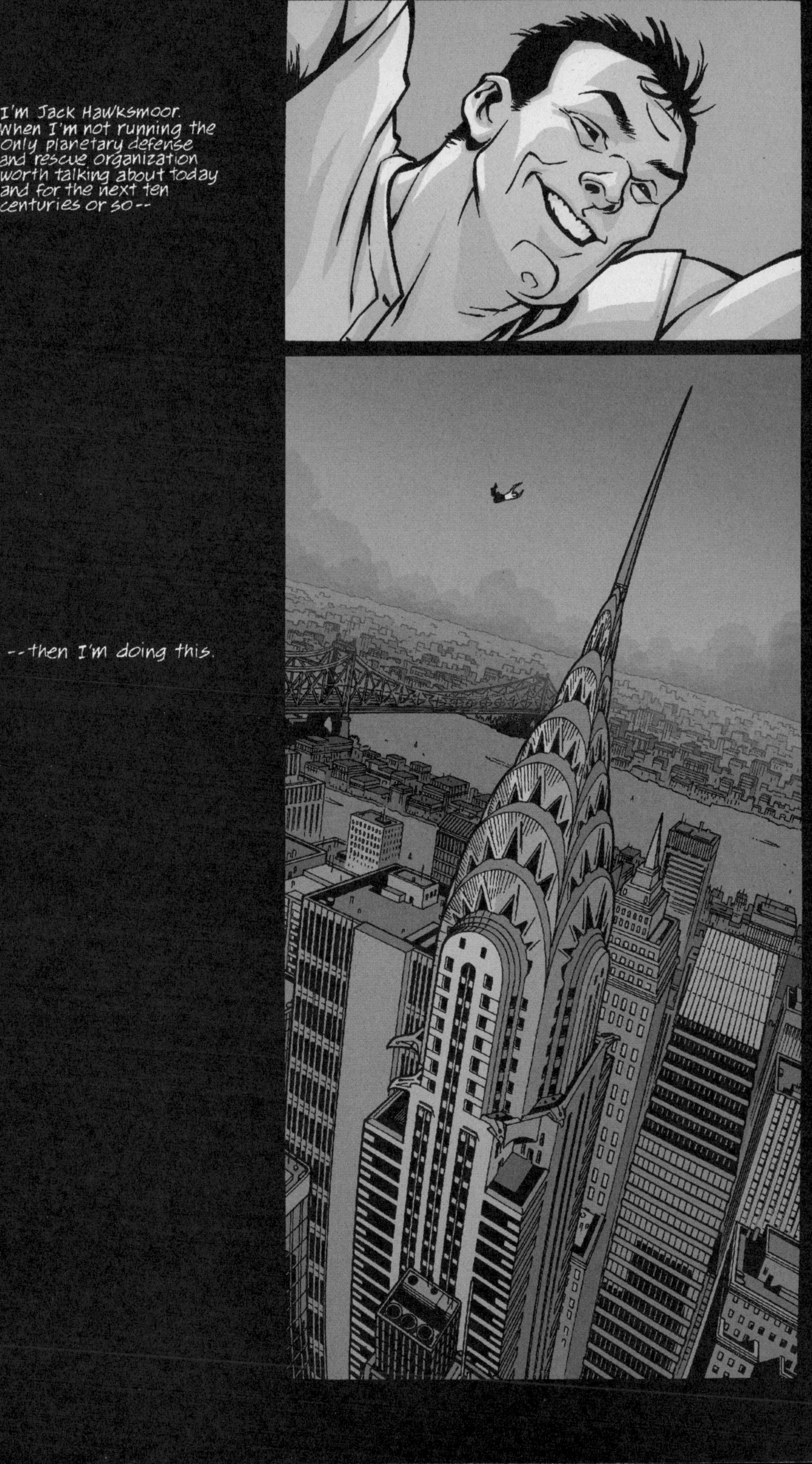
I'm Jack Hawksmoor. When I'm not running the only planetary defense and rescue organization worth talking about today and for the next ten centuries or so--
--then I'm doing this.

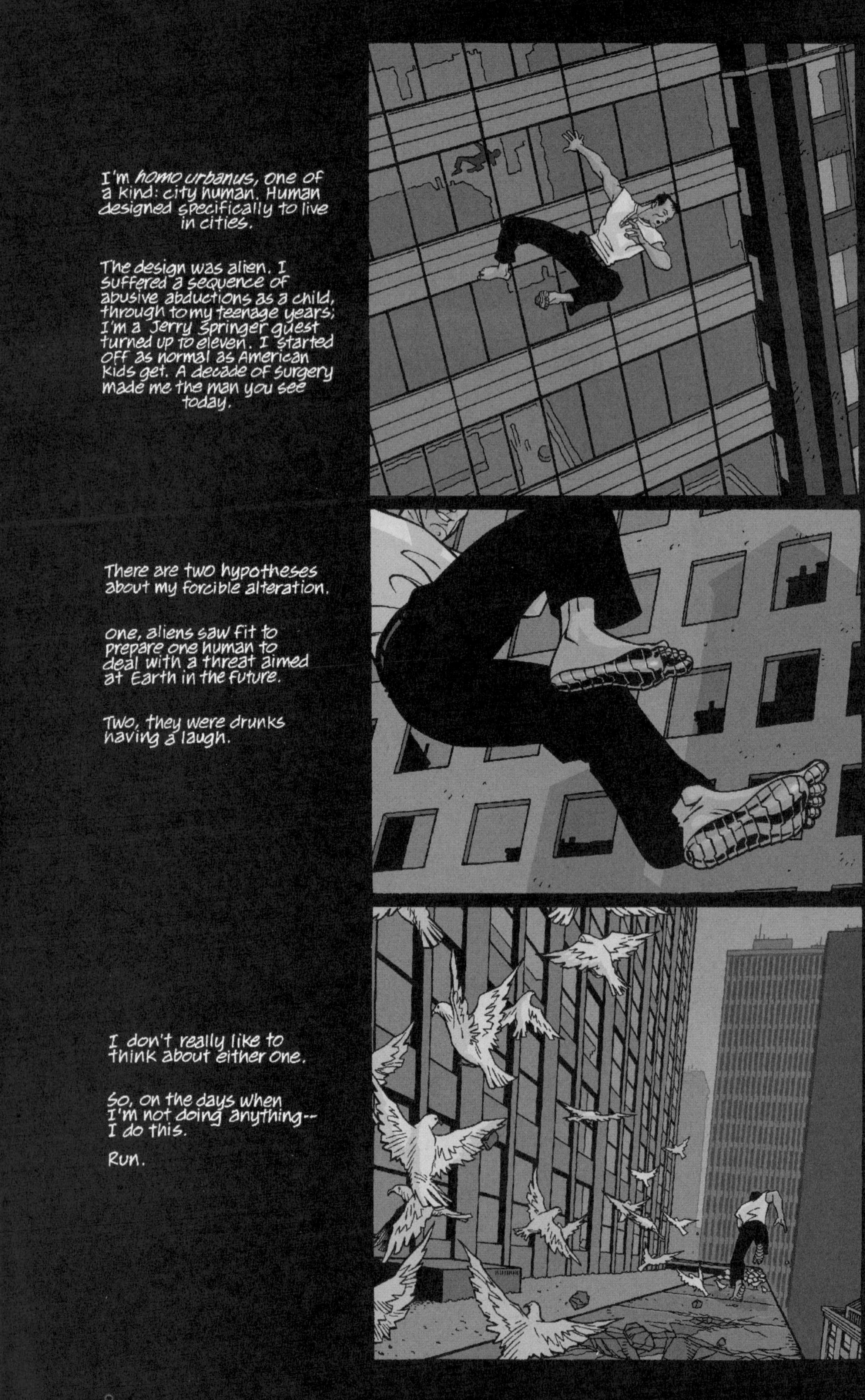
I'm *homo urbanus*, one of a kind: city human. Human designed specifically to live in cities.
The design was alien. I suffered a sequence of abusive abductions as a child, through to my teenage years; I'm a Jerry Springer guest turned up to eleven. I started off as normal as American kids get. A decade of surgery made me the man you see today.
There are two hypotheses about my forcible alteration.
One, aliens saw fit to prepare one human to deal with a threat aimed at Earth in the future.
Two, they were drunks having a laugh.
I don't really like to think about either one.
So, on the days when I'm not doing anything-- I do this.
Run.

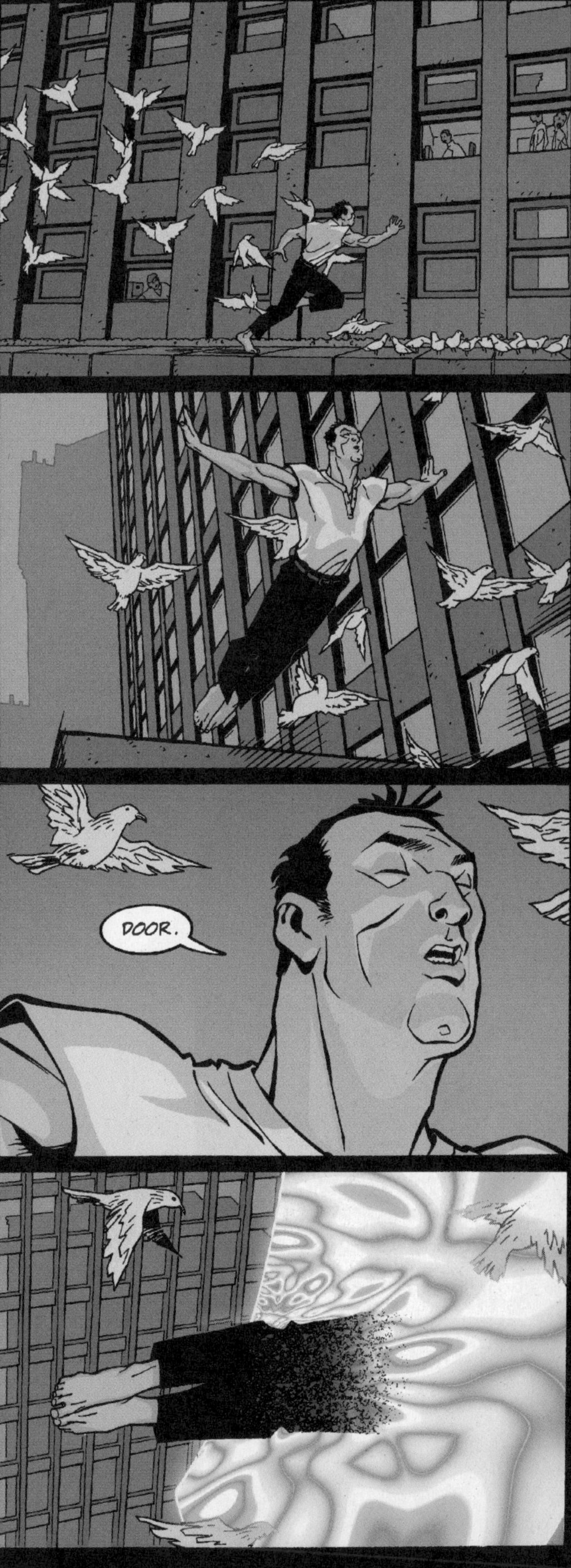
DOOR.

An engineer friend of mine has tried to explain this bit to me several times, and each time I just get a headache. My organization's base of operations comes equipped with what she calls a superpositioned teleportation system; it is everywhere at all times, and can therefore put me anywhere by opening a door from here to there.

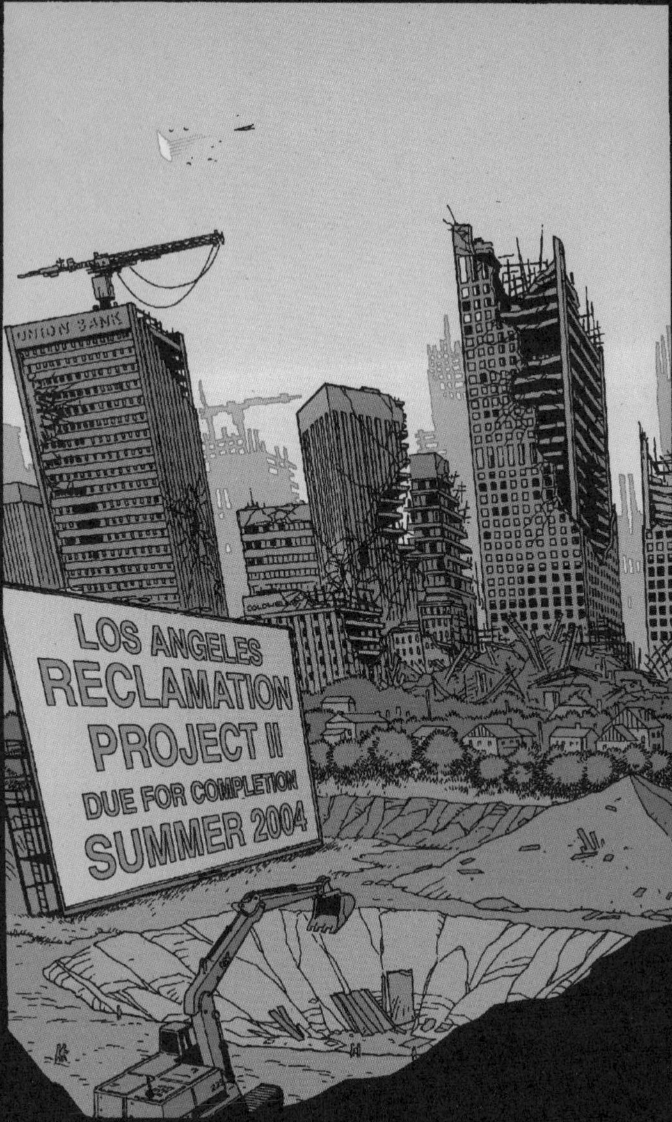
UNION BANK
LOS ANGELES
RECLAMATION
PROJECT II
DUE FOR COMPLETION
SUMMER 2004

Thinking about it for more than two minutes really just makes you want to unroll your brain out in front of a television someplace. Sticking around for the point in the explanation where she starts talking about ten-dimensional supercavitation will put anyone -- *anyone* -- in need of a fat wrap of crack.

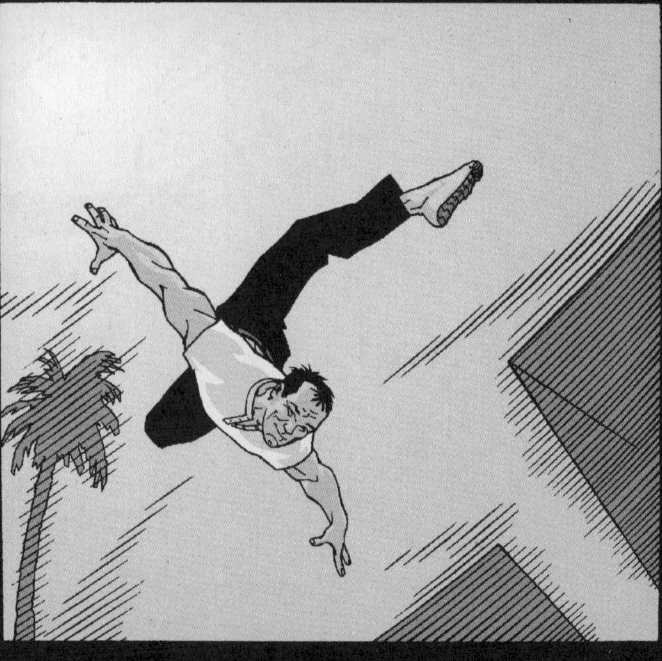

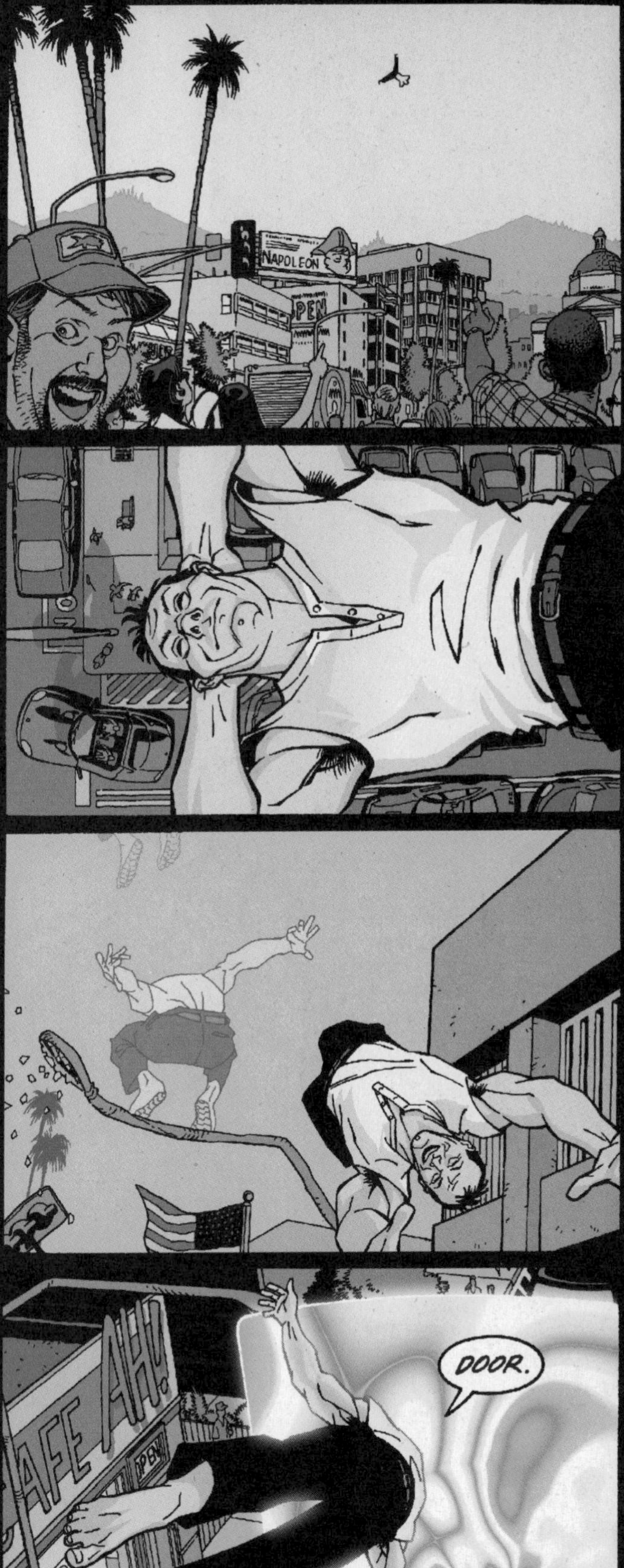
NAPOLEON
DOOR.

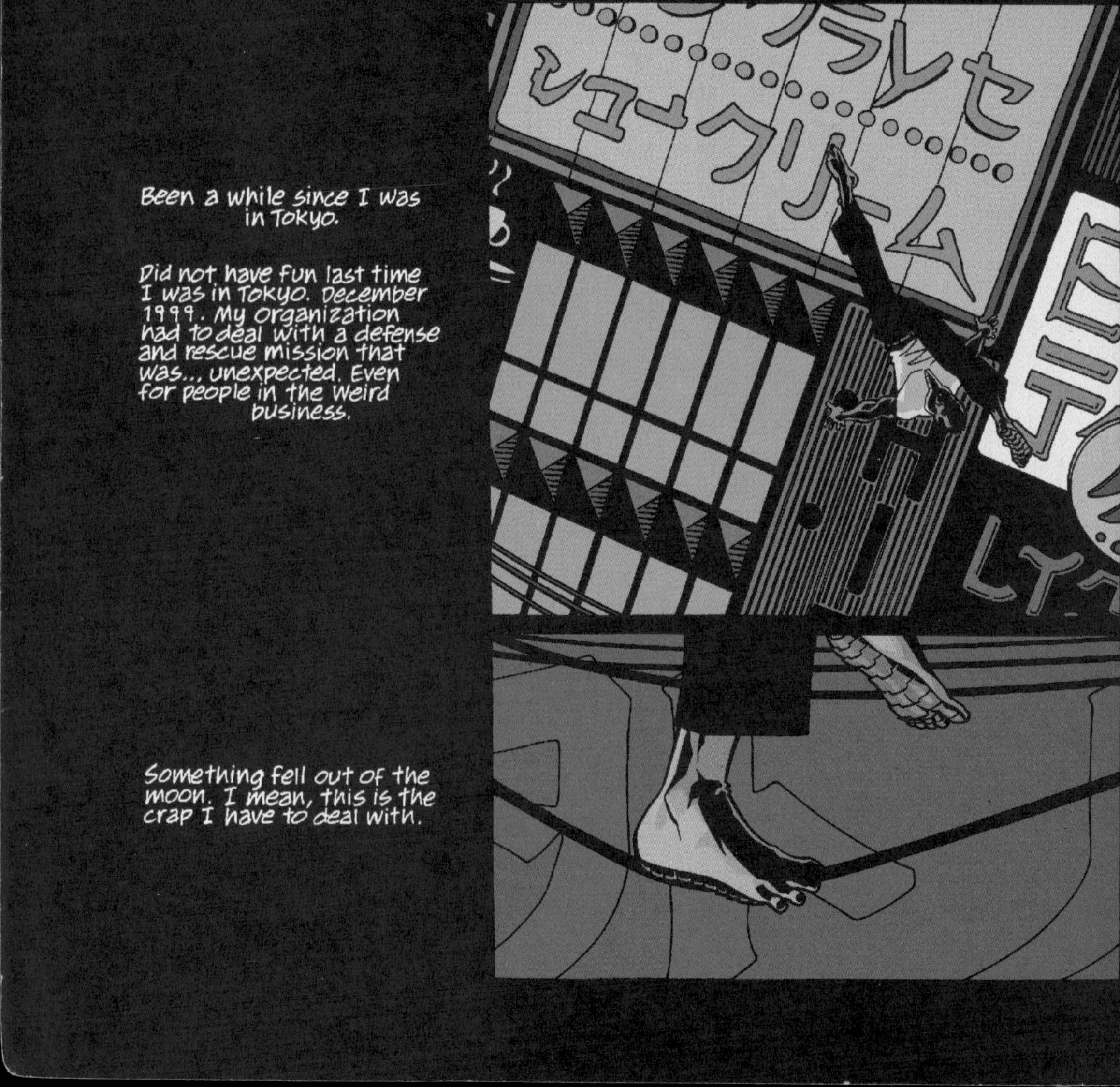
Been a while since I was in Tokyo.
Did not have fun last time I was in Tokyo. December 1999. My organization had to deal with a defense and rescue mission that was..., unexpected. Even for people in the weird business.
Something fell out of the moon. I mean, this is the crap I have to deal with.

It was basically God's self-cleaning system. Organic animal-projectiles hidden beneath the moon's regolith that, on command, fired themselves into transEarth injection. They impregnated and conceived en route, and gave birth to ground attack organisms seconds before final impact.

Seven hundred people died. But there's a hell of a lot more people than that in Tokyo.

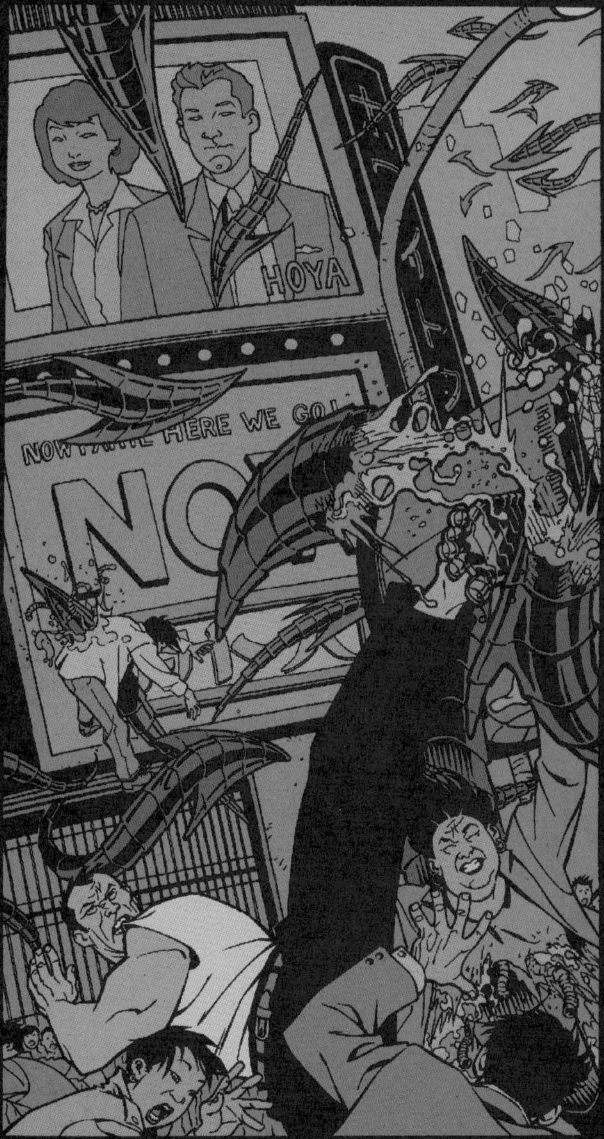
HOYA
HERE WE GO
NO

These are the mathematics of my job. Me and my team win if we've only seen hundreds die, instead of millions. Some people say that makes us bastards.

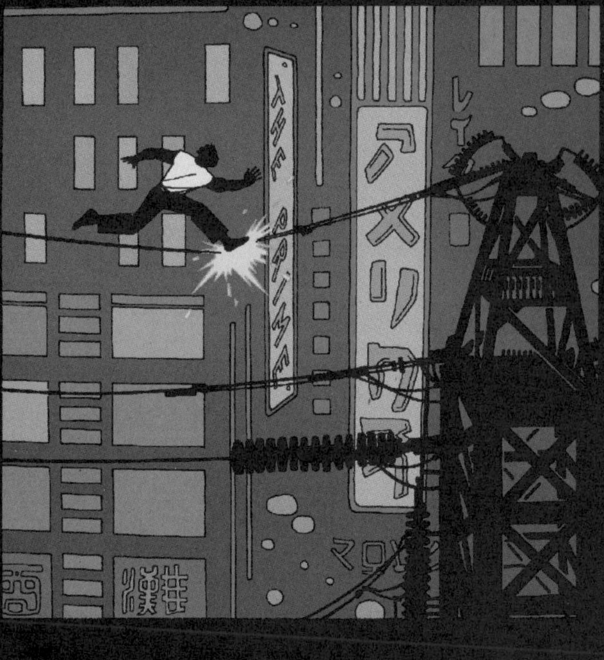
THE PRIME

Some people...

...don't.

This is the one we couldn't get to. We weren't ready for it. Had no warning.

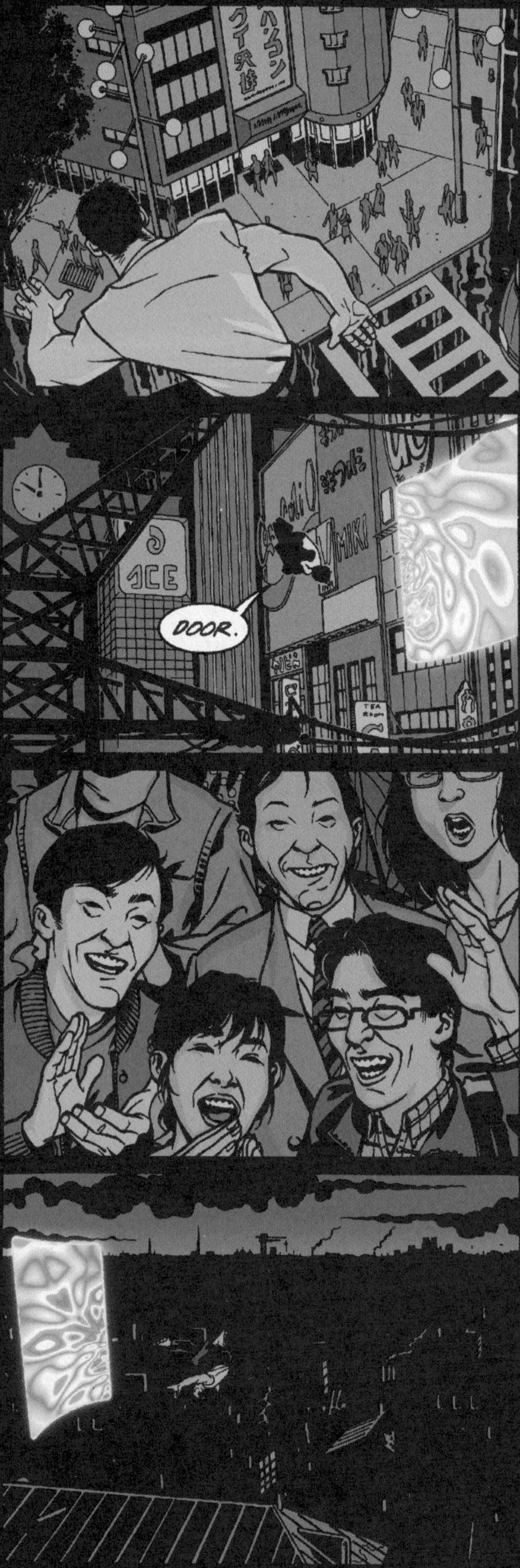
DOOR.
MIKI

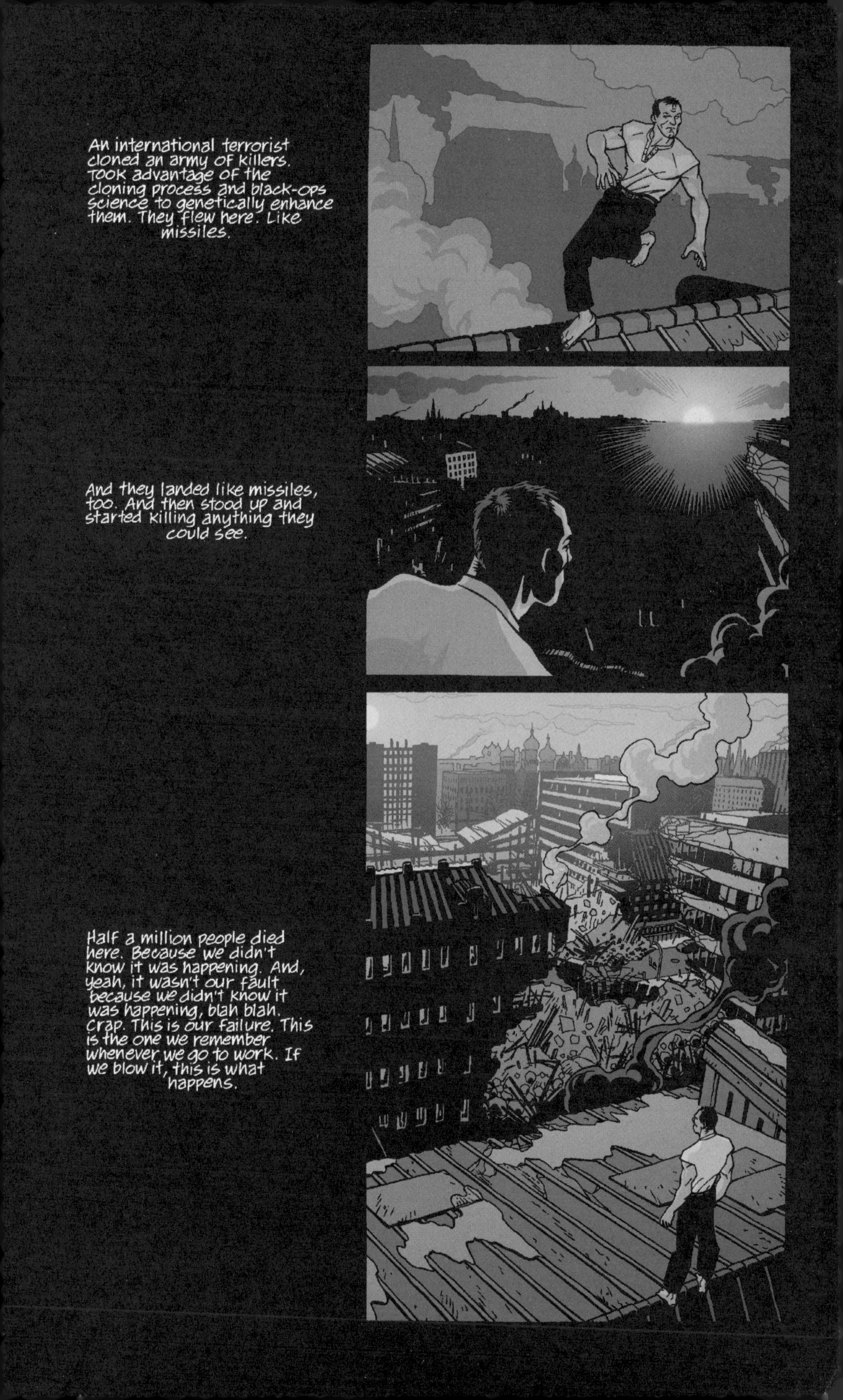
An international terrorist cloned an army of killers. Took advantage of the cloning process and black-ops science to genetically enhance them. They flew here. Like missiles.
And they landed like missiles, too. And then stood up and started killing anything they could see.
Half a million people died here. Because we didn't know it was happening. And, yeah, it wasn't our fault because we didn't know it was happening, blah blah. Crap. This is our failure. This is the one we remember whenever we go to work. If we blow it, this is what happens.

DOOR.

Here's where we did it right. After Moscow, the terrorists aimed at London. And we took the scumbags, right here. A hundred of them came in. Twelve civilian fatalities.

Of course, we caused a little property damage. That newer-seeming area of sidewalk indicates the point where a friend of mine ripped up the original sidewalk and hit ten people in the brains with it.

We did good here. We killed a lot of people, but defense implies war. And this was war, here. It was us versus people who were intent only on killing and killing and killing. Twelve civilian fatalities in a city of, what, seven or eight million? I'll live with that.

DOOR.

I'll try to live with that.

And on the days when I can't, when I feel chased by all the dead people I wasn't there for or weren't good enough for...

I run.

End